Lecture Notes in Artificial Intelligence 3963

Edited by J. G. Carbonell and J. Siekmann

Subseries of Lecture Notes in Computer Science

Oğuz Dikenelli   Marie-Pierre Gleizes
Alessandro Ricci (Eds.)

Engineering Societies in the Agents World VI

6th International Workshop, ESAW 2005
Kuşadasi, Turkey, October 26-28, 2005
Revised Selected and Invited Papers

 Springer

Series Editors

Jaime G. Carbonell, Carnegie Mellon University, Pittsburgh, PA, USA
Jörg Siekmann, University of Saarland, Saarbrücken, Germany

Volume Editors

Oğuz Dikenelli
Ege University
Department of Computer Engineering
35100 Bornova, Izmir, Turkey
E-mail: oguz.dikenelli@ege.edu.tr

Marie-Pierre Gleizes
Université Paul Sabatier
IRIT
118 route de Narbonne, 31062 Toulouse Cedex 9, France
E-mail: gleizes@irit.fr

Alessandro Ricci
Università di Bologna
DEIS, Alma Mater Studiorum
Via Venezia 52, 47023 Cesena, Italy
E-mail: aricci@deis.unibo.it

Library of Congress Control Number: 2006926506

CR Subject Classification (1998): I.2.11, I.2, C.2.4, D.1.3, D.2.2, D.2.7, D.2.11, I.6

LNCS Sublibrary: SL 7 – Artificial Intelligence

ISSN   0302-9743
ISBN-10   3-540-34451-9 Springer Berlin Heidelberg New York
ISBN-13   978-3-540-34451-3 Springer Berlin Heidelberg New York

This work is subject to copyright. All rights are reserved, whether the whole or part of the material is
concerned, specifically the rights of translation, reprinting, re-use of illustrations, recitation, broadcasting,
reproduction on microfilms or in any other way, and storage in data banks. Duplication of this publication
or parts thereof is permitted only under the provisions of the German Copyright Law of September 9, 1965,
in its current version, and permission for use must always be obtained from Springer. Violations are liable
to prosecution under the German Copyright Law.

Springer is a part of Springer Science+Business Media

springer.com

© Springer-Verlag Berlin Heidelberg 2006
Printed in Germany

Typesetting: Camera-ready by author, data conversion by Scientific Publishing Services, Chennai, India
Printed on acid-free paper   SPIN: 11759683   06/3142   5 4 3 2 1 0

Preface

ESAW 2005 took place at the Pine Bay Hotel in Kusadasi, Turkey at the end of the October 2005. It was organized as a stand-alone event as were ESAW 2004 and ESAW 2003. Following the initial ESAW vision, which was set in 1999, by the members of the working group on "Communication, Coordination and Collaboration" of Agentlink, ESAW 2005 continued to focus on the engineering of complex software systems in terms of multi-agent societies, especially the social and environmental aspects of such societies. The number of participants (40 researchers from 10 countries) and the highly interactive discussions held during the workshop showed the augmented importance of the initial vision as well as the effectiveness of ESAW as a well-established research forum.

It is obvious that today's interconnected world increases the importance of approaches concerning the engineering of complex and distributed software systems. These kinds of large scale systems, made up of massive numbers of autonomous components, force us to discover new and novel approaches to model and engineer such systems as agent societies. It is very likely that such innovations will exploit lessons from a variety of different scientific disciplines, such as sociology, economics, organizational science and biology: ESAW 2005 included presentations from these domains in addition to its traditional research topics.

The following themes were addressed during the three-day meeting:

- *Agent Oriented System Development.* The presentations of this session focused on the environment concept and the role of the environment was discussed from applied and historical perspectives throughout the session.
- *Methodologies for Agent Societies.* This session hosted presentations and discussions on the two critical concepts of agent societies, which are role models and artifacts, in terms of the usage of these concepts within the methodologies of agent system development.
- *Deliberative Agents and Social Aspects.* The papers of this session concentrated on the employment of deliberative agents from an architectural perspective, such as in detecting inconsistencies in reasoning, and from an applied perspective, such as in realizing human-centric systems using deliberative agents.
- *Agent Oriented Simulation.* This session covered the presentations on the methodological and architectural issues of specific simulation areas such as crowd simulation and the evaluation of a population of sexual agents.
- *Adaptive Systems.* This session elaborated on the techniques and infrastructures that are designed to make an agent society adaptable against unpredictable events in its environment and illustrated some case studies of adaptive systems.

– *Coordination, Negotiation, Protocols.* This session collected the presentations about the applications of traditional topics of research on agent societies, such as coordination, negotiation and interaction protocols.
– *Agents, Networks and Ambient Intelligence.* This session focused on the usage of intelligent agents within two flourishing areas: mobile ad-hoc networks (MANETs) and ambient intelligence.

Three invited presentations underlined the interdisciplinary nature of research on agent societies by considering social insects, human economical and social systems, and privacy issues of MASs. The first invited talk was given by Guy Theraulaz, who is a professor at the Centre de Recherche sur la Cognition Animale group of the Université Paul Sabatier, Toulouse, France. In his talk, he presented some of the basic coordination mechanisms used by social insects to collectively make a decision or to build a nest architecture, paying particular attention to information processing within a colony.

The second invited talk was presented by Peter McBurney, who is a faculty member of the Agent Applications, Research and Technology (Agent ART) Group of the Department of Computer Science at the University of Liverpool, Liverpool, UK. During the talk, he first defined the properties of the anticipatory and reflective systems and then explored the use of recent MAS technologies for representing and designing anticipatory and reflective complex, adaptive systems.

The third invited presentation by Federico Bergenti, now senior researcher at CNIT (Consorzio Nazionale Interuniversitario per le Telecomunicazioni), Parma, Italia, discussed the latest studies related to management of security, trust and privacy in real-world multi-agent systems.

The original contributions, the slides of the presentations and more information about the workshop are available online on the ESAW 2005 Web site[1]. These post-proceedings continue the series published by Springer (ESAW 2000: LNAI 1972, ESAW 2001: LNAI 2203, ESAW 2002: LNAI 2577, ESAW 2003: LNAI 3071, ESAW 2004: LNAI 3451). This volume contains the revised, reworked and extended versions of selected papers from ESAW 2005.

The ESAW 2005 organization would not have been possible without the financial support of the following institutions:

– Agentlink III
– EBILTEM (Ege University of Science and Technology Applications and Research Center)
– EMO (Chamber of Turkish Electrical Engineers)
– TUBITAK (Turkish Scientific and Technical Research Organization)
– Netsis, Turkey.

As well as the scientific support of DEIS, Università di Bologna, and IRIT, Université Paul Sabatier, and of all the members of the Program Committee, our

---

[1] http://esaw05.ege.edu.tr

thanks also go to Alfred Hofmann and all his Springer crew for their essential role during the realization of these post-proceedings.

March 2006   Oguz Dikenelli
                                                   Marie-Pierre Gleizes
                                                     Alessandro Ricci

Organization

ESAW 2005 Workshop Organizers and Program Chairs

Oguz Dikenelli   Department of Computer Engineering,
Ege University, Izmir, Turkey

Marie-Pierre Gleizes   IRIT, Université Paul Sabatier, Toulouse,
France

Alessandro Ricci   DEIS, Università di Bologna, Cesena, Italy

ESAW 2005 Steering Committee

Marie-Pierre Gleizes   IRIT, Université Paul Sabatier, Toulouse,
France

Andrea Omicini   DEIS, Università di Bologna, Cesena, Italy

Paolo Petta   Austrian Research Institute for Artificial
Intelligence, Austria

Jeremy Pitt   Imperial College London, UK

Robert Tolksdorf   Free University of Berlin, Germany

Franco Zambonelli   Università di Modena e Reggio Emilia, Italy

ESAW 2005 Local Organizing Committee

Oguz Dikenelli (Local Chair)   Department of Computer Engineering,
Ege University, Izmir, Turkey

Riza Cenk Erdur   Department of Computer Engineering,
Ege University, Izmir, Turkey

Özgür Gümüs   Department of Computer Engineering,
Ege University, Izmir, Turkey

Ali Murat Tiryaki   Department of Computer Engineering,
Ege University, Izmir, Turkey

Önder Gürcan   Department of Computer Engineering,
Ege University, Izmir, Turkey

Inanç Seylan   Department of Computer Engineering,
Ege University, Izmir, Turkey

ESAW 2005 Program Committee

Ronald Ashri   University of Southampton, UK

Patrick Albert   ILOG, France

Alexander Artikis   Imperial College London, UK

Federico Bergenti	Università di Parma, Italy
Carole Bernon	IRIT, Université Paul Sabatier, France
Monique Calisti	Whitestein Technologies, Switzerland
Jacques Calmet	University of Karlsruhe, Germany
Valrie Camps	IRIT, Université Paul Sabatier, France
Cristiano Castelfranchi	CNR Roma, Italy
Luca Cernuzzi	Universidad Catòlica de Asunciòn, Paraguay
Vincent Chevrier	LORIA, France
Paolo Ciancarini	Università di Bologna, Italy
Helder Coelho	University of Lisbon, Portugal
Scott Cost R.	University of Maryland Baltimore County, USA
Paul Davidsson	Blekinge Institute of Technology, Sweden
Riza Cenk Erdur	Ege University, Izmir, Turkey
Rino Falcone	CNR Roma, Italy
Stephan Flake	ORGA Systems, Paderborn, Germany
Zahia Guessoum	LIP6/CReSTIC, France
Anthony Karageorgos	University of Thessaly, Greece
Barbara Keplicz	Polish Academy of Science, Poland
Peter McBurney	University of Liverpool, UK
Pablo Noriega	IIIA CSIC, Spain
Michel Occello	Université Mendés France, Grenoble, France
Eugenio Oliveira	University of Porto, Portugal
Sascha Ossowski	Universidad Rey Juan Carlos, Spain
Van Dike Parunak	ALTARUM, USA
Michal Pechoucek	Czech Technical University, Prague, Czech Republic
Onn Shehory	IBM, Haifa Research Labs, Israel
Kostas Stathis	City University London, UK
Paola Turci	Università di Parma, Italy
Luca Tummolini	CNR Roma, Italy
Leon Van der Torre	CWI Amsterdam, The Netherlands
Mirko Viroli	DEIS, Università di Bologna, Cesena, Italy
Danny Weyns	Katholieke Universiteit Leuven, Belgium
Pinar Yolum	Bogazici University, Istanbul, Turkey

Table of Contents

Agent Oriented Simulation

Networks, Ambient Intelligence

Deliberative Agents and Social Aspect

Developing Multi Agent Systems on Semantic Web Environment Using SEAGENT Platform

Oguz Dikenelli[1], Riza Cenk Erdur[1], Geylani Kardas[2], Özgür Gümüs[1],
Inanç Seylan[1], Önder Gürcan[1], Ali Murat Tiryaki[1], and Erdem Eser Ekinci[1]

[1] Ege University, Department of Computer Engineering,
35100 Bornova, Izmir, Turkey
{oguz.dikenelli, cenk.erdur, ozgur.gumus, inanc.seylan, onder.gurcan,
ali.murat.tiryaki}@ege.edu.tr, erdemeserekinci@gmail.com
[2] Ege University, International Computer Institute,
35100 Bornova, Izmir, Turkey
geylani.kardas@ege.edu.tr

Abstract. In this paper, we discuss the development of a multi agent system working on the Semantic Web environment by using a new framework called SEAGENT. SEAGENT is a new agent development framework and platform, which includes built-in features for semantic web based multi agent system development. These features provide semantic supports such as a new specific content language for transferring semantic knowledge, specifically designed agent's internal architecture to handle semantic knowledge, a new directory facilitator architecture based on semantic service matching engine and ontology management service to provide ontology translations within the platform's ontologies. The implemented case study shows the effectiveness of these features in terms of semantically enriched multi agent system development.

1 Introduction

The standardization effort on Semantic Web [2] aims to transform the World Wide Web into a knowledge representation system in which the information provided by web pages is interpreted using ontologies. This creates an environment in which knowledge is defined in terms of these ontologies and information systems are designed and implemented in a way that these ontologies are used, transferred and regenerated. In these environments, agents place a critical role to autonomously collect, interpret and use semantic knowledge as a part of future's information systems.

In this paper, we discuss how to develop MASs in such semantically enriched environments with a new framework called SEAGENT. SEAGENT, which is introduced in [8], is a new agent development framework and platform that is specialized for semantic web based MAS development. The communication and plan execution infrastructure of SEAGENT looks like other existing agent development frameworks such as DECAF [10], JADE [1], and RETSINA [16]. However, to support and ease semantic web based MAS development, SEAGENT

O. Dikenelli, M.-P. Gleizes, and A. Ricci (Eds.): ESAW 2005, LNAI 3963, pp. 1–13, 2006.
© Springer-Verlag Berlin Heidelberg 2006

includes the following built-in features that the existing agent frameworks and platforms do not have:

* SEAGENT provides a specific feature within the agent's internal architecture to handle the agent's internal knowledge using OWL (Web Ontology Language) [13].
* The directory service of SEAGENT stores agent capabilities using specially designed OWL based ontologies and it provides a semantic matching engine to find the agents with semantically related capabilities.
* Based on FIPA-RDF [9], a content language called Seagent Content Language (SCL) has been defined to transfer semantic content within the agent communication language messages.
* SEAGENT introduces a new service called Ontology Management Service (OMS). The most important feature of this service is to define mappings between platform ontologies and external ontologies. Then it provides a translation service to the platform agents based on these defined mappings.
* SEAGENT supports discovery and dynamic invocation of semantic web services by introducing a new platform service for semantic service discovery and a reusable agent behavior for dynamic invocation of the discovered services.

The paper is organized as follows: Section 2 gives a brief overview of the related work. Section 3 explains the overall architecture of the SEAGENT framework. In section 4, a case study on MAS development using SEAGENT is discussed in detail. This case study demonstrates the MAS implementation taking into account of platform initialization, agent plan development using semantic knowledge and semantic capability matching on platform's Directory Facilitator (DF). Conclusion is given in section 5.

2   Related Work

The idea of integrating the semantic web and agent research has already been realized and some systems have been developed. ITtalks [5] system offers access to information about activities such as talks and seminars related with information technology. ITtalks uses DAML+OIL for knowledge representation and lets agents to retrieve and manipulate information stored in the ITtalks knowledge base. The smart meeting room system [4] is a distributed system that consists of agents, services, devices and sensors that provide relevant services and information to the meeting participants based on their contexts. This system uses semantic web languages for representing context ontologies. Both the ITtalks and the smart meeting room system use a multi-agent development framework in their underlying infrastructure. For example, ITtalks uses Jackal [6] and smart meeting room system uses Jade [1]. In these systems, semantic web functionality is hard coded into the system together with the domain knowledge, because the agent frameworks used in the implementation of these systems do not have a built-in support for semantic web. For example, it is difficult for these systems' developers to support basic semantic web functionalities such as discovering and dynamically invoking of semantic web services inside an agent or performing an ontology translation between different platform ontologies. Moreover, it requires knowledge for ordinary developers to handle the semantic web and agent technology details in addition to the application domain related knowledge.

There have been a few implementations to integrate web services and FIPA compliant agent platforms. WSDL2JADE [22] can generate agent ontologies and agent codes from a WSDL input file. WSIG (Web Services Integration Gateway) [19] supports bi-directional integration of web services and Jade agents. WS2JADE [21] allows deployment of web services as Jade agents' services at run time. But these tools only deal with agent and web service integration and do not provide any mechanism to use semantic web knowledge during MAS development.

There is an attempt called as "JADE Semantic Agent" [20], to integrate FIPA ACL semantics into a multi agent development framework. It is implemented on top of the JADE framework and it has a built-in mechanism to interpret the semantics of FIPA messages. This is a very noble attempt but it is highly dependent on the FIPA-SL language which seems to be a problem when sending OWL content between agents. We believe that it still remains a problem to define ACL semantics in a way compatible with OWL.

We can conclude from this discussion that there must be environments, which will simplify semantic web based multi agent system (MAS) development for ordinary developers and which will support the basic semantic web functionalities.

3   Platform Architecture

In this section, we explain SEAGENT's layered software architecture briefly. Each layer and packages of the layers have been specially designed to provide build-in support for MAS development on Semantic Web environment. The overall architecture is shown in Fig. 1. Although the given architecture is the implemented architecture of the SEAGENT platform, we believe that it is generic enough to be considered as a conceptual architecture of MASs those are developed and deployed for semantic web environment. In the following subsections, we discuss each layer with an emphasis on the semantic support given by that layer.

3.1   Communication Infrastructure Layer

This bottom layer is responsible of abstracting platform's communication infrastructure implementation. SEAGENT implements FIPA's Agent Communication and Agent Message Transport specifications [9] to handle agent messaging. Although Communication Infrastructure Layer can transfer any content using FIPA ACL and transport infrastructure, SEAGENT platform only supports Seagent Content Language (SCL) by default. SCL itself is a specific OWL ontology to define the ACL content. It is based on the FIPA-RDF but extends the FIPA-RDF by defining new concepts and relations. So, the language itself is not OWL like Zou et. al's work [18], but it is serialized into OWL. This allows content to be easily parsed and takes advantage of directly inserting

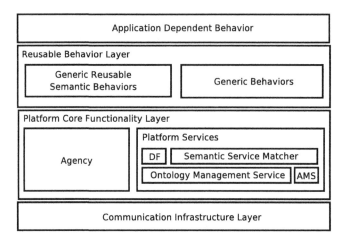

Fig. 1. SEAGENT Platform Overall Architecture

concepts/individuals from OWL ontologies which form the knowledge bases of services and agents.

In order to be used with FIPA-ACL, a content language must satisfy three requirements [3]. The first two states that the language must be capable of representing propositions and actions. This is done in SEAGENT by defining those two concepts in the SCL ontology. The third requirement is that it must be capable of representing objects, including identifying referential expressions to describe objects. To achieve this, we have defined a query and match ontology in OWL which is called "Seagent Match Ontology". The concepts of this ontology are used to define required content and are directly inserted into SCL based content to represent objects.

3.2   Platform Core Functionality Layer

Agency Package. The second layer includes packages, which provide the core functionality of the platform. The first package, called as Agency, handles the internal functionality of an agent. Agency package supports the creation of general purpose and goal directed agents. In this sense, Agency package provides a built-in "agent operating system" that matches the goal(s) to defined plan(s), which are defined using HTN planning formalism [14]. It then schedules, executes and monitors the plan(s). From semantic web based development perspective, an agent's internal architecture must support semantic web ontology standards for messaging and internal knowledge handling to simplify semantic based development. For this purpose, Agency package provides a build-in support to parse and interpret SCL content language to handle semantic web based messaging. On the other hand, Agency provides two interfaces for semantic knowledge handling, one for local ontology management and the other one for querying. Although the current version includes the JENA [11] based implementation of these interfaces, other semantic knowledge management environments and query engines can be integrated to the platform by implementing these interfaces.

Platform Services. The second package of the Core Functionality Layer includes service sub-packages, one for each service of the platform. SEAGENT provides all standard MAS services such as DF Service and Agent Management Service (AMS) following the previous platform implementations and FIPA standards. But these standard services are implemented in a different way by using the capabilities of a semantic web infrastructure.

In SEAGENT implementation, DF uses an OWL ontology to hold agent capabilities and includes a semantic matching engine to be able to return agent(s) with semantically similar capabilities to the requested ones. Matchmaking process in case is realized within the built-in capability matching engine of the DF which is called *Seagent Matching Engine*. This engine matches advertised agent services with the received service request. It stores agent service definitions in a database. Actually this database is an ontology model of the agent services in which agent service ontology individuals are included. Therefore each agent service that is registered to the DF is also represented in this ontology with an individual as it is discussed above. The matching engine uses those individuals and compares them with given service requests semantically. Seagent Matching Engine uses a basic reasoner called *Ontolog* to determine semantic relation between agent services. We have adapted the service matching algorithm originally proposed in [15] for semantic web services into the matchmaking process of agent services. The Ontolog works on ontology hierarchy tree of service concepts and finds distance between any given two classes (i.e. service types of requested and advertised agent services). Based on the results returned from the Ontolog, Seagent Matching Engine defines and uses a degree of match function named $DoM(C_1, C_2)$ which determines semantic match degree between concepts, C_1 and C_2:

$DoM(C_1, C_2) =$ EXACT if C_1 is a direct subclass of C_2 or $C_1 = C_2$,
$DoM(C_1, C_2) =$ PLUG-IN if C_1 is a distant subclass of C_2,
$DoM(C_1, C_2) =$ SUBSUMES if C_2 is a direct or distant subclass of C_1,
$DoM(C_1, C_2) =$ FAIL otherwise.

Matching engine of the agent platform takes the above defined relations into account and determines the suitability of the advertised agent services with the requested one. The internal architecture and theoretical base of the engine is introduced in [12].

Similarly, AMS stores descriptions of agents in OWL using FIPA Agent Management Ontology [9] and can be queried semantically to learn descriptions of any agent that is currently resident on the platform.

Besides implementing standard services in a semantic way, SEAGENT platform provides two new services to simplify semantic web based MAS development. The first one is called as Semantic Service Matcher (SSM). SSM is responsible for connecting the platform to the semantic web services hosted in the outside of the platform. SSM uses "service profile" construct of the Web

Ontology Language for Semantic Web Services (OWL-S) [17] standard for service advertisement and this knowledge is also used by the internal semantic matching engine for discovery of the service(s) upon a request. SSM and DF services are implemented by extending a generic semantic matching engine architecture, which are introduced in [7] and [12] in detail.

The second unique service is the Ontology Management Service (OMS). It behaves as a central repository for the domain ontologies used within the platform and provides basic ontology management functionality such as ontology deployment, ontology updating and querying etc. The most critical support of the OMS is its translation support between the ontologies. OMS handles the translation request(s) using the pre-defined mapping knowledge which is introduced through a specific user interface. Through the usage of the ontology translation support, any agent of the platform may communicate with MAS and/or services outside the platform even if they use different ontologies.

3.3 Reusable Behaviour Layer

Third layer of the overall architecture includes pre-prepared generic agent plans. We have divided these generic plans into two packages. Generic Behavior package collects domain independent reusable behaviors that may be used by any MAS such as well known auction protocols (English, Dutch etc.). On the other hand, Generic Semantic Behaviors package includes only the semantic web related behaviors. In the current version, the most important generic semantic behavior is the one that executes dynamic discovery and invocation of the external services. This behaviour is defined as a pre-prepared HTN structure and during its execution, it uses SSM service to discover the desired service and then using OWL-S "service grounding" construct, it dynamically invokes the found atomic web service(s). Detail of this behaviour is explained in [7]. Hence, developers may include dynamic external service discovery and invocation capability to their plan(s) by simply inserting this reusable behavior as an ordinary complex task into their HTN based plan definition(s).

4   Developing a MAS with Using SEAGENT Through a Case Study

In this section, development of a simple MAS using SEAGENT framework is discussed to demonstrate semantic knowledge handling capability of the framework. We first describe scenario of the implemented case study. Then initialization of the MAS on semantic web enviroment, plan and behaviour structure of the working agents and internal workflow of the system's semantic DF service are explained respectively.

4.1   Scenario

The agent environment in case is about Tourism domain in which traveler agents try to reserve hotel rooms on behalf of their users while some other agents are offering hotel services for those ones. In our prototype MAS, we have a traveler agent and four hotel agents. Initially each one is unaware of the others. Those four hotel agents are registered to the DF of the MAS with their service advertisements. Those agents use an agent description ontology called "fipa-agent-management.owl" to advertise themselves (including their services and related information) in DF. "df-agent-description" and "service-description" concepts defined in this ontology are given in Fig. 2. This ontology involves the concepts given in FIPA Agent Management Specification [9], thus making the platform compatible with FIPA Specifications.

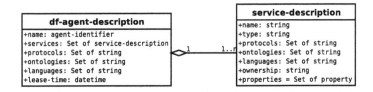

Fig. 2. DF Agent Description and Agent Service Description concepts

On the other hand, we use two properties of service description *(type* and *properties)* to define agent services semantically. Values of these properties may come from various domain ontologies. Therefore they involve URI of related ontology concepts. For example in our case, hotel agents use "HotelInfoService" concept which is defined in the OWL ontology called "TourismServices.owl" to set *type* property of service description instance and to advertise themselves in DF. This means that hotel agents provide a service called "HotelInfoService" to other agents.

According to our scenario, hotel agents in here provide activities to their customers. Hence, service descriptions include a service property called "activity" within the set of service description *properties.* The range of the *activity* property is an individual of the concept that comes from another domain ontology called "Hotel.owl". TourismServices ontology and a fragment of Hotel Ontology are given in Fig. 3 and Fig. 4 respectively. Service types and activities available in each hotel agent's service description are given in Table 1.

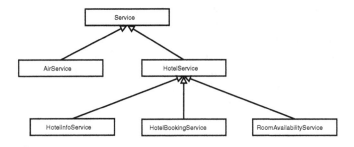

Fig. 3. TourismServices ontology

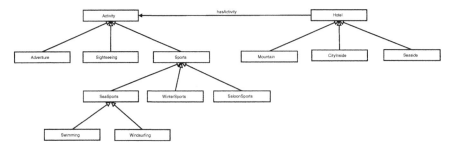

Fig. 4. A Fragment of Hotel Ontology

Table 1. Four hotel agent services registered into the directory facilitator

Agent's name	Service type	Activity type
hotel1@seagent.com	TourismServices.owl#HotelInfoService	Hotel.owl#Windsurf
hotel2@seagent.com	TourismServices.owl#HotelInfoService	Hotel.owl#WinterSports
hotel3@seagent.com	TourismServices.owl#HotelInfoService	Hotel.owl#Swimming
hotel4@seagent.com	TourismServices.owl#HotelInfoService	Hotel.owl#SeaSports

In the scenario, our traveler agent looks for suitable hotels in which "Sea-Sports" activity is available. Hence, it first communicates with DF of the MAS, receives DF descriptions of the suitable agents and then calls "HotelInfoService" service of those agents to get further information about the hotel.

4.2 Initiating the Platform

To instantiate the platform, the standard platform services are started first. These are AMS, ACC (Agent Communication Channel) and DF in order. Agents and services which aren't registered to an AMS are not considered to be a part of a platform, therefore registration to AMS is the initial behavior of all entities (agents and services). The AMS maintains an OWL instance of the FIPA Agent Management Ontology. When agents register themselves, their agent descriptions are kept in this instance. The interaction between AMS and the agents are as stated by FIPA specification [9]. If there is no problem with the content delivered to AMS, it sends an *agree* message and if the agent is successfully registered, an *inform* message is sent back by the AMS.

After the initialization of AMS, ACC is started. All communication is done through ACC, thus it is needed when agents send their "register to AMS" message. Finally, DF is created. It is not mandatory that agents register themselves with DF on their creation as in AMS. This is why all entities take AMS and ACC address in the construction but not the DF address. After the DF starts its operation, it broadcasts that it is working. Then platform's AMS and ACC advertises their service descriptions to the DF. The types of these services are reserved – *fipa-acc* and *fipa-ams* – so no other agent can advertise themselves with those parameters.

When the instance of the standard Seagent platform is ready, it is then populated with five agents mentioned above. These agents are supplied with their AMS agent descriptions when they are created. They then use these agent descriptions to register to AMS, which is already stated as a mandatory operation. The agents are also planned to register their services with the DF. As in AMS, the knowledge base of DF is an OWL ontology. This ontology has instances of DF agent descriptions. An instance of DF agent description for one of the hotel agents in N3 format is given in Fig. 5.

```
@prefix ts:        <http://aegeants.ege.edu.tr/ont/TourismServices.owl#> .
@prefix xsd:       <http://www.w3.org/2001/XMLSchema#> .
@prefix hotel:     <http://aegeants.ege.edu.tr/ont/Hotel.owl#> .
@prefix am: <http://aegeants.ege.edu.tr/ont/fipa-agent-management.owl#>.
@prefix rdfs:      <http://www.w3.org/2000/01/rdf-schema#> .
@prefix rdf:       <http://www.w3.org/1999/02/22-rdf-syntax-ns#> .
@prefix :          <#> .
@prefix owl:       <http://www.w3.org/2002/07/owl#> .

[]      a          am:DFAgentDescription ;
        am:language  "http://aegeants.ege.edu.tr/ont/scl.owl" ;
        am:name [ a         am:AgentIdentifier ;
                  am:name "hotel4@seagent.com" ] ;
        am:ontology _:b1 ;
        am:service
                [ a         rdf:Bag ;
                  rdf:_1    [ a         am:ServiceDescription ;
                             hotel:activity hotel:SeaSports ;
                             am:name "sea sports service" ;
                             am:ontology _:b1 ;
                             am:ownership "Foo Co." ;
                             am:type ts:HotelInfo ] ] .
_:b1    a          rdf:Bag ;
        rdf:_1     "http://aegeants.ege.edu.tr/ont/TourismServices.owl" ;
        rdf:_2     "http://aegeants.ege.edu.tr/ont/Hotel.owl" .
```

Fig. 5. DF Agent Description of a Hotel Agent in N3 format

4.3   Internal Plan of the Traveler Agent

In the Seagent Platform, there is a generic plan in which agents query on DF and evaluate the match results to select agent(s) with appropriate service(s). This plan simply contains one behaviour called "Find Agent from DF" and this behaviour is composed of two actions: "Create Query and Send It to DF" and "Select Agent". The HTN structure of this plan is given in Fig. 6.

In the first action, the agent retrieves search criteria provision which is created according to the previously mentioned Seagent Match Ontology. The search criteria in here can define anything that can be retrieved from DF such as a service description or an agent DF description. To model the criteria, a concept which is called SeagentMatchRequest as a part of the Seagent Match Ontology is used [12]. A SeagentMatchRequest has properties such as "hasPremise", "hasQuery" and "hasSemanticMatch" to define RDF (Resource Description Framework) triples which will be used in semantic match on DF. In "hasPremise" and

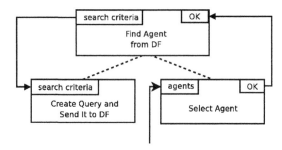

Fig. 6. HTN strcuture of the generic "Find Agent" plan

"hasQuery" lists, the requester defines RDF sentences of the RDQL (RDF Data Query Language) [11] query which will be executed before semantic match to filter result set according to non-semantic parameters. On the other hand, the requester specifies each semantic parameter and its ontological value in "hasSemanticMatch" list to be used during semantic match on filtered query results. Result type and desired semantic match degree of the match process is given in "mustBindVariable" and "matchDegree" properties of the SeagentMatchRequest.

In our scenario, the traveler agent prepares the proper SeagentMatchRequest instance in which a DF Agent Description is requested with *Tourism-Services.owl#HotelInfoService* service and *Hotel.owl#SeaSports* activity. In this request, match degree is emphasized as *SUBSUMES* and semantic matching is requested on these two fields. That means the traveler agent accepts all agent services which are semantically related with *TourismServices.owl#HotelInfoService* service. Likewise the traveler agent also requests hotel activities which are semantically related with *Hotel.owl#SeaSports* activity.

In order to be sent to DF, the instance of SeagentMatchRequest is serialized in the outgoing ACL message based on Seagent Match Ontology. The content of the message is shown in Fig. 7. Due to space limitations, the namespaces in Fig. 5 are not given here again. As it is seen, the content language (SCL) itself is an OWL ontology. Therefore the SeagentMatchRequest instance corresponds to an individual in this ontology. It is the argument of the *search* action that is requested from DF.

In the second action, the traveler agent receives DF Agent Descriptions those are matched with the above request in a SeagentMatchResultSet instance. Each element in this result set is a SeagentMatchResult and they are ordered according to their match degrees. It should be noted that the DF of the MAS uses OWL representations of those results to put them into the ongoing ACL message. So the traveler agent parses the content and de-serializes each result object to proceed on its task. During this de-serialization it uses "seagent-match-ontology.owl" to understand ontological content of the result objects. Since match results are also semantically defined in the "seagent-match-ontology" as match requests, the traveler agent retrieves query results to properly use in its plan execution. After all, the traveler agent successfully retrieves appropriate services and it communicates with hotel agents starting from the first element of the result set.

```
@prefix match:     <http://aegeants.ege.edu.tr/ont/
                    seagent-match-ontology.owl#> .
@prefix scl:       <http://aegeants.ege.edu.tr/ont/scl.owl#> .

[]      a     scl:Action ;
        scl:act "search" ;
        scl:actor
           [ a         am:AgentIdentifier ;
             am:name "df@seagent.com" ] ;
        scl:argument _:m1 .
_:m1    a     match:SeagentMatchRequest ;
        match:hasPremise
           [ match:object "fipa-agent-management.owl#ServiceDescription" ;
             match:predicate "http://www.w3.org/02/22-rdf-syntax-ns#type";
             match:subject "?s" ] ;
        match:hasPremise
           [ match:object "fipa-agent-management.owl#DFAgentDescription" ;
             match:predicate "http://www.w3.org/02/22-rdf-syntax-ns#type";
             match:subject "?x" ] ;
        match:hasPremise
           [ match:object "http://.../ont/Hotel.owl#Activity" ;
             match:predicate "http://www.w3.org/02/22-rdf-syntax-ns#type";
             match:subject "?a" ] ;
        match:hasQuery
           [ match:object "?a" ;
             match:predicate "http://.../ont/Hotel.owl#activity" ;
             match:subject "?s" ] ;
        match:hasQuery
           [ match:object "?s" ;
             match:predicate "http://../fipa-agent-management.owl#service
                ";
             match:subject "?x" ] ;
        match:hasSemanticMatch
           [ match:object "http://.../ont/TourismServices.owl#HotelInfo" ;
             match:predicate "http://.../fipa-agent-management.owl#type" ;
             match:subject "?s" ] ;
        match:hasSemanticMatch
           [ match:object "http://.../ont/Hotel.owl#SeaSports" ;
             match:predicate "http://www.w3.org/02/22-rdf-syntax-ns#type";
             match:subject "?a" ] ;
        match:matchDegree "SUBSUMES" ;
        match:mustBindVariable "?x" .
```

Fig. 7. N3 formatted Seagent Match Request transferred in the ACL Message content

4.4 Semantic Capability Matching on DF

When DF of the MAS receives request of the traveler agent; it determines proper
hotel agents - that means semantically "right" agents - and returns their descriptions back to the traveler agent. As first, the engine performs an RDQL query
on the advertised hotel agent services and filters them according to the non-
semantic parameters. Then, it uses its reasoner (Ontolog) to determine semantic
relationship between the given request and recently filtered service advertisements. As given in the request of the traveler, semantic query is performed on
service type and activity property of the descriptions. For both semantic parameters, match degree is desired as "SUBSUMES" in the request. Semantic match
on service type is straightforward and all the advertised services are acceptable.
However, the traveler agent have asked for the hotel info services those have at
least a subsumes relationship between the given request activity type (SeaSports

in case). So, the engine matches the service descriptions hotel1, hotel3 and hotel4 with the given request and sorts the match results starting from the most exact one(s) in the following order: hotel4, hotel1, hotel3 with EXACT, SUBSUMES and SUBSUMES match degrees respectively. Each match result is returned in a SeagentMatchResult object.

5 Conclusion

The main contribution of this study is to present how to develop a MAS running on the Semantic Web environment. The case study, that is discussed in here, has been implemented successfully by using the semantic features of the SEAGENT platform. SEAGENT both presents a new development framework and a platform that developers can use to create semantically enriched MASs. That means ACL content transfer, agent service discovery and agent planning would all be performed via processing the semantic knowledge of the environment.

Acknowledgments

This work is supported in part by the Scientific and Technical Research Council of Turkey (TÜBITAK), Project Number: 102E022. This support is gratefully acknowledged.

References

1. Bellifemine, F., Poggi, A., and Rimassa, G.: Developing Multi-agent Systems with a FIPA-compliant Agent Framework, Software Practice and Experience, 31 (2001) 103–128
2. Berners-Lee, T., Hendler, J. and Lassila, O.: The Semantic Web, Scientific American, 284(5) (2001) 34–43
3. Botelho, L., Willmott, S., Zhang, T., and Dale, J.: A review of Content Languages Suitable for Agent-Agent Communication, EPFL I&C Technical Report #200233.
4. Chen, H., et al.: Intelligent Agents Meet Semantic Web in a Smart Meeting Room, in the proc. of Autonomous Agents and Multi Agent Systems 2004 (AAMAS'04), NY, USA
5. Cost, R. S., et al.: Ittalks: A Case Study in the Semantic Web and DAML+OIL, IEEE Intelligent Systems, January-February (2002) 40–46
6. Cost, R. S., et al.: Jackal: A Java-Based Tool for Agent Development, in the proc. workshop tools for Developing Agents (AAAI98), AAAI Pres, Calif. (1998) 73–82
7. Dikenelli, O., Gümüs, O., Tiryaki, A. M. and Kardas, G.: Engineering a Multi Agent Platform with Dynamic Semantic Service Discovery and Invocation Capability, Multiagent System Technologies - MATES 2005, Lecture Notes in Computer Science (Subseries: Lecture Notes in Artificial Intelligence), Springer-Verlag, Vol. 3550 (2005) 141–152
8. Dikeneli, O., Erdur, R. C., Gumus, O., Ekinci, E. E., Gurcan, O., Kardas, G., Seylan, I. and Tiryaki, A. M.: SEAGENT: A Platform for Developing Semantic Web Based Multi Agent Systems, AAMAS'05, ACM AAMAS (2005) 1271–1272

 9. FIPA (Foundation for Intelligent Physical Agents): FIPA Specifications, available at: http://www.fipa.org
10. Graham, J. R., Decker, K. S. and Mersic, M.: DECAF - A Flexible Multi Agent Systems Infrastructure, Journal of Autonomous Agents and Multi-Agent Systems, 7 (2003) 7–27
11. JENA - A Semantic Web Framework for Java, available at: http://jena.sourceforge.net
12. Kardas, G., Gümüs, Ö. and Dikeneli, O.: Applying Semantic Capability Matching into Directory Service Structures of Multi Agent Systems", Computer and Information Sciences - ISCIS 2005, Lecture Notes in Computer Science, Springer-Verlag, Vol. 3733 (2005) 452–461
13. McGuiness, D. L., and van Harmelen, F.: OWL Web Ontology Language Overview, (2004), available at: http://www.w3.org/TR/owl-features/
14. Paolucci, M., et al.: A Planning Component for RETSINA Agents, Intelligent Agents VI, LNAI 1757, N. R. Jennings and Y. Lesperance, eds., Springer-Verlag, 2000
15. Sycara, K., Paolucci, M., Ankolekar, A., and Srinavasan, N.: Automated discovery, interaction and composition of Semantic Web Services, Journal of Web Semantics, Elsevier 1 (2003) 27–46
16. Sycara, K., Paolucci, M., Van Velsen, M. and Giampapa, J.: The RETSINA MAS Infrastructure, Journal of Autonomous Agents and Multi-Agent Systems, 7 (2003) 29–48
17. The OWL Services Coalition: OWL-S: Semantic Markup for Web Services, availabe at: http://www.daml.org/services/owl-s/1.1/
18. Zou, Y., Finin, T., Ding, L., Chen, H., and Pan, P.: Using Semantic Web Technology in Multi-Agent Systems: A Case Study in the TAGA Trading Agent Environment, ICEC 2003, Oct 2003, Pittsburgh PA.
19. Greenwood, D., and Calisti, M.: Engineering Web Service - Agent Integration, IEEE Systems, Cybernetics and Man Conference, 10–13 October, 2004, The Hague, The Netherlands.
20. Louis, V. and Martinez, T.: An Operational Model for the FIPA-ACL Semantics, Proceedings of the AAMAS'05 Workshop on Agent-Communication (AC'2005), Utrecht, The Netherlands. (2005)
21. Nguyen, T. X. and Kowalczyk, R.: WS2JADE: Integrating Web Service with Jade Agents, Proceedings of the AAMAS'05 Workshop on Service-Oriented Computing and Agent-Based Engineering (SOCABE'2005), Utrecht, The Netherlands (2005)
22. Varga, L. Zs., Hajnal, A.: Engineering Web Service Invocations from Agent Systems, Proceedings of the 3rd International Central and Eastern European Conference on Multi-Agent Systems, CEEMAS 2003, June 16–18, Prague, Czech Republic (2003) 626–635

Agent Information Server: A Middleware for Traveler Information

Mahdi Zargayouna[1,2], Flavien Balbo[1,2], and Julien Saunier Trassy[2]

[1] Inrets - Gretia, National Institute of Transportation Research and their Security,
2, avenue du Général Malleret-Joinville,
F-94114 Arcueil Cedex
[2] Lamsade, Paris Dauphine University,
Place du Maréchal de Lattre de Tassigny,
75775 Paris Cedex 16, France
{zargayou, balbo, saunier}@lamsade.dauphine.fr

Abstract. This paper proposes an Agent Traveler Information Server (ATIS) for a daily trip in an urban area. It is based on the multi-agent paradigm and is using the Environment as Active Support of Interaction (EASI) model. It instantiates the mutual awareness concept. The purpose is to allow services, information sources and human travelers to be represented by a unified agent structure and to allow them to interact homogeneously although they are conceptually different. Given that the whole information process must be envisaged in a real time configuration, the increase of the interactions has to be taken into account and the classical interaction modes become rapidly inefficient. The EASI model enables agents to build their interaction interests egocentrically and delegates the interaction management to the multi-agent environment.

1 Introduction

Traveler Information Systems (TIS) are applications of great interest for the multi-agent paradigm. The multiplication of independent transportation services and of the information resources in the network are suitable to the design of distributed systems. These applications and the human users connected to the system try to achieve independent goals; they correspond to the agent conception in Multi-Agent Systems (MAS). In a TIS, the main purpose of an agent is to get the information concerning its context at the right time. The information flow management is then crucial, especially when the number of agents is very high (services, information resources and users) and very changing (users' agents are present temporarily, just as long as the traveler is not yet at his destination). The management of interactions between these heterogeneous agents is therefore the main task to be fulfilled by the system. The problem is to know which agent can match the other's functional needs. In MAS, the use of specialized agents (called middle-agents) that help others to locate service providers is a solution that is frequently used. The advantage of this approach is to locate an agent by its capabilities, thus allowing a matching with the needs of the agents.

O. Dikenelli, M.-P. Gleizes, and A. Ricci (Eds.): ESAW 2005, LNAI 3963, pp. 14–28, 2006.
© Springer-Verlag Berlin Heidelberg 2006

During the interaction step, mobile agents can also be used to reduce the communication cost by limiting the number of remote interactions and the amount of data exchanged over the network. Our proposition combines the advantages of the middle agents and the mobile agents' approaches. It solves the problems dealing with a dynamic informational context and more generally each real time information management. Such problems include the fact that the information management process must take into account the reactivity of agents not to information sources only but to the information content too, and moreover the reactivity of agents may be based on a combination of information provided by different sources.

Our middleware belongs to the field of Distributed Agent Environment [18], and interaction within the platform is based on the EASI - Environment as Active Support of Interaction - model, which enables each agent to perceive information that is available in the environment [2]. The remainder of the paper is structured as follows: section 2 presents the traveler information domain, section 3 presents the EASI model; section 4 shows our Agent Traveler Information Server application; and section 5 draws general conclusions.

2   Application Domain

The design of a Traveler Information System (TIS) should meet the growing needs of travelers, helping them to choose a mode of transportation, and facilitating their use of the networks [1]. In fact, travelers' requirements are on the rise, since the volume of information sources are increasing rapidly and with new technologies it should theoretically be possible for everyone to receive the information wherever he is. Thus, a TIS should provide two types of information: first, information before the trip starts providing the global offer over all transportation modes for a given request; second, it should provide information during the user's trip, notifying him about events that could occur on his route. Conscious of the importance of the traveler information in their relationship with their customer, the transport operators propose an answer which is adapted to their needs as it is presented in the next section. However, this answer is heterogeneous and disseminated and MAS are a solution to propose an aggregated answer to this problem as we describe it in the section 2.2.

2.1   The Operators' Approach

Operators' responses include passive information - such as variable message boards - and/or interactive information such as web servers or Personal Assistants. However, the information provided by the operators usually only concerns their own transportation mode(s): each operator has access to his own data and provides information to his own customers. The advantage of this type of management is to facilitate information update and to ensure a good quality service for their customer. In addition, the operator traveler information is generally based on existing information provided and used by their operating system. For instance the Dynasty[1] project aims to establish a demonstration of an Integrated Traffic Information Platform in China, including traffic data collection, modelling and communication. The broadcast of real time traffic information is one part of the project and will be specific to this information system. In the ITISS[2] project five partner cities share their knowledge and experience. Every partner has already a number of existing services and databases of travel information; and the main emphasis of this project will be to deliver information from these systems to a range of media, particularly to mobile devices. The project will also consider making multi-lingual information available and using natural language interfaces to systems and services. The objective for each of the cities is to open its databases, but not to propose an information system enabling the integration of other information sources. However, operator information makes the mutual management of different sources difficult, and requires the user to be adaptable, that is why preparing a trip is still a hard task [12]. The multi-agent paradigme offers solutions for automating certain tasks of the travelers and to design advanced services that the multi agent paradigm offers solutions.

2.2   The Multi-agent Approach

The multi-agent paradigm offers solutions to these kinds of problems and MAS are frequently used to develop systems that are adapted to the transportation domain [16, 5] and particularly to the traveler information domain [4, 6, 11]. Two European projects are based on a multi-agent approach: Ask-IT[3] and Imagine@ IT[4] [15]. In the traveler information context, the first function for the system is to collect the information from heterogeneous and distributed systems. In fact, the user should have the possibility to express his needs without necessarily knowing the information sources that are able to answer it. In order to build a personalised answer, the second function is to integrate the obtained data. The traveler should be able to specify his preferences and to receive answers according to his profile. Finally, the last function is to ensure an information follow-up in order to supervise the good unfolding of the traveler's move. The traveler has to be notified about any event that could occur on his route, which is able to disturb it, and solutions (alternatives) have to be proposed to him.

This adequacy between the traveler information domain and the recognized characteristics of agents is at the origin of the application part of the work of the FIPA (Foundation for Intelligent Physical Agents). One example of this formalization allows a human user to book a trip simply by indicating the detail of his need to his PTA (Personal Travel Assistant) [13]. The organization proposed by FIPA is efficient for obtaining pre-trip information: it proposes a solution to the problem of collecting and customizing the information and an advanced function automating the negotiation phase, all of the process is ensured by a dyadic interaction, following a request-response pattern. But though this is essential for the

---

[1] http://www.ertico.com/en/activities/projects_and_fora/dynasty.htm
[2] http://www.itiss-eu.com/
[3] http://www.ask-it.org/
[4] http://www.imagineit-eu.org/

automation of the activities of a travel agency, it is impractical for information about daily travel. For a traveler in a city or suburban network, the problem is not to identify the information sources (that are known) but to manage his moves dynamically, so he can receive personalized information only when the information concerns him. The second phase of the traveler's information process, i.e. providing him with real-time personalized information about a given trip, cannot efficiently be achieved in the same way as pre-trip information. In a real-time configuration, the request/response pattern becomes expensive especially in a very dynamic context like daily information in an urban area. In Im@gine IT, the MAS forwards events generated by Service and Content Providers to B2C Operators. B2C Operators will find out the users that are interested in the particular event by looking at the database of registered user subscriptions, which is stored together with the user profile. This organisation is close to our proposition and answers to the efficiency criticism. Nevertheless, the use of a database limits the personalization possibilities to the traveller profile. The possibility to link independent events is in this project the task of specialized agents (service agent) and is not directly possible for the traveller.

To solve this problem, we use the mutual awareness concept to convey the right information to the right user i.e. the one who is concerned by the information according to its own preference.

3   The EASI Model

Interaction is in the center of the design of a multi-agent system. It should allow agents to locate each others corresponding to their needs. Also, as much as it is possible, it should not be scale sensitive and should avoid message overloads and communication bottlenecks. In open environments such as internet, where agents don't know each others a priori, middle-agents are used mostly as a service tracker [8]. They are based on the capability-based coordination which is a preference/ability matching, in order to identify the best provider for a given capability search. However, assimilating preference and capability is not sufficient when the problem is not the location of the information but the content itself. If in [15] a middle-agent is used to find a specialized service, the event management is done in another way: a push mechanism based on a database, with the limits that have already been described. The receiver can gain efficiency by choosing itself its sources and criteria. In addition, with a middle-agent, dynamic information rapidly increases the number of message exchanges in order to maintain a valid representation of the world for the agents [3]. This could lead to the apparition of bottlenecks when the agents' interactional needs are high and varying rapidly. Dugdale [9] has proved that, in a dynamic informational context like regulation, a large part of the interactions derive from the concept of mutual awareness, the ability of the agents to take into account not only the messages but also the information itself, as the unit of treatment to be processed. Some systems provide a partial answer to this problem of dynamic information sharing through distributed systems, like LIME [14] or Javaspaces[10]. The first is a system which permits tuple-space sharing among distributed platforms, without necessarily knowing which tuple-spaces are accessible. The second is a java-based technology which makes it possible to share spaces containing objects between distributed agents. It is based on object put and retrieval, with an inscription/notification system. Even if these two technologies are close to our interaction needs, LIME doesn't ensure the consistency of the tuple-space. It is a sort of distributed blackboard, which means that the agents have to read the blackboard explicitly instead of receiving their messages, and it does not correspond to a whole unified communication system. This second statement also applies to Javaspaces, although there is a template-based notification system. Because the templates cannot be composed, it is not possible for agents to have a combined interest for several sources simultaneously. In addition, it has been proved that the serialisability of the system was not guaranteed.

As an agent knows better than any other agents what its interactional needs are, it should be able to choose which messages it wants to pay attention to, decided according to its interests and independently of the sender. As a mirror, the sender should be given the same possibility about the receivers and, since broadcast costs a lot, both in terms of network occupation and to every agent of the system obliged to process it even if it's not interested in the message content, mutual awareness should be enabled inside the environment itself. The matching of the relevant receivers should no longer be based on preference and abilities, but on the content of the message itself and the interests of the agents.

The solution proposed here is based on distant clients who communicate with representative agents located on the server-side. This scheme enables computation-based communication to occur only on the server side and allows the agents to use local technologies fully, thus making possible to use the mutual awareness interaction model. The Agent Traveler Information Server (ATIS) proposed in section 4 is based on these features.

3.1   The Interaction Model

Mutual awareness is based on the sharing of interactions. To be efficient, this principle implies that agents share a common communication media. As a consequence, an agent has to find among all messages only those that it is interested in. In the reactive agent community, the environment is already used as a common media of interaction. In the cognitive agent community, we have proposed the EASI model [2]. It enables cognitive agents to use the environment to exchange messages and, more precisely, it enables an agent to send messages to an other agent that is located by the environment and it enables agents to perceive every exchanged message. To find useful information from a very large data set, we have grounded our model on symbolic data analysis theory. This theory is aimed at discovering information by modelling both qualitative and quantitative data grouped into what is named symbolic object. In our research, we consider that environment contains symbolic descriptions of messages and agents. The interactional problem is to make possible for agents the use of these descriptions to locate messages according to the environment state.

Let us introduce basic symbolic data analysis definitions that we found in [7]. A symbolic object is a triple $s = (a, R, d)$ where R is a comparison operator between descriptions, d is a description and a is a mapping from Ω (set of individuals, also called entities) in L ($L = \{true, false\}$ or $L = [0, 1]$). An assertion is a special case of a symbolic object and is written as follows: $\forall w \in \Omega$ $a(w) = \wedge_{i=1,\ldots,p}[y_i(w)R_id_i]$ where $y_i(w)$ is the value of the individual w for the symbolic variable y_i. When an assertion is asked of any particular entity $w \in \Omega$, it assumes a value true ($a(w) = 1$) if that assertion holds for that entity, or false ($a(w) = 0$) if not.

In our EASI model, we have added this notation to formalize the knowledge about the description of interaction components (messages and agents). Because it enables to represent the agents, it is possible for agents to create their own interactional context as a set of assertions. In EASI, the set of individuals is the environment (noted E). It contains two types of entities: agents and messages. Symbolic variables will be called visible properties and noted Pv_j, $j = 1, \ldots, p$. Let $M = (Pv_j)$, $j = 1, \ldots, r$ ($r <= p$) be the definition of the message class and $A = (Pv_j)$, $j = r + 1, \ldots, p$ the definition of the agent class. This last one may be composed of several agent' subclasses, each of them is described by a subset of visible properties and has a null value for the other. Each agent description is updated by the agent itself, modifying dynamically the value of its visible properties. In E, filters co-exist with agents and messages, this will make possible to link a particular message with particular agents. Because an assertion concerns only one entity at the same time, we propose to define a filter as an extension of an assertion. For each agent $e_a \in A$, each message $e_m \in M$ and (e_j), $j = 1, \ldots, ll \subset E$ when the filter $f_k(e_a, e_m, (e_j))$ is true, agent e_a is interested by message e_m, and $(e_j)j = 1, \ldots, ll$ verify the imposed relations ((e_j) is optional).

A message put in the environment will be perceived by every agent that has a filter that is matched in the current informational context. The next section describes how we use the dynamicity in the interaction to propose an information server that is controlled by its users.

3.2 The Middleware Architecture: Agent Information Server (AIS)

Because, in the EASI interactional model, the environment contains filters (created by agents) and entities (public description of agents and messages), we can propose an information middleware dynamically parameterized by its users. An efficient management of information exchange between several requesters and providers means taking into account the dynamicity of the interests of the requesters for heterogeneous providers and also the cost of the information exchange. Our architecture meets these requirements. The mutual awareness model proposed by EASI makes it possible to put together all the information, each agent perceiving only that information which, according to its filters, concerns its interests. This Agent Information Server (AIS) architecture does not duplicate information from the provider but organizes its use in a defined context. Our server is a common place where requesters and providers exchange information through a common environment.

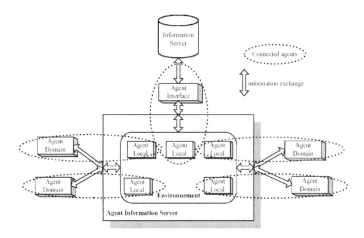

Fig. 1. Agent Information Server (AIS)

Within our proposition, according to the dynamicity of their information, two types of provider behaviours are possible. For static information, a provider waits for users' requests. In this case, the server is used by requesters in order to identify the provider (with the use of the visible properties) and to interact with it in a normalized way. For dynamic information, a provider puts updated information into the environment. In this case, the server is used by requesters to identify which information has some interest for them from among all data available in the environment. New information is put in the environment once and is received by all interested users.

The multi-agent system upon which our architecture is based is made up of three types of agents (Figure 1). The first, *Interface* agent, is the link between an existing information server and our own. This agent is used by the others to interact with the external server in a normalized way (static information) and/or to gather relevant information for the MAS and to put it in the environment (dynamic information). Using an *Interface* agent within our multi-agent system makes it possible to keep a homogeneous system with heterogeneous components. Agents do not have to know the external server to interact with it; they only need to know which kind of service it provides. This implies that the server may be changed and that the technical means used to interact (http, ftp, SOAP, etc.) is hidden from the users' agents.

The second type of agent is the *Domain* agent. Contrary to *Interface* agents which are not interested in using information coming from the environment (they are only information providers), *Domain* agents may be requesters and/or providers of information. These two agent categories are not located on the server. Using them in our proposal solves the problem of provider identification and standardizes interaction with heterogeneous information providers. Nevertheless the communication cost remains high because each interaction has to be carried out with a message exchange between distant agents.

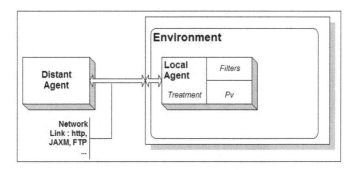

Fig. 2. Relation between distant and local agent

To solve this problem our multi-agent system has a third category of agent, *Local* agent, which is located on the server. Thus, a part of the processing may be done on the server, reducing the communication cost (as with mobile agents). Each distant agent (*Interface* and *Domain* agent) has a representative (*Local* agent) on the server (Figure 2).

The role of this entity is to manage interaction for the distant agent, by creating/deleting filters according to the needs of the distant agent. For each perceived message, it decides what to do with it. Alternative is to deal with it or to forward it to the distant agent. In that way, the exchanged messages are limited to those that are essential for distant agents. The role of the *Local* agent implies a hybrid architecture, since this agent is the link between the informational environment (it can put and perceive messages inside the middleware) and the application environment (it can send and receive messages to and from distant applications).

Sharing responsibility for interaction processing between local and distant agents means that distant agents may participate in several MAS. For each participation they delegate their interaction needs to their local agent.

4   Agent Information Server

4.1   The Software Architecture

In order to use the AIS architecture to implement an agent-traveler information server, we have to introduce which agent in our architecture is equivalent to which agent in AIS. The distant information systems can be *Interface* or *Domain* agents. The MPTA (Mobile Personal Travel Assistants) are *Domain* agents, whose role is to "link" the human user to the system. They are the software interlocutors of our system (Figure 3).

In order to test our proposal, we have implemented three information systems. The first is an application that is an *Interface* agent with an existing web service[5] - working following a request/response model - and that creates a trip

---

[5] http://patriceb.users.mcs2.netarray.com

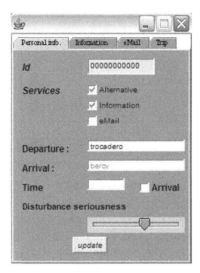

Fig. 3. Preference user interface

as an answer to a request. The result of the http request is an xml file containing the sequence of transportation modes to be taken by the user to reach his destination. The second, the traffic system, is also an *Interface* agent connected to an existing service [17] that gives information about the traffic (accidents, deceleration, etc.) and the corresponding seriousness of the disruptions. The messages sent by this service are broadcasted through the environment with no specified receiver. The third and last system - called "alternative" - is specific to our application and gives the nearest alternative station rather than the one which has been received as a request parameter. This last agent is a *Domain* agent which uses information coming from the middleware to find the best alternative for travelers when there are disruptions.

For each of these distant agents (*Interface* or *Domain*), *Local* agents representing them are created. *Local* agents are divided into two categories: the first are the agents that we called LA which are permanent, because they represent a distant information system. The second, that we have called PTA (Personal Travel Assistant), are agents which are transitory because they represent an MPTA: they are created the first time a user connects to the server and erased at the end of his session. The first time the user connects, his profile and preferences are uploaded from his MPTA to the corresponding newly created PTA.

The users' preferences are entered via a standard interface where he is asked to determine the categories of services that interest him (warning announcement, alternative) (figure 3). His choice determines the behaviour of his associated PTA. For instance, the seriousness of the disturbance determines in which cases the PTA will warn him. If the value is high, he will only receive the information on disturbances that changes his travel-plans considerably. The relation between MPTA and PTA underlines the information filtering process that a Local agent enables. The first level concerns the filters and visible properties. At this level only useful information (according to the Distant agent preferences) are perceived by the Local agent. To do that, a PTA will use the kind of services the user needs, the trip properties (departure and arrival location) and the seriousness value. This information will be used to create the personalized filters like this one: (f2) fPTA (ea, em) = [networkPosition(em) networkPosition(ea)] [seriousness(ea) ? seriousness(em)][6]. The second level concerns the Local agent behaviour. If the human user chooses the alternative service it will forward not the filtered information that it receives about a disruption but an alternative to the initial trip if it exists (see section 4.2).

We focus now on the few technologies used to implement our traveler information server. Some problems had to be solved in order to instantiate the EASI model onto a real implementation. First, a problem is the synchronisation between distant application and the server. Since in the EASI model, messages are caught by filters without the intervention of the owner distant agent, we have to find a way to convey the message to the distant agent asynchronously, what cannot be done upon http which is a synchronous protocol. We chose to send our messages via an api (JAXM[7]) which enables us to send our messages via a provider in an asynchronous way, which releases our server and the distant agent of the synchronisation of http. Second, we want to do the same with the distant users, they shouldn't be obliged to wait for a response of the server i.e. to wait for a response to their messages, since the remainder of the interaction is asynchronous. The solution is to use an intermediate xml page dedicated to the user, page that is refreshed periodically (e.g. a few seconds, 10 in our test application). The messages exchanged over the network are SOAP[8] messages.

4.2   The Scenario of Execution

Figure 2 illustrates our matter. The numbers show the chronologic order of the exchanges. Figure 3 focuses on the internal interactions -the messages exchanged inside the middleware, presented by an AUML diagram. Chronologically, the traveler connects to the server (via his MPTA) and a PTA representing him is created. We suppose that our user is interested in the three services described above. After specifying his departure and destination points, he is asked to wait until his request is processed. His PTA creates a message with this information and deposits it in the environment. In this case, the message is intended to the LAs which have a planning capability - only one in our case (1). When the planning LA receives the message, it forwards it to the *Interface* planning agent. To do so, the request is wrapped into a SOAP message and sent via the Web (2). Then, the distant *Interface* agent requests the planning service for a plan (via http) and the latter sends it back in a message containing an xml trip plan (3). This is transformed - by the LA - into a message obeying the environment syntax,

---

[6] The visible property networkPosition not really exist but regroups all data that are useful to locate an information on a network.

[7] http://java.sun.com/xml/downloads/jaxm.html

[8] http://www.w3.org/TR/SOAP

addressed to the user's PTA (4). Note here that the presence of the *Interface* agent between the LA agent and the planning system has the advantage that the same *Interface* agent can have more than one LA agent representing it in different middleware servers, covering different transportation networks. This way, the user connects in exactly the same way to different networks, and the presence of different services is transparent to him.

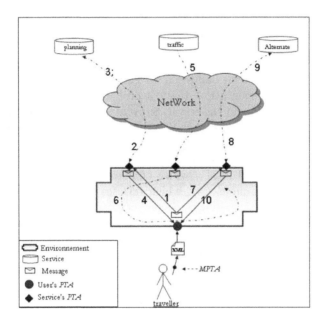

Fig. 4. Example of messages routing

When the user's PTA receives the xml plan corresponding to its initial user's request, it forwards it to its MPTA to inform the user, then it parses it and generates a filter for every plan segment (a plan segment is a part of a trip, provided by only one transport mode). This way, the PTA of a user restricts its reception conditions just to the information concerning its own trip. For each of the interaction within the AUML interaction diagram Figure 3, we have noted the visible properties that an agent uses to receive a message. For instance, each agent has an identifier and it is a visible property that can be used to address a message. This diagram is only related to the interaction between agents within the information server and based on the EASI model.

The *Interface* traffic agent collects information - via ftp - on CLAIRE SITI [17] and forwards it to the middleware. If a warning concerns a part of the user's trip (which is the case in Figure 2(5)), the message is intercepted by its PTA (Figure 3 (6)). The type of a message (in this case a warning) is a visible property. Note that this information is also used by alternative LA to intercept this message in order not to send another station concerned by a traffic problem. This interaction is based on the mutual awareness paradigm because this is

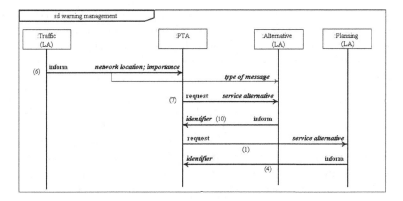

Fig. 5. Warning management protocol

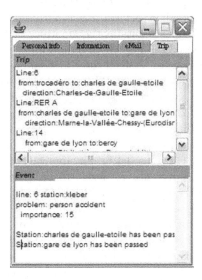

Fig. 6. Trip information interface

directed by the receiver and not by the sender of the message. This last one gives several visible properties to its messages and their values are used by receivers to choose which of the messages has interest for them. The network location and disturbance seriousness are visible properties for a warning message. Each PTA according to these values can intercept this information. This interaction directed by the receiver is also based on the mutual awareness paradigm. That implies that agents share the global environment knowledge that the visible properties are. This kind of interaction is represented by the double connection (Figure 3 (6)).

When there is no problem, the basic behaviour of the Local agent is to update its filters according to the traveler trip. The figure 4 pictures this comportment because each event relative to a station being passed corresponds to the corresponding rules removing from the environment. For instance when the station Charles-de-Gaulle has been passed the filter concerning the trip relative to the the line 6 has been removed.

In our example, we suppose that the disturbance is serious enough to be intercepted by the user's PTA (superior to the value of the disturbance seriousness given by the user). As the alternative service has been chosen by the user, the PTA puts in the environment a message "addressed" to the agent which has the alternative capabilities (7–8–9–10). Once the alternative station is received, the PTA sends an addressed message to the planning LA asking for a plan with the alternative station as a departure point (1–2). These interactions are based on a preference ability matching like with a middle-agent and thus EASI enables the same advantage to dissociate a service from a particular agent. Each LA has a visible property (called service) that is a list where all their abilities are recorded. Because each request contains the identifier of the sender, the answer of a LA to the PTA is based on a dyadic interaction.

When receiving the new plan (3–4), if the additional cost with the alternative trip is less than the current delay, the PTA proposes it to the human user and asks him if he wants to avoid the disrupted station. In this case, and if the new plan is validated by the user, the old filters are replaced by the new ones concerning the new plan; only the events concerning this new plan will henceforth be received.

Thus, with the use of EASI model in our application, it is possible, for the interaction of an agent (representing a user), to be dynamically parameterized by its context, through the update of its filters. Our middleware enables agent to interact in a normalized way. The use of existing classical web services is totally transparent to him; interaction with any kind of service is homogenized by the environment interaction protocol. Moreover, using the same middleware, agents can communicate through dyadic and ability matching if the sender and receiver are interested in the interaction or mutual awareness interaction if only the receiver is interested. Using AIS also enabled us to build a complex service based on different sources that had not been pre-defined to offer such a service.

5   Conclusion and Perspectives

The basic principles behind our Agent Information Server (AIS) described in this paper are principles generally acknowledged to be of interests in the multi-agent community. The operationalisation of these principles for a dynamic informational context imposes to take into account the update of information and/or of the agents' interest. Our proposition to use mutual awareness to create a communication space where representative of distant agents interact limits the communication cost. Our mutual awareness model (called EASI) is based on a property-based interaction model, which generalizes the capability-based coordination model. In that way, our model enables to take into account the content of information and so, more specific interaction.

A real application of a Transportation Information System illustrates our proposition. This specialized middleware integrates several information servers and enables normalized interaction with them. Because a middleware regroups services relative to a local network, an information server may be used in a specific middleware or in several ones. For instance, the planning *Interface* gives information for several networks whereas a server for a local taxi network will have only one representative. On the same idea, a user making a trip between two towns will have a representative within the two networks.

We have several directions for future works. We plan to investigate the consequences of the admission or the exit of agents on services management that implies that a distant agent constructs its representative in a dynamic way. We also plan to propose a management process for taxonomy of available services. This process will have to take into account that our environment has to remain open with no specialized agent controlling its activity.

Concerning the implementation perspectives, we plan to apply our work to other domains whose problems are suitable to our interests. We think about Agent-Based Marketplaces where the attention of agents according to information varies very rapidly during a day, and could suitably be managed using our approach.

References

1. Adler, J. L., Blue, V. J.: Toward the design of intelligent traveler information systems. Transportation Research Part C 6 (1998) 157–172
2. Balbo, F., Pinson, S.: Toward a Multi-Agent Modelling Approach for Urban Public Transportation Systems. Omicini A., Petta P. et Tolksdorf R. (eds), Engineering Societies in the Agent World II, LNAI **2203**, Springer Verlag (2001) 160–174
3. Balbo F.: A new interaction model for agent based simulation. In European Simulation Multiconference, (2004)
4. Coyle, L., Cunningham, P. and Hayes, C.: A Case-Based Personal Travel Assistant for Elaborating User Requirements and Assessing Offers. Proceedings of the 6th European Conference, ECCBR 2002, Susan Craw, Alun Preece (eds.). LNAI volume **2416**, Springer-Verlag (2002) 505–518
5. Davidsson, P., Henesey, L., Ramstedt, L., Trnquist, J., Wernstedt,F. : An Analysis of Agent-Based Approaches to Transport Logistics. Transportation Research Part C: Emerging Technologies, **Vol. 13(4)**, Elsevier, (2005) 255–271
6. Dia, H.: An agent-based approach to modelling driver route choice behaviour under the influence of real-time information. Transportation Research Part C10 (2002) 331–349
7. Diday, E., Hébrail, G.: Symbolic Data Analysis: some in and out. Kesda'98 Eurostat Luxembourg, April (1998) 19–24
8. Decker, K., Sycara, K. and Williamson, M.: Middle-Agent for the Internet. In Fifteenth International Joint Conference on Artificial Intelligence, Morgane Kaufmann (1997) 578–583.

9. Dugdale, J., Pavard, J., Soubie, B.: A Pragmatic Development of a Computer Simulation of an emergency Call Center Designing Cooperative System, Frontiers in Artificial Intelligence and Applications, Rose Dieng et al., IOS Press' (2000)

10. Freeman E., Hupfer S., Arnold K. : JavaSpaces(TM) Principles, Patterns, and Practice. Pearson Education; 1st edition (June 15, 1999)

11. Moraitis, P., Petraki, E. and Spanoudakis, N.: Providing Advanced, Personalised Infomobility Services Using Agent Technology. Proceedings of the 23rd SGAI International Conference on Innovative Techniques and Applications of AI (AI'2003), Cambridge, UK, 15th–17th 2003.

12. O'Brien, P. D., Nicol, R. C.: FIPA - towards a standard for software agents. BT Technol J, 16, 3 (1998) 51–59

13. O'Sullivan, D., Nnez-Surez, J., brochoud, H., Cros, P., Moore, C.and Byrne, C.: Experiences in the use of the FIPA agent technologies for the development of a Personal Travel Application. In proceeding of international conference on autonomous agents (Agents), Barcelone, (2000)

14. Picco, G.P., Buschini, M.L.: Exploiting Transiently Shared Tuple Spaces for Location Transparent Code Mobility. In Proceedings of the 5th International Conference on Coordination Models and Languages, York (UK), F. Arbab and C. Talcott, eds., LNCS **2315** Springer Verlag (2002) 258–273

15. Raimondi M., Manzato M., Petraki E., Spanoudakis N., Kauber M. : Services specification design and System architecture. Technical report, January (2004)

16. Schleiffer, R.: Intelligent agents in traffic and transportation. Transportation Research part C: emerging technologies (special issue), Schleiffer R. (Guest) editor, Volume 10C, Numbers 5–6 (2002)

17. Scemama, G., Carles, O.: CLAIRE-SITI, Public and Road Transport Network Management Control: A Unified Approach. IEE Road Transport Information and Control Conference, London (2004)

18. Weyns, D., Parunak, H.V.D., Michel, F., Holvoet, T. Ferber, J.: Environments for Multiagent Systems, State-of-the-art and Research Challenges. Proceedings of Workshop on Environments for Multi-Agent Systems (E4MAS) LNAI **3374** Springer Verlag (2004) 1–47

A Role Model for Description of Agent Behavior and Coordination

Yunus Emre Selçuk and Nadia Erdoğan

Istanbul Technical University, Faculty of Electrical and Electronic Engineering,
Computer Engineering Department, Maslak, TR-34469, Istanbul, Turkey
selcukyu@itu.edu.tr, erdogan@cs.itu.edu.tr

Abstract. This paper presents a role model implementation, JAWIRO (JAva WIth ROles), which enhances Java with role support. After a brief introduction to role models and the capabilities of JAWIRO, the paper proceeds to a comparison of our model with another role model and a design pattern for implementing roles. These three approaches are compared on the basis of their abilities and performances. It is shown that role models are valuable tools for modeling dynamic real world entities as they provide many useful abilities without a significant performance overhead. The dynamic nature of agents represents a good domain for using roles to describe both behavior and coordination issues. The paper ends with a sample application for agents that demonstrates how characteristics of roles may be employed.

1 Introduction

Software systems are constantly getting more complex in order to keep up with the ever changing, dynamic and heterogeneous nature of the current real world scenarios. Complex systems become easier to understand when they are described in terms of acts and responsibilities of the elements they contain [1]. Such a description leads to a better separation of concerns and therefore to better modeling. Roles allow agents to dynamically acquire capabilities to perform specific tasks, and therefore enable separation of concerns and code reusability in software development and maintenance [2].

Separation of concerns leads to the separation between the algorithmic issues and the interaction ones [3]. Roles represent a good paradigm for modeling interactions among agents. A role can be built to represent an interface for interactions, providing a set of common instruments for dealing with and allowing interactions among entities. Furthermore, roles help the modularization and the organization of MAS, separating responsibilities and rights among entities involved [4].

Agent oriented techniques are well suited for modeling complex and distributed systems [5]. As the notion of role is frequently applied for conceptualizing the behavior of human individuals, roles can be used for describing the behavior of individual agents in a multiple agent system [6]. MAS implementations such as [3, 7] can be found in literature which use roles in their approaches. Roles are also used for encapsulating the interactions between agents [7, 8]. In ROPE; roles provide a well

O. Dikenelli, M.-P. Gleizes, and A. Ricci (Eds.): ESAW 2005, LNAI 3963, pp. 29–48, 2006.
© Springer-Verlag Berlin Heidelberg 2006

defined interface between agents and cooperation processes, which enable an agent to read and follow the normative rules given by the cooperation process even if not known to the agent before [8].

This paper presents a role model implementation, JAWIRO, which enhances Java with role support for better modeling of dynamically evolving real world systems. JAWIRO provides all expected requirements of roles, as well as providing additional functionalities without a performance overhead when executing methods. An example application is also described in order to demonstrate how roles can be used in MAS.

2   Related Work

The BRAIN framework [7] covers the development of agent-based systems while modeling agent interactions with roles. The RoleX extension [3] introduces an interaction infrastructure for the BRAIN framework for Java mobile agents using bytecode manipulation for role operations. Although bytecode manipulation proves itself to be useful, it can breach the Java security mechanism. Therefore, bytecode manipulation is not used in JAWIRO.

An agent can be thought as a role or a set of roles [6]. However, having agents as roles is somewhat controversial. A role is defined as a class that defines a normative behavioral repertoire of an agent in [9]. We believe that roles are useful for representing both the coordination and the responsibilities of agents as they provide a good separation of concerns.

3   The Role Concept from the Role Models' Viewpoint

The role concept comes from the theoretical definition where it is the part of a play that is played by an actor on stage. Roles are different types of behavior that different types of entities can perform. Kristensen [10] defines a role as follows: a role of an object is a set of properties which are important for an object to be able to behave in a certain way expected by a set of other objects.

A *role model* specifies a style of designing and implementing roles. As such, coding by using roles can be called as *role based programming* (RBP). RBP provides a direct and general way to separate internal and external behaviors of objects. When a role model is built in an object oriented environment, RBP extends the concepts of OOP naturally and elegantly.

Object oriented programming is based on specialization at the class level, e.g. *(class level) inheritance*. However, specialization at the instance level is a better approach than specialization at the class level when evolving entities are to be modeled. In this case, an entity is represented by multiple objects, each executing a different role that the real-world entity is required to perform. In role based programming, an object evolves by acquiring new roles and this type of specialization at the instance level is called *object level inheritance*. When multiple objects are involved, the fact that all these objects represent the same entity is lost in the regular OOP paradigm unless the programmer takes extra precaution to keep that information such as utilizing a member in each class for labeling purposes. Role models take this burden from the programmer and provide a mechanism for object level inheritance.

Object level inheritance successfully models the *IsPartOf* [11] relation where class level inheritance elegantly models the *IsA* [11] relation. As both types of relationship are required when modeling real world systems, both types of inheritance should coexist in an object-oriented environment. Therefore, many role models are implemented by extending an object-oriented language of choice, such as INADA [12], DEC-JAVA [13], the works of Schrefl and Thalhammer [14] and Lee and Bae [15], etc.

4   Overview of JAWIRO

Our role model JAWIRO extends the Java programming language with role support. Java has been chosen as the base language because even though it has advanced capabilities that help to its widespread use, it lacks features to design and implement roles in order to model dynamic object behaviors. JAWIRO implements all basic features of roles as well as additional capabilities that can be expected from roles, e.g. the extended features of roles.

4.1   Features of Roles

Definition of the basic features of roles varies slightly among different researchers [10, 14]. We believe the basic features of a role model should contain the following:

- Roles can be gained and abandoned dynamically and independently of each other.
- Roles can be organized in various hierarchical relationships. A role can play other roles, too.
- The notion that a real world object is defined by all its roles is preserved, e.g. each   role object is aware of its owner and the root of the hierarchy.
- An entity can switch between its roles any time it wishes. This means that any of the roles of an object can be accessed from a reference to any other role.
- A role can access member variables and methods of other roles by means of the two previously described features.
- Class level inheritance can be used together with object level inheritance.
- Entities can be queried whether they are currently playing a certain type of role or a particular role object.
- An entity can have more than one instance of the same role type. Such roles are called aggregate roles and are distinguished from each other with an identifier.
- Different roles are allowed to have member variables and methods with same names without conflicts.

In addition to the basic features listed above, JAWIRO implements the following extended features as well:

- Roles can be suspended and then resumed.
- A role can be transferred to another owner without dropping its sub roles.
- Multiple object level inheritance is supported.

- Any public member variable or method of any participant of a role hierarchy can be accessed solely by its name, without a direct reference to its owner. In case of identical names, the most evolved member is returned.
- Previously mentioned behavior can be overridden by setting dominant nodes in a role hierarchy.
- Both consultation and delegation mechanisms are supported.
- Abnormal role bindings are prevented.
- Persistence is supported, so that users are able to save entire role hierarchies to secondary storage devices for later use.

More details and usage examples of the features of roles can be found in the following sections.

Kendall is one of the researchers who pointed out some useful properties of roles that can be used in MAS [16]. In compliance with Kendall's statements, the role model of JAWIRO does not exist to replace class models. On the contrary, JAWIRO extends the strongly typed and class based nature of Java with the basic and extended features of roles. Roles are implemented as first class objects so that they can be instantiated, generalized, specialized and aggregated; just as Kendall stated [16].

Another compliance of JAWIRO with Kendall's statements [16] is the dynamic nature of JAWIRO. Role hierarchies can be evolved by means of gaining, transferring, suspending, resuming and resigning roles. The ability of JAWIRO to access members of a participant of a role hierarchy without referencing that particular participant, combined with the dominance ability, ensures this evolution. Roles in JAWIRO can constrain each other with the use of constraint managers, again as mentioned in [16].

4.2 Role Model of JAWIRO

JAWIRO models relational hierarchies of roles with a tree representation. Such hierarchical representation enables better modeling of role ownership relations. This leads to easier and more robust implementation of roles' basic and extended characteristics.

The UML schema of JAWIRO API is given in Figure 1. The Actor class models the real world objects which can be the root of a role hierarchy. The Role class

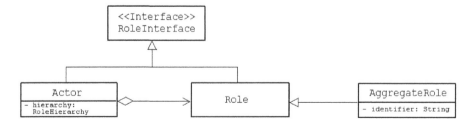

Fig. 1. The UML schema of JAWIRO API

models the role objects. The `Actor` and `Role` classes implement the `RoleInterface` as these two classes share some characteristics of roles. The aggregate roles are implemented by deriving a namesake class via class-level inheritance from `Role` class. The backbone of the role model is implemented in the `RoleHierarchy` class, where each `Actor` object has one member of this type.

4.3   Using Roles with JAWIRO

This section shows how the basic and extended features of roles can be used with JAWIRO. The examples in this section use the sample role hierarchy given in Figure 2.

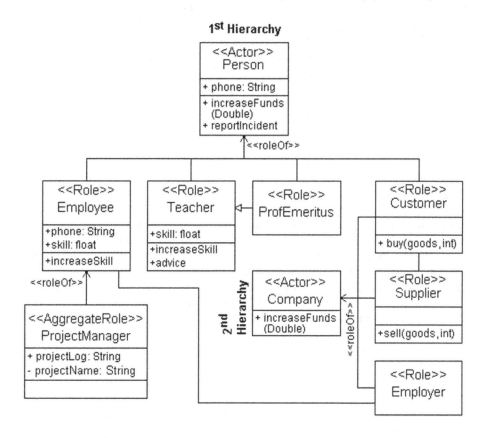

Fig. 2. A system consisting in two intersecting role hierarchies

4.3.1   Building Role Hierarchies Via Gaining and Loosing Roles
A real world entity gains and looses some roles during its lifetime and therefore may follow a different evolution path than the other entities of the same type. In case of this object level specialization, a real world entity is defined by all of the roles it currently plays. In order to build a role hierarchy in JAWIRO, an object of a class which is created by class level inheritance from the `jawiro.Actor` class and the necessary

role objects of different types which inherit from the jawiro.Role class are required. All of these objects can be created any time before they participate in a role hierarchy. Afterwards, the necessary role adding operations dictated by the requirements of the modeled system are carried out through the public boolean RoleInterface.addRole(Role aNewRole) method. If a role is no longer required, it can be dissociated from the role hierarchy by using the public boolean Role.resign() method of that role, so that it does not participate in this role hierarchy. A sample code fragment featuring these operations is given in Figure 3.

```
import jawiro.*;                     Person peTom;
class Person extends Actor {         Teacher teTom;
   String name, phone;               peTom = new Person("Thomas
   public Person( String n,              Anderson", "843-663");
       String p )                    teTom = new
   { name = n; phone = p; }}             Teacher("Physics");
class Teacher extends Role {         peTom.addRole(teTom);
   String course;                    teTom.teach();
   public Teacher( String c )        teTom.resign();
   { course = c; }                   //Tom is now retired
   public void teach() {
      /*carry out the role*/ }}
```

Fig. 3. Building a role hierarchy

4.3.2 Aggregate Roles

Sometimes it is necessary for a real world entity to be able to play the same kind of role in different contexts. For example, a person can be the leader of various projects. Aggregate roles address this need. Unlike regular roles, multiple instances of the same aggregate role type can participate in the same role hierarchy. JAWIRO uses the jawiro.AggregateRole class for this purpose. The instances of the same aggregate role are distinguished from each other with an identifier, namely the String AggregateRole.identifier member. The code fragment in Figure 4 is an example of using the aggregate roles.

```
class ProjectManager               peTom = new Person("Thomas
     extends                           Anderson", "843-663");
     AggregateRole {                pmAI = new ProjectManager(
   String projectName;                "Artificial
   public ProjectManager              Intelligence","AI");
      (String id) {                 pmVR = new ProjectManager(
      super(id);                       "Virtual Reality","VR");
      projectName = id; } }         peTom.addRole(pmAI);
Person peTom;                       peTom.addRole(pmVR);
ProjectManager pmAI, pmVR;
```

Fig. 4. Using aggregate roles. The class Person is defined in Figure 3.

4.3.3 Run Time Role Checking and Role Switching

A real world entity is modeled with multiple objects which form a role hierarchy. Each participant of a role hierarchy can be queried whether that entity is playing a particular role or not. If the entity has the desired role type, the user can ask for a reference to the object representing that role and send it a message with the obtained reference. This process is called role switching.

The various types of `public boolean RoleInterface.canSwitch` method are used for role checking, which return `true` if the desired role or aggregate role instance exists in the hierarchy. Afterwards, the user can access the desired role by using an appropriate version of the `public Object RoleInterface.as` method. Figure 5 gives examples of these methods, both for a regular and an aggregate role.

```
package test;
Person peTom;
create_hierarchy(); /*Create the role hierarchy*/
if( peTom.canSwitch("test.Teacher") )
    ((Teacher)peTom.as("test.Teacher")).introduce();
if( peTom.canSwitch("test.ProjectManager","VR") )
    ((Teacher)peTom.as("test.ProjectManager", "VR")).manage();
```

Fig. 5. Role checking and switching. The role classes are defined in Figures 3 and 4.

4.3.4 Using Class Level and Instance Level Inheritance Together

The `ProfEmeritus` class of Figure 2 shows how class level and instance level inheritances are supported together in JAWIRO. This class is created via class level inheritance from the `Teacher` role, yet it can be a part of an instance level inheritance relationship by participating in the first role hierarchy of Figure 2.

4.3.5 Suspending and Resuming Roles

According to the rules dictated by the environment, a role can be suspended temporarily and then resumed without loosing the state information and the subroles of that role. The code fragment in Figure 6 shows how to suspend and resume a role.

```
package test;
Person peTom; Teacher teTom;
peTom = new Person("Thomas Anderson","843-663");
teTom = new Teacher("Physics");
peTom.addRole(teTom);
teTom.suspend();
if( peTom.canSwitch("test.Teacher") )
   System.out.println("This is not supposed to happen!");
teTom.resume();
if( peTom.canSwitch( "test.Teacher") )
   teTom.introduce();
```

Fig. 6. Suspending and resuming role

```
Person peGordon;
peGordon = new Person("Gordon Freeman","712-257");
pmVR.transfer(peGordon);
```

Fig. 7. Role transfer

4.3.6 Role Transfer

A real world entity can transfer some of its responsibilities to another entity. JAWIRO lets a role to be transferred to another owner without dropping its sub roles. Consider the example in Figure 4 where the person Tom is given the lead of two projects. However, Tom becomes overwhelmed with his duties and transfers the leadership of one of those projects to a colleague. This case is shown in Figure 7, which represents the code fragment that is to follow the code fragment in Figure 4.

4.3.7 Preventing Abnormal Role Bindings

Abnormal role bindings are role relationships which violate the rules of the modeled system. The following restrictions are hard-coded into the JAWIRO role model as they contradict with the expected usage of roles:

- A role instance is not added to a hierarchy where that instance already exists.
- A suspended role cannot be used with commands of JAWIRO API, e.g. it cannot be transferred or switched.
- A role instance can participate in only one hierarchy at the same time.

JAWIRO also allows users to take additional precautions by defining a constraint manager. The role model implements this mechanism via the strategy design pattern [17]. If a constraint manager is assigned via Actor.setConstraintStrategy method, it will be invoked before each addRole, resign, suspend and resume command to approve the operation. If the manager implemented by the user does not approve the operation, the operation is cancelled. The interface that a constraint manager should implement is given in Figure 8.

```
public interface ConstraintStrategy {
    public boolean approveAddRole( String parentClassName, String
        childClassName );
    public boolean approveResign( String parentClassName, String
        childClassName );
    public boolean approveSuspend( String parentClassName, String
        childClassName );
    public boolean approveResume( String parentClassName, String
        childClassName );
    public void setActor( Actor anActor );}
```

Fig. 8. The interface for constraint managers

The ConstraintStrategy.setActor method is called automatically when the Actor.setConstraintStrategy method is executed. The sole parameter of the setActor method gives the coder of the constraint manager a chance to obtain a reference to the root of the role hierarchy. That reference enables the user to access any other participant of the role hierarchy and execute thorough checks when an operation such as resuming a role is being considered for approval.

4.3.8 Member Access by Name

JAWIRO allows to access a member variable or method of an object which participates in a role hierarchy, without explicitly referencing the actual object. In this case, referencing any participant of the role hierarchy is sufficient. The `Object RoleInterface.bringMember(String name)` method searches a member variable with the given name in all the participants of the role hierarchy and returns a reference to this variable. If none of the participants has such a variable, `bringMember` returns `null`. The most evolved member is returned if more than one participant of the role hierarchy have a variable with this name.

A member method is accessed in similar fashion with the `Object RoleInterface.executeMethod( String name, Object... parameters )` method. This time, the method with the given signature is searched within the role hierarchy. If the desired method is found, it is executed and its result is returned by the `executeMethod` method. Figure 9 shows the usage of this feature.

```
Person p;
Incident anIncident = new Incident("Fire");
Authority anAuthority = new Authority("Fire Brigade");
p = new Person("Yunus Emre Selçuk","212-2891990");
p.add_Teacher_or_ProfEmeritus_Role(); /* Person gains either a
teacher or a professor role, according to the events happened at
run-time. */
p.executeMethod("reportIncident",anIncident,anAuthority);
```

Fig. 9. Member method access by name

The feature of member access by name is necessary when the types of the participants of a role hierarchy are not known exactly. Object level multiple inheritance, which will be explained later, is such a case. This feature can be thought such as an order in spoken English such as "I am not interested in what you are, just give me that service if you can".

4.3.9 Dominant Roles

The previously described behaviour of accessing the most evolved member when a command of member access by name is issued can be overridden by specifying some participants of a role hierarchy to be dominant. This is achieved by executing the `RoleInterface.dominateSearch(boolean dominate)` method of a participant. When an `Actor` instance is dominant, it searches the requested member firstly in itself and returns immediately if the search succeeds. Otherwise, the rest of the role hierarchy is searched. A dominant `Role` instance acts likewise, but only when the root of its role hierarchy is not also dominant. Otherwise the search order followed is first the root, then the role itself, and finally the rest of the role hierarchy.

Figure 10 can be examined in order to understand the rules of dominance. In the left side of the Figure 10, the root of the role hierarchy is shown as a rectangle, roles are shown as ellipses and aggregate roles are shown as double ellipses with their identifiers given after a comma. Members and methods of the objects are also attached to their right. The right side of Figure 10 shows a sample code and the outcome of an instruction is shown in its remark.

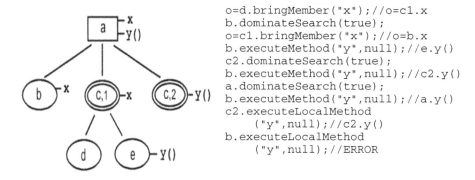

```
o=d.bringMember("x");//o=c1.x
b.dominateSearch(true);
o=c1.bringMember("x");//o=b.x
b.executeMethod("y",null);//e.y()
c2.dominateSearch(true);
b.executeMethod("y",null);//c2.y()
a.dominateSearch(true);
b.executeMethod("y",null);//a.y()
c2.executeLocalMethod
      ("y",null);//c2.y()
b.executeLocalMethod
      ("y",null);//ERROR
```

Fig. 10. Using dominant roles

4.3.10 Object Level Multiple Inheritance

JAWIRO supports multiple object-level inheritance, where owners from different classes are allowed to play the same type of role object, whenever it is required for better modeling of a real world system. This feature will not cause any logical ambiguities since only one owner can play a particular role instance at the same time. Moreover, the ability of accessing member methods and variables presented above removes the typing ambiguities.

```
class Customer extends Role {
   Supplier supplier;
   public Customer(Supplier supplier) {this.supplier=supplier;}
   public void buy( Goods aGood, int amount ) {
     if( supplier.sell(aGood,amount) )
        getActor().executeLocalMethod( "increaseFunds",
           -myGood.getUnitPrice()*amount ); }}
class Supplier extends Role {
   public boolean sell( Goods aGood, int amount ) {
     if( sale_possible() ) {
        getActor().executeLocalMethod( "increaseFunds",
           +myGood.getUnitPrice()*amount );
        return true;
     } else return false; }}
class Person extends Actor { //partial code of the class
   private double funds;
   public void increaseFunds(Double incr) { funds += incr; } }
class Company extends Actor { // partial code of the class
   private double funds;
   public void increaseFunds(Double incr) { funds += incr; } }
```

Fig. 11. Solving the typing ambiguity created by a multiple object level inheritance case

The Customer role of Figure 2 is an example as both Person and Company instances can acquire a role of this type. In this example, the cash amount available for a person and a company are kept in the Company.funds and Person.funds members, respectively. That amount should be modified after a transaction between a customer and a supplier, which is initiated by the Customer.buy method. The increaseFunds(Double incr) method of either the Person or the Company class is used for increasing or decreasing the value of the member `funds`. However, the type of the entity whose budget is to be modified can only be known at run time. Figure 11 shows how to overcome this typing ambiguity. An alternative solution is to move the `increaseFunds` method to another role such as `FundOwner`. Yet another solution would be to have the `Person` and `Company` classes to conform to a common interface such as `IntfFundOwner`. The disadvantage of these alternative solutions is their requirement of another type to be added into the modeled system.

4.3.11 Using Delegation and Consultation
By default, JAWIRO works with the consultation mechanism [12] shown in Figure 12a, where the implicit "this" parameter points to the object that the method call has been forwarded to. JAWIRO supports the alternative mechanism as well, where the implicit "this" parameter points to the original receiver of the message. This is called the delegation mechanism and shown in Figure 12b.

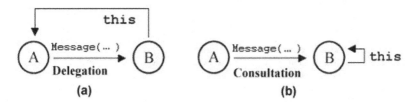

Fig. 12. Delegation (a) and consultation (b) mechanisms

Fig. 13. Different scenarios (i. and ii.) requiring different mechanisms (consultation and delegation, respectively)

JAWIRO allows to change the current mechanism for individual role hierarchies at run time. Both `Actor` and `Role` classes have an `Object` member named `self`. The `as` role switching command assigns either the former receiver of the message or the latter to the `self` member variable of the final recipient of the message, according to the current mode of operation. When writing "delegation-and-consultation-sensitive" code, users must send the messages to the `self` member.

Delegation and consultation mechanisms should not be mutually exclusive, as both may be needed for better modeling of a real-world system. Consider Figure 13, which shows a role hierarchy of a person with an employee and a professor role. Both the

ProfEmeritus and the Employee classes have a skill variable and an increaseSkill method. Two scenarios are defined in Figure 13 with roman numerals. The first one suggests that the person is in the company at the time being but he is required to give an academic advice to a student. This means that we need switching from the employee role to the professor role. The consultation mechanism should be used in this case in order to have the person's academic skill increased.

On the other hand, the second scenario suggests that the person is again is in the company at the time being and he is required to report an incident to authorities. This action requires the person to give his phone number. As the person is in the office when the incident happens, the second scenario requires switching to Person role from Employee role. This time we need to use delegation mechanism in order to give the correct phone number to the authorities, which is the work phone of the person. Otherwise, home phone would be stated. The first part of Figure 14 shows the implementation of the classes and methods mentioned in the two scenarios while the second part shows how the scenario is executed.

```
public class Employee extends Role {
   double skill; String phone;
   public Employee( String p ) { phone = p; skill = 1.0;    }
   public void increaseSkill(Double d) {skill+=d.doubleValue();}
   public String givePhone( ) { return phone;    } }
public class ProfEmeritus extends Teacher {
   public double skill;
   public ProfEmeritus(Teacher t) {super(t.course);skill=1.0;}
   public void advice( ) { //give academic advice
     ((RoleInterface)self).executeMethod("increaseSkill",0.1);}
   public void increaseSkill(Double
d){skill+=d.doubleValue();}}
public class Person extends Actor {
   String name, phone;
   public Person(String n,String p) {name = n; phone = p;}
   public void reportIncident( ) { //report the incident
     String currentPhone = (String) ((RoleInterface)self).
          ExecuteMethod ("givePhone",null);
     System.out.println("You can call me from"+currentPhone);}}
//...
Person p; Employee e; Teacher t; ProfEmeritus pre;
p = new Person("Yunus Emre Selçuk","216-7891976");
e = new Employee( "212-2853300" );
p.addRole( e ); pre = new ProfEmeritus( t ); p.addRole( pre );
p.enableDelegation( true ); p.useConsultation();
((ProfEmeritus)e.as("test.ProfEmeritus")).advice();
p.useDelegation();
((Person)e.as("test.Person")).reportIncident();
```

Fig. 14. Writing "delegation-and-consultation-sensitive" code

4.3.12   Persistent Role Hierarchies

Persistence capability is added to JAWIRO, so that users are able to save entire role hierarchies to secondary storage devices for later use. The PersistenceManager (PM) class is responsible from secure storage and retrieval of role hierarchies. A PM instance has a *persistency table* where an entry for each Actor instance that needs to be persistent is kept. The persistency table is stored in an encrypted file. The following information is automatically generated and kept in the table:

- The class name of the `Actor` object.
- The name of the file where the `Actor` object is to be serialized.
- The name of the file where the information about the role hierarchy is kept. This file is called the *information file* and it is encrypted as well.

If persistency is needed in an application, the first task to do is to create a PM instance by using the `PersistenceManager(String path, String name)` constructor. If the given persistency file does not exist, PM creates a new file. The second task is to register the root of the hierarchy with the `PersistenceManager.register(Object anActor, String key)` method. The PM instance saves the persistency table after each registration. The final task for the programmer is to upload the root of the hierarchy to the PM instance with the correct *key*, given in the previous step. This procedure is illustrated in Figure 15. JAWIRO handles the rest as follows:

- The PM instance serializes the `Actor` object to disk and encrypts the file.
- The `Actor.hierarchy` member serializes the rest of the hierarchy and encrypts all files. It creates and encrypts the information file as well.
- The PM instance encrypts all created files with the 64-bit DES algorithm.

```
PersistenceManager pm;
A a = new A(); //Class A extends Actor
construct_hierarchy(); //create the role hierarchy
pm = new PersistenceManager( "C:\\Temp\\", "test_a" );
pm.register( a, "key_a" );
pm.upload( a, "key_a" );
```

Fig. 15. Code for saving a role hierarchy to disk

If a role hierarchy is no longer needed to be persistent, the `public void PersistenceManager.unregister(String key)` method is used. This method removes the `Actor` object with the given key from the persistence table and deletes all associated files from the disk.

When a persistent role hierarchy is needed later, the user creates a PM instance and a new instance of the root class and then uploads the entire hierarchy by using the `public Object PersistenceManager.download (String key)` method, provided that the correct key is given. Figure 16 gives an example of how this is done. JAWIRO handles the rest of the procedure as follows:

- The root instance is deserialized from the secondary storage.
- The PM instantiates and deserializes the role objects belonging to the rest of the hierarchy.
- The PM instance adds the role objects to the role hierarchy in correct order.

The persistence capability of JAWIRO is implemented by using the serialization API of Java, which has a drawback: suppose that a class A has a member variable of

```
PersistenceManager pm;
A a = new A();
pm = new PersistenceManager("C:\\Temp\\","test_a");
a = (A) pm.download("key_a");
```

Fig. 16. Code for loading a role hierarchy from disk

class B. Further assume that another class C has also a member variable of class B. Let an instance of A named obj_a and an instance of C named obj_c exist and point to the same instance of B named obj_b. When obj_a and obj_c are serialized to disk and then deserialized, obj_a and obj_c no longer point to the same object obj_b but they point to two different objects having the same state as the object obj_b. The coder must explicitly check the copies and merge those two copies into one object. As a consequence; if a participant of a role hierarchy has one or more references to other Role or Actor instances, these references no longer show the original instances after serialization. The user should write additional code to correct those references.

5   Evaluating JAWIRO

This section evaluates JAWIRO in terms of both its features and performance. Schrefl and Thalhammer's role model [14] for Java and an implementation of a design pattern for roles, *role relationship* [18], are used for comparison. The role relationship pattern is extended from the role object pattern [18].

Schrefl and Thalhammer's role model [14] is implemented in Java and is available for academic use. This role model is based on Gottlob, Schrefl and Rock's previous work [19] in Smalltalk. Schrefl's recent work with Thalhammer [14] supports all primary features of roles.

5.1 Feature Comparison

JAWIRO is an extended role model which supports both the basic and extended features of roles. Table 1 shows some key features of the compared approaches, as well as other recent role models for Java.

We have kept the implementation of the role relationship pattern [18] as its original. This pattern can be extended to support additional features of roles, but we think this would cause us to loose our focus on JAWIRO. Another important work, Schrefl and Thalhammer's role model [14], supports all basic features of roles. However, it does not support the extended features of roles. This role model is available for download as a JAR file, together with its documentation.

5.2 Performance Comparison

The objective of the performance comparison is twofold. Firstly, we need to compare JAWIRO's performance with that of another role model. Secondly, we need to determine whether a significant overhead is introduced or not when roles are incorporated in an application.

Table 1. Feature based comparison of recent role models in Java

	Jawiro	Schrefl et al. [14]	Role Rel. Pattern [18]	Dec-Java [12]	Lee& Bae [15]
Base language	Java	Java	Java	Java	Java
Aggregate roles	+	+	+	+	−
Hierarchy support	+	+	−	+	−
Run-time role checking	+	+	+	−	−
Preventing role binding anomalies	+	−	−	−	+
Object level multiple inheritance	+	−	−	−	−
Member/method access without referring its owner.	+	−	−	−	−
Dominant roles	+	−	−	−	−
Delegation and consultation support	+	−	−	−	−
Role transfers	+	−	−	−	−
Suspending and resuming roles	+	−	−	−	−
Persistency	+	−	−	−	−
Role searching optimization	+	−	−	−	−

The benchmarking code first creates a role hierarchy with a given depth and degree. The tree representing the hierarchy is a balanced one. However, the role relationship pattern does not support hierarchies of depth greater than two. In this case, the code creates an equal number of role objects but adds all of them to the same object, the root. The benchmarking code then executes commands representing the basic features of roles.

In order to see how changes in the size of a role hierarchy affect performances, we should be able to create hierarchies with arbitrary depth and degree. This need leads to an arbitrary number of role objects as well. Even trees with small values of depth and degree can lead to thousands of role objects. It is practically impossible to create such great numbers of different role classes. Therefore, we've used *aggregate roles,* as defined in Section 3.1 among the basic features of roles and named as *qualified roles* in Schrefl's model [14], as role objects in the benchmark. The results of our benchmarks are given in Table 2. They are obtained by using an Intel platform with 2.8 GHz Pentium 4 CPU, i865 chipset, 512MB RAM and JDK 1.5.0_03.

There is a slight difference in creating role hierarchies between JAWIRO and Schrefl's model [14]. In JAWIRO, role objects are instantiated with an arbitrary constructor and added to an owner any time the programmer wishes by issuing the `RoleInterface.addRole(Role)` call. These two calls represent the first and the second stages given in Table 2. On the other hand, role objects must be bound with an owner during instantiation when using Schrefl's model. This represents the third stage given in Table 2. For easier comparison, the third stage for JAWIRO is calculated by adding the execution times of stages 1 and 2 in Table 2. We will name the first three stages *building phase* and the others *running phase.*

JAWIRO uses an optimization mechanism which will be explained shortly. For now, consider the un-optimized results given in Table 2 first. These results show that

Table 2. Benchmark results in Intel platform. Hierarchy depth is 6 and its degree is 3.

Stages	Average exec. time (msec.)					
	Without Optimization			With Optimization		
	Jawiro	Schrefl	Pattern	Jawiro	Schrefl	Pattern
Create members	0,009	N/A	0,009	0,0044	N/A	0,000
Add roles	0,009	N/A	0,000	0,004	N/A	0,000
Construct hierarchy	0,017	0,082	0,009	0,009	0,073	0,000
Role checking	0,018	0,009	0,041	0,0002	0,009	0,041
Role switching	0,018	0,030	0,041	0,0002	0,030	0,041
Role execution	0,006	0,005	0,004	0,003	0,003	0,002
Switching execution	0,043	0,047	0,056	0,004	0,033	0,044
Checking switching execution	0,068	0,092	0,110	0,006	0,065	0,087

using role models instead of a pattern introduces two or three-fold overhead during the building phase. However, this overhead diminishes as the running phase is more important than the building phase. The building phase is executed only once at the beginning of the application code but the operations in the running phase will be repeated continuously during the lifetime of the application program. Table 2 also shows that role models are always faster in the running phase and JAWIRO is usually faster than Schrefl's model. It is also seen that the overhead of role execution is virtually zero in all role based approaches.

One of the unique features of JAWIRO is an optimization mechanism for searching and switching roles. It is a wise choice in dynamic and persistent systems such as JAWIRO to search for existence of a role before switching to that role. Whenever the existence of a role is checked, JAWIRO keeps this particular role in a private member. When handling a following role switching command, JAWIRO first checks that private member. If the requested role is the one kept in the private member, that role is returned without searching the role hierarchy. Subsequent switching requests to this same role also return the role kept in the private member. The optimized results given in Table 2 show that this mechanism proves itself to be useful. Execution times of the benchmark stages are either halved or shortened tenfold when commands are rearranged in an order that makes use of the optimization mechanism.

The same benchmark code gives different results in AMD platforms. In a PC with Athlon XP 2500+ CPU, nForce2 chipset, 512MB RAM and JDK 1.5.0_03; performance of Schrefl's model [14] becomes 25% better and performance of the role relationship pattern [18] becomes 40% better while JAWIRO's performance becomes 20% poorer.

In order to investigate how changes in the size of a role hierarchy affect performance, the benchmarks for the running phase are repeated for trees with different depth values on the Intel platform. The results obtained for JAWIRO are presented in Table 3.

Table 3 shows that JAWIRO causes no overhead when executing roles, regardless of the size of the role hierarchy. Even if there are one million roles in the hierarchy, the biggest overhead that JAWIRO introduces is as small as one tenth of a millisecond.

Table 4 shows the same benchmark in the Intel platform, using Schrefl's model and the role relationship pattern.

Table 4 shows that the results for Schrefl's model and the role relationship pattern are similar with the results for JAWIRO, with one exception. Schrefl's role model uses hash tables to keep track of roles, therefore its performance for role checking operations are unaffected with the growing sizes of the role hierarchies.

Table 3. Effects of hierarchy size on JAWIRO, using Intel platform. n represents number of the role objects in the hierarchy.

Degree=3 (constant)	n=39; $n^2=1,521$	n=120; $n^2=14,400$	n=363; $n^2=131,769$	n=1,092; $n^2=1,192,464$
Depth	**4**	**5**	**6**	**7**
Role checking (n^2 operations)	0,003	0,012	0,018	0,058
Role switching (n^2 operations)	0,003	0,003	0,018	0,055
Role execution (n operations)	0,000	0,000	0,001	0,001
Switching execution (n^2 operations)	0,000	0,011	0,018	0,055
Checking switching execution (n^2 ops.)	0,005	0,003	0,020	0,055

Table 4. Effects of hierarchy size on Schrefl's role model and the role relationship pattern, using Intel platform

Degree=3 (constant)	Schrefl's model				Role relationship pattern			
Depth	**4**	**5**	**6**	**7**	**4**	**5**	**6**	**7**
Role checking	0,008	0,008	0,010	0,011	0,009	0,014	0,041	0,131
Role switching	0,014	0,017	0,030	0,073	0,003	0,017	0,041	0,130
Role execution	0,000	0,000	0,000	0,000	0,000	0,000	0,001	0,002
Switching execution	0,013	0,017	0,031	0,074	0,008	0,016	0,044	0,135
Checking switching execution	0,022	0,033	0,061	0,147	0,006	0,031	0,088	0,273

6 Describing Behavior with Roles in a Simple Team Application

This section demonstrates how roles can be employed for a team of agents by using JAWIRO. Consider a multiplayer shooter game where the team members are computer controlled entities, i.e. bots. There can be mobile bots representing soldiers, as well as immobile turrets and medical stations. Figure 14 shows a role hierarchy for modeling such an environment.

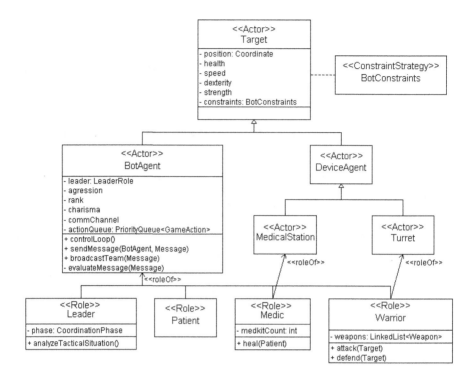

Fig. 14. A role hierarchy for modeling agents in a shooter game

All agent types are created from the `Target` class which contains the common properties of different bot types. The `Target` class extends the `jawiro.Actor` class; so that a `Target` instance can be root of a role hierarchy. Mobile bots are instances of the `BotAgent` class, which can play all available roles. The `Leader` role can be played by only one member of a team, while there can be multiple bots playing the `Warrior` or the `Medic` role. Moreover, a `BotAgent` instance in need of medical treatment can play the `Patient` role.

There are also immobile bots in the application domain, i.e. medical stations which heal nearby patients and turrets which attack the enemies in its range. These devices are modeled with namesake classes. The `Medic` role can be reused for the medical stations; therefore a `MedicalStation` instance can play the `Medic` role but it cannot become a `Warrior`. Similarly, a `Turret` instance can play the `Warrior` role but it cannot become a `Medic`.

Let's examine some possible situations where the characteristics of roles can be put into good use. A warrior who noticed that he is moderately injured broadcasts a call for a medic and it gains the `Patient` role. If his health is further dropped, he can become crippled. In such case, his `Warrior` role is suspended until he is attended by a bot playing the `Medic` role. However, he can heal himself if he plays a `Medic` role, too.

The behavior of a bot is determined by its current roles. The control loop of each bot checks the owned roles and determines which actions to be taken. The specific commands of the leader are executed in topmost priority, as long as the necessary roles exist. For example, a bot attacks to or defends a target with an appropriate weapon if it has the `Warrior` role. If there are no specific orders, bots make decisions which fit the current situation. For example, a bot having the `Medic` role looks for nearby allies to heal.

The example application domain imposes some rules on role binding operations. These rules can be enforced by the constraint managers of JAWIRO, given in detail in [13]. Briefly; constraint managers are called before a role is gained, lost, suspended or resumed so that they have a chance to allow or disallow the operation. The `BotConstraints` class contains the rules of the restricted role bindings previously described. Moreover, it can automate actions such as resuming the `Warrior` role after loosing the `Patient` role if the soldier was previously crippled.

Roles can be used for representing and/or implementing the coordination of multiple agents as well. Just as roles representing individual behavior can be added to individual agents; roles representing cooperation and coordination rules can be added to agents, too. The way how the individual agents cooperate can be altered according to the current state of the environment by defining the roles modeling the coordination rules necessary at that instant as dominant to the rest.

7 Results

Role models provide an abstraction that can unify diverse aspects of an agent system such as collaboration protocols and task models. Additionally, agents, objects, and people can all play roles, so that a role model can span multiple layers in a software system [16]. The results of our assessment show that role models are valuable tools in modeling dynamically evolving systems. Role models introduce no overhead when executing roles and the overhead introduced in the running phase is quite insignificant. As patterns and ad-hoc approaches do not support all features of roles, they can be only used in situations where they cover all required abilities. When a project needs the basic features of roles, role models become the obvious choice. Any role model can be chosen at this stage, considering the platform that the software is targeted. However, when some of the extended features are needed as well, JAWIRO becomes a significant alternative with its rich set of extended features. Moreover, JAWIRO presents a runtime performance good enough for non real-time systems. The JAWIRO role package, along with its API documentation and usage examples, is available in http://www.yunusemreselcuk.com/jawiro/index.html. Currently, we are working on tailoring JAWIRO for agent based systems to be used in describing both the responsibilities and the coordination of agents.

References

1. Pacheco, O., Carmo, J.: A Role Based Model for the Normative Specification of Organized Collective Agency and Agents Interaction. Autonomous Agents and Multi-Agent Systems 6 (2003) 145–184
2. Cabri, G., Ferrari, L., Leonardi, L.: Applying security policies through agent roles: A JAAS based approach. Science of Computer Programming (Article in Press)

3. Cabri, G., Ferrari, L., Leonardi, L.: Exploiting runtime bytecode manipulation to add roles to Java agents. Science of Computer Programming. 54 (2005) 73–98
4. Zhu, H.: A Role Agent Model for Collaborative Systems. Proc. Int'l Conf. on Information and Knowledge Engineering, (2003)
5. Jennings, N.R.: An agent-based approach for building complex software systems. Communications of the ACM 44/4 (2001) 35–41
6. Odell, J.J., Parunak, H.V.D., Brueckner, S., Sauter, J.: Temporal Aspects of Dynamic Role Assignment. Proc. 4th Int'l Workshop on Agent-Oriented Software Engineering. (2003) 201–213
7. Cabri, G., Leonardi, L., Zambonelli, F.: BRAIN: a Framework for Flexible Role-based Interactions in Multiagent Systems. Proc. Conf. On Cooperative Information Systems. (2003)
8. Becht, M., Gurzkil, T., Klarmann, J., Muscholl, M.: ROPE: Role Oriented Programming Environment for Multiagent Systems. Fourth IECIS Int'l Conf. on Cooperative Information Systems. (1999) 325–333
9. Odell, J.J., Parunak, H.V.D., Fleischer, M.: The Role of Roles in Designing Effective Agent Organizations. In Software Engineering for Large-Scale Multi-Agent Systems, Springer-Verlag (2003)
10. Kristensen, B.B.: Conceptual Abstraction Theory and Practical Language Issues. Theory and Practice of Object Systems 2/3 (1996)
11. Zendler, A.M.: Foundation of the Taxonomic Object System. Information and Software Technology 40 (1998) 475–492
12. Aritsugi, M., Makinouchi, A.: Multiple-Type Objects in an Enhanced C++ Persistent Programming Language. Software - Practice and Experience. 30/2 (2000) 151–174
13. Bettini, L., Capecchi, S., Venneri, B.: Extending Java to Dynamic Object Behaviours. Electronic Notes in Theoretical Computer Science. 82/8 (2003)
14. Schrefl, M., Thalhammer, T.: Using roles in Java. Software - Practice and Experience. 34 (2004) 449–464
15. Lee, J-S., Bae, D-H.: An Enhanced Role Model for Alleviating the Role-Binding Anomaly. Software - Practice and Experience. 32 (2002) 1317–1344
16. Kendall, E.A.: Role Models – Patterns of Agent System Analysis and Design. BT Technology Journal. 17/4 (1999) 46–57
17. Gamma, E., Helm, R., Johnson, R, Vlissides, J.: Design Patterns Elements of Reusable Object Oriented Software. AddisonWesley, Massachussets (1994)
18. Fowler, M.: Dealing with Roles. Unpublished paper. http://martinfowler.com/apsupp/roles.pdf
19. Gottlob, G., Schrefl, M., Röck, B.: Extending object-oriented systems with roles. ACM Trans. on Information Systems. 14/3 (1996) 268–296

SODA: A Roadmap to Artefacts

Ambra Molesini[1], Andrea Omicini[2], Enrico Denti[1], and Alessandro Ricci[2]

[1] DEIS, Alma Mater Studiorum – Università di Bologna,
Viale Risorgimento 2, 40136 Bologna, Italy
ambra.molesini@unibo.it, enrico.denti@unibo.it
[2] DEIS, Alma Mater Studiorum – Università di Bologna a Cesena,
Via Venezia 52, 47023 Cesena, Italy
andrea.omicini@unibo.it, a.ricci@unibo.it

Abstract. An *artefact* for MASs is an entity not driven by an inner goal (as agents are), but *used* by agents to achieve their own goals. In this paper, we assume agents and artefacts as first-class entities in MAS engineering, and claim that agent-oriented methodologies should exploit these two abstractions as the basic bricks for the whole engineering process. As a first testbed, we take the SODA agent-oriented methodology and draw a possible roadmap for its extension toward the notion of artefact.

1 Agents and Artefacts for MAS Engineering

Agents never live alone. Agents coexist with other agents in a MAS (multi-agent system) within an *environment* where they act and interact. Independently of the specific agent definition adopted—among the many available—, the agent abstraction alone is not enough to fully model the *environment* in a natural way. In fact, many environmental items, simply, are *not* agents: instead, they are something inherently different, entities (objects, instruments, tools) that are to be *used* by agents, rather than agents themselves. Following the lexicon originally introduced by Activity Theory [1] and later borrowed by MAS coordination [2], we refer to such items as *artefacts*.

Artefacts are objects explicitly designed to provide some function, which guides their use [3]. Typically, artefacts take the form of objects or tools that agents share and use to support their activities, and to achieve their (individual and social) objectives. By adopting a cognitive perspective over systems [4], agents are the entities of a system that are characterised by some goals to be pursued, whereas artefacts are the entities that are not intrinsically characterised by a goal (they are not goal-oriented). Instead, artefacts are characterised by the concept of *use*, where an agent using an artefact for its own goals implicitly (and temporarily) associates an external goal to the artefact itself.

Coordination artefacts are a case of particular interest in the context of agent societies, where they are usually exploited to achieve or maintain a global behaviour which is coherent with the society's social goal [5]. As such, a coordination artefact is an essential abstraction for building social activities, in that it

O. Dikenelli, M.-P. Gleizes, and A. Ricci (Eds.): ESAW 2005, LNAI 3963, pp. 49–62, 2006.
© Springer-Verlag Berlin Heidelberg 2006

is crucial both for enabling and mediating agent interaction, and for governing the social activities by ruling the space of agent interaction. Indeed, at a closer sight, any activity carried on by the components of a system—individually or cooperatively—cannot be really understood (sometimes, even conceived) without considering the artefacts that govern the components' actions and interactions [5]. More precisely, on the one hand, coordination artefacts mediate the interaction between individual agents and their environment (including other agents); on the other, they capture, express and embody those parts of the environment that are to be designed and controlled in order to support agent's activities.

In the end, along with agents, artefacts constitute the basic building blocks both for MAS analysis and modelling, and for MAS development and actual construction—i.e., real first-class abstractions available to engineers throughout MAS design and development process, down to run-time. So, agents and artefacts can be assumed as the two fundamental abstractions required to model and shape the structure of MASs: a MAS is made by agents *speaking* with other agents and *using* artefacts in order to achieve their goals. However, in order to show this conceptual framework worthwhile, and prove its effectiveness, we should be able to show how a MAS could be actually built using agents and artefacts: for instance, experimenting with some well-founded agent-oriented approach adopting agents and artefacts as its basic abstractions. The fact is that, no known agent-oriented methodology [6, 7, 8, 9] does this today: as a result, to put our framework to test, we are required either to invent a new agent-oriented methodology, or to extend an existing one with the notion of artefact.

Among the many others, SODA [10] (whose basics are recalled in Section 3) is an agent-oriented methodology for the analysis, design and engineering of agent-based systems, specifically focussing on inter-agent issues. As such, SODA heavily relies on the notion of *coordination model* [11], which deeply influences its abstractions and mechanisms, leading engineers to build MAS social infrastructure on top of a coordination infrastructure. So, in particular, social rules are expressed as coordination laws, and embedded into *coordination media*.

Since coordination media are to be seen as a sort of ancestors of coordination artefacts (and more generally of artefacts for MASs [3]), it seems quite natural to choose SODA as our testbed methodology for extension toward artfacts. In fact, the original SODA formulation does not include artefacts explicitly as such— mostly because the full development of the artefact notion in the MAS context is subsequent to the first articulated definition of SODA [10]. Furthermore, a recent research development has lead us to introduce a simple layering principle (called *zooming*) in SODA, which makes it possible to scale the representation details with the complexity of task description (SODA+zoom [12]). This development has clearly shown that a re-formulation of SODA in terms of artefacts could not be delayed any longer, for both theoretical and practical reasons, apart from obvious reasons of coherence and conceptual elegance.

Accordingly, this paper traces a roadmap toward the forthcoming SODA+ artefacts. First, we shortly outline the most relevant features of artefacts and discuss a possible taxonomy (Section 2), then we recall SODA basics and briefly present the novel SODA+zoom (Section 3). In Section 4 we show the impact of the introduction of artefacts in the SODA approach, sketching a possible re-formulation which also relies on SODA+zoom. In particular, we investigate the meaning and the consequences of introducing the artefact notion onto the above-mentioned zooming principle (Subsection 4.1), and onto the several SODA models—role, society, resource, and interaction models (Subsections 4.2 through 4.4). Conclusions and future lines of research are finally drawn in Section 5.

2   Artefacts: Features and Classification

The sources for a theory of artefacts can be found in a number of different research fields, ranging from organisational/psychological theories [1] to anthropology [13,14], and obviously including the area of coordination models [15]. Such a theory, first developed for coordination artefacts [5] then generalised to artefacts for MASs [3], is shortly sketched in the remainder of this section. In particular, Subsection 2.1 outlines the main features of artefacts for MAS, and lists a number of desirable artefact properties. Subsection 2.2 outlines a possible taxonomy for artefacts, meant to be used both as a classification criterion and as a model for a well-principled methodology for agent-oriented engineering. Finally, Subsection 2.3 discusses in principle the impact of the notion of artefact upon an agent-oriented methodology.

2.1   Features

According to [3], an artefact for MAS exposes *(i)* a usage interface, *(ii)* operating instructions, and *(iii)* a function/service description.

Usage Interface — The set of operations provided by an artefact defines what is called its usage interface. Through its usage interface, an artefact is used by agents (and never the other way round) and is driven by their control, automatising a specific service in a predictable way, without the freedom of autonomy.

Operating Instructions — Operating instructions are a (possibly formal) description of the procedure an agent has to follow to meaningfully interact with an artefact over time, working as a sort of manual for an agent using an artefact.

Function Description — A function description is a description of the functionality provided by the artefact, which agents can use essentially for artefact selection. In fact, differently from operating instructions, which describe *how* to exploit an artefact, function description tells an agent about *what* can be obtained by using an artefact.

In addition, artefacts should exhibit further relevant properties, which enhance MAS engineers' but also agents' ability to use them for their own purposes. For instance, it should be possible to *monitor* artefacts as an observable part of the environment, so as to check the development of the activities, track the system history, and evaluate the overall system performance. Desirable artefact features can then be listed as follows:

Inspectability — The state of an artefact, its content, the laws governing its behaviour, its usage interface, operating instructions and function description might be all or partially inspectable by agents.

Controllability — The operational behaviour of an artefact should be controllable so as to allow engineers and agents to monitor its proper functioning: it should be possible to stop and restart an artefact working cycle, to trace its inner activity, and to observe and control a step-by-step execution.

Malleability — The behaviour of an artefact should be modifiable at execution time in order to adapt to the changing needs or mutable external conditions of a MAS.

Predictability — The behaviour of an artefact should be predictable by an agent as well as by a MAS engineers—while the same assumption is not applicable in general to agents, given their autonomy. So, usage interface, operating instructions and function description of an artefact can be used by an agent as a contract with an artefact.

Formalisability — Predictability is easily related with formalisability. When a formal model of the behaviour of an artefact is available, artefact is obviously predictable. In addition, features like automatic verification of the properties of the services provided by an artefacts easily follow from formalisability.

Linkability — Artefacts can be used encapsulate and model reusable services in a MAS. To scale up with complexity of an environment, it might be useful to compose artefacts, by allowing artefacts to invoke operations on other artefacts.

Distribution — For the same reasons advocated for linkability, artefacts could be distributed. In particular, a single, distributed artefact can in principle be used to model a distributed service, accessible from more nodes of the network.

As a final remark, it should be noted that all the artefact properties presented above play a different role when seen from the different viewpoints of agents and of MAS engineers. For instance, operating instructions are to be seen as mostly a design tool for engineers, as well as a run-time support for rational agents.

2.2 Taxonomy of Artefacts

Many sorts of different artefacts populate a MAS, providing agents with a number of different services, embodying a variety of diverse models, technologies and tools, and addressing a wide range of application issues. So, different categorisations could be made. For instance, for coordination artefacts, which entail a form of mediation among the agents using a given artefact and enact some coordination policy, two basic aims can be identified: the *constructive* artefact, as an abstraction aimed at creating and composing social activities; and the *normative* artefact, essential for ruling social activities. This distinction is particularly relevant when dealing with the concept of norm, however for our purposes a different classification seems more useful. The taxonomy of artefacts presented in [3] distinguishes among *individual artefacts*, *social artefacts*, and *resource artefacts*.

Individual artefacts are artefacts exploited by one agent, and mediate between an individual agent and the environment. In general, individual artefacts are not directly affected by the activity of other agents, but can, through linkability, interact with other artefacts in the MAS.

Social artefacts are instead artefact exploited by more than one agent, and mediate between two or more agents in a MAS. In general, social artefacts typically provide MASs with a service which is in the first place meant to achieve a social goal of the MAS, rather than an individual agent goal.

Resource artefacts are artefacts that conceptually wrap external resources, and mediate between agents of a MAS and the external resources. In principle, resource artefacts can be conceived as a means to raise external MAS resources up to the agent cognitive level. In fact, they can equip external resources with an usage interface, operating instructions, and a service description, and realise their task by dynamically mapping high-level agent interactions upon lower-level interactions.

In the end, individual, social and resource artefacts can be used as the basis for building the glue keeping agents together in a MAS, and for structuring the environment where agents live and interact: altogether, they can be taken as the conceptual, layered foundation for artefact design in MAS engineering.

2.3   Artefacts for AOSE: A First Insight

Looking at the current state of agent technologies and methodologies [16], artefacts of many sorts (like web services, coordination media, mailboxes, ontologies, directory services, and so on) are widespread in MASs today, and are typically provided as infrastructural abstractions.

However, they lack a shared common model, and as a direct consequence there is no general methodological approach enabling MAS engineers to design artefacts for MAS in a systematic way. Once such a model has been devised out, however (Section 2), the question is how it impacts on the theory and practise of AOSE (agent-oriented software engineering).

First of all, artefacts are the means for modelling and shaping the agent environment [3]. This means that any AOSE methodology exploiting the notion of artefact should in principle model the environment as a first-class entity, and use then artefacts to this end. SODA is in fact one of the few AOSE methodology (if not the only one) explicitly modelling MAS environment, and promoting its engineering (perhaps not surprisingly) through coordination media.

Furthermore, artefacts promote the engineering of the space of interaction among agents — thus enabling more articulated schemata for agent communication. AOSE methodologies should then allow for less trivial communication models than mere conversations between agents, and exploit artefacts to promote the design and development of complex agent interaction patterns. In the original SODA formulation, for instance, the interaction model in the analysis stage accounts for social interaction in terms of the rules governing interactions within groups of agents, which are then mapped upon coordination laws embedded within coordination media in the design stage.

More generally, artefacts make it easier to enrich MAS design with social/organisational structures, as well as complex security models: roles, permissions, policies, commitments, and the like can be represented explicitly as first-class entities, and encapsulated within artefacts that both embody and enforce them within a MAS. AOSE methodologies should then enable and promote the design of specialised artefacts from general-purpose abstractions, which could take in charge specific MAS aspects such as workflows, topology, security policies, and so on. An obvious source of inspiration for SODA, for instance, was the notion of coordination medium as provided by the TuCSoN coordination infrastructure [17]—which was shown to be expressive enough to capture a number of different issues, from organisation to security [18], from intelligent environment to workflow management.

3   SODA: An Outline

SODA (Societies in Open and Distributed Agent spaces [10]) is an agent-oriented methodology for the analysis and design of agent-based systems. SODA focuses on inter-agent issues, like the engineering of societies and infrastructures for MASs. Since this conceptually covers all the interactions within an agent system, the design phase deeply relies on the notion of *coordination model* [11]. In particular, coordination models and languages are taken as a source of the abstractions and mechanisms required to engineer agent societies: social rules are designed as coordination laws and embedded into coordination media, and the social infrastructure is built upon coordination system.

The analysis phase is characterised by three models: the *role model*, the *resource model* and the *interaction model*. In particular:

- in the **role model**, first the application goals are modelled in terms of the (*individual* and *social*) *tasks* to be achieved, in turn expressed in terms of the responsibilities they involve, of the competence they require, and of the resources they depend upon. Each individual task is associated to an *individual role*, analogously, social tasks are assigned to *groups*. Groups are defined in terms of the social roles participating in the group. A social role describes the role played by an individual within a group.
- in the **resource model**, the application environment is modelled in terms of available services, associated to *abstract resources*. These are further associated to a *policy*, intended as a set of access permissions/protocols associated to a role or group.
- the **interaction model** is aimed at capturing interaction among roles, groups and resources. Each interaction protocol is defined in terms of the information required/provided by roles and resources. Analogously, interaction rules govern interaction within groups.

The *design* phase is based on three strictly-related models, deriving from the models defined in the analysis phase. In particular, the analysis' role model maps on the design's *agent model* and *society model*, while the analysis' resource model maps on the design's *environment model*. So, more precisely:

- in the **agent model**, individual and social roles are mapped upon *agent* classes: each agent class is then characterised by the task, the interaction protocols associated to its role, and the resources that need be accessed, with the corresponding set of permissions.
- in the **society model**, groups are mapped onto agent societies, each organised around a *coordination abstraction* [19] along with the corresponding coordination rules—these are the design counterpart of the analysis' interaction rules.
- in the **environment model**, the resources identified in the analysis phase (along with the corresponding policies) are mapped onto *concrete resource* at the design phase—for instance, databases, expert systems, physical sensors, and so on. Furthermore *concrete resources* are associated to *topological abstractions*.

For the sake of simplicity, we skip here further details: we forward interested readers to [10], and to [12] for the tabular representation of SODA+zoom.

3.1   SODA+zoom

The recent extension of SODA is SODA+zoom [12], where we introduce a simple layering principle with the specific aim of scaling with the complexity of tasks description.

MAS design in SODA+zoom can be layered. Each layer contains a description of the models (role, resource, interaction) at a given level of abstraction, and is labelled with a number: as a convention, the uppermost layer is layer 0—which represents the most abstract view of the MAS: so, zooming a model at layer L results in a model at either layer L+1 (in-zooming) or layer L-1 (out-zooming). The zooming principle comes from the basic intuition that what can be described as a (complex) individual task T assigned to a role R at layer L, can also be zoomed into a social task ST assigned to a group Gr at the layer L+1—and viceversa. That is, zooming allows for different viewpoints over the system at different levels of abstraction (see Figure 1).

It is worth noting that the zooming rule includes a sort of *consistency rule* for which if R is the role at layer L zoomed as group Gr at layer L+1, then *(i)* the set IN(R) of the information required characterising the interaction protocol of R must be a subset of the union of all the sets describing the information required by the social roles SR of the group Gr; *(ii)* the set OUT(R) of the information provided characterising the interaction protocol of R must be a subset of the union of all the sets describing the information provided by the social roles SR of the group Gr.

The zooming mechanism provided for the model at the analysis stage directly impacts on the models and diagrams identified at the design stage. For each

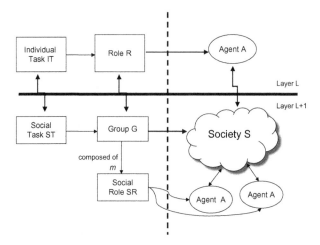

Fig. 1. Zooming: the basic intuition

layer defined at the analysis stage, in fact, there is a corresponding layer at the design stage, which maps the models described in SODA. As a result, the effect of the zooming principle at the design stage basically accounts for describing agent classes C—mapping a role R at the layer L—as a society S at the layer L+1, mapping the group Gr which results from in-zooming R.

4   Roadmap

As argued in Subsection 2.3, the introduction of the concept of artefact in a AOSE methodology has several consequences. In this section, we perform a conceptual experiment by discussing the potential impact of artefacts when they are introduced in the SODA+zoom methodology.

First, here we conceive artefacts mostly as design abstractions, and we consequently choose to introduce them since the design phase. As a result, the models of the design stage have to be suitably adapted and extended: as one may easily expect now, we introduce *(i)* social artefacts in the society model, *(ii)* resource artefacts in the environment model, and *(iii)* individual artefacts in the agent model. Furthermore, even the models of the analysis stage are not exempted from the influence of artefacts—in particular, the interaction model. Only the resource model is essentially left unchanged.

So, in the remainder of this section we outline a possible re-structuring of all the models used by SODA (in particular, by taking its SODA+zoom extension as our reference), which works as a practical roadmap for the full exploitation of the artefact notion in the methodology—toward SODA+artefacts.

4.1   Artefacts and Zoom

As mentioned above, one may expect that artefacts have a relevant impact on any AOSE methodology, SODA included. What might be not-so-obvious is that the very notion of artefact is itself affected by the principles of the methodology, as it happens when they are introduced in SODA.

This is particularly evident when applying the zooming principle to artefacts. For instance, a resource artefact at layer L could be zoomed and become a composition of one or more social artefacts (managing the resource access policy) and one or more resource artefacts at layer L+1.

Zooming artefacts also allows for different levels of abstraction over resources. As a simple example, taken from human world, one may think of a simple desktop computer as an artefact: at layer L, it may be seen as a single resource artefact, but would become a composition of different resource artefacts (a CPU, a hard-disk, a DVD unit, wires, and so on) when zoomed at layer L+1. If we further

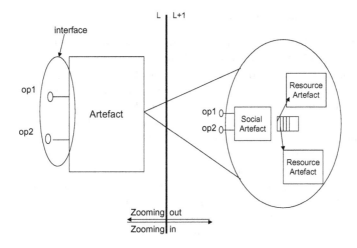

Fig. 2. Zooming: exploding/imploding artefacts

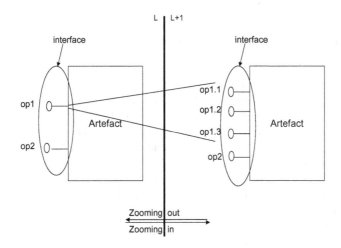

Fig. 3. Zooming: refining artefacts

zoom in the hard-disk, this could be seen at layer L+2 as the composition of a case, disks, heads—just to mention a few; and zooming could continue until the desired/required level of detail/abstraction is reached.

However, zooming artefacts is not restricted only to "exploding" artefacts (Figure 2)—i.e., an artefact that "generates" several artefacts. Instead, it could involve a refinement of the artefact's features (Figure 3), such as its usage interface. So, an artefact could expose at layer L an interface that provides all the operations required at that layer, whereas at layer L+1 the same artefact could expose further, more detailed operations according to the level of abstraction required. For instance, an individual artefact operation could result into a number of (more refined) artefact operations at layer L+1.

4.2   Artefacts and Role/Society Models

The society model deals with the issues of how to design *social rules* so as to make agent societies accomplish their social tasks.

In the following, we re-formulate the model by introducing social artefacts, which can be roughly assumed as a *generalisation* of coordination media as found in the original definition of SODA. A social artefact, in fact, embodies and extends the facilities of a coordination medium, that is, mainly the automation of coordination services that allow the activities of a society of agents to be governed in an effective way. Furthermore, it may provide for a certain *quality of coordination* in terms of e.g., performance, robustness, reliability—as well as of the above-mentioned artefact's features—, and can also act as a kind of "social memory", which could be inspected for analysis of global behaviours.

Back to our re-formulation, the original coordination rules associated to the coordination medium become here the *social rules* associated to the social artefacts. So, groups are still mapped onto agent societies, but societies are organised around social artefacts, enforcing social rules—the design counterparts of the analysis' interaction rules.

4.3   Artefacts and Resource/Environment Models

The SODA environment model deals with the issues of how to design the environment where the agents and societies live.

The introduction of resource artefacts (instead of concrete resources) allows the SODA environment model to be re-formulated so as to provide MAS engineers with a better tool to represent the environment for a MAS. In fact, resource artefacts directly represent and embody external MAS resources and raise them up to the agent cognitive level. However, it is quite frequent that resource artefacts are strictly connected with social artefacts (for instance, as a result of a zooming), because they are passive entities not supporting coordination processes of any sort—relying instead on social artefacts for this. This re-formulation has no immediate consequence on the resource model, however the presence of social artefacts as the managers of resource artefacts (through artefact linkability) emphasises the role played by policies in the resource model, i.e., the set of admissible (protocols of) actions associated to the roles. In fact, given the nature of resource and social artefacts, the definition of a policy in the resource model at the analysis stage also results in the definition of social rules embodied in social artefacts that govern the access to shared resource artefacts.

As a consequence of introduction of artefacts, the need for the definition of a *topological model* that represents the geography of a MAS environment becomes even more stringent. Given the nature of artefacts—as design abstractions meant to survive the whole engineering process down to deployment—, it is almost mandatory to allow MAS engineers to model the topology of a system since the design phase. This would make it possible to early understand the MAS physical constraints, and better face that deployment stage which represents one of the most trouble-making phases in the engineering of today complex software systems. However, given the aim of this paper, the definition of a general topological model for SODA is definitely out of the scope of this work, and will deserve a treatment on its own in the future.

4.4 Artefacts and Interaction Model

Given that artefacts mostly deal with agent interaction, and that SODA is an AOSE methodology focussing on agent interaction, it seems quite obvious that introducing artefacts in SODA requires modifications in the interaction model.

A first distinction comes to be useful, that is, separating the interaction protocols related to roles from those related to abstract resources: here, we rename them as *role interaction protocols* and *resource interaction protocols*, respectively. An interaction protocol is a composition of *elementary actions* for roles, and *elementary operations* for resources. What is elementary, however, strictly depends on the considered layer.

Since agents in a MAS can either *(i)* speak with other agents or *(ii)* use artefacts according to their own goals, actions may take two forms, *communicative action* and *use action*: communicative actions model agents speaking with agents, while use actions model agents using resources (artefacts).

Further consequences come from the application of zooming. For the sake of discipline, we let zooming be applied on single dimensions only: that is, only a single sort of abstraction should be in-zoomed at a time. For instance, it is not allowed to in-zoom a role and an interaction protocol together. So, two different situations may occur:

In-zooming protocols — If we in-zoom role interaction protocols at layer L, we obtain a refinement of interaction protocols at layer L+1, which may result in further actions added, a different action composition, or both things together.

In-zooming roles — If we in-zoom role R at layer L, we obtain a group Gr at layer L+1, so we should define both social roles and social rules associated to Gr. Role interaction protocols of R should be exploded into several role interaction protocols associated to the social roles of Gr: there is no univocal association between them, in particular a role interaction protocol at layer L could be exploded into a number (at most n, if n is the number of social roles of Gr) of role interaction protocols at layer L+1, associated to different social roles. Furthermore, in-zooming role interaction protocols at layer L could require the introduction of new social rules to preserve the coherence of the role interaction protocols originated by the zooming at layer L+1.

Basically, the same happens for abstract resources and resource interaction protocols: when we zoom on resource interaction protocols we obtain at layer L+1 a refinement of the resource interaction protocols. When we in-zoom an abstract resource at layer L, we obtain a number (say n) of other abstract resources at layer L+1, and the resource interaction protocols can be then exploded into n resource interaction protocols. In addition, in-zooming resource interaction protocols at layer L may require the introduction of new rules (called *resource rules*) to preserve the coherence of the resource interaction protocols at layer L+1, originated by the zooming.

In the design phase, resource rules can be mapped onto social artefacts that govern the resource artefacts generated by the zooming of an artefact at a higher level of abstraction. It is worth noting that this social artefact works essentially as an *access and coordination point* aimed at the preservation of the coherence among resource interaction protocols: if the resource artefacts need resource access policies, it is then necessary (in principle) to add other dedicated social artefacts—which may possibly collapse in a unified run-time abstraction after the development stage. Here, "access and coordination point" means that the social artefact coordinates the agent access to several resource artefacts so that the single operation on a single artefact done by the agent at layer L is carried out correctly once the operation is exploded in a number operations on a number of artefacts at layer L+1.

Finally, the agent model is to be modified so as to adopt individual artefacts, aimed at associating role interaction protocols to the agents playing roles. Role interaction protocols, in fact, could be suitably embedded within individual artefacts and so associated to individual agents: each agent would then be connected to a single individual artefact containing all the role interaction protocols associated to the roles played by agent in the MAS. The choice of individual artefact as the *locus* where to place role interaction protocols is not only the most natural and obvious: it also brings some further potential result, in particular when individual artefacts come equipped with features like inspectability and malleability—so that, for instance, an intelligent agent could know and understand its admissible actions in the MAS, and possibly reason about it to find the best possible course of actions. Even more, individual artefacts promote a systematic approach to the problems of security (as shown by agent coordination contexts in [20]), allowing for instance the introduction of a Role-Base Access Control (RBAC) model aimed at developing safe MASs.

5   Conclusions

This paper investigates the impact of assuming the artefact notion as the second milestone for MAS modelling and engineering, side-by-side to agents, clearly distinguishing between agents and the entities they use—i.e., between goal-driven entities, and entities whose goal is assigned by agents at the time of their usage. The SODA methodology, in its more advanced version that includes zooming, is taken as the case study to test the effectiveness of this approach, reformulating its original definition in terms of artefacts. In this paper we started exploring the consequences of this choice onto the analysis and the design models, with special regard to its adequacy in capturing the effects of zooming. Early results seem promising: artefacts appear to fit well the SODA role, society, and environment models—although in the latter case the need of a topological model arises, indicating one first open issue. Further work will also be needed to better understand all the implications of the impact of artefacts onto the SODA interaction model, since this is where the relationships between most SODA concepts (roles, protocols, resources—to cite just some) interlace together more strictly—and also where many other relevant aspects (e.g. RBAC model, security issues) are likely to insist in the future.

References

1. Nardi, B.: Context and Consciousness: Activity Theory and Human-Computer Interaction. MIT Press (1996)
2. Ricci, A., Omicini, A., Denti, E.: Activity Theory as a framework for MAS coordination. In Petta, P., Tolksdorf, R., Zambonelli, F., eds.: Engineering Societies in the Agents World III. Volume 2577 of LNCS. Springer (2003) 96–110 3rd International Workshop (ESAW 2002), Madrid, Spain, 16–17 September 2002. Revised Papers.
3. Omicini, A., Ricci, A., Viroli, M.: *Agens Faber*: Toward a theory of artefacts for MAS. Electronic Notes in Theoretical Computer Sciences (2005) 1st International Workshop "Coordination and Organization" (CoOrg 2005), COORDINATION 2005, Namur, Belgium, 22 April 2005. Post-proceedings.
4. Conte, R., Castelfranchi, C.: Cognitive and Social Action. UCL Press Limited, University College London, UK (1995)
5. Omicini, A., Ricci, A., Viroli, M., Castelfranchi, C., Tummolini, L.: Coordination artifacts: Environment-based coordination for intelligent agents. In Jennings, N.R., Sierra, C., Sonenberg, L., Tambe, M., eds.: 3rd international Joint Conference on Autonomous Agents and Multiagent Systems (AAMAS 2004). Volume 1. ACM, New York, USA (2004) 286–293
6. Wood, M.F., DeLoach, S.A.: An overview of the Multiagent Systems Engineering methodology. In Ciancarini, P., Wooldridge, M.J., eds.: Agent-Oriented Software Engineering. LNCS, Springer (2001) 207–221 1st International Workshop (AOSE 2000), Limerick, Ireland, 10 June 2000. Revised Papers.
7. Zambonelli, F., Jennings, N.R., Wooldridge, M.: Developing multiagent systems: The Gaia methodology. ACM Transactions on Software Engineering and Methodology (TOSEM) **12** (2003) 317–370
8. Padgham, L., Winikof, M.: Prometheus: A methodology for developing intelligent agents. In Giunchiglia, F., Odell, J., Weiss, G., eds.: Agent-Oriented Software Engineering III. Volume 2585 of LNCS. Springer (2003) 174–185 3rd International Workshop (AOSE 2002), Bologna, Italy, 15 July 2002. Revised Papers and Invited Contributions.

9. Bresciani, P., Giorgini, P., Giunchiglia, F., Mylopoulos, J., Perini, A.: Tropos: An agent-oriented software development methodology. Autonomous Agent and Multi-Agent Systems (8) **3** (2004) 203–236
10. Omicini, A.: SODA: Societies and infrastructures in the analysis and design of agent-based systems. In Ciancarini, P., Wooldridge, M.J., eds.: Agent-Oriented Software Engineering. Volume 1957 of LNCS. Springer (2001) 185–193 1st International Workshop (AOSE 2000), Limerick, Ireland, 10 June 2000. Revised Papers.
11. Ciancarini, P., Omicini, A., Zambonelli, F.: Multiagent system engineering: The coordination viewpoint. In Jennings, N.R., Lespérance, Y., eds.: Intelligent Agents VI. Agent Theories, Architectures, and Languages. Volume 1757 of LNAI. Springer (2000) 250–259 6th International Workshop (ATAL'99), Orlando, FL, USA, 15–17 July 1999. Proceedings.
12. Molesini, A., Omicini, A., Ricci, A., Denti, E.: Zooming multi-agent systems. In Müller, J.P., Zambonelli, F., eds.: 6th International Workshop "Agent-Oriented Software Engineering" (AOSE 2005), AAMAS 2005, Utrecht, The Netherlands (2005) 193–204 Proceedings.
13. Hewes, G.W.: A history of speculation on the relation between tools and languages. [14] 20–31
14. Gibson, K.R., Ingold, T., eds.: Tools, Language & Cognition in Human Evolution. Cambridge University Press (1993)
15. Omicini, A., Zambonelli, F., Klusch, M., Tolksdorf, R., eds.: Coordination of Internet Agents: Models, Technologies, and Applications. Springer (2001)
16. Henderson-Sellers, B., Giorgini, P.: Agent Oriented Methodologies. Idea Group Publishing, Hershey, PA, USA (2005)
17. Omicini, A., Zambonelli, F.: Coordination for Internet application development. Autonomous Agents and Multi-Agent Systems **2** (1999) 251–269
18. Cremonini, M., Omicini, A., Zambonelli, F.: Multi-agent systems on the Internet: Extending the scope of coordination towards security and topology. In Garijo, F.J., Boman, M., eds.: Multi-Agent Systems Engineering. Volume 1647 of LNAI. Springer (1999) 77–88 9th European Workshop on Modelling Autonomous Agents in a Multi-Agent World (MAAMAW'99), Valencia, Spain, 30 June – 2 July 1999. Proceedings.
19. Ciancarini, P., Omicini, A., Zambonelli, F.: Coordination technologies for Internet agents. Nordic Journal of Computing **6** (1999) 215–240
20. Ricci, A., Viroli, M., Omicini, A.: An RBAC approach for securing access control in a MAS coordination infrastructure. In Barley, M., Massacci, F., Mouratidis, H., Scerri, P., eds.: 1st International Workshop "Safety and Security in MultiAgent Systems" (SASEMAS 2004), AAMAS 2004, New York, USA (2004) 110–124 Proceedings.

From Reactive Robotics to Situated Multiagent Systems

A Historical Perspective on the Role of Environment in Multiagent Systems

Danny Weyns and Tom Holvoet

AgentWise, DistriNet, Katholieke Universiteit Leuven,
Celestijnenlaan 200 A, B-3001 Leuven, Belgium
{danny.weyns, tom.holvoet}@cs.kuleuven.be

Abstract. Historically, the idea of situated multiagent systems—in which the environment gets a prominent role—originates from the domain of reactive robotics. In this paper, we give a historical perspective of research on agency that devotes pertinent attention to the environment, and show how the role of the environment evolved along with subsequent evolutions of agent systems. Today, it is quite obvious that the environment offers opportunities and challenges for all types of agency. We discuss recent research in this area, which advocates that the environment is not only an essential part of every multiagent system, but also provides an exploitable design abstraction to build multiagent systems. The notion of environment exceeds specific types of agency, and as such offers opportunities for synergetic research in the interest of multiagent systems in general.

1 Introduction

Recently, the environment became subject of active research in multiagent system [1, 2, 3, 4]. Research on environments, however, is not new. In situated multiagent systems the environment has always been a central part of the system. Historically, the idea of situated multiagent systems originates from the domain of reactive robotics. Throughout the different stages in the evolution, from single robotic systems to situated multiagent systems, the role of the environment evolved along with subsequent evolutions of agent systems. Whereas the environment was initially considered as "the external world" in which agents were situated, gradually researchers became aware that the environment provides a medium that could be exploited for building multiagent systems. Today, it is quite obvious that the environment offers opportunities and challenges for all types of agency.

This paper provides a background on the role of the environment in multiagent systems, aiming to help researchers to improve their understanding of the notion of environment in multiagent systems. We give a historical overview of research on agency that devotes pertinent attention to the environment. We show how the role of the environment evolved along with subsequent evolutions of agent systems, and we discuss recent developments in research on environments. The notion of environment exceeds specific types of agency, and as such offers opportunities for synergetic research in the interest of multiagent systems in general.

This paper is structured as follows. In Sect. 2, we give an overview of single agent systems that originate from the principles of reactivity. Section 3 discusses the evolution of multiagent systems, starting from collective reactive behavior to today's situated

O. Dikenelli, M.-P. Gleizes, and A. Ricci (Eds.): ESAW 2005, LNAI 3963, pp. 63–88, 2006.
© Springer-Verlag Berlin Heidelberg 2006

multiagent systems. In Sect. 4, we discuss recent developments in research on environments and we point to a number of challenging domains for future research.

2   Single Agent Systems

Around 1985, several researchers pointed to fundamental problems with deliberative approaches to build agent systems [5, 6, 7]. Reasoning on internal symbolic models and action planning turned out to be insufficient for agents that have to operate in a dynamic and unpredictable environment. These researchers proposed radical new architectures for building agents. Whereas deliberative approaches emphasize explicit knowledge and rational choice, the emphasis of these new architectures was on direct coupling of perception to action, modularization of behavior, and dynamic interaction with the environment. Initially, the focus of this research was on single agent systems. In this section, we give an overview of the subsequent evolutions of single agent architectures and we discuss the role of the environment in this evolution.

2.1   Reactive Robotics

In the mid 1980s, researchers were faced with the problem of how to build autonomous robots that are able to generate robust behavior in the face of uncertain sensors, an unpredicted environment, and a changing world [8]. Attempts to build such robots with traditional techniques from artificial intelligence showed deficiencies such as brittleness, inflexibility, and no real-time reaction [9]. Besides, these systems suffered from several theoretical problems, such as the frame problem and the problem of non-monotonic reasoning within realistic time constraints [10]. This brought a number of researches to the conclusion that reasoning on symbolic internal models, and planning the sequence of actions to achieve the goals is unfeasible for agents with many—often conflicting—goals that have to operate in complex, dynamic environments. This conclusion led to the development of a radically new approach to build autonomous agents. The key characteristics of this approach are described by Brooks in [8]:

- *Situatedness.* The robots are situated in the world, they do not deal with abstract descriptions, but with the here and now of the world directly influencing the behavior of the system.
- *Embodiment.* The robots have bodies and experience the world directly, their actions are part of a dynamic with the world.
- *Intelligence.* Robots are observed to be intelligent. The source of intelligence is not limited to the agents internal system, it also comes from physical coupling of the robot with the world.
- *Emergence.* The intelligence of the system emerges from the system's interactions with the world and from indirect interactions between its components.

Architectures for these robots emphasize a direct coupling of perception to action and the dynamic interaction with the environment. The environment is not only taken into account dynamically, but its characteristics are exploited to serve the functioning of the system. The internal machinery of the robots typically consists of combinatorial circuits completed with a timing circuitry. Each circuit represents a simple behavior of the agent. These circuits are hard-wired or pre-compiled from specifications. The resulting structure allows robots to *react* in real-time to the changing conditions of the world in which they are embedded. Representative examples of approaches for reactive agents are Pengi [6] and Situated Automata [7]. In Pengi, the penguin's situated actions are coded in the form of simple rules. The expressions of the rules use so called indexical-functional representations of the environment. Pengi does not associate symbols with individual objects in the world, but uses expressions that describe causal relationships between the agent and indexically or functionally entities in the world. An example of a situated action is "if there is an ice-cube-besides-me then push ice-cube-besides-me". In Situated Automata, an agent is specified declaratively in the Gapps language [11]. From this specification a runtime program is generated, which satisfies the declarative specification. This program achieves real-time performance, it acts reactively without doing any symbol manipulation.

As an illustration of reactive robots, we discuss the Subsumption Architecture developed by Brooks [5]. The Subsumption Architecture is organized as a series of parallel working layers, each layer is responsible for a specific behavior of the agent. The priority of layers—behaviors—increases from bottom to top. Higher layers are able to inhibit lower layers, giving priority to more important behavior. Fig. 1 depicts an example of a Subsumption Architecture for a simple robot that has to collect packets and deliver them at a destination. On its way, the robot must avoid obstacles in the environment.

A layer in the architecture directly connects perception to action by means of a finite state machine augmented with timing elements. Each layer collects its own sensor data that is written in registers. The arrival of specific data, or the expiration of a timer, can trigger a change of state in the interior finite state machine and possibly produce output commands to actuators. Inhibition and suppression mechanisms resolve conflicts between actuator commands from different layers. In the original version of the Subsumption Architecture, finite state machines could not share any state, each layer encapsulated its registers and clock. Later this restriction was relaxed, allowing clusters of finite state machines to share state and clocks. The Subsumption Architecture has successfully been used in many practical robots.

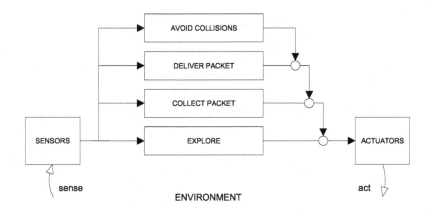

Fig. 1. Subsumption Architecture for a Simple Robot

2.2 Behavior-Based Agents

In the early 1990s, researchers raised important limitations of the initial reactive approaches. In [9], Maes points to a number of problems with the wired or pre-compiled action selection structures of reactive architectures. Although these approaches demonstrate very good performance, they are typically very specific solutions, leaving little room for reuse. For complex agents in complex environments, the architectures are very hard to build. Another important shortcoming is the lack of explicit goals and goal-handling. The designer must anticipate what the best action is to take in all occurring situations. However, for complex systems much of the necessary information will only be available at runtime. Goals may vary over time and now goals may come into play.

Different approaches that support run-time decision making have been developed, usually referred to as behavior-based or situated agents. Prominent examples are Motor Schemas [12], Distributed Architecture for Mobile Navigation [13] (DAMN), and Free-Flow Architectures [14, 15]. Motor schemas is based on schema theory that explains a robot's motor behavior in terms of the concurrent control of different activities [16]. A schema-based robot consists of a number of parallel executing motor schemas, each schema providing a behavior. Schemas can be added or removed at runtime. Each motor schema has as output an action vector that defines the way the robot should move in response to the perceived stimuli. The sum of output vectors determines the behavior of the robot. In DAMN different behaviors generate outputs as a collection of votes. Behavior arbitration is a winner-take-all strategy in which the largest number of votes for an action is selected for execution. Multiple parallel arbiters for different control functions can be combined, e.g. for speed, turning, etc. A free-flow architecture consists of a hierarchy of nodes which receive information from internal and external stimuli in the form of activity. The nodes feed their activity down through the hierarchy until the activity arrives at the action nodes (i.e. the leaf nodes of the tree) where a winner-take-all process decides which action is selected. A free-flow architectures allows an agent to take into account different preferences simultaneously.

As an illustration of behavior-based agents, we discuss Maes' Agent Network Architecture [9] (ANA). ANA combines the robot-oriented principles of reactivity such as decomposition along tasks, de-emphasizing of internal world models and emergent functionality with goal-handling at runtime, and puts this approach in a broader context of software agent systems. An ANA consists of a network of competence modules. A competence module is a node in the network with its own specific competence. A competence module has a list of preconditions which have to be true before the competence module becomes executable. In addition, each competence module has a level of activity. When the activation level of an executable competence module reaches a certain threshold, it may be selected for execution, resulting in some actions. Fig. 2 shows a simple example of an agent network architecture.

Competence modules are linked through different types of links. Modules use these links to activate and inhibit each other, so that after some time the activation energy accumulates in the modules that represent the best actions to take, given the current situation and goals. The spreading of activation among modules, as well as the input of

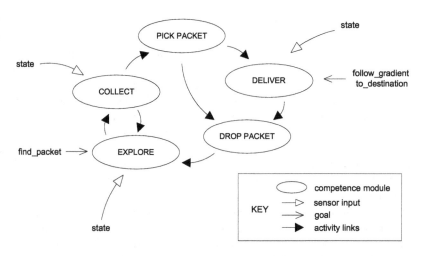

Fig. 2. Agent Network Architecture for a Simple Robot [17]

new activation energy into the network is determined by the current observations and the goals of the agent. Note that goals may change at runtime. Through the cumulative effect of forward and backward spreading of activation energy along sequences of competence modules, the network exhibits implicit "planning" capabilities. The continuous re-evaluation of environmental input ensures that the action selection easily adapts with changing situations. However, ANA suffers also from a number of limitations, a detailed discussion is given by Tyrrell in [15]. One problem is the loss of information because the approach assumes binary sensor data. However, many properties of realistic environments are continuous. Tyrrell has demonstrated that ANA suffers from an inherent unbalance of competition among competence modules, resulting in inefficient behavior. Another problem with ANA is the lack of compromise actions, i.e. ANA does not consider preferences of more then one competence module at a time. From our experiences [17], we learned that it is very difficult to design an agent network architecture for a non-trivial agent. ANA offers little support for structuring the behavior of complex agents. Moreover, adding a competence module to an existing network is almost impossible without affecting the existing structure.

2.3   Explicit World Models and Hybrid Agent Architectures

The use of explicit world models in reactive-based agent architectures has been subject of debate from the early start of reactive agents. Brooks argued against the need for any kind of world model or cognitive level at all [5]. Other researchers showed how knowledge may be compiled into non-symbolic implementations, see e.g. [18]. In [19], Steels states that "autonomous agents without internal models will always be severely limited". He proposes to use analogical instead of symbolic representations, and demonstrates his approach for a simple robot that has to acquire a map of the environment by wandering around. Another argumentation for the necessity of knowledge representation was given by Arkin in [20]. Arkin states that "despite the assumptions of early work in reactive control, representational knowledge *is important* for robot navigation", and he demonstrates how a priori and dynamically acquired world knowledge can be exploited to increase flexibility and efficiency of reactive navigation.

Related to the issue of explicit world models is the position of plans. In [21], Agre and Chapman elaborate on the use of plans in agents' decision making. The authors contrast two views on plans: plans as a resource to the agent versus plans for actions. In the view of plans as a resource, agents use plans as a resource among others in continually re-deciding what to do. In the view of plans for action, agents execute plans to achieve goals, i.e. a plan is a prescription of subsequent actions to achieve a goal. The analysis of Agre and Chapman laid the foundation for the work on reactive planning [22, 23].

In [24], Malcolm and Smithers introduced the notion of hybrid architecture. A hybrid architecture combines a deliberative subsystem with a behavior-based subsystem. The deliberative subsystem permits representational knowledge to be used for planning purposes in advance of execution, while the behavior-based subsystem maintains the responsiveness, robustness, and flexibility of purely reactive systems. Over the years, many hybrid behavior-based architectures have been developed. Today, the approach is common in the domain of robotics, for an overview see [25]. A key function in hybrid architectures is the interface between deliberation and reactivity since it links rapid reaction and long-range planning. A common approach to balance reactivity with planning is to introduce an explicit third layer that coordinates among the reactive and deliberative layer. In general however, coordination of deliberation and reactivity is not yet well understood and is subject of active research.

2.4 Reflection

Starting from the initial principles of reactivity, a wide range of architectural approaches have been developed. Three classes of approaches are identified:

1. *Reactive robots* emphasize the dynamic interaction with the environment. The internal machinery of the robots directly couples perception to action, enabling real-time reaction.
2. *Behavior-based agents* stress the need for dynamic and flexible action selection, aiming to cope with complex environments. Architectures for behavior-based agents support runtime arbitration among parallel executing behaviors and allow goals to vary dynamically over time.
3. *Hybrid agents* exploit representational knowledge of static aspects of the environment. Architectures for hybrid agents integrate cognition (reasoning over internal representations of the world and planning) with reactivity (real-time reaction to stimuli) aiming to combine the advantages of planning and quick responsiveness.

These approaches share two properties:

1. The focus is on the *architecture* of *single* agents. Architectures differ in the way they solve the problem of *action selection*. Architectures do not support social interaction.
2. The approaches stress the importance of *environmental dynamics*. However, the environment itself is considered as *external* to the system, i.e. the environment is not an explicit part of the models or architectures.

3   From Collective Reactive Behavior to Situated Multiagent Systems

Since the early 1990s, researchers which devote pertinent attention to the environment have been investigating systems in which multiple agents work together to realize the system's functionality. In these systems, the agents *exploit* the environment to share information and coordinate their behavior. In this section, we take a look at a number of relevant approaches that have been developed.

3.1   Collective Reactive Behavior

In [26], Reynolds demonstrated flocking behavior between a set of agents. The aggregate behavior of the multiagent system emerged from the interaction of multiple agents that each follows a set of simple behavioral rules. Mataric adopted these techniques to real robots [27], showing how a set of robots produced pack behavior. Each robot was provided with a set of simple behaviors from which it selects the most suitable behavior according to its current environmental context, i.e. its current position relative to other robots. In [28], Zeghal demonstrated another form of reactive coordination. Zeghal used vector fields to control the landing and movements of a large group of aircrafts in a simulation. In this approach, each agent is guided by a potential field that it constructs based on attracting and repulsing forces resulting from goals and obstacles (including other agents) respectively. An advanced example of behavior-based coordination among unmanned guided vehicles is demonstrated in the DARPA UGV programme.[1] In this case, a DAMN arbiter was used to coordinate the vehicle's behavior given its position in the formation. Although very attractive, several researchers have pointed to the complexity of designing collective reactive behavior, see e.g. [30, 29].

3.2   Stigmergic Agent Systems

In [31], Grassé introduced the term *stigmergy* to explain nest construction in termite colonies. The concept indicates that individual entities interact indirectly through a shared environment: one individual modifies the environment and others respond to the modification, and modify it in turn. Deneubourgh [32] and Steels [33] demonstrated how explorer robots can improve the search of target objects by putting marks in the environment. When a robot finds a source of target objects, it puts a trail of marks in the environment from the source of objects toward the robot base, while returning home with an object. This trail allows other exploring robots to find the source of objects efficiently, similar to ants that inform each other about sources of food by depositing pheromone trails in the environment. To ensure that the robots are not mislead when the source becomes exhausted, the marks must be dynamical elements that vanish over time. This mechanism of indirect coordination through the environment combines positive feedback (reinforcement of the trail) with negative feedback (decay of the trail over time).

Stigmergy has been a source of inspiration for many researcher in the multiagent systems. In [34], Parunak describes how principles of different natural agent systems

---

[1] For a detailed discussion see [29].

(ants, wasps, wolves, etc.) can be applied to build self-organizing artificial agent systems. Example applications of stigmergy are ant colony optimization [35], routing calls through telecommunication networks [36], supply chain systems [37], manufacturing control [38], and peer to peer systems [39].

We illustrate the use of marks in the environment with two prominent examples from literature: first we look at Synthetic Ecosystem developed by Brueckner [38], after that we briefly discuss the Co-Fields approach proposed by Mamei and Zambonelli [40].

Synthetic Ecosystem. A synthetic ecosystem enables indirect coordination among software agents in the same way social ants coordinate, the software environment emulates the "services" provided by the real world of ants. The part of the software environment realizing the services is called the pheromone infrastructure. The pheromone infrastructure models a discrete spatial dimension. It comprises a finite set of places and a topological structure linking the places. A link connecting two places has a downstream and an upstream direction. Each agent in a synthetic ecosystem is mapped to a place, i.e. the current location of the agent, which may change over time. The pheromone infrastructure models a finite set of pheromone types. A pheromone type is a specification of a software object comprising a strength-slot (real number) and other data-slots. For each pheromone type, a propagation direction (downstream or upstream) is specified. The pheromone infrastructure handles a finite set of software pheromones for each pheromone type. Every data-slot is assigned a value of a finite domain to form one pheromone (type, direction, propagation, evaporation, etc.). The strength value (i.e. the value in the strength-slot) is interpreted as a specific amount of the pheromone. Different pheromones of a synthetic ecosystem may be stored in each place.

The pheromone infrastructure manipulates the values in the strength-slot of the pheromones at each place in three different ways:

1. External input (aggregation): Based on a request by an agent, the strength of the specified pheromone is changed by the specified value.
2. Internal propagation (propagation/diffusion): When an agent injects pheromone at a place, the input event is immediately propagated to the neighbors of that place in the direction of the pheromone. There the local strength of the pheromone is increased with the arriving pheromone value reduced by the propagation parameter. This process is recursively repeated until the remaining pheromone value crosses a minimal threshold.
3. Without taking changes caused by external input or propagation into account, the strength of each pheromone is constantly reduced in its absolute value (evaporation). The reduction is influenced by the evaporation parameter of the pheromone.

The pheromone infrastructure realizes an application-independent support for synthetic ecosystems designed according to a number of design principles, such as decentralization, locality, parallelism, indirect communication, information sharing, feedback, randomization and forgetting. In [38, 34], Brueckner and Parunak describe a set of engineering principles for designing synthetic ecosystems, including: agents are things, not functions – keep agents small – decentralize control – support agent diversity – enable information sharing – support concurrency.

The principles of synthetic ecosystems and the proposed pheromone infrastructure are applied to a manufacturing control system [38]. V. Parunak and his colleagues have applied digital pheromones in many other practical applications, for an overview we refer to [41].

Co-fields. Computational Fields (Co-Fields) is an approach to model and engineer the coordinated movements of a group of agents such as mobile devices (possibly carried by users), mobile robots, or sensors of a dynamic sensor network. In Co-Fields, the movements of the agents are driven by abstract (computational) force fields. By letting agents follow the shape of the fields, global coordination and self-organization can emerge.

The Co-Fields model is essentially based on the following three principles:

1. The environment is represented by fields that can be spread by agents or by the environment itself. These fields convey useful information for the agents to coordinate their behavior.
2. The coordination among agents is essentially realized by letting the agents following the waveform of these fields.
3. Environment dynamics and movements of the agents induce changes in the surface of the fields, realizing a feedback cycle that influences agents' movement. This feedback cycle enables the system (agents and environment) to auto-organize.

A field is defined as a distributed data structure composed of a unique identifier, a value that represents the field magnitude, and a propagation rule. Fields can be generated by the agents or by the environment, and are propagated through the space according to the propagation rule. The propagation rule determines the shape of the field surface. Fields can be static or dynamic. A field is static if its magnitude does not change over time, while a the magnitude of a dynamic field may change. Agents combine the values of the fields they perceive, the resulting new field is called the agents coordination field. Agents follow (deterministically or probabilistically) the shape of their coordination field. Agents can follow the coordination field downhill, uphill, or along one of the equipotential lines of the field. Complex movements are achieved by dynamically re-shaping the surface of the field.

In principle, the approach can be generalized toward coordination fields spread in abstract spaces to encode coordination among agents that is related to actions differently from physical movements. In such a case, the agents follow their coordination field, not by moving from one place to another, but by making other kinds of actions.

The Co-Fields model is applied to a number of experimental applications, including a case study in urban traffic management [42] and a video game [43].

3.3 Situated Multiagent Systems

Stigmergic agent systems have proven their value in practice, yet, a number of comments are in order:

- Stigmergic agents are considered as "simple" entities. However, there is little or no attention for the architecture of agents.

- Stigmergic agents are not able to set up explicit collaborations to exploit contextual opportunities.
- The environment is considered as *infrastructure for coordination*, typically supporting one particular form of coordination. However, these infrastructures are not concerned with other environmental aspects such as perception, direct communication, or synchronization of actions. As for agents, there is little or no attention for the architecture of the environment.

Motivated by these considerations, researchers have extended the vision of stigmergic agents and developed architectures for a family of agent systems that is generally referred to as situated multiagent systems.

Multilayered Multi Agent Situated System. In the Multilayered Multi Agent Situated System [44, 45] (MMASS) agents and the environment are explicitly modelled. MMASS introduces the notion of agent type which defines agent state, perceptual capabilities and a behavior specification. Agent behavior can be specified with a behavior specification language [46] that defines a number of basic primitives, such as emit (starts the diffusion of a field), transport (defines the movement of the agent), or trigger (specifies state change when a particular condition is sensed in the environment). MMASS models the environment as a multi-layered structure, where each layer is represented as a connected graph of sites. Layers may represent abstractions of a physical environment, but can also represent logical aspects, e.g. the organizational structure of a company. Between the layers specific connections (interfaces) can be defined that are used to specify that information generated in one layer, may propagate into other layers. In MMASS, agents can (1) interact through a reaction among adjacent entities, (2) emit fields that are diffused in the environment, and (3) can be perceived by other agents.

Influence–Reaction Model. In [47], Ferber and Müller propose a basic architecture for situated multiagent systems. This architecture builds upon earlier work of Genesereth and Nilson [48]. Ferber and Müller distinguish between tropistic and hysteric agents. Tropistic agents are essentially reactive agents without memory, whereas hysteric agents may have complex behaviors that use past experiences for decision making. Central to the model is the way actions are modelled. The action model distinguishes between influences and reactions to influences. Influences are produced by agents and are attempts to modify the course of events in the world. Reactions, which result in state changes, are produced by the environment by combining influences of all agents, given the local state of the environment and the laws of the world. This clear distinction between the products of the agents' behavior and the reaction of the environment provides a way to handle simultaneous activity in the multiagent systems. In [49], Ferber uses the BRIC formalism (Block-like Representation of Interactive Components) to model situated multiagent systems. In BRIC, a multiagent system is modelled as a set of interconnected components that can exchange messages via links. BRIC components encapsulate their own behavior and can be composed hierarchically. An interesting model for action that extends the influence–reaction model with the notion of *activity* as first-class concept is proposed in [50].

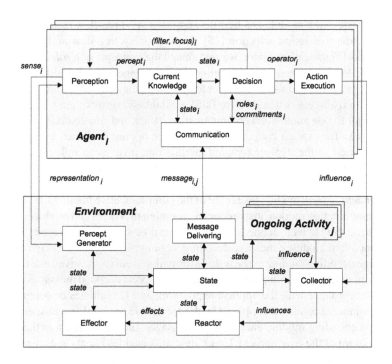

Fig. 3. Reference Architecture for Situated Multiagent Systems

Reference Architecture for Situated Multiagent Systems. Inspired by the work of Ferber and Müller, in our research we have developed a reference architecture for situated multiagent systems. This reference architecture generalizes and extracts common functions and structures from various applications we have studied and built, including the Packet-World [51], a peer-to-peer file sharing system [52], a number of simple robot applications [53], and an simulator for Automatic Guided Vehicle systems [54]. Fig. 3 shows a high-level module view of the reference architecture. The architecture integrates three primary abstractions: agents, ongoing activities and the environment. We successively look at the architecture of each abstraction.

Agents. The agent architecture models different concerns of the agent (perception, decision making and communication) as separate modules. The *Perception* module maps a local representation of the state of the environment to a percept for the agent. We developed a model for *selective perception* that enables an agent direct its perception at the most relevant aspects in the environment according to its current task [55]. To sense its environment, the agent selects a set of *foci*. Sensing results in a representation of the agent's surrounding that can be interpret by the agent producing a percept. Finally, the percept is filtered by a set of selected *filters*, restricting the perceived data according to specific context relevant selection criteria.

The *CurrentKnowledge* module integrates percepts to update the current knowledge of the agent. The *Decision* module is responsible for action selection [56, 57]. We developed the decision module as a free-flow architecture. Free-flow architectures allow flexible and adaptive action selection [15]. Since existing free-flow architectures lack explicit support for social behavior, we introduced the concepts of a *role* and a *situated commitment*. A role covers a logical functionality of the agent, while a situated commitment allows an agent to adjust its behavior towards the role in its commitment. An agent can commit to itself, e.g. when it has to fulfill a vital task. However, in a collaboration, agents commit to one another via communication. Roles and situated commitments are building blocks for explicit collective behavior. The operator selected by the decision module is passed to the *ActionExecution* module that invokes an influence in the environment. The action model is based on the influence—reaction model of Ferber and Müller [47].

The *Communication* module takes care of the communicative interactions. We developed a communication module that processes incoming messages and produces outgoing messages according to well-defined communication protocols [58]. The module consists of three functional modules: message decoding, communicating and message encoding. The message decoding module extracts the information from the received messages. The core of the model, the communicating module (1) interprets decoded messages and reacts to them in accordance with the applicable protocol, and (2) initiates or continues conversations when the conditions imposed by the applicable protocol are satisfied. Finally, the message encoding module encodes new messages and passes them to the message transport system of the environment. Communication enables agents to exchange information, and set up collaborations reflected in mutual situated commitments.

Ongoing Activities. Next to agents, we introduced the concept of an ongoing activity [59]. An ongoing activity provides an abstraction for an environmental process that happens independent of agents. An ongoing activity is defined by an *Operation* that produces influences in the environment according to the state of the world. Examples of ongoing activities are an evaporating pheromone, a self-managing gradient field, a moving object, or a timer. Ongoing activities are generic building blocks for indirect coordination, and as such it forms a basis for collective behavior.

Environment. The environment architecture decomposes the environment into different functional modules (perception, communication, action and interaction). The *Percept-Generator* module is responsible for perception management [55]. When an agent is interested in perceiving its surroundings, it invokes a *sense* command in the environment. Such a sense command contains a set of foci that expresses the agent's current interests of perception. The PerceptGenerator then composes a representation based on the foci, the current state of the environment and a set of perceptual laws. A perceptual law constrains the composition of a representation according to the requirements of the modelled domain. An example of a perceptual law in the context of a simulation is a law that specifies how an area behind an obstacle is out of scope of a perceiving agent. However, perceptual laws can also serve as an instrument for the designer to introduce "synthetic" constraints on perception. E.g., for reasons of efficiency a designer can introduce default limits for perception in order to restrain the amount of information that has to be processed, or to limit the occupied bandwidth.

The *MessageDelivering* module is responsible for message transfer. When a message arrives, the MessageDelivering module passes the message to the list of addressees indicated in the message. It is possible to provide communication laws that are applied when messages are transferred. An examples is a communication law that specifies the maximal distance that messages can be delivered. Communication laws are interesting for simulation purposes, but can also be a useful instrument for designers, e.g. to regulate the message transfer.

The *Collector—Reactor—Effector* modules take care of action handling [59]. The Collector collects the influences of simultaneously performed activity in the system and passes them to the Reactor. Simultaneity of activity can be based on transactional semantics, or it can be determined by a synchronization mechanism, see e.g. [47, 60]. The Collector passes the influences to the Reactor that calculates, according to a set of domain specific interaction laws, the reaction, i.e. state changes in the environment. An example of an interaction law in the context RoboCup soccer is a law that determines the effects of two football players that kick the ball simultaneously. The Reactor finally passes the effects to the Effector that applies the outcome of the interaction by updating the state of the environment.

It is important to notice that the module view of the architecture as depicted in Fig. 3 abstracts from distribution. For a practical application, the state of the environment, the delivering of messages, ongoing activities, etc., have to be implemented according to the domain at hand, i.e. centralized or distributed. Another important remark is that the presented model also abstracts from physical resources, external to the multiagent system. The state of the environment may represent external resources. Support to keep the state of the representation consistent with external resources is not covered by the presented model.

The reference architecture for situated multiagent systems has been applied in an industrial system for logistics services in warehouses and manufactories. This real-world application uses a situated multiagent system to control an automated guided vehicle (AGV) transportation system [61, 62]. We briefly discuss this application in Sect. 4.2.

3.4 Reflection

In multiagent systems, multiple agents work together to realize system functionality. We identified three classes of systems in which the environment has a central role:

- Agents with *collective reactive behavior* follow a set of simple behavioral rules. Each agent is driven by what it perceives in the environment. The aggregate behavior of the multiagent system emerges from the local behavior of agents.
- In *stigmergic agent systems*, the environment serves as a medium for coordination. Stigmergic agents coordinate their behavior through the manipulation of marks in the environment. The environment is an active entity that maintains processes independent of the activity of the agents. Stigmergic coordination combines positive feedback (reinforcement of interesting information) with negative feedback (decay of information over time).
- *Situated multiagent systems* emphasize the importance of architecture for agents and the environment. Basic concerns of agent architecture are perception, communication, and decision making. Advanced types of situated agents support social

behavior enabling them to set up explicit collaborations. Basic concerns of the environment include perception management, message delivering, action handling, and maintenance of processes independent of agents. Laws represent domain specific constraints, but can also be used as a design instrument to impose rules in the multiagent system.

Important characteristics of these multiagent systems are:

- Agents and the environment are explicit parts of the system, each with its specific responsibilities.
- System functionality emerges from the indirect interactions of agents through the environment.

Along the evolution from collective reactive behavior to situated multiagent systems, the role of the environment evolved from (1) the context that drives the agents, to (2) an active coordination medium, to (3) an explicit abstraction with its specific concerns that differ from agent concerns.

Today's situated multiagent systems integrate the architectural perspective of the earlier reactive and behavior-based agent systems with the explicit role of environment of stigmergic agent systems. Moreover, architectures for situated agents extend the initial architectures for single agents by (1) providing support not only for action selection, but for different concerns of agents (perception, communication, etc.), and (2) providing support for explicit social behavior (roles, situated commitments, etc.). Similarly, architectures for the environment extend the role of the environment from a an infrastructure for coordination to a design abstraction that covers specific concerns that differ from agent concerns (perception management, action handling, maintenance of processes, laws, etc.).

Fig. 4 shows a time line with the introduction of subsequent agent systems, together with the main steps in the evolution of the role of the environment in the agent systems.

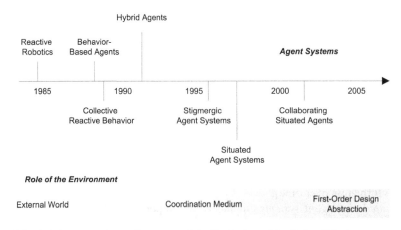

Fig. 4. Subsequent Agent Systems and the Evolution of the Role of Environment

4   Environment, a First-Order Abstraction in Multiagent Systems

Originating from research on behavior-based agent systems and multiagent systems, and stimulated by a number of recent efforts [1, 2, 3], the environment is now a focus of research in multiagent systems in general. In this section, we first zoom in on the role of the environment in multiagent systems. After that, we discuss a real-world application in which the environment is exploited for coordinating agents behavior. The section concludes with a number of pointers to interesting domains for future research on environments for multiagent systems.

4.1   Role of the Environment in Multiagent Systems

Today's research on environments considers a dual role of the environment in multiagent systems. On the one hand, the environment is an *essential* part of every multiagent system that encapsulates parts of a multiagent system that conceptually do not belong to agents, such as infrastructure for communication, the topology of a spatial domain, or laws of an e-institution. Basically, the environment provides the surrounding conditions for agents to exist, it offers an abstraction of the external world to agents in which they can act and interact. This abstraction bridges the conceptual gap between the agent abstraction and low-level issues, such as details of communication, or resources access. On the other hand, the environment provides an *exploitable* design abstraction to build multiagent systems. The environment can serve as a medium for agents to share information and coordinate their behavior.

Distinguishing between agents and the environment supports *separation of concerns* in multiagent systems. A clean separation of agent and environment concerns helps to manage the huge complexity of engineering complex real-world applications. To clarify the role of the environment in multiagent systems, we list a number of important functionalities of the environment:

The Environment Structures the Multiagent System. The environment is first of all a shared "space" for the agents, resources and services, which structures the whole system. Resources are objects with a specific state. Services are considered as reactive entities that encapsulate functionality. The agents as well as resources and services are dynamically interrelated to each other. It is the role of the environment to define the rules which these relationships have to comply to. As such the environment acts as a *structuring* entity for the multiagent system. In general, different forms of structuring can be distinguished:

- *Physical structure* refers to spatial structure, topology, and possibly distribution, see e.g. [38, 44].
- *Communication structure* refers to infrastructure for message transfer, infrastructure for stigmergy [38, 40], or support for implicit communication [63, 64].
- *Social structure* refers to the organizational structure of the environment in terms of roles, organizations, and societies, e.g. [65, 66].

Structuring is a fundamental functionality of the environment. Structures of the environment may be imposed by constraints of the domain at hand, or they may be carefully considered design choices.

The Environment Manages Recourses, Services, and Dynamics. The environment embeds resources and services. An important functionality of the environment is to enable and control the access to these resources and services, hiding the complexity of low-level issues to agents. In general, resources can be read/perceived, written/modified or generated/consumed by agents. Services on the other hand provide functionality to the agents on their request. The extent to which agents are able to access a particular resource or service may depend on several factors such as the nature of the resource or service, the capabilities of the agent, the (current) interrelationships with other resources, services or agents, etc.

The environment also embeds the agents. The environment may provide support for maintaining external state of agents, examples are tags for coordination or reputation mechanisms.

Besides the activity of the agents, the environment can assign particular activities to resources as well. A digital pheromone, for example, is a dynamic structure as it aggregates with additional pheromone that is dropped, it diffuses in space and it evaporates over time. Other examples of environmental activities are a self-managing field in a network, or in the context of simulation a rolling ball that moves on, or the local temperature that evolves over time. Maintaining such dynamics is an important functionality of the environment.

The Environment is Locally Observable to Agents. Contrary to agents, the environment must be observable. Agents must be able to inspect the different structures of the environment, as well as resources, services, and possibly external state of other agents. Observation of a structure is typically limited to the current context (spatial context, communication context and social context) in which the agent find itself. In general, agents should be able to inspect the environment according to their current tasks. Examples of selective perception are [55] where "foci" are proposed to enable agents to perceive their environment according to their current tasks, and [67, 68] where "views" are proposed as selector for perception. Perception is constrained not only by agents' capabilities, but also by environmental properties. In [55], the perceptual constraints are made explicit in the form of "perceptual laws".

Related to observability is the semantic description of the domain, which can be defined by an environment ontology, see e.g. [69]. The ontology must cover the different structures of the environment as well as the observable characteristics of resources, services and agents, and possibly the regulating laws. In an open system, it would be useful for agents to be able to understand at run-time a new environment they are discovering. For symbolically-oriented agents, an explicit ontology should be available to the agents to enable them to interpret their environment and reason about it. For non-reasoning agents, the designer/developer applies the ontology to encode the agents' internal structures. As such, these kinds of agents have an implicit ontology that enables them to make decisions.

The Environment is Locally Accessible to Agents. Agents must be able to access the different structures of the environment, as well as resources, services, and possibly external state of other agents. As for observability, accessing a structure is limited to the current context in which the agent find itself. Access to spatial structure refers to support for metrics, mobility, etc. Access to communication infrastructure refers to support for direct communication (message transfer), support for indirect communication (pheromones, etc.), or support for implicit communication (over-hearing, over-sensing, etc.). Access to social structures refers to group membership, etc.

The Environment Can Defines Rules for the Multiagent System. The environment can define different types of rules on all entities in the multiagent system. Rules may refer to constraints imposed by the domain at hand (e.g. mobility in a network), or refer to "synthetic laws" imposed by the designer (e.g. limitation of access to neighboring nodes in a network for reasons of performance). Rules may restrict access to specific resources or services to particular types of agents, or determine the outcome of agents' interactions.

Dealing with interactions in multiagent systems in general is a very complex matter. [70] points out the difficulties to control the activities of agents operating in distributed systems and propose coordination policies to deal with control. According to the authors, coordination policies need to be formulated explicitly rather than being implicit in the code of the agents involved and they should be enforced by means of a generic, broad spectrum mechanism. The environment is the natural candidate to embed such control mechanism.

In electronic institutions [71], agents interact through agent group meetings that are called scenes. Interactions in a scene have to follow a well-defined communication protocol. Scenes can be composed in a performative structure. The specification of a performative structure contains a description of how the different roles can legally move from scene to scene. Agents within a performative structure may participate in different scenes at the same time with different roles. Agent actions in the context of an institution may have consequences that either limit or enlarge its subsequent acting possibilities. Such consequences will impose obligations to the agents and affect its possible paths within the performative structure. The environment can define and enforce the rules imposed on the movements and interactions of agents in an electronic institution.

A particular problem is the regulation of simultaneous actions in simulations. To allow multiple agents to act in the environment in parallel, explicit models are needed to deal with actions that range far beyond the scope of state changes based on simple individual manipulation of objects. [47, 59, 50] discusses models for simultaneous actions.

4.2 Exploiting the Environment in Practice

In this section, we illustrate how the reference architecture for situated multiagent systems discussed in Sect. 3.3 is applied to an automated transportation system for warehouse logistics. This real-world application is developed in a joint R&D project between the AgentWise research group and Egemin, a manufacturer of automating logistics services in warehouses and manufactories [61, 72].

The automated transportation system uses automatic guided vehicles (AGVs) to transport loads through a warehouse. Typical applications are distributing incoming goods to various branches, or distributing manufactured products to storage locations. An AGV is provided with a battery as its energy source. AGVs can move through a warehouse, following fixed paths on the factory floor, typically guided by a laser navigation system, or by magnets or cables that are fixed in the floor. The low-level control of the AGVs in terms of sensors and actuators (such as staying on track on a path, turning, and determining the current position, etc.), is handled by the AGV control software. Fig. 5 depicts a high-level model of the situated multiagent system. The situated

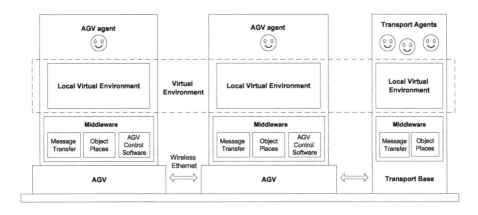

Fig. 5. High-level model of the AGV transportation system

multiagent system consists of two kinds of agents, *transport agents* and *AGV agents*. Transport agents are located at *transport bases*. AGV agents are located in AGVs that are situated on the factory floor. The communication infrastructure provides a wireless network that enables mobile AGVs to communicate with each other and with transport agents on transport bases.

A transport agent represents a transport that needs to be handled by an AGV. AGV agents are responsible for executing the assigned transports. AGVs are situated in a physical environment, however, this environment is very constrained: AGVs cannot manipulate the environment, except by picking and dropping loads. This restricts how AGV agents can exploit their environment. Therefore, a virtual environment was introduced for agents to live in. This virtual environment offers a medium that agents can use to exchange information and coordinate their behavior. Besides, the virtual environment serves as a suitable abstraction that shields the AGV agents form low-level issues, such as the physical control of the AGV. The AGV control software that deals with the low-level control of the AGVs is fully reused. As such, the AGV agents control the movement and actions of AGVs on a fairly high level.

In the AGV application, the only physical infrastructure available to the AGVs is a wireless network for communication. In other words, the virtual environment is necessarily distributed over the AGVs and transport bases. In effect, each AGV and each transport base maintains a *local virtual environment*, which is a local manifestation of the virtual environment. Local virtual environments are merged with other local virtual environments opportunistically, as the need arises. In other words, *the* virtual environment as a software entity does not exist; rather, there are as many local virtual environments as there are AGVs and transport bases. Some of these local virtual environments may have been synchronized recently with each other, while others may not. From the agent perspective, the virtual environment appears as one entity. The synchronization of the state of neighboring local virtual environments is supported by the ObjectPlaces middleware [68].

We now illustrate the use of the virtual environment with a couple of examples.

Routing. For routing purposes, the virtual environment has a static map of the paths through the warehouse. This graph-like map corresponds to the layout used by low-level AGV control software. To allow agents to find their way through the warehouse efficiently, the virtual environment provides signs on the map that the agents use to find their way to a given destination. These signs can be compared to traffic signs by the road that provide directions to drivers. At each node in the map, a sign in the virtual environment represents the cost to a given destination for each outgoing segment. The cost of the path is the sum of the static costs of the segments in the path. The cost per segment is based on the average time it takes for an AGV to drive over the segment. The agent perceives the signs in its environment, and uses them to determine which segment it will take next.

Traffic Information. Besides the static routing cost associated with each segment, the cost is also dependent on dynamic factors, such as congestion of a segment. To warn other agents that certain paths are blocked or have a long waiting time, agents mark segments with a dynamic cost on a *traffic map* in the virtual environment. Agents mark the traffic map by dropping pheromones on the applicable segments. When AGVs come in each others neighborhood, the information of the traffic maps is exchanged and merged to provide up-to-date information to the AGV agents. Since pheromones evaporate over time, outdated information automatically vanishes over time. AGV agents take the information on the traffic map into account when they decide how to drive through the warehouse.

Collision Avoidance. AGV agents avoid collisions by coordinating with other agents through the virtual environment. AGV agents mark the path they are going to drive in their environment using *hulls*. The hull of an AGV is the physical area the AGV occupies. A series of hulls then describes the physical area an AGV occupies along a certain path. If the area is not marked by other hulls (the AGV's own hulls do not intersect with others), the AGV can move along and actually drive over the reserved path. Afterwards, the AGV removes the markings in the virtual environment. [62] discusses collision avoidance through the virtual environment in detail.

In summary, the virtual environment serves as a flexible coordination medium, which hides much of the complexity of the system (distribution, mobility, etc.) from the agents: agents coordinate by putting marks in the environment, and observing marks from other agents. The virtual environment creates opportunities beyond a physical environment that situated AGV agents can exploit.

4.3 Challenging for Future Research on Environments

Many issues are open for future research on environments in multiagent systems. [73] gives an extensive overview of challenges in the domain. One particular challenge we stress here is environment engineering. Environment engineering poses challenges a three levels: (1) Architectural design, (2) Detailed design, and (3) Implementation. Successively, we zoom in on each level.

Architectural Design. Starting from system requirements, including functional and quality requirements (robustness, flexibility, openness, etc.) as well as project and business constraints (budgets, schedules, etc.), the first step in environment engineering is defining a suitable *software architecture* [74]. Software architecture urges engineers to think first in abstract terms about the structure of the environment, distilling away low-level design and implementation details. Software elements of the software architecture provide the functionality of the environment, while the required quality requirements are primarily achieved through the structures of the software architecture. Integration with legacy systems and middleware are important issues when designing the software architecture of an environment. An important challenge for research on environments will be the development of reusable architectural approaches for architectural design of environments. Architectural patterns [75] (or architectural styles) are recurring architectural approaches with particular quality attributes that can be reused for building software architectures of environments. A reference architecture combines a set of architectural patterns and can serve as a blueprint for developing software architectures for a family of environments that share a common base of functional and quality attributes. One interesting challenge is to develop support for the architectural design of different environment structures (physical, communication, social; see Sect. 4). Interesting work on architectural design of environments is discussed in [76, 62, 77, 78].

Detailed Design. A software architecture constrains the concrete development of an environment, yet, it does not *define* it. Detailed design is concerned with the concrete design of the software architectures of environments. One important challenge here is the development of suitable description languages. Examples of open problems for detailed design of environments are support for indirect interaction or environmental laws. Another interesting area for research are the development of specific design and implementation patterns for environments [79, 80].

Implementation. Support for the implementation of environments can come from frameworks, libraries, and development platforms. Existing agent tools can be extended with explicit support for environments, or new tools can be developed that support environments within which different kinds of agents can interact. An important aspect of implementation of environments is the integration with middleware platforms. Middleware hides hardware and platform details, and offers powerful capabilities such as remote method invocation, threading, transaction, etc. Moreover, middleware provides a software platform on which distributed environments can run, hiding complex issues such as low-level details of communication or mobility. A number of proven middleware infrastructures for multiagent systems are [81, 82, 83, 68, 84].

5 Concluding Remarks

In this paper, we discussed the evolution of the role of the environment in multiagent systems from an historical perspective of situated multiagent systems. We have showed how the role of the environment evolved along with subsequent types of agent systems. We identified three phases in the evolution of the role of the environment:

1. Single agent systems emphasize environmental dynamics. The environment is considered as "the external world", which is not an explicit part of models and architectures.
2. In stigmergic agent systems, the environment is considered as coordination infrastructure. Stigmergic agents coordinate their behavior through the manipulation of marks in the environment.
3. In situated multiagent systems, agents and the environment are first-order abstractions, each with its own specific responsibilities. Basic concerns of the environment include perception management, message delivering, action handling, and maintenance of processes independent of agents.

Originating from the area of situated multiagent systems, research on environments today exceeds specific types of agency. Distinguishing between agents and the environment supports *separation of concerns* in multiagent systems. Separating agent and environment concerns helps to manage the huge complexity of engineering complex real-world applications. Today's research on environments considers a dual role of the environment in multiagent systems:

1. The environment is an *essential* part of every multiagent system that provides the surrounding conditions for agents to exist.
2. The environment provides an *exploitable* design abstraction to build multiagent systems.

We illustrated how the environment is exploited in a industrial system for logistic services in warehouses. This practical application shows how a virtual environment creates opportunities for agents to share information and coordinate their behavior an a way that would be impossible in a physical environment.

Environments offers numerous opportunities for future research. Interesting challenges for environment engineering are the development of reusable architectural approaches, including architectural patterns and reference architectures for environments; the development of description languages for environment concerns such as indirect interaction or laws; and the development of frameworks and libraries to support the implementation of environments. Developing such reusable tools for environment engineering is the result of extensive practical experiences with building concrete environments in practical multiagent system applications.

We hope that this paper helps researchers to improve their understanding of the notion of environment in multiagent systems. The notion of environment provides a challenging area for synergetic research in multiagent systems, the environment offers opportunities for all types of agency, from ant systems to rational agent systems such as BDI agents. Understanding the background of environments is essential to carry on the exploration and exploitation of environments in multiagent systems.

References

1. Weyns, D., Parunak, V., Michel, F., eds.: Proceedings of the First International Workshop on Environments for Multi-Agent Systems, New York, 2004. Volume 3374 of Lecture Notes in Computer Science., Springer-Verlag (2005)
2. Weyns, D., Parunak, V., Michel, F., eds.: Proceedings of the Second International Workshop on Environments for Multi-Agent Systems, Utrecht, 2005. Volume 3830 of Lecture Notes in Computer Science., Springer-Verlag (to appear)
3. AgentLink III Technical Forum Group on Environments for Multiagent Systems. (http://www.cs.kuleuven.ac.be/~distrinet/events/e4mas/tfg2005/)
4. Weyns, D., Schumacher, M., Ricci, A., Viroli, M., Holvoet, T.: Environment in Multiagent Systems. Knowledge Engineering Review **20** (2005)
5. Brooks, R.A.: Achieving Artificial Intelligence through Building Robots. AI Memo 899, MIT Lab (1986)
6. Agre, P.E., Chapman, D.: Pengi: An Implementation of a Theory of Activity. In: Proceedings of National Conference on Artificial Intelligence, Seattle, WA. (1987)
7. Rosenschein, S.J., Kaelbling, L.P.: The Synthesis of Digital Machines With Provable Epistemic Properties. In: Proceedings of the First Conference on Theoretical Aspects of Reasoning about Knowledge, Monterey, CA. (1986)
8. Brooks, R.A.: Intelligence Without Reason. In: Proceedings of 12th International Joint Conference on Artificial Intelligence, Sydney, Australia (1991)
9. Maes, P.: Situated Agents Can Have Goals. Designing Autonomous Agents, MIT Press (1990)
10. Pylyshyn, Z.: The Robot's Dilemma. The Frame Problem in Artificial Intelligence. Ablex Publishing Corp., Norwood, New Jersey (1987)
11. Kaelbling, L.P., Rosenschein, S.J.: Action and Planning in Embedded Agents. Designing Autonomous Agents, MIT Press (1990)
12. Arkin, R.C.: Motor Schema-Based Mobile Robot Navigation. International Journal of Robotics Research **8** (1989)
13. Rosenblatt, J.: DAMN: A Distributed Architecture for Mobile Navigation. In: Proceedings of the Spring Symposium on Lessons Learned from Implemented Software Architectures for Physical Agents, AAAI Press (1995)
14. Rosenblatt, K., Payton, D.: A Fine Grained Alternative to the Subsumption Architecture for Mobile Robot Control. Proceedings of the International Joint Conference on Neural Networks, IEEE (1989)
15. Tyrrell, T.: Computational Mechanisms for Action Selection. University of Edinburgh (1993)
16. Arbib, M.A.: Schema Theory. Encyclopedia of Artificial Intelligence (1992)
17. Custers, R.: The Agent Network Architecture Extended for Cooperating Robots. Master Thesis, Katholieke Universiteit Leuven, Belgium (2004)
18. Kaelbling, L.P.: Goals as Parallel Program Specifications. In: Proceedings of the Seventh National Conference on Artifical Intelligence, Minneapolis, Minnesota. (1988)
19. Steels, L.: Exploiting Analogicl Representations. Designing Autonomous Agents (1990)
20. Arkin, R.: Integrating Behavioral, Perceptual, and World Knowledge in Reactive Navigation. Designing Autonomous Agents, MIT Press (1990)

21. Agre, P.E., Chapman, D.: What are Plans for? Designing Autonomous Agents, MIT Press (1990)
22. Nilsson, N.J.: Teleo-Reactive Programs for Agent Control. Journal of Artificial Intelligence Research **1** (1994)
23. Bryson, J.J.: Intelligence by Design, Principles of Modularity and Coordination for Engineering Complex Adaptive Agents. PhD Dissertation: MIT (2001)
24. Malcolm, C., Smithers, T.: Symbol Grounding via a Hybrid Architecture in an Autonomous Assembly System. Designing Autonomous Agents, MIT Press (1990)
25. Arkin, R.: Bahavior-Based Robotics. MIT Press (1998)
26. Reynolds, C.: Flocks, Herds and Schools: A Distributed Behavior Model. Computer Graphics **21** (1996)
27. Mataric, M.: Leaning to Behave Socially. In: From Animals to Animats, Proceedings of the 3th International Conference on Simulation of Adaptive Behavior, MIT Press (1994)
28. Zeghal, K., Ferber, J.: CRAASH: A Coordinated Collision Avoidance System. In: Proceedings of European Simulation Conference, Lyon, France. (1993)
29. Arkin, R.: Behavior-Based Robotics. Massachusetts Institute of Technology, MIT Press, Cambridge, MA, USA (1998)
30. Wavish, P.R., Connah, D.M.: Representing Multiagent Worlds in ABLE. Technical Note, TN2964, Philips Research Laboratories (1990)
31. Grassé, P.P.: La Reconstruction du nid et les Coordinations Inter-Individuelles chez Bellicositermes Natalensis et Cubitermes sp. La theorie de la Stigmergie. Essai d'interpretation du Comportement des Termites Constructeurs. Insectes Sociaux **6** (1959)
32. Deneubourg, J.L., Goss, S.: Collective Patterns and Decision Making. Ecology, Ethology and Evolution **1** (1989)
33. Steels, L.: Cooperation between Distributed Agents through Self-Organization. Decentralized Artificial Intelligence (1989)
34. Parunak, V.: Go to the Ant: Engineering Principles from Natural Agent Systems. Annals of Operations Research **75** (1997)
35. Dorigo, M., Gambardella, L.: Ant Colony System: A Cooperative Learning Approach to the Traveling Salesman Problem. IEEE Transactions on Evolutionary Computation **1** (1997)
36. Bonabeau, E., Hnaux, F., Gurin, S., Snyers, D., Kuntz, P., Theraulaz, G.: Routing in Telecommunications Networks with Ant-Like Agents. IATA (1998)
37. Sauter, J., Parunak, H.: ANTS in the Supply Chain. Agent based Decision Support for Managing the Internet-Enabled Supply Chain, Seattle, WA (1999)
38. Brueckner, S.: Return from the Ant, Synthetic Ecosystems for Manufacturing Control. Ph.D Dissertation, Humboldt University, Berlin, Germany (2000)
39. Babaoglu, O., Meling, H., Montresor, A.: Anthill: A Framework for the Development of Agent-Based Peer-to-Peer systems. In: Proceedings of the 22nd International Conference on Distributed Computing Systems, Vienna, Austria, IEEE Computer Society, Digital Library (2002)
40. Mamei, M., Zambonelli, F.: Co-Fields: A Physically Inspired Approach to Distributed Motion Coordination. IEEE Pervasive Computing **3** (2004)
41. V. Parunak, home page. (http://www.erim.org/ vparunak/)
42. Mamei, M., Zambonelli, F., Leonardi, L.: Distributed Motion Coordination with Co-Fields: A Case Study in Urban Traffic Management. In: 6th IEEE Symposium on Autonomous Decentralized Systems, Pisa, Italy, IEEE Press (2003)
43. Mamei, M., Zambonelli, F.: Motion Coordination in the Quake3 Arena Environment. In: Environments for Multiagent Systems, E4MAS. Volume 3374 of Lecture Notes in Computer Science., Springer (2005)

44. Bandini, S., Manzoni, S., Simone, C.: Dealing with Space in Multiagent Systems: A Model for Situated Multiagent Systems. In: Proceedings of the First International Joint Conference on Autonomous Agents and Multiagent Systems, ACM Press (2002)
45. Bandini, S., Manzoni, S., Vizzari, G.: MultiAgent Approach to Localization Problems: the Case of Multilayered Multi Agent Situated System. Web Intelligence and Agent Systems **2** (2004)
46. Bandini, S., Federici, M.L., Manzoni, S., Vizarri, G.: Towards a Methodology for Situated Cellular Agent Based Crowd Simulations. In: Sixth International Workshop on Engineering Societies in the Agents World, ESAW. (2005)
47. Ferber, J., Muller, J.: Influences and Reaction: a Model of Situated Multiagent Systems. Second International Conference on Multi-agent Systems, Japan, AAAI Press (1996)
48. Genesereth, M.R., Nilsson, N.: Logical Foundations of Artificial Intelligence. Morgan Kaufmanns (1997)
49. Ferber, J.: An Introduction to Distributed Artificial Intelligence. Addison-Wesley (1999)
50. Helleboogh, A., Holvoet, T., Berbers, Y.: Simulating actions in dynamic environments. In: Conceptual Modeling and Simulation Conference, CMS2005, Track on Agent Based Modeling and Simulation in Industry and Environment. (2005)
51. Weyns, D., Helleboogh, A., Holvoet, T.: The Packet-World: A Test Bed for Investigating Situated Multiagent Systems. In: Software Agent-Based Applications, Platforms and Development Kits, Whitestein Series in Software Agent Technology (2005)
52. P2P Simulator. (http://trappie.studentenweb.org/andy/www/site mai/main.php)
53. Helsen, E., Deschacht, K.: The DELTA Framework for Situated Multiagent Systems. Master Thesis, Katholieke Universiteit Leuven, Belgium (2005)
54. AGV Simulator. (http://www.cs.kuleuven.ac.be/~distrinet/taskforces/agentwise/agvsimulator/)
55. Weyns, D., Steegmans, E., Holvoet, T.: Towards Active Perception in Situated Multi-Agent Systems. Journal on Applied Artificial Intelligence **18** (2004)
56. Weyns, D., Steegmans, E., Holvoet, T.: Integrating Free-Flow Architectures with Role Models Based on Statecharts. In: Environments for Multiagent Systems. Volume 3374 of Lecture Notes in Computer Science., Springer-Verlag (2005)
57. Steegmans, E., Weyns, D., Holvoet, T., Berbers, Y.: A Design Process for Adaptive Behavior of Situated Agents. Agent-Oriented Software Engineering, Lecture Notes in Computer Science **3382** (2005)
58. Weyns, D., Steegmans, E., Holvoet, T.: Protocol Based Communication for Situated Multiagent Systems. 3th Joint Conference on Autonomous Agents and Multi-Agent Systems, New York (2004)
59. Weyns, D., Holvoet, T.: Formal Model for Situated Multi-Agent Systems. Fundamenta Informaticae **63** (2004)
60. Weyns, D., , Holvoet, T.: Regional Synchronization for Situated Multi-agent Systems. In: Third International Central and Eastern European Conference on Multi-Agent Systems, Prague, Czech Republic. Volume 2691 of Lecture Notes in Computer Science., Springer-Verlag (2004)
61. EMC^2: Egemin Modular Controls Concept. (http://emc2.egemin.com/)
62. Weyns, D., Schelfthout, K., Holvoet, T.: Exploiting a Virtual Environment in a Real-World Application. Second International Workshop on Environments for Multiagent Systems, Utrecht (2005)
63. Tummolini, L., Castelfranchi, C., Omicini, A., Ricci, A., Viroli:, M.: "Exhibitionists" and "Voyeurs" do it Better: a Shared Environment for Flexible Coordination with Tacit Messages. In: Environments for Multiagent Systems. Volume 3374 of Lecture Notes in Computer Science, Springer-Verlag (2005)

64. Platon, E., Sabouret, N., Honiden, S.: Oversensing with a Softbody in the Environment: Another Dimension of Observation. In: Proceedings of Modeling Others from Observation at International Joint Conference on Artificial Intelligence, Edinburgh, Scotland (2005)

65. Ferber, J., Michel, F., Baez, J.: AGRE: Integrating environments with organizations. In: Environments for Multiagent Systems. Volume 3374 of Lecture Notes in Computer Science, Springer-Verlag (2005)

66. Zambonelli, F., Jennings, N., Wooldridge, M.: Developing Multiagent Systems: The Gaia Methodology. ACM Transactions on Software Engineering and Methodology **12** (2003)

67. Julien, C., Roman, G.C.: Egocentric Context-Aware Programming in Ad-Hoc Mobile Environments. In: Proceedings of the 10th Symposium on Foundations of Software Engineering, Charleston, South Carolina, USA, ACM Press, New York, NY, USA (2002)

68. Schelfthout, K., Holvoet, T.: Views: Customizable Abstractions for Context-Aware Applications in MANETs. Software Engineering for Large-Scale Multi-Agent Systems, St. Louis, USA (2005)

69. Chang, P., Chen, K., Chien, Y., Kao, E., Soo, V.: From Reality to Mind: A Cognitive Middle Layer of Environment Concepts for Believable Agents. In: Environments for Multiagent Systems. Volume 3374 of Lecture Notes in Computer Science., Springer-Verlag (2005)

70. Minsky, N., Ungureanu, V.: Law-Governed Interaction: A Coordination and Control Mechanism for Heterogeneous Distributed Systems. ACM Transactions on Software Engineering Methodologies **9** (2000)

71. Noriega, P., Sierra, C.: Electronic Institutions: Future Trends and Challenges. In: Proceedings of the 6th International Workshop on Cooperative Information Agents. Volume 2446 of Lecture Notes in Computer Science., Springer-Verlag, London, UK (2002) 14–17

72. Weyns, D., Schelfthout, K., Holvoet, T., Lefever, T.: Decentralized control of E'GV transportation systems. In: 4th Joint Conference on Autonomous Agents and Multiagent Systems, Industry Track, Utrecht, The Netherlands, ACM Press, New York, NY, USA (2005)

73. Weyns, D., Parunak, V., Michel, F., Holvoet, T., Ferber, J.: Environments for Multiagent Systems, State-of-the-Art and Research Challenges. In: Environments for Multiagent Systems. Volume 3374 of Lecture Notes in Computer Science., Springer-Verlag (2005)

74. Bass, L., Clements, P., Kazman, R.: Software Architecture in Practice. Addison Wesley Publishing Comp. (2003)

75. Shaw, M., Garlan, D.: Software architecture: perspectives on an emerging discipline. Prentice-Hall (1996)

76. Valckenaers, P., Van Brussel, H.: Holonic Manufacturing Execution Systems. CIRP Annals-Manufacturing Technology **54** (2005) 427–432

77. Viroli, M., A.Omicini, Ricci, A.: Engineering MAS Environment with Artifacts. In Weyns, D., Parunak, V., Michel, F., eds.: 2nd International Workshop Environments for Multi-Agent Systems, AAMAS 2005, Utrecht, The Netherlands (2005)

78. Molesini, A., Omicini, A., Denti, E., Ricci, A.: SODA: A Roadmap to Artifacts. In: Sixth International Workshop on Engineering Societies in the Agents World, ESAW. (2005)

79. Kendall, E., Jiang, C.: Multiagent System Design Based on Object Oriented Patterns. Journal of Object Oriented Programming (1997)

80. Schelfthout, K., Coninx, T., Helleboogh, A., Holvoet, T., Steegmans, E., Weyns, D.: Agent Implementation Patterns. In: OOPSLA Workshop on Agent-oriented Methodologies, Seattle, WA USA. (2002)

81. Murphy, A., Picco, G., Roman, G.: LIME: a Middleware for Physical and Logical Mobility. 21th International Conference on Distributed Computing Systems (2001)

82. Omicini, A., Ossowski, S., Ricci, A.: Coordination infrastructures in the engineering of multiagent systems. In Bergenti, F., Gleizes, M.P., Zambonelli, F., eds.: Methodologies and Software Engineering for Agent Systems: The Agent-Oriented Software Engineering Handbook. Volume 11 of Multiagent Systems, Artificial Societies, and Simulated Organizations. Kluwer Academic Publishers (2004) 273–296

83. Mamei, M., Zambonelli, F.: Programming pervasive and mobile computing applications with the tota middleware. 2nd IEEE International Conference on Pervasive Computing and Communication (2004)

84. Schelfthout, K., Weyns, D., Holvoet, T.: Middleware for Protocol-based Coordination in Dynamic Networks. In: Proceedings of the 3rd International Workshop on Middleware for Pervasive and Ad-hoc Computing, Grenoble, France, ACM Press (2005)

Consistency Verification of the Reasoning in a Deliberative Agent with Respect to the Communication Protocols

Jaime Ramírez and Angélica de Antonio

Technical University of Madrid,
Madrid, Spain
{jramirez, angelica}@fi.upm.es
http://decoroso.ls.fi.upm.es

Abstract. The paper presents a method that can detect inconsistencies in the reasoning carried out by a deliberative agent in a changing environment. The verified agent operates on a description of the world represented by means of an OWL Lite ontology, and utilizes production rules to take decisions related to its future behaviour. The considered kind of rules allows for representing non-monotonic reasoning and linear arithmetic constraints in the rule antecedents. The proposed method can specify the scenarios in which the agent would deduce an inconsistency. A scenario is defined to be a description of the initial agent's state (in the agent life cycle), a deductive tree of rule firings, and a partially ordered set of messages and/or stimuli schemas that the agent must receive from other agents and/or the environment. Besides, the method will make sure that the scenarios will be valid w.r.t. the communication protocols in which the agent is involved.

1 Introduction

The aim of this paper is to present a method to detect inconsistencies in the reasoning that a deliberative agent can perform. We assume the agent to own a hybrid knowledge base (KB) that comprises an ontology expressed in OWL Lite, and a set of production rules. These rules not only can add new facts to the Fact Base (FB), but they can also remove facts from the FB. Hence, a certain kind of non monotonic reasoning can be represented in the KB.

We suppose that the agent to be verified needs to carry out a reasoning process in order to decide its next action according to its goals. During this reasoning process, in order to fire rules, the agent takes into account innate facts and acquired facts, that is, information coming from its perception or requested to other agents. It is clear that, as the reasoning process evolves, it would be perfectly possible and valid that the agent obtains contradictory facts from these sources w.r.t. previously acquired facts. In this case, the new knowledge would

O. Dikenelli, M.-P. Gleizes, and A. Ricci (Eds.): ESAW 2005, LNAI 3963, pp. 89–105, 2006.
© Springer-Verlag Berlin Heidelberg 2006

replace the obsolete knowledge. However, the agent should not be allowed to deduce a set of contradictory facts from the acquired facts.

The proposed method finds scenarios in which the agent would deduce an inconsistency. We define a scenario to be a description of the initial agent's state (in the agent life cycle), a deductive tree of rule firings, and a partially ordered set of messages and/or stimuli (expressed as schemas) that the agent must receive from other agents and/or the environment. We assume the agent's state to be a Fact Base (FB). In addition, the proposed method will make sure that the partially ordered set of messages and/or stimuli schemas included as part of a scenario will be valid w.r.t. the communication protocols in which the verified agent is involved.

Some methods or tools intended to verify the consistency of a Knowledge Base System (KBS) (mostly rule based systems) build a model of the KBS (Graph, Petri Net, etc.), and execute the model for each valid input, in order to identify possible inconsistencies during the reasoning process. This approach in many cases turns to be computationally very costly. Thus, we decided to follow another approach in which the starting point is one of the inconsistencies that might be possibly deduced by the verified KBS, and the goal is to compute a description of the scenarios in which the KBS included in the agent would deduce that inconsistency. This approach takes some ideas from the ATMS designed by de Kleer [1] since it uses the concept of label as a way to represent a description of a set of FBs. Other methods for verifying rule-based systems that follow a similar approach were proposed in [2] [3] [4] [5] [6].

In section 2, some aspects are explained related to the agent's KBS. Section 3 explains how the communication protocols will be specified. Section 4 describes how to specify the inconsistencies that are verified by this method. In section 5 a case study, which will be used as context in the explanation of the operation of the method, is presented. Section 6 explains how this method specifies the way in which an agent can deduce an inconsistency, if possible. In section 7, the procedure for detecting an inconsistency is outlined. We end with some conclusions about our work.

2   Characteristics of the Agent's KBS to be Verified

The agent's KBS is made up of a KB and an inference engine. In turn, the agent's KB consists of an OWL Lite ontology and a set of production rules. Let us describe each part in more detail.

2.1   OWL Lite Ontology

OWL language[1] was intended to associate meaning to the web contents, so as to improve the performance of applications such as search engines, e-commerce,

---

[1] http://www.w3.org/TR/owl-features/

navigation or web services. In addition, OWL allows for defining a shared vocabulary that several agents can process and utilize to exchange information.

OWL is a layered language because it specifies a hierarchy of three sublanguages. They are, sorted by decreasing degree of expressiveness, OWL Full, OWL DL and OWL Lite. Although OWL Full and OWL DL are more expressive than OWL Lite, the utilization of OWL Lite for reasoning purposes is more recommended, as long as the entailment problem for OWL Full is undecidable, and quite inefficient for OWL DL.

An OWL Lite ontology consists of a set of axioms and a set of facts. The axioms define some class taxonomies where each class comprises a set of properties, whereas each fact defines an individual by specifying the names of the classes that it belongs to, and the values for some of its attributes. The facts can be also used to specify synonymous individuals, since by default the individuals with different names are considered different individuals.

An OWL property is either a data-valued property (or datatype property) or an object-valued property. In OWL Lite, the cardinality of the properties must be 0 or 1. Moreover, a property can be defined to be transitive, symmetrical or inverse of another property. The properties can be arranged to make up taxonomies of properties, for example, the property *HasFather* can be defined as a subproperty of the property *HasRelative*.

2.2 Production Rules

The rule form considered by the proposed method is:

$$(l_{11}, l_{12}, ..., l_{1w} \vee ,..., \vee l_{m1}, l_{m2}, ..., l_{ms}) \rightarrow a_1, a_2, ..., a_t$$

where the antecedent part contains a disjunction of m conjunctions of literals (l_{ij}), and the consequent part contains a list of actions (a_k). A *literal* is an atom, a negated atom (except when the atom is $Different(I1, I2)$) or a linear arithmetic constraint. The variables must be preceded by ?, and the types of the variables can be determined taking into account the OWL Lite axioms. The kinds of atoms that can occur in the antecedent part are outlined in the table below:

Atom	Meaning
$SubClass(C1, C2)$	The class C1 is subclass of the class C2
$SubProperty(P1, P2)$	The property P1 is subproperty of the property P2
$Instance(I, C)$	The individual I is an instance of the class C
$Different(I1, I2)$	The individual I1 is not the same as the individual I2
$PROPERTY(I1, VALUE)$	The individual I1 has a property PROPERTY with value VALUE

In the table above, each argument written in capital letters can be a variable or an object name (a numeric constant would be a particular case of object name). Hence, $PROPERTY$ may be a variable representing any property. Besides, if any of the arguments of the $Different(I1, I2)$ atom is a variable, it must occur also in another type of atom.

The intended meaning for the literal $\neg PROPERTY\ (I1, VALUE)$ is:

$\neg PROPERTY(I1, VALUE) \equiv \exists VALUE1(PROPERTY(I1, VALUE1) \wedge Different(VALUE,$ $VALUE1))$. This meaning is established taking into account that the maximum cardinality for the OWL Lite properties is 1.

The linear arithmetic constraints are intended to represent complex relationships over some data-valued properties on real domain. The syntax for these constraints is the same as the syntax specified for the DL reasoner RACER[2].

Basically, we admit actions in the consequent part to be addition actions or deletion actions. By means of an addition action, a rule can add a fact to the FB, whereas by means of a deletion action, a rule can remove a fact from the FB. Syntactically, an action can take the form $Add(Individual\_Atom)$ or $Del(Individual\_Atom)$ where $Individual\_Atom$ is either $Instance(I, C)$ or $PROPERTY(I1, Value)$.

2.3   Dynamic Aspects

The agent's KBS is assumed to contain an inference engine able to execute the rules following a forward or backward chaining. Furthermore, the agent's KBS must support a DL reasoner able to deal with the entailment problem. When a rule is fired, we assume that all the actions belonging to the consequent of the rule are executed sequentially.

As an OWL Lite ontology can be translated into the description logic $\mathcal{SHIF}$ [7], DL reasoners such as RACER can be used to instantiate a literal of a rule on demand if possible. If a certain literal cannot be instantiated with the facts entailed by the ontology, and the KBS utilizes a backward chaining, the rule inference engine will try to find a rule that deduces that literal.

As the logical foundation for OWL Lite is description logic, the way of dealing with the negation is established by open-world semantics (OWS) instead of closed-world semantics [8] [9]. This means that a fact can have three different truth values, true, false, or unknown if the ontology does not entail neither the fact nor the negated fact.

We assume that two kinds of facts can appear during the agent's execution: *static facts* and *dynamic facts*. A static fact is a fact whose truth value does not change from true to false or from false to true during the reasoning process, whereas the truth value of a dynamic fact actually may change those ways. In this sense, some acquired facts will be dynamic facts. In the table below, the source of each kind of knowledge is outlined:

---

[2] http://www.franz.com/products/racer/racer_features.lhtml

	Static	**Dynamic**
Acquired	messages/stimuli	messages/stimuli (non-monotonically)
Deducible	rules	rules (non-monotonically)
Innate	agent's developer	*no allowed*

A literal is static/dynamic/deducible/acquired/innate iff any fact derived from this literal is also static/dynamic/deducible/acquired/innate. For example, if $F(x,y)$ is a static literal, then the facts $F(a,b)$, $F(c,d)$, etc. are also static. The method needs to know both whether a literal is static or dynamic, and whether a literal is acquired, innate or deduced, so a classification must be provided.

2.4   Non-monotonicity and Inconsistency

Rules can introduce new facts in the agent's state, but they can also delete already existing facts. This provides the agent's designer with the capability of building agents with non-monotonic reasoning. Consequently, we could find production rules of the form $p \rightarrow Add(\neg p)$ under Open World Assumption (OWA). This kind of rules (when p is assumed to hold) are not admissible in a monotonic KB, since they are logical inconsistencies. If we admit rules of the form $p \rightarrow Add(\neg p)$, we situate ourselves quite far from the concept of inconsistency in monotonic KBS as defined in other works, so we are going to clarify the meaning of inconsistency in this work:

A deductive tree T that deduces a conjunction of facts F and F' is *tree consistent* iff:

1. T does not contain a set of contradictory static facts, or
2. the deductive subtree of T that deduces F must not deduce $\neg F'$ in the end, and vice versa.

This definition implies that the deductive subtree that deduces a fact F must not deny the other fact F' that must hold at the same time than F, and vice versa.

When the agent executes a reasoning process, a deductive tree is evaluated and a sequence of rules is fired. A deductive tree defines a partial order for firing rules, so many sequences may match with a certain deductive tree. The definition showed above is not more than a structural property to be fulfilled by the deductive trees built by the agent that we want to verify using the method. We will call this property $Tree\_Consistency(dt)$ where dt is a tree of rule firings defined recursively by means of the constructor $tree(rule\ firing, list\ of\ subtrees)$ and the constant NIL_TREE (empty tree). As the method will simulate the agent's reasoning, it will discard any deductive process that implies the creation of an invalid deductive tree. Next, we will formally define this property:

$$Tree\_Consistency(dt) \equiv Tree\_Consistency\_Aux1(Boundary(dt))$$
$$\wedge\, Tree\_Consistency\_Aux2(dt, \emptyset)$$

$$Tree\_Consistency\_Aux1(B) \equiv$$
$$AF = \bigcup_{r \in B} Assumed\_Facts(r),$$
$$\neg(((OWL\_AXMS \cup AF) \vDash \bot) \vee$$
$$(\exists is \in INCONSISTENT\_SETS\ is \subset \bigcup_{r \in B} Assumed\_Facts(r)))$$
$$Tree\_Consistency\_Aux2(dt, scope) \equiv (dt = NIL\_TREE) \vee$$
$$\exists r \exists a_1, \exists a_2 ... \exists a_n (dt = tree(r, [a_1, a_2, ..., a_n]),$$
$$scope\_in\_rule = scope \setminus Deduced\_Facts(r),$$
$$\neg(((scope\_in\_rule \cup Assumed\_Facts(r) \cup OWL\_AXMS) \vDash \bot) \vee$$
$$(\exists f \in Deduced\_Facts(r), (f \cup scope \cup OWL\_AXMS) \vDash \bot) \vee$$
$$(\exists acc \in Actions(r), (acc = Del(f), f \in scope))),$$
$$Tree\_Consistency\_Aux2(a_1, scope\_in\_rule \cup Assumed\_Facts(r)),$$
$$Tree\_Consistency\_Aux2(a_2, scope\_in\_rule \cup Assumed\_Facts(r)),$$
$$...$$
$$Tree\_Consistency\_Aux2(a_n, scope\_in\_rule \cup Assumed\_Facts(r)))$$

where $INCONSISTENT\_SETS$ is the set of the different semantic inconsistencies to be considered according to the application domain, the OWL_AXMS is the set of the axioms defined in the ontology, $A \vDash \bot$ means that A is an inconsistent set of OWL Lite axioms, OWL Lite facts and linear arithmetic constraints, the function $Boundary(dt)$ returns the set of rule firings that are leaves of the tree dt, the function $Deduced\_Facts(r)$ returns the facts deduced by the rule firing r and the function $Assumed\_Facts(r)$ returns all the facts that must hold to execute the rule firing r except for the acquired dynamic facts.

In the definition above, the property $Tree\_Consistency\_Aux1$ formalizes the condition (1) in the previous definition of the inconsistent deductive tree, and the property $Tree\_Consistency\_Aux2$ formalizes the condition (2).

Let us see an example of an inconsistent set of rules. For the sake of clarity, a simplified notation for the rules will be employed in this example. According to this notation, $\neg p$ denotes a fact that is contradictory with the fact p w.r.t. the ontology axioms. Let us take the production rules $R1$: $r, s \rightarrow Del(p), Add(\neg p)$; $R2$: $t \rightarrow Add(p)$; $R3$: $\neg p \rightarrow Add(q)$ under OWA. In figure 1 we can see the deductive tree for a conjunction $p \wedge q$ that is supposed to be the antecedent of another rule. The facts p and q are deducible and all the other facts are static. Obviously (see rule R3), in order to deduce q, $\neg p$ must be deduced beforehand, and after having deduced $\neg p$ it is not possible to deduce p.

Lets see an example of a RB that is consistent according to our definition, but inconsistent according to other definitions. Lets take the production rules $R1$: $n, u \rightarrow Add(q)$; $R2$: $s, \neg q \rightarrow Add(q)$; $R3$: $q, m, t \rightarrow Del(p), Add(\neg p)$; $R4$: $v \rightarrow Del(q), Add(\neg q)$ under OWA. In the figure 2 we can see the deductive tree for the conjunction $\neg p \wedge q$ that is supposed to be the antecedent of another rule.

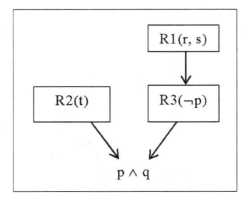

Fig. 1. Example of an invalid deductive tree

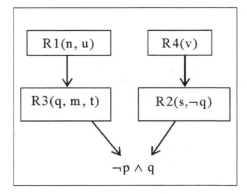

Fig. 2. Example of a valid deductive tree

We assume that $\neg p$ and q are deducible facts, and all the other facts are static. Although the truth value of q changes during the reasoning process (in rule R2, the antecedent requires $\neg q$ to hold, and in the end, q must hold), it does not matter w.r.t. the fulfilment of the tree-consistency property since rule R2 is a valid rule, and it can be used to change the truth value of q without problems. Moreover, no other rule associated with the reasoning of $\neg p$ can annul the effect of rule R2.

3   Specification of the Communication Protocols

A state machine view for the verified agent must be provided as an input to the method. Each state transition of the state machine has a label that specifies the kind of messages that fire the transition. Each kind of message is specified by a message schema. This state machine will be more complete if the state transitions provoked by the stimuli that the agent may perceive in its environment are represented as well as the transitions provoked by inter-agent communication and agent-human communication.

In addition to the state machine, a correspondence between message/stimulus schemas and queries must be supplied. A query is a conjunction of literals that contains at least an acquired literal. If a message/stimulus schema corresponds to a query $\{l_i\}_{i=1,..,n}$, any message/stimulus that matches that schema contains a model for the formula $\exists x_{k1} \ldots \exists x_{km} \bigwedge_{i=1,\ldots,n} l_i$ where the variables $x_{k1} \ldots x_{km}$ are all the free variables in $\bigwedge_{i=1,\ldots,n} l_i$. If the supplied model is empty, the previous formula is to be interpreted as unsatisfiable. During the reasoning process, the acquired literals in the rules will be completely instantiated with the objects provided by the messages/stimuli.

4   Specification of Semantic Inconsistencies

Each semantic inconsistency that must be considered is represented by means of an Integrity Constraint (IC). The IC form is: $\exists x_1 \exists x_2 ... \exists x_n$ $(l_1(scope_1) \wedge l_2(scope_2) \wedge ... \wedge l_k(scope_k)) \Rightarrow \perp$. A scope is associated with each literal to specify the kind of data referenced in the literal (input or output). A literal with input scope states something about the initial FB, while a literal with output scope states something about the final FB (resulting after the execution of the KBS). Let us see a simple example of IC:

$$\exists ?x(Instance(?x, MAN)(I), NumberOfPregnancies(?x, ?n)(O), ?n > 0(O)) \Rightarrow \perp$$

This IC expresses that it is inconsistent to assume that a man has ever been pregnant. The information of that the person $?x$ is a man is provided as input, and the agent is supposed to deduce that $?x$ is pregnant.

Moreover, pairs of message/stimulus schemas, called *contradictory message/ stimulus schemas*, that contain pairs of contradictory models must be also provided to the proposed method.

5   Case Study

We will present an abstract example that will be used as context for the explanation of the method. let us have rules R1 and R2, and the IC defined in the figure 4. We assume that literals $T(?X, ?Y)$ and $\neg T(?X, ?Z)$ are deducible literals; literals $R(?X, ?Y)$ and $\neg R(?X, ?Y)$ are acquired dynamic literals that correspond to the message schemas M and M' respectively, which, in turn, are contradictory message schemas; literal $Instance(?X, A)$ is an acquired static literal that corresponds to the stimulus schema S; and the rest of the literals make up innate knowledge.

We also assume that the OWL Lite ontology encompasses at least the definition of the class A; the individual a; the object properties R, V and T; the datatype property D and some other datatype properties defined to be subproperties of D.

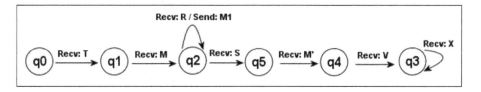

Fig. 3. Fragment of the Agent's State Machine for the case study

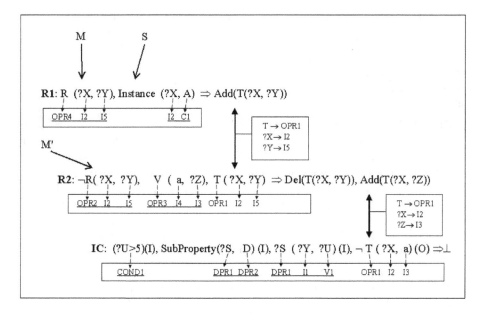

Fig. 4. Deductive tree of the case study

In this example, we suppose that the verified agent communicates with other agents by exchanging messages, and perceives stimuli coming from its environment. The communication protocols view of the verified agent is specified by the state machine of the figure 3.

6   Specification of the Scenarios

6.1   Describing Fact Bases

The proposed method will construct an object called *subcontext* to specify how the initial agent's state must be and which deductive tree must be executed in order to cause an inconsistency. There can be different initial agent's states and different deductive trees that lead to the same inconsistency. An object called *context* will gather all the different ways to violate a given IC. Consequently, a context will be composed of n subcontexts. In turn, a subcontext is defined as a pair *(environment, deductive tree)* where an environment is composed of a set of *metaobjects*, and a deductive tree is a tree of rule firings.

A metaobject describes characteristics that one object that can be present in the agent's state should have. For each type of OWL Lite object there will be a different type of metaobject. In order to describe an OWL Lite object, a metaobject must include a set of constraints on the characteristics of the OWL Lite object. All the metaobjects's attributes are outlined below:

Metaclass = (identifier, subclass_of, metaindividuals)

MetaObjectProperty = (identifier, pairs_of_metaindividuals, subproperty_of)

MetaDataTypeProperty = (identifier, pairs_of_metaindividual-value, subproperty_of)

MetaIndividual = (identifier, instance_of, objectproperties, datatypeproperties, differentfrom)

MetaValue =(conditions)

Given that certain constraints expressed as arithmetic inequations can restrict the datatype property values, a different kind of metaobject called *condition* will represent them. The attributes of a condition are *expression* and *values*.

Let us see an example of an environment describing a FB in which the formula $Instance(?X, House) \land Belongs(?X, Peter) \land Costs(?X, ?pr) \land ?pr > 120000$ holds. If there exists an OWL Lite object in the FB for each metaobject in the environment, that satisfies all the requirements imposed on it, then the given formula will hold in the FB. The environment is defined as {CLASS1, IND1, IND2, OPRO1, DTPRO1, VALUE1, COND1} where:

$CLASS1 = (House, , \{IND1\})$
$IND1 = (, \{CLASS1\}, \{OPRO1\},$
$\{DTPRO\},)$
$IND2 = (Peter, \{OPRO1\}, ,)$
$OPRO1 = (Belongs, \{(IND1, IND2)\},)$

$DTPRO1 = (Costs,$
$\{(IND1, VALUE1)\},)$
$VALUE1 = (\{COND1\})$
$COND1 = ("?pr > 120000", [VALUE1])$

CLASS1 is a metaclass, IND1 and IND2 are metaindividuals, OPRO1 is a metaobjectproperty, DTPRO1 is a metadatatypeproperty, VALUE1 is a meta Value1, and finally COND1 is a condition. As defining the metaobjects, two consecutive commas or a comma just before or after a parenthesis represents an empty field.

A *goal* g is a pair (l, A) where l is a literal and A is a set of metaobjects, associated with the object names and variables in l, that specifies the FBs in which the literal l is satisfied without using DL reasoning. Moreover, a goal (l, A) is static/dynamic/deducible/acquired/innate iff the literal l is static/dynamic/ deducible/acquired/innate.

6.2   Dealing with Acquired Information

Sometimes, in order to execute a deductive tree, it may be required that a dynamic acquired fact f holds in a rule, and later on, that another fact f' in conflict with f holds in another rule. This situation may yield an apparently contradictory environment. To determine if it is a real contradiction, *temporal labels* (a temporal label identifies a rule firing, and specifies that the constraint comes from a dynamic acquired fact) will be associated with some constraints included in the goals (l, A) and (l', A') that entail f and f' respectively, to represent that these constraints must be satisfied in different rule firings (or moments). In addition, the method will specify, as part of the resulting scenario, that a message/stimulus that matches schema M and allows literal l to hold must be received <u>before</u> a message/stimulus that matches schema M' and allows literal l' to hold is received, formally $M < M'$. *Temporal constraints*, like the one stated in the previous sentence, will define a partially ordered set of messages and/or stimuli schemas, in which the relationship $<$ expresses temporal precedence. In the example proposed in section 5, we assume the following sequence of rule firings [R1, R2]. As the message schemas M and M' are contradictory, and they allow the acquired dynamic literals $R(?X, ?Y)$ in R1 and $\neg R(?X, ?Y)$ in R2 respectively to hold, the method will compute the temporal constraint $M < M'$.

For each static acquired literal included in the KB, it will be needed to generate a temporal constraint to express that the message/stimulus schema allowing the static acquired literal to hold must be received before the end of the deductive process. For this reason, some temporal labels must be also associated with the constraints derived from static acquired literals, so that the method can obtain the proper temporal constraints later. In addition, these labels must specify that the constraints have been obtained from a static acquired fact. For the example in section 5, a temporal constraint $S < End$ is computed.

Moreover, the method has to generate temporal constraints to express that some messages/stimuli allowing static acquired literals to hold must be received before the message/stimulus that allows a certain dynamic acquired literal to hold. Let $(R1, R2, ..., RN)$ be the sequence of rules that are fired as a result of evaluating a deductive tree according to the control mechanisms. Let Ri *s.t.* $1 \leqslant i < N$ be a rule whose antecedent requires the dynamic acquired literal Ld to hold, and let M be a message/stimulus schema that entails Ld; let Rj *s.t.* $i < j \leqslant N$ be a rule whose antecedent requires the dynamic acquired literal $L'd$ to hold, and let M' be a message/stimulus schema that entails $L'd$ and that is contradictory with M. Then, it is clear that any message/stimulus schema $M1$ that entails a static acquired literal Ls belonging to the antecedent of a rule Rk *s.t.* $i \leqslant k < j$ must satisfy $M1 < M'$. In the example of section 5, a temporal constraint $S < M'$ is computed.

6.3   Contexts Operations

We will define the following contexts operations: creation of a context, concatenation of a pair of contexts and combination of a list of contexts. These operations will be employed by the method to compute the scenarios, as we will see later on.

a) *Creation*: a context with an unique subcontext is created from an acquired/ innate goal $g = (l, A)$ and a rule $r: C(g, r) = \{(E, EMPTY\_TREE)\}$ where the environment E comprises all the metaobjects included in g. The rule r must be a rule that comprises the literal l in its antecedent. If the literal l is not innate (so it is related to a message/stimulus), some constraints of the metaobjects must be labeled with a temporal label indicating that these constraints must be satisfied at least in the firing of the rule r; in particular, the constraints that require: the presence of a pair in an object property or a datatype property; or an individual to be or not to be an instance of a class.

b) *Concatenation of a pair of contexts*: let C_1 and C_2 be a pair of contexts and $Conc(C_1, C_2)$ be the context resulting from the concatenation, then: $Conc(C_1, C_2) = C_1 \cup C_2$.

c) *Combination of a list of contexts*: Let $C_1, C_2, ..., C_n$ be the list of contexts, and $Comb(C_1, C_2, ..., C_n)$ be the context resulting from the combination. The form of this resulting context is: $Comb(C_1, C_2, ..., C_n) = \{(E_{k1} \cup E_{k2}... \cup E_{kn}, DT_{k1} * DT_{k2}... * DT_{kn})$ s.t. $(E_i, DT_i) \in C_i\}$

   c.1) *Union of environments* $(E_i \cup E_j)$: this operation consists of the union of the sets of metaobjects E_i and E_j. After the union of two sets, it is necessary to check whether any pair of metaobjects can be merged. A pair of metaobjects will be merged if they contain a pair of constraints c_1 and c_2, respectively, such that $(c_1 \wedge c_2)$ entail that both metaobjects represent the same OWL Lite object. This will happen if both metaobjects should have the same value in the *identifier* attribute according to the ontology axioms. Finally, if the resulting environment represents an invalid initial agent state, then this environment will also be discarded. This last check will be carried out with the help of the DL reasoner RACER.

   c.2) *Combination of deductive trees* $(DT_i * DT_j)$: let DT_i and DT_j be deductive trees, then $DT_i * DT_j$ is the deductive tree that results from constructing a new tree whose root node represents an empty rule firing, and whose two subtrees are DT_i and DT_j.

7   Computing the Scenarios

The process to compute the scenarios associated with an IC is divided into four steps. Next, these steps will be explained.

7.1   First Step

The first step can be considered as a pre-processing of the set of rules. In the second step, a backward chaining simulation of the real rule firings is carried out without making calls to the DL reasoner (except for consistency checks in the union of environments, see 6.3, or in the updates of the set of assumed individuals, see 7.2). However, in a real execution of the KBS some literals in the rule antecedents are instantiated thanks to these DL reasoner calls. In order to fill this gap in the simulation, some new rules derived from the ontology axioms and already existing rules are added to the set of rules. In particular, the generation of new rules is related to the presence of deduced literals in the rules. Sometimes, a rule adds a new fact to the FB that matches a literal in another rule's antecedent; in that case, we will say in the simulation that the first rule can be chained with the literal. In other cases, a rule adds a new fact to the FB that does not match directly a literal in a rule antecedent, but it actually does it indirectly, because the new fact allows the DL reasoner to deduce another fact that does match the literal. For the purpose of simulating properly this kind of inference situations, the set of rules must be pre-processed. Next, we will explain how the new rules are computed from the ontology axioms and already existing rules:

Deducing the Literal $\neg Instance(ID1, C)$:
According to the syntactical restrictions explained in 2.2, no rules can deduce directly this kind of literals, but KBS actually can indirectly deduce it these ways:

1. $R(ID1, ID2), \neg subclass(C, Domain(R)) \rightarrow \neg Instance(ID1, C)$
2. $R(ID2, ID1), \neg subclass(C, Range(R)) \rightarrow \neg Instance(ID1, C)$

Where R is any property. Thus, in each rule whose antecedent contains a conjunction c where the deducible literal $\neg Instance(ID1, C)$ occurs, the conjunction c will be replaced with the new conjunctions:

$Substitute(c, "\neg Instance(ID1, C)", "R(ID1, ID2), \neg subclass(C, Domain(R))")$ and, $Substitute(c, "\neg Instance(ID1, C)", "R(ID2, ID1), \neg subclass(C, Range(R))")$

where the function $Substitute(c, s1, s2)$ returns the conjunction resulting from replacing the string $s1$ with the string $s2$ in the conjunction c.

Deducing the Literal $Instance(ID, C)$:
Following an analogous reasoning to the previous replacement, in each rule whose antecedent contains a conjunction c where the deducible literal $Instance(ID1, C)$ occurs, two new conjunctions must be added:

$Substitute(c, "Instance(ID1, C)", "R(ID1, ID2), subclass(C, Domain(R))")$ and, $Substitute(c, "Instance(ID1, C)", "R(ID2, ID1), subclass(C, Range(R))")$

Furthermore, given that any individual a that is instance of a class A is also instance of any superclass of A, then another conjunction must be added:

$Substitute(c, "Instance(ID1, C)", "Instance(ID1, C1), subclass(C, C1)")$

Deducing Transitive Object Properties:
If the object property R is defined to be transitive, then in each rule whose antecedent contains a conjunction c where the deducible literal $R(ID1, ID2)$ occurs, the new conjunction must be added:

$Substitute(c,$ "$R(ID1, ID2)$", "$R(ID1, ?X), R(?X, ID2$") st. the variable X does not occur in the conjunction c.

Deducing Symmetric Object Properties:
If the object property R is defined to be symmetric, then in each rule whose antecedent contains a conjunction c where the deducible literal $R(ID1, ID2)$ occurs, the new conjunction must be added:

$Substitute(c,$ "$R(ID1, ID2)$", "$R(ID2, ID1)$") .

Deducing Inverse Object Properties:
If the object property R^{-1} is defined to be inverse of the object property R, then in each rule whose antecedent contains a conjunction c where the deducible literal $R^{-1}(ID1, ID2)$ occurs, the new conjunction must be added:

$Substitute(c,$ "$R^{-1}(ID1, ID2)$", "$R(ID2, ID1)$") and vice versa.

7.2   Second Step

Basically, the second step can be divided into two phases. In the first phase, the AND/OR decision tree associated with the IC is expanded following a backward chaining simulation of the real rule firings. The leaves of this tree are rules that only contain acquired/innate facts in their antecedents. At this point, the difference between a deductive tree and an AND/OR decision tree should be explained. While a deductive tree can be viewed as one way and only one way for achieving a certain goal (that is, for deducing a bound formula or for firing a rule), an AND/OR decision tree comprises one or more deductive trees, therefore it specifies one or more ways to achieve a certain goal. During the first phase, metaobjects are built corresponding with each variable of a rule/IC and each referenced OWL Lite name, and these metaobjects are propagated from a rule to another one. In this propagation, some constraints are added to the metaobjects due to the rule literals, and some constraints are removed from the metaobjects due to the rule actions, because any constraint deduced by an action is not required to be satisfied by the initial FB any more. In addition to the metaobjects, a set of assumed individuals (SAI) is propagated and updated. The aim of SAI is to warrant that the expanding deductive tree fulfills the second condition of the *Tree Consistency* property. The first condition of the *Tree Consistency* property is checked in the union of environments (see 6.3) during the next phase.

Figure 4 shows the expanded deductive tree for the example proposed in 5. This figure shows the names of the metaobjects build for the variables and the OWL Lite names, as well as the two propagations of metaobjects through the two goal-action chainings. We will follow the trajectory of metaindividual I2 from the IC, where it is created for the variable $?X$, to the rule R1. In the IC, I2 is created as $(,, objectproperties \rightarrow \{OPR1\}, ,)$ (see the format of the metaobjects in section 6.1). Then, the reference to $OPR1$ is removed from I2 in the first chaining, because the action deduces a pair of the object property T in which I2 is involved. Next, in the rule R2, I2 is required to appear in two pairs, one of the object property R, and another of the object property T; therefore I2 is updated to $I2 = (,,objectproperties \rightarrow \{OPR1, OPR2\},,)$. Now, I2 is involved in another chaining, this time from R2 to R1, and in this chaining the reference to $OPR1$ is removed from I2 due to the simulation of the action effect. Finally, in the rule R1, a reference to the object property R and a constraint stating that the individual I2 is instance of class A are added to I2.

For the example of the figure 4, a SAI is created in the IC, so that $SAI = \{SubProperty(DPR1, DPR2), DPR1(I1, V1), V1 > 5, T(I2, I3), Different(I3, a)\}$. Then, in the first chaining the action removes $T(I2, I3)$ from SAI, and when SAI gets to the conjunction of R2, it is updated so that $SAI = \{SubProperty (DPR1, DPR2), DPR1(I1, V1), V1 > 5, V(a, I3), T(I2, I5), Different(I3, a)\}$. Finally, in R1, $SAI = \{SubProperty(DPR1, DPR2), DPR1 (I1, V1), V1 > 5, V(a, I3), Different(I3, a), Instance(I2, C1)\}$. As we can just see in this paragraph, the example of the figure 4 does not raise any inconsistency propagating SAI. However, if the innate literal $V(a, a)(I)$ was added to IC, in the antecedent of R2, SAI would be $\{SubProperty(DPR1, DPR2), DPR1(I1, V1), V1 > 5, V(a, I3), T(I2, I5), Different(I3, a), V(a, a)\}$, which is inconsistent because it forces the object property V to have two pairs $(a, I3)$ and (a, a) st. $Different (I3, a)$. If SAI turns to be inconsistent w.r.t. the ontology axioms, the $Tree\ Consistency$ property does not hold for the current deductive tree, and then the current rule must be discarded.

In the second phase, the AND/OR decision tree is contracted by means of context operations, so that metaobjects in acquired/innate goals and conditions related to metaobjects in acquired/innate goals are inserted in the subcontexts of the context associated with the IC. Basically, the creation operation is employed to work out the context associated with an acquired/innate goal; the combination operation is employed to work out the context associated with a conjunction of literals from the contexts associated with the literals; and the concatenation operation is employed to work out the context associated with a disjunction from the contexts associated with the formulas involved in the disjunction.

Let us see the context associated with the IC in the example of the figure 4: $C(IC) = \{SUBC1\} = \{((\{C1, I1, I2, I3, I5, I5', I6, DPR1, DPR2, OPR3, OPR5, V1, COND1\}, tree(R1, [tree(R2, [EMPTY\_TREE])]))\}$ where:

$C1 = (A,, \{I2\})$

$I1 = (,,,\{DPR1\},)$

$I2 = (, \{A(static, R1)\}, \{OPR5\},,)$

$I3 = (,, \{OPR3\},, \{I6\})$

$I5' = (,,,,\{I5\})$

$I5 = (,, \{OPR5\},, \{I5'\})$

$I6 = (a,, \{OPR3\},, \{I3\})$

$/ * I6 = I4 + I3' * /$

$DPR1 = (, \{(I1, V1)\}, \{DPR2\})$

$DPR2 = (D,,)$

$OPR3 = (V, \{(I6, I3)\},)$

$OPR5 = (R, \{(I2, I5)(dynamic, R1),$

$(I2, I5')(dynamic, R2)\},)$

$/ * OPR5 = OPR2 + OPR4 * /$

$V1 = (\{COND1\})$

$COND1 = ("?U > 5", \{V1\})$

The two phases of the second step are explained in detail for a frame-like knowledge representation formalism called CCR-2 in [10].

7.3 Third Step

In the third step of the method, a different scenario is derived from each sub-context in the context associated with the IC by adding a partially ordered set of message and/or stimulus schemas to the subcontext. In this step, some subcontexts may be discarded if they are impossible w.r.t. the control mechanisms. The partial order on the message/stimulus schemas reflects the temporal constraints derived from the control mechanisms and the deductive tree. These temporal constraints are built as it was explained in section 6.2. The temporal constraints for the example of section 5 were already worked out in section 6.2. Thus, the partially ordered set is $\{M < M', S < M', S < End\}$, and the scenario is $(SUBC1, \{M < M', S < M', S < End\})$.

7.4 Fourth Step

Now, the fourth step must be applied. So far, some scenarios have been obtained for an IC. However, it could happen that some scenario obtained in the previous step describes impossible sequences of messages or stimuli w.r.t. the communication protocols. In order to check this, at least one path that satisfies all the temporal constraints must be found in the state machine. The first state of this path must be the state in which the agent begins its reasoning process. It is clear that there is a path in the state machine of the figure 3 that satisfies all the temporal constraints imposed in the scenario computed in the previous step, so the scenario in this example is consistent with the state machine.

8   Conclusion and Future Work

In this paper, a formal method to verify the consistency of the reasoning process of a deliberative agent w.r.t. communication protocols has been presented. To the best of our knowledge, there is no other method or tool that also addresses this kind of verification. It is also noteworthy that the agent to be verified encompasses a hybrid KB that permits the representation of non-monotonic reasoning and arithmetic constraints.

We think that the proposed approach can be applied to large deliberative agents with a reasonable efficiency. As the proposed method only focuses on the deduction of an inconsistency by using the available rules, the computational cost will not depend on the size of the whole rule base in the average case, but it will depend on the size of the decision tree expanded for the IC, which normally will involve a small percentage of the total set of rules. In addition, as it was commented in section 1, the proposed method will not need to consider all the different initial states of the verified agent, as other methods actually would do.

We are currently investigating how to improve the generation of the temporal constraints from the contexts and the control mechanisms of the KBS. This works are addressing the treatment of metarules, as control mechanisms, and the deletion of redundant temporal constraint by using transitive dependencies.

References

1. de Kleer, J.: An assumption based TMS. Artificial Intelligence **28** (1986) 127–162
2. Rousset, M.: On the consistency of knowledge bases: The COVADIS system, Proceedings ECAI-88, Munich, Alemania (1988) pp. 79–84.
3. Ginsberg, A.: Knowledge-base reduction: A new approach to checking knowledge bases for inconsistency and redundancy, Proceedings of the AAAI-88 (1988) pp. 585-589.
4. Meseguer, P.: Incremental verification of rule-based expert systems, Proceedings of the 10th. European Conference on AI (ECAI'92) (1992) pp. 840–844.
5. Dahl, M., Williamson, K.: A verification strategy for long-term maintenance of large rule-based systems, Workshop Notes of the AAAI92 WorkShop on Verification and Validation of expert Systems (1992) pp. 66–71.
6. Ayel, M., Laurent, J.P.: Validation, Verification and Test of Knowledge-Based Systems: SACCO-SYCOJET: Two Different Ways of Verifying Knowledged-Based Systems. John Wiley publishers (1991)
7. Horrocks, I., Patel-Schneider, P.F.: Three theses of representation in the semantic web. In: Proc. of the Twelfth International World Wide Web Conference (WWW 2003), ACM (2003) 39–47
8. Baader, F., Nutt, W.: Basic description logics. in [9], chapter 2 (2003) 43–95
9. Baader, F., et al.: The Description Logic Handbook. Cambridge University Press (2003)
10. Ramírez, J., de Antonio, A.: Knowledge base semantic verification based on contexts propagation, Notes of the AAAI-01 Symposium on Model-based Validation of Intelligence (2001) http://ase.arc.nasa.gov/mvi/abstracts/index.html.

Security Protocols Verification
in Abductive Logic Programming:
A Case Study*

Marco Alberti[1], Federico Chesani[2], Marco Gavanelli[1],
Evelina Lamma[1], Paola Mello[2], and Paolo Torroni[2]

[1] ENDIF, Università di Ferrara - Via Saragat, 1 - 44100 Ferrara, Italy
{marco.alberti, marco.gavanelli, evelina.lamma}@unife.it
[2] DEIS, Università di Bologna - Viale Risorgimento, 2 - 40126 Bologna, Italy
{fchesani, pmello, ptorroni}@deis.unibo.it

Abstract. In this paper we present by a case study an approach
to the verification of security protocols based on Abductive Logic
Programming.

We start from the perspective of open multi-agent systems, where the
internal architecture of the individual system's components may not be
completely specified, but it is important to infer and prove properties
about the overall system behaviour. We take a formal approach based
on Computational Logic, to address verification at two orthogonal levels:
'static' verification of protocol properties (which can guarantee, at design
time, that some properties are a logical consequence of the protocol),
and 'dynamic' verification of compliance of agent communication (which
checks, at runtime, that the agents do actually follow the protocol).

In order to explain the approach, we adopt as a running example the
well-known Needham-Schroeder protocol. We first show how the protocol
can be specified in our previously developed *SOCS-SI* framework, and
then demonstrate the two types of verification.

We also demonstrate the use of the *SOCS-SI* framework for the static
verification of the NetBill e-commerce protocol.

1 Introduction

The recent and fast growth of network infrastructures, such as the Internet, is
allowing for a new range of scenarios and styles of business making and transaction management. In this context, the use of security protocols has become
common practice in a community of users who often operate in the hope (and
sometimes in the trust) that they can rely on a technology which protects their
private information and makes their communications secure and reliable. A large

---

* This paper is a revised version of work discussed at the Twentieth Italian Symposium
on Computational Logic, CILC 2005, whose informal proceedings are available from
the URL: http://www.disp.uniroma2.it/CILC2005/

O. Dikenelli, M.-P. Gleizes, and A. Ricci (Eds.): ESAW 2005, LNAI 3963, pp. 106–124, 2006.
© Springer-Verlag Berlin Heidelberg 2006

number of formal methods and tools have been developed to analyse security protocols, achieving notable results in determining their strengths (by showing their security properties) and their weaknesses (by identifying attacks on them).

The need for well defined protocols is even more apparent in the context of multi-agent systems. By "well defined", we mean that they guarantee some desirable properties (assuming that agents act according to them). In order to achieve reliability and users' trust, formal proofs of such properties need to be provided. We call the generation of such formal proofs *static verification of protocol properties*.

Open agent societies are defined as dynamic groups of agents, where new agents can join the society at any time, without disclosing their internals or specifications, nor providing any formal credential of being "well behaved" [1]. Open agent societies are a useful setting for heterogenous agent to interact; but, since no assumptions can be made about the agents and their behaviour, it cannot be assumed that the agents will follow the protocols. Therefore, at run-time, the resulting agent interaction may not exhibit the protocol properties that were verified statically at design time. In order to know whether the desired "static" properties hold at run-time, we need to be able to verify that agents do follow the protocols. In other words, we can do what Guerin and Pitt call *on-the-fly verification of compliance* [2]. This kind of verification should be performed by a trusted entity, external to the agents.

In previous work, and in the context of the EU-funded SOCS project [3] we developed a Computational Logic-based framework, called *SOCS-SI* (where *SI* stands for *Social Infrastructure*), for the specification of agent interaction. In order to make *SOCS-SI* applicable to open agent societies, the specifications refer to the *observable* agent behaviour, rather than to the agents' internals or policies, and do not over-constrain the agents' behaviour. We have shown that *SOCS-SI* is suitable for semantic specification of agent communication languages [4], and that it lends itself to the definition of a range of agent interaction protocols [5].[1]

In this paper, we demonstrate by a case study on the well known Needham-Schroeder security protocol [7] how the *SOCS-SI* framework supports both static verification of protocol properties and on-the-fly verification of compliance. The two kinds of verifications are achieved by means of the operational counterpart of the *SOCS-SI* framework, consisting of two abductive proof-procedures ($\mathcal{S}$CIFF and g-$\mathcal{S}$CIFF). Notably, the same specification of the protocol in our language is used for both kinds of verification: in this way, the protocol designer is relieved from a time consuming and error-prone translation step.

SOCS-SI can thus be viewed as a tool for protocol designers, which can be used to automatically verify: (i) at design time, that a protocol enjoys some desirable properties, and (ii) at runtime, that the agents follow the protocol, so making the interaction indeed exhibit the properties.

The paper is structured as follows. In Sect. 2, we describe an implementation of the well-known Needham-Schroeder Public Key authentication protocol in our framework, and in Sect. 3 we show how we perform on-the-fly verification

---

[1] A repository of protocols is available on the web [6].

of compliance and static verification of properties of the protocol. In Sect. 4, as a further example, we propose the static verification of the NetBill e-commerce protocol. Related work and conclusions follow.

2   Specifying the Needham-Schroeder Public Key Encryption Protocol

In this section, we show how the *SOCS-SI* framework can be used to represent the well-known Needham-Schroeder security protocol [7]. The purpose of the protocol is to ensure mutual authentication while maintaining secrecy. In other words, once agents A and B have successfully completed a run of the protocol, A should believe his partner to be B if and only if B believes his partner to be A.

(1) $A \rightarrow B : \langle N_A, A \rangle_{pub\_key(B)}$
(2) $B \rightarrow A : \langle N_A, N_B \rangle_{pub\_key(A)}$
(3) $A \rightarrow B : \langle N_B \rangle_{pub\_key(B)}$

Fig. 1. The Needham-Schroeder protocol (simplified version)

The protocol consists of seven steps, but, as other authors do, we focus on a simplified version consisting of three steps, where we assume that the agents know the public key of the other agents. A protocol run can be represented as in Figure 1.

$A \rightarrow B : \langle M \rangle_{PK}$ means that A has sent to B a message M, encrypted with the key PK. A message of form N_X represents a *nonce*: a message whose content is assumed impossible to guess (such as a long binary string), and thus known only to the agent that synthesized it and to those who received it.

In step (1), A sends to B a new nonce N_A, together with A's identifier, encrypted with B's public key. In step (2), B sends N_A back to A, together with a new nonce N_B, encrypted with A's public key. A is now sure about B's identity, since only B can have decrypted the first message and know N_A. Similarly, B is sure about A's identity after step (3), because only A can have decrypted the second message and have read N_B to send it back to B.

At the end of the protocol, seemingly, A and B are mutually authenticated.

Lowe's attack on the protocol. Eighteen years after the publication of the Needham-Schroeder protocol, Lowe [8] proved it to be prone to a security attack. Lowe's attack on the protocol is presented in Figure 2, where a third agent i (standing for *intruder*) manages to successfully authenticate itself as agent a with a third agent b, by exploiting the information obtained in a legitimate dialogue with a.

It is important to notice that Lowe's attack is effective even if the nonces and keys are not compromised, differently from other kinds of attack (see, for instance, those exemplified by Denning and Sacco [9]).

(1) $a \rightarrow i : \langle N_a, a \rangle_{pub\_key(i)}$
(2) $i \rightarrow b : \langle N_a, a \rangle_{pub\_key(b)}$
(3) $b \rightarrow i : \langle N_a, N_b \rangle_{pub\_key(a)}$
(4) $i \rightarrow a : \langle N_a, N_b \rangle_{pub\_key(a)}$
(5) $a \rightarrow i : \langle N_b \rangle_{pub\_key(i)}$
(6) $i \rightarrow b : \langle N_b \rangle_{pub\_key(b)}$

Fig. 2. Lowe's attack on the Needham-Schroeder protocol

2.1 The Social Model

In this section we give a brief summary of the *SOCS-SI* social framework developed within the EU-funded SOCS project [3][2] to specify interaction protocols for open societies of agents in a declarative way.

Since in open societies the agents' internal state is not observable, the *SOCS-SI* framework is aimed at specifying and verifying the agents' observable behaviour. The verification is performed by an external entity, the *social infrastructure*, which can observe the agent behaviour.

The agent interaction is recorded by the social infrastructure in a set **HAP** (called *history*), of *events*. Events are represented as ground atoms

$$\mathbf{H}(Event[, Time])$$

The term *Event* describes the event that has happened, according to application-specific conventions (e.g., a message sent or a payment issued); *Time* (optional) is a number, meant to represent the time at which the event has happened.

For example,

$$\mathbf{H}(send(a, b, content(key(k_b), agent(a), nonce(n_a))), 1)$$

could represent the fact that agent a sent to agent b a message consisting its own identifier (a) and a nonce (n_a), encrypted with the key k_b, at time 1.

While events represent the actual agent behaviour, the desired agent behaviour is represented by *expectations*. Expectations are "positive" when they refer to events that are expected to happen, and "negative" when they refer to events that are expected *not* to happen. The following syntax is adopted

$$\mathbf{E}(Event[, Time]) \qquad \mathbf{EN}(Event[, Time])$$

for, respectively, positive and negative expectations. Differently from events, expectations can contain variables (we follow the Prolog convention of representing variables with capitalized identifiers) and CLP [11] constraints can be imposed on the variables. This is because the desired agent behaviour may be under-specified (hence variables), yet subject to restriction (hence CLP constraints).

For instance,

$$\mathbf{E}(send(a, b, content(key(k_b), nonce(n_b), empty(0))), T)$$

---

[2] The reader can refer to [10] for a more detailed description.

could represent the expectation for agent a to send to agent b a message consisting of a nonce (n_b) and an empty part $(empty(0))$, encrypted with a key k_b, at time T. A CLP constraint such as $T \leq 10$ can be imposed on the time variable, to express a deadline.

Explicit negation can be applied to expectations ($\neg\mathbf{E}$ and $\neg\mathbf{EN}$).

In the *SOCS-SI* framework, the agent interaction is specified by means of interaction protocols.

A protocol specification $\mathcal{S} = \langle KB_S, \mathcal{IC}_S \rangle$ is composed of:

- the *Social Knowledge Base* (KB_S) is a logic program whose clauses can have expectations and CLP constraints in their bodies. It can be used to express domain-specific knowledge (such as, for instance, deadlines);
- a set $\mathcal{IC}_S$ of *Social Integrity Constraints* (also SICs, for short, in the following): rules of the form *Body → Head*. SICs are used to express how the actual agent behaviour generates expectations on their behaviour; examples can be found in the following sections.

In abductive logic frameworks [12], *abducibles* represent hypotheses, a logic program specifies which set of hypotheses entail a goal, and integrity constraints rule out inconsistent set of hypotheses. The abductive reasoning is successful if it finds a set of hypotheses which entail the goal while not violating the integrity constraints.

In our (abductive) framework, we map expectations to abducibles, and the abductive semantics is used to select a desired behaviour which entails a social goal, while not violating the SICs. In addition, we require the desired behaviour to be matched by the actual agent behaviour.

In particular, we say that a history **HAP** is *compliant* to a specification $\mathcal{S} = \langle KB_S, \mathcal{IC}_S \rangle$ iff there exists a set **EXP** of expectations that is

- $\mathcal{IC}_S$-*consistent*: it must entail $\mathcal{IC}_S$, for the given $\mathcal{S}$ and **HAP**;
- $\neg$-*consistent*: for any ground p, **EXP** cannot include $\{\mathbf{E}(P), \neg\mathbf{E}(p)\}$ or $\{\mathbf{EN}(p), \neg\mathbf{EN}(p)\}$ (this requirement implements explicit negation for expectations);
- **E**-*consistent*: for any ground p, **EXP** cannot include $\{\mathbf{E}(p), \mathbf{EN}(p)\}$ (an event cannot be both expected to happen and expected not to happen);
- *fulfilled*: for any ground p, **EXP** cannot contain $\mathbf{EN}(p)$ if **HAP** contains $\mathbf{H}(p)$, and **EXP** cannot contain $\mathbf{E}(p)$ if **HAP** does not contain $\mathbf{H}(p)$ (happened events are required to match the expectations).

In order to support goal-oriented societies, **EXP** is also required to entail, together with KB_S, a *goal* $\mathcal{G}$ which is defined as a conjunction of literals.

2.2 Representing the Needham-Schroeder Protocol in the *SOCS-SI* Social Model

In the following, we show a specification of the Needham-Schroeder protocol in the *SOCS-SI* language.

With the atom:

$$\mathbf{H}(send(X, Y, content(key(K), Term1, Term2)), T_1)$$

we mean that a message is sent by an agent X to an agent Y; the content of the message consists of the two terms $Term_1$ and $Term_2$ and has been encrypted with the key K. T_1 is the time at which Y receives the message.

The interaction of Figure 1, for instance, can be expressed as follows:

$$\mathbf{H}(send(a, b, content(key(k_b), agent(a), nonce(n_a))), 1)$$
$$\mathbf{H}(send(b, a, content(key(k_a), nonce(n_a), nonce(n_b))), 2)$$
$$\mathbf{H}(send(a, b, content(key(k_b), nonce(n_b), empty(0))), 3)$$

A first group of SICs, depicted in Figure 3, defines the protocol itself, i.e, the expected sequence of messages.

```
  H( send( X, B, content( key( KB), agent( A), nonce( NA))), T1)
--->
  E( send( B, X, content( key( KA), nonce( NA), nonce( NB))), T2)
  /\ NA!=NB /\ T2 > T1.

  H( send( X, B, content( key( KB), agent( A), nonce( NA))), T1)
  /\ H( send( B, X, content( key( KA), nonce( NA), nonce( NB))), T2)
  /\ T2 > T1
--->
  E( send( X, B, content( key( KB), nonce( NB), empty( 0))), T3)
  /\  T3 > T2.
```

Fig. 3. Social Integrity Constraints defining the Needham-Schroeder protocol

The first SIC of Figure 3 states that, whenever an agent B receives a message from agent X, and this message contains the name of some agent A (possibly the name of X himself), and some nonce N_A, encrypted with B's public key K_B, then a message is expected to be sent at a later time from B to X, containing the original nonce N_A and a new nonce N_B, encrypted with the public key of A.

The second SIC of Figure 3 expresses that if two messages have been sent, with the characteristics that: a) the first message has been sent at the instant T_1, from X to B, containing the name of some agent A and some nonce N_A, encrypted with some public key K_B; and b) the second message has been sent at a later instant T_2, from B to X, containing the original nonce N_A and a new nonce N_B, encrypted with the public key of A; then a third message is expected to be sent from X to B, containing N_B, and encrypted with B's public key.

The second group of SICs consists of the one in Figure 4, which expresses the condition that an agent is not able to guess another agent's *nonce*. The predicate *one_of(A, B, C)*, defined in the KB_S, is true when A unifies with at least one of B and C. The SIC says that, if agent X sends to another agent Y a

```
    H( send( X, Y, content( key( KY), Term1, Term2)), T0)
    /\ one_of(NX, Term1, Term2) /\ not isNonce( X, NX)
--->
    E( send( V, X, content( key( KX), Term3, Term4)), T1)
    /\ X!=V /\ isPublicKey( X, KX) /\ T1 < T0
    /\ one_of (nonce(NX), Term1, Term2)
\/
    E( send( V, X, content( key( KY), Term1, Term2)), T2)
    /\ T2 < T0
```

Fig. 4. Social Integrity Constraint expressing that an agent cannot guess a *nonce* generated by another agent (after Dolev-Yao [13])

message containing a nonce that X did not create, then X must have received N_X previously in a message encrypted with X's public key, or X must be forwarding a message that it has received.

3   Verification of Security Protocols

In this section we show the application of the *SOCS-SI* social framework to on-the-fly verification of compliance and static verification of protocol properties, adopting the Needham-Schroeder security protocol, specified in 2.2 as a case study.

By "static verification of protocol properties" we mean a verification (by means of a formal proof, performed at design time) that a protocol enjoyes desirable properties. If the agents follow the protocol, then the agent interaction will itself exhibit the properties. However, since in open agent societies it cannot be assumed that the agents will follow the protocols, it becomes necessary to verify the agents' compliance to the protocol by means of an external trusted entity, able to observe the agent behaviour at runtime. Following Guerin and Pitt [2], we call this process "on-the-fly verification of compliance".

In our approach, both types of verification are applied to the same specification of the protocol, without the need for a translation: the protocol designer, in this way, can be sure that the protocol for which he or she has verified formal properties will be the same that the agents will be required to follow.

The two types of verification are achieved by means of two abductive proof-procedures, $\mathcal{S}$CIFF and g-$\mathcal{S}$CIFF, which are closely related. In fact, the proof-procedure used for the static verification of protocol properties (g-$\mathcal{S}$CIFF) is defined as an extension of the one used for on-the-fly verification of compliance ($\mathcal{S}$CIFF): for this reason, we first present on-the-fly verification, although, in the intended use of *SOCS-SI*, static verification would come first.

3.1   On-the-Fly Verification of Compliance

In this section, we show examples where the $\mathcal{S}$CIFF proof-procedure is used as a tool for verifying that the agent interaction is *compliant* to a protocol.

```
h(send( a, b, content( key( kb), agent( a), nonce( na))), 1).
h(send( b, a, content( key( ka), nonce( na), nonce( nb))), 2).
h(send( a, b, content( key( kb), nonce( nb), empty( 0))), 3).
```

Fig. 5. A compliant history

```
h(send( a, b, content( key( kb), agent( a), nonce( na))), 1).
h(send( b, a, content( key( ka), nonce( na), nonce( nb))), 2).
```

Fig. 6. A non-compliant history (the third message is missing)

$\mathcal{S}$CIFF verifies compliance by trying to generate a set **EXP** which fulfils the four conditions defined in Section 2.1.

The $\mathcal{S}$CIFF proof-procedure [14] is an extension of the IFF proof-procedure[3] [15]. Operationally, if the agent interaction has been compliant to the protocol, $\mathcal{S}$CIFF reports success and the required set **EXP** of expectations; otherwise, it reports failure. The proof-procedure has been proven sound and complete with respect to the declarative semantics. A result of termination also holds, under acyclicity assumptions.

The following examples can be verified by means of $\mathcal{S}$CIFF. Figure 5 shows an example of a history compliant to the SICs of Figure 3 and Figure 4.

Figure 6 instead shows an example of a history that is not compliant to such SICs. The reason is that the protocol has not been completed. In fact, the two events in the history propagate the second integrity constraints of Figure 3 and impose an expectation

```
e(send( a, b, content( key( kb), nonce( nb), empty( 0))), T3)
```

(with the CLP constraint T3>2), not fulfilled by any event in the history.

The history in Figure 7, instead, while containing a complete protocol run, violates the integrity constraint of Figure 4 because agent a has used a nonce (nc) that it cannot know, being not one of its own nonces (as defined in the KB_S), nor one of those a received in any previous message (or better, we have no evidence of it). In terms of integrity constraints, the history satisfies those in Figure 3, but it violates the one in Figure 4.

Based on $\mathcal{S}$CIFF, $SOCS$-SI is able to capture at run-time violation cases such as these.

Figure 8 depicts Lowe's attack, which is compliant both to the protocol and to the SICs in Figure 4.

A number of experiments made on a number of protocols can be downloaded from the SOCS Protocol Repository [6].

---

[3] Extended because, unlike IFF, it copes with (*i*) universally quantified variables in abducibles, (*ii*) dynamically incoming events, (*iii*) consistency, fulfillment and violations, and (*iv*) CLP-like constraints.

```
h(send( a, b, content( key( kb), agent( a), nonce( nc))), 1).
h(send( b, a, content( key( ka), nonce( nc), nonce( nb))), 2).
h(send( a, b, content( key( kb), nonce( nb), empty( 0))), 3).
```

Fig. 7. A non-compliant history (agent **a** has used a nonce that it cannot hold)

```
h(send( a, i, content( key( ki), agent( a), nonce( na))), 1).
h(send( i, b, content( key( kb), agent( a), nonce( na))), 2).
h(send( b, i, content( key( ka), nonce( na), nonce( nb))), 3).
h(send( i, a, content( key( ka), nonce( na), nonce( nb))), 4).
h(send( a, i, content( key( ki), nonce( nb), empty( 0))), 5).
h(send( i, b, content( key( kb), nonce( nb), empty( 0))), 6).
```

Fig. 8. Lowe's attack, recognized as a compliant history

3.2   Static Verification of Protocol Properties

In order to verify protocol properties, we have developed an extension of the $\mathcal{SCIFF}$ proof-procedure, called g-$\mathcal{SCIFF}$. Besides verifying whether a history is compliant to a protocol, g-$\mathcal{SCIFF}$ is able to generate a compliant history, given a protocol. g-$\mathcal{SCIFF}$ has been proved sound [16], which means that the histories that it generates (in case of success) are guaranteed to be compliant to the interaction protocols while entailing the goal. Note that the histories generated by g-$\mathcal{SCIFF}$ are in general not only a collection of ground events, like the **HAP** sets given as an input to $\mathcal{SCIFF}$. They can, in fact, contain variables, which means that they represent *classes* of event histories.

In order to use g-$\mathcal{SCIFF}$ for verification, we express the property to be verified as a conjunction of literals. If we want to verify if a formula f is a property of a protocol $\mathcal{P}$, we express the protocol in our language and $\neg f$ as a g-$\mathcal{SCIFF}$ goal. Then either:

- g-$\mathcal{SCIFF}$ returns success, generating a history **HAP**. Thanks to the soundness of g-$\mathcal{SCIFF}$, **HAP** entails $\neg f$ while being compliant to $\mathcal{P}$: f is not a property of $\mathcal{P}$, **HAP** being a counterexample; or
- g-$\mathcal{SCIFF}$ returns failure, suggesting that f is a property of $\mathcal{P}$[4].

In the following, we exemplify such a use of g-$\mathcal{SCIFF}$ by showing the automatic generation of Lowe's attack by g-$\mathcal{SCIFF}$, obtained as a counterexample of a property of the Needham-Schroeder protocol. The property that we want to disprove is $\mathcal{P}_{trust}$ defined as $trust_B(X, A) \rightarrow X = A$, i.e., if B trusts that he is communicating with A, then he is indeed communicating with A.

Thanks to the properties of public keys (a message encrypted with a public key can only be decrypted by the owner of the corresponding private key) and nonces (a nonce cannot be guessed), the notion of $trust_B(X, A)$ can be characterized as follows:

---

[4] If we had a completeness result for g-$\mathcal{SCIFF}$, this would indeed be a proof and not only a suggestion.

Definition 1 $(trust_B(X, A))$. *B trusts that the agent X he is communicating with is A, once two messages have been exchanged at times T_1 and T_2, $T_1 < T_2$, having the following sender, recipient, and content:*

(T_1) $B \to X : \{N_B, \dots\}_{pub\_key(A)}$
(T_2) $X \to B : \{N_B, \dots\}_{pub\_key(B)}$

where N_B is a nonce generated by B.

In order to check whether $\mathcal{P}_{trust}$ is a property of the protocol, we ground $\mathcal{P}_{trust}$ and define its negation $\neg\mathcal{P}_{trust}$ as a goal, g, where we choose to assign to A, B, and X the values a, b and i:

$g \leftarrow isNonce(NA), NA \neq nb,$
$\quad \mathbf{E}(send(b, i, content(key(ka), nonce(NA), nonce(nb))), 3),$
$\quad \mathbf{E}(send(i, b, content(key(kb), nonce(nb), empty(0))), 6).$

This goal negates $\mathcal{P}_{trust}$, in that b has sent to an agent one of its nonces, encrypted with a's public key, and has received the nonce back unencrypted, so being entitled to believe the other agent to be a; whereas the other agent is, in fact, i.

Besides defining g for three specific agents, we also assign definite time points (3 and 6) in order to improve the efficiency of the proof by exploiting constraint propagation.

Running the g-$\mathcal{S}$CIFF on g results in a compliant history:

$\mathbf{HAP}_g = \{ \ h(send(a, i, content(key(ki), agent(a), nonce(na))), 1),$
$h(send(i, b, content(key(kb), agent(a), nonce(na))), 2),$
$h(send(b, i, content(key(ka), nonce(na), nonce(nb))), 3),$
$h(send(i, a, content(key(ka), nonce(na), nonce(nb))), 4),$
$h(send(a, i, content(key(ki), nonce(nb), empty(0))), 5),$
$h(send(i, b, content(key(kb), nonce(nb), empty(0))), 6)\},$

that is, we generate Lowe's attack on the protocol.

$\mathbf{HAP}_g$ represents a counterexample which shows that the Needham-Schroeder protocol does not have the property $\mathcal{P}_{trust}$, being a history that is compliant to the protocol while violating the property.

4   Verifying the NetBill Protocol

In this section, we further demonstrate the specification and verification of agent interaction protocols in the *SOCS-SI* framework, on the NetBill (see [17]) protocol.

NetBill is a security and transaction protocol optimized for the selling and delivery of low-priced information goods, like software or journal articles. The protocol rules transactions between two agents: *merchant* and *customer*. A Net-Bill server is used to deal with financial issues such as those related to credit card accounts of customer and merchant.

In the following, we focus on the type of the NetBill protocol designed for non zero-priced goods, and do not consider the variants that deal with zero-priced goods.

A typical protocol run is composed of three phases:

1. *price negotiation*. The customer requests a quote for a good identified by *PrId* (`priceRequest(PrId)`), and the merchant replies with (`priceQuote(PrId,Quote)`).
2. *good delivery*. The customer requests the good (`goodRequest(PrId,Quote)`) and the merchant delivers it in an encrypted format (`deliver(crypt(PrId,Key),Quote)`).
3. *payment*. The customer issues an Electronic Payment Order (EPO) to the merchant, for the amount agreed for the good (`payment(epo(C,crypt(PrId,K),Quote))`); the merchant appends the decryption key for the good to the EPO, signs the pair and forwards it to the NetBill server (`endorsedEPO(epo(C,crypt(PrId,K),Quote),M)`); the NetBill server deals with the actual money transfer and returns the result to the merchant (`signedResult(C,PrID,Price,K)`), who will, in her turn, send a receipt for the good and the decryption key to the customer (`receipt(PrId,Price,K)`).

The customer can withdraw from the transaction until she has issued the *EPO* message; the merchant until she has issued the *endorsedEPO* message.

4.1 NetBill Protocol Specification in *SOCS-SI*.

The NetBill protocol is implemented in the *SOCS-SI* framework by means of SICs of two types:

- *backward integrity constraints* (Fig. 9), i.e., integrity constraints that state that if some set of event happens, then some other set of event is expected to have happened before.

  For instance, the first backward integrity constraints imposes that, if M has sent a `priceQuote` message to C, stating that M's quote for the good identified by `PrId` is `Quote`, in the interaction identified by `Id`, then C is expected to have sent to M a `priceRequest` message for the same good, in the same interaction, at an earlier time.

- *forward integrity constraints* (Fig. 10), i.e., constraints that state that if some conjunction of event has happened, then some other set of event is expected to happen in the future.

  For instance, the first forward integrity constraint in Fig. 10 imposes that an `endorsedEPO` message from M to the *netbill* server be followed by a `signedResult` message, with the corresponding parameters.

We only impose forward constraints from the `endorsedEPO` message onwards, because both parties (merchant and customer) can withdraw from the transaction at the previous steps.

```
H(tell(M,C,priceQuote(PrId,Quote),Id),T)
--->
E(tell(C,M,priceRequest(PrId),Id),T2) /\ T2 < T.

H(tell(C,M,goodRequest(PrId,Quote),Id),T)
--->
E(tell(M,C,priceQuote(PrId,Quote),Id),Tpri) /\ Tpri < T.

H(tell(M,C,goodDelivery(crypt(PrId,K),Quote),Id),T)
--->
E(tell(C,M,goodRequest(PrId,Quote),Id),Treq) /\ Treq < T.

H(tell(C,M,payment(C,crypt(PrId,K),Quote),Id),T)
--->
E(tell(M,C,goodDelivery(crypt(PrId,K),Quote),Id),Tdel) /\ Tdel <
T.

H(tell(netbill,M,signedResult(C,PrId,Quote,K),Id),Tsign)

/\ M != netbill
--->
E(tell(M,netbill,endorsedEPO(epo(C,PrId,Quote),K,M),Id),T) /\ T
< Tsign.

H(tell(M,C,receipt(PrId,Quote,K),Id),Ts)
--->
E(tell(netbill,M,signedResult(C,PrId,Quote,K),Id),Tsign) /\
Tsign < Ts.
```

Fig. 9. NetBill protocol: backward integrity constraints

```
H(tell(M,netbill,endorsedEPO(epo(C,PrId,Quote),K,M),Id),T)
--->
E(tell(netbill,M,signedResult(C,PrId,Quote,K),Id),Tsign) /\ T <
Tsign.

H(tell(netbill,M,signedResult(C,PrId,Quote,K),Id),Tsign)
--->
E(tell(M,C,receipt(PrId,Quote,K),Id),Ts) /\ Tsign < Ts.
```

Fig. 10. NetBill protocol: forward integrity constraints

4.2 Verification of NetBill Properties

In this section, we show how a simple property of the NetBill protocol can be
expressed, and verified, in the *SOCS-SI* framework.

We want to verify the following property: *the merchant receives the payment for
a good G if and only if the customer receives the good G*, as long as the protocol
is respected.

Since the $\mathcal{S}$CIFF deals with (communicative) events and not with the states of the agents, we need to express the properties in terms of happened events. To this purpose, we can assume that merchant has received the payment once the NetBill server has issued the *signedResult* message, and that the the customer has received the good if she has received the encrypted good (with a *deliver* message) and the encryption key (with a *receipt* message).

Thus, the property that we want to verify can be espressed as

$$\mathbf{H}(tell(netbill, M, signedResult(C, PrId, Quote, K), Id), Tsign)$$
$$\Longleftrightarrow \mathbf{H}(tell(M, C, goodDelivery(crypt(PrId, K), Quote), Id), T) \qquad (1)$$
$$\wedge \mathbf{H}(tell(M, C, receipt(PrId, Quote, K), Id), Ts)$$

whose negation is

$$(\neg\mathbf{H}(tell(netbill, M, signedResult(C, PrId, Quote, K), Id), Tsign)$$
$$\wedge \mathbf{H}(tell(M, C, goodDelivery(crypt(PrId, K), Quote), Id), T)$$
$$\wedge \mathbf{H}(tell(M, C, receipt(PrId, Quote, K), Id), Ts))$$
$$\vee$$
$$(\mathbf{H}(tell(netbill, M, signedResult(C, PrId, Quote, K), Id), Tsign) \qquad (2)$$
$$\wedge \neg\mathbf{H}(tell(M, C, goodDelivery(crypt(PrId, K), Quote), Id), T)$$
$$\vee$$
$$(\mathbf{H}(tell(netbill, M, signedResult(C, PrId, Quote, K), Id), Tsign)$$
$$\wedge \neg\mathbf{H}(tell(M, C, goodDelivery(crypt(PrId, K), Quote), Id), T))$$

In other words, a history that entails Eq. (2) is a counterexample of the property that we want to prove. In order to search for such a history, we define a g-$\mathcal{S}$CIFF goal as follows:

$$g \leftarrow \mathbf{EN}(tell(netbill, M, signedResult(C, PrId, Quote, K), Id), Tsign),$$
$$\mathbf{E}(tell(M, C, goodDelivery(crypt(PrId, K), Quote), Id), T),$$
$$\mathbf{E}(tell(M, C, receipt(PrId, Quote, K), Id), Ts)).$$
$$g \leftarrow \mathbf{E}(tell(netbill, M, signedResult(C, PrId, Quote, K), Id), Tsign), \qquad (3)$$
$$\mathbf{EN}(tell(M, C, goodDelivery(crypt(PrId, K), Quote), Id), T).$$
$$g \leftarrow \mathbf{E}(tell(netbill, M, signedResult(C, PrId, Quote, K), Id), Tsign),$$
$$\mathbf{EN}(tell(M, C, goodDelivery(crypt(PrId, K), Quote), Id), T))$$

and run g-$\mathcal{S}$CIFF.

The result of the call is a failure. This suggests that there is no history that entails the negation of the property while respecting the protocol, i.e., the property is likely to hold if the protocol is respected. However, yet no guarantee can be given, because g-$\mathcal{S}$CIFF has not been proven complete.

If we remove the second forward integrity constraints (which imposes that a `signedResult` message be followed by a `receipt` message), then g-$\mathcal{S}$CIFF reports success, and the following history is generated:

```
h(tell(_E,_F,priceRequest(_D),_C),_M),
h(tell(_F,_E,priceQuote(_D,_B),_C),_L),
h(tell(_E,_F,goodRequest(_D,_B),_C),_K),
h(tell(_F,_E,goodDelivery(crypt(_D,_A),_B),_C),_J),
h(tell(_E,_F,payment(_E,crypt(_D,_A),_B),_C),_I),
h(tell(_F,netbill,endorsedEPO(epo(_E,_D,_B),_A,_F),_C),_H),
h(tell(netbill,_F,signedResult(_E,_D,_B,_A),_C),_G),
_I<_H, _H<_G,
_L>_M, _K>_L, _I>_J, _J>_K,
```

The *receipt* event is missing, which would violate the integrity constraint that has been removed. In other words, without that integrity constraint, the protocol no longer has the desired property.

In this way, a protocol designer can make sure that an integrity constraint is not redundant with respect to a desired property of the protocol.

5   Related Work

The focus of our work is not on security protocols themselves, for which there exist many efficient specialised methods, but on a language for describing protocols, for verifying the compliance of interactions, and for proving general properties of the protocols. To the best of our knowledge, this is the first comprehensive and fully operational approach addressing both types of verification, and using the same protocol definition language in both cases. Security protocols and their proof of flawedness are, in our viewpoint, instances of the general concepts of agent protocols and their properties.

However, in this section we will discuss some related logic-based approaches to automatic verification of security properties.

Russo *et al.* [18] discuss the application of abductive reasoning for analysing safety properties of declarative specifications expressed in the Event Calculus. In their abductive approach, the problem of proving that, for some invariant I, a domain description D entails I ($D \models I$), is translated into an equivalent problem of showing that it is not possible to consistently extend D with assertions that particular events have actually occurred (i.e., with a set of abductive hypotheses Δ), in such a way that the extended description entails $\neg I$. In other words, there is no set Δ such that $D \cup \Delta \models \neg I$. They solve this latter problem by a complete abductive decision procedure, thus exploiting abduction in a refutation mode. Whenever the procedure finds such a set Δ, the assertions in Δ act as a counterexample for the invariant. Our work is closely related: in fact, in both cases, goals represent negation of properties, and the proof-procedure attempts to generate counterexamples by means of abduction. However, we rely on a different language (in particular, ours can also be used for checking compliance on the fly without changing the specification of the protocol, which is a demanding task) and we deal with time by means of CLP constraints, whereas Russo *et al.* employ a temporal formalism based on Event Calculus.

In [19] the authors present a new approach, On-the-Fly Model Checker, to model check security protocols, using two concepts quite related to our approach:

the concept of lazy data types for representing a (possibly) infinite transition system, and the use of variables in the messages that an intruder can generate. In particular, the use of unbound variables reduces the state space generated by every possible message that an intruder can utter. Protocols are represented in the form of transition rules, triggered by the arrival of a message: proving properties consists of exploring the tree generated by the transition rules, and verifying that the property holds for each reachable state. They prove results of soundness and completeness, provided that the number of messages is bounded. Our approach is very similar, from the operational viewpoint. The main difference is that the purpose of our language is not limited to the analysis of security protocols. Moreover, we have introduced variables in all the messages, and not only in the messages uttered by the intruder; we can pose CLP constraints on these variables, whereas OFMC can only generate equality/inequality constraints. On the downside, OFMC provides state-of-the-art performance for security protocol analysis; our approach instead suffers for its generality, and its performance is definitely worse than the OFMC.

A relevant work in computer science on verification of security protocols was done by Abadi and Blanchet [20, 21]. They adopt a verification technique based on logic programming in order to verify security properties of protocols, such as secrecy and authenticity in a fully automatic way, without bounding the number of sessions. In their approach, a protocol is represented in extensions of pi calculus with cryptographic primitives. The protocol represented in this extended calculus is then automatically translated into a set of Horn clauses [21]. To prove secrecy, in [20, 21] attacks are modelled by relations and secrecy can be inferred by non-derivability: if $attacker(M)$ is not derivable, then secrecy of M is guaranteed. More importantly, the derivability of $attacker(M)$ can be used, instead, to reconstruct an attack. This approach was later extended in [22] in order to prove authenticity. By first order logic, having variables in the representation, they overcome the limitation of bounding the number of sessions. We achieve the same generality of [20, 21], since in their approach Horn clause verification technique is not specific to any formalism for representing the protocol, but a proper translator from the protocol language to Horn clause has to be defined. In our approach, we preferred to directly define a rewriting proof-procedure ($\mathcal{S}$CIFF) for the protocol representation language. Furthermore, by exploiting abduction and CLP constraints, also in the implementation of g-$\mathcal{S}$CIFF transitions themselves, in our approach we are able to generate proper traces where terms are constrained when needed along the derivation avoiding to impose further parameters to names as done in [21]. CLP constraints can do this more easily.

Armando *et al.* [23] compile a security program into a logic program with choice lp-rules with answer set semantics. They search for attacks of length k, for increasing values of k, and they are able to derive the flaws of various flawed security protocols. They model explicitly the capabilities of the intruder, while we take the opposite viewpoint: we explicitly state what the intruder cannot do (like decrypting a message without having the key, or guessing the key or the nonces of an agent), without implicitly limiting the abilities of the intruder.

Our social specifications can be seen as intensional formulations of the possible (i.e., compliant) traces of communication interactions. In this respect, our way of modeling protocols is very similar to the one of Paulson's inductive approach [24]. In particular, our representation of the events is almost the same, but we explicitly mention time in order to express temporal constraints. In the inductive approach, the protocol steps are modeled as possible extensions of a trace with new events and represented by (forward) rules, similar to our SICs. However, in our system we have expectations, which allow us to cope with both compliance on the fly and verification of properties without changing the protocol specification. Moreover, SICs can be considered more expressive than inductive rules, since they deal with constraints (and constraint satisfaction in the proof), and disjunctions in the head. As far as verification, the inductive approach requires more human interaction and expertise, since it exploits a general purpose theorem prover, and has the disadvantage that it cannot generate counterexamples directly (as most theorem prover-based approaches). Instead, we use a specialized proof-procedure based on abduction that can perform the proof without any human intervention, and can generate counterexamples.

Millen and Shmatikov [25] define a sound and complete proof-procedure, later improved by Corin and Etalle [26], based on constraint solving for cryptographic protocol analysis. g-$\mathcal{S}$CIFF is based on constraint solving as well, but with a different flavour of constraint: while the approaches by Millen and Shmatikov and by Corin and Etalle are based on abstract algebra, our constraint solver comprises a CLP(FD) solver, and embeds constraint propagation techniques to speed-up the solving process.

In [27], Song presents Athena, an approach to automatic security protocol analysis. Athena is a very efficient technique for proving protocol properties: unlike other techniques, Athena copes well with state space explosion and is applicable with an unbounded number of peers participating in a protocol, thanks to the use of theorem proving and to a compact way to represent states. Athena is correct and complete (but termination is not guaranteed). Like Athena, the representation of states and protocols in g-SCIFF is non ground, and therefore general and compact. Unlike Athena's, the g-SCIFF's implementation is not optimised, and suffers from the presence of symmetrical states. On the other hand, a clear advantage of the SOCS approach is that protocols are written and analyzed in a formalism which is the same used for run-time verification of compliance.

Özkohen and Yolum [28] propose an approach for the prediction of exceptions in supply chains which builds upon the well-known commitment-based approach for protocol specification (see, for instance, Yolum and Singh [29]); their approach is related in many aspects to our on-the-fly verification. They represent the expected agent behaviour by means of commitments between agents; commitments have timeouts, i.e., they must be fulfilled by a deadline, and can be composed by means of conjunction and disjunction. In this perspective, commitments are similar to our expectations, which can have deadlines represented by CLP constraints, and which are composed in disjunctions of conjunctions in the head of the social integrity constraints. However, our expectations can regard any kind of events expected to happen, not only those that can be represented as a commitment of a debtor towards a creditor; and we can also represent negative expectations. Operationally, in [28] the reasoning about commitments is centralized in a monitoring agents; in our framework, a similar task in performed by the social infrastructure.

6   Conclusion and Future Work

In this paper, we have shown how the *SOCS-SI* abductive framework can be applied to the specification and verification of security protocols, using, as a running example, the Needham-Schroeder Public Key authentication protocol.

The declarative framework is expressive enough to specify both which sequences of messages represent a legal protocol run, and constraints about the messages that a participant is able to synthesize.

Based on the *SOCS-SI* framework, we have implemented and experimented with two kinds of automatic verification: on-the-fly verification of compliance (by means of the sound and complete $\mathcal{S}$CIFF proof-procedure), and static verification of protocol properties (by means of the sound g-$\mathcal{S}$CIFF proof-procedure). In this way, our approach tackles both the case of agents misbehaving (which, in an open society, cannot be excluded) and the case of a flawed protocol (which can make the interaction exhibit an undesirable feature even if the participants follow the protocol correctly).

We believe that the main contribution of this work consists of providing a unique framework to both the two types of verification. The language used for protocol definition is the same in both the cases, thus lowering the chances of errors introduced in the protocol translation from one notation to a different one. The protocol designer can benefit of our approach during the design phase, by proving properties, and during the execution phase, where the interaction can be proved to be compliant with the protocol, and thus to exhibit the protocol properties.

Future work will be aimed to investigate a result of completeness for g-$\mathcal{S}$CIFF, and to extend the experimentation on proving protocol properties to a number of security and e-commerce protocols, such as SPLICE/AS [30].

Acknowledgments

This work has been supported by the European Commission within the SOCS project (IST-2001-32530), funded within the Global Computing Programme and by the MIUR COFIN 2003 projects *La Gestione e la negoziazione automatica dei diritti sulle opere dell'ingegno digitali: aspetti giuridici e informatici* and *Sviluppo e verifica di sistemi multiagente basati sulla logica*.

References

1. Davidsson, P.:   Categories of artificial societies.   In Omicini, A., Petta, P., Tolksdorf, R., eds.: Engineering Societies in the Agents World II. Volume 2203 of Lecture Notes in Artificial Intelligence, Springer-Verlag (2001) 1–9 2nd International Workshop (ESAW'01), Prague, Czech Republic, July 7, 2001, Revised Papers

2. Guerin, F., Pitt, J.: Proving properties of open agent systems. In Castelfranchi, C., Lewis Johnson, W., eds.: Proceedings of the First International Joint Conference on Autonomous Agents and Multiagent Systems (AAMAS-2002), Part II, Bologna, Italy, ACM Press (2002) 557–558

3. Societies Of ComputeeS (SOCS): a computational logic model for the description, analysis and verification of global and open societies of heterogeneous computees. IST-2001-32530 (2001) Home Page: http://lia.deis.unibo.it/Research/SOCS/

4. Alberti, M., Ciampolini, A., Gavanelli, M., Lamma, E., Mello, P., Torroni, P.: A social ACL semantics by deontic constraints. In Mařík, V., Müller, J., Pěchouček, M., eds.: Multi-Agent Systems and Applications III. Proceedings of the 3rd International Central and Eastern European Conference on Multi-Agent Systems, CEEMAS 2003. Volume 2691 of Lecture Notes in Artificial Intelligence, Prague, Czech Republic, Springer-Verlag (2003) 204–213

5. Alberti, M., Gavanelli, M., Lamma, E., Mello, P., Torroni, P.: Specification and verification of agent interactions using social integrity constraints. Electronic Notes in Theoretical Computer Science **85** (2003)

6. The socs protocol repository (2005) Available at http://lia.deis.unibo.it/research/socs/partners/societies/protocols.html

7. Needham, R., Schroeder, M.: Using encryption for authentication in large networks of computers. Communications of the ACM **21** (1978) 993–999

8. Lowe, G.: Breaking and fixing the Needham-Shroeder public-key protocol using CSP and FDR. In Margaria, T., Steffen, B., eds.: Tools and Algorithms for the Construction and Analysis of Systems: Second International Workshop, TACAS'96. Volume 1055 of Lecture Notes in Artificial Intelligence, Springer-Verlag (1996) 147–166

9. Denning, D.E., Sacco, G.M.: Timestamps in key distribution protocols. Communications of the ACM **24** (1981) 533–536

10. Alberti, M., Gavanelli, M., Lamma, E., Mello, P., Torroni, P.: An Abductive Interpretation for Open Societies. In Cappelli, A., Turini, F., eds.: AI*IA 2003: Advances in Artificial Intelligence, Proceedings of the 8th Congress of the Italian Association for Artificial Intelligence, Pisa. Volume 2829 of Lecture Notes in Artificial Intelligence, Springer-Verlag (2003) 287–299

11. Jaffar, J., Maher, M.: Constraint logic programming: a survey. Journal of Logic Programming **19–20** (1994) 503–582

12. Kakas, A.C., Kowalski, R.A., Toni, F.: Abductive Logic Programming. Journal of Logic and Computation **2** (1993) 719–770

13. Dolev, D., Yao, A.C.C.: On the security of public key protocols. IEEE Transactions on Information Theory **29** (1983) 198–207

14. Alberti, M., Gavanelli, M., Lamma, E., Mello, P., Torroni, P.: The sciff abductive proof-procedure. In: Proceedings of the 9th National Congress on Artificial Intelligence, AI*IA 2005. Volume 3673 of Lecture Notes in Artificial Intelligence, Springer-Verlag (2005) 135–147

15. Fung, T.H., Kowalski, R.A.: The IFF proof procedure for abductive logic programming. Journal of Logic Programming **33** (1997) 151–165
16. Alberti, M., Chesani, F., Gavanelli, M., Lamma, E., Mello, P., Torroni, P.: On the automatic verification of interaction protocols using g-$\mathcal{S}$CIFF. Technical Report DEIS-LIA-04-004, University of Bologna (Italy) (2005) LIA Series no. 72.
17. Cox, B., Tygar, J., Sirbu, M.: Netbill security and transaction protocol. In: Proceedings of the First USENIX Workshop on Electronic Commerce, New York (1995)
18. Russo, A., Miller, R., Nuseibeh, B., Kramer, J.: An abductive approach for analysing event-based requirements specifications. In Stuckey, P., ed.: Logic Programming, 18th International Conference, ICLP 2002. Volume 2401 of Lecture Notes in Computer Science, Berlin Heidelberg, Springer-Verlag (2002) 22–37
19. Basin, D.A., Mödersheim, S., Viganò, L.: An on-the-fly model-checker for security protocol analysis. In Snekkenes, E., Gollmann, D., eds.: ESORICS. Volume 2808 of Lecture Notes in Computer Science, Springer (2003) 253–270
20. Blanchet, B.: Automatic verification of cryptographic protocols: a logic programming approach. In: PPDP '03: Proceedings of the 5th ACM SIGPLAN international conference on Principles and practice of declaritive programming, New York, NY, USA, ACM Press (2003) 1–3
21. Abadi, M., Blanchet, B.: Analyzing security protocols with secrecy types and logic programs. J. ACM **52** (2005) 102–146
22. Blanchet, B.: From secrecy to authenticity in security protocols. In: SAS '02: Proceedings of the 9th International Symposium on Static Analysis, London, UK, Springer-Verlag (2002) 342–359
23. Armando, A., Compagna, L., Lierler, Y.: Automatic compilation of protocol insecurity problems into logic programming. In Alferes, J.J., Leite, J.A., eds.: Logics in Artificial Intelligence, 9th European Conference, JELIA 2004, Lisbon, Portugal, September 27–30, 2004, Proceedings. Volume 3229 of Lecture Notes in Artificial Intelligence, Springer-Verlag (2004) 617–627
24. Paulson, L.C.: The inductive approach to verifying cryptographic protocols. Journal of Computer Security **6** (1998) 85–128
25. Millen, J.K., Shmatikov, V.: Constraint solving for bounded-process cryptographic protocol analysis. In: CCS 2001, Proceedings of the 8th ACM Conference on Computer and Communications Security, ACM press (2001) 166–175
26. Corin, R., Etalle, S.: An improved constraint-based system for the verification of security protocols. In Hermenegildo, M.V., Puebla, G., eds.: Static Analysis, 9th International Symposium, SAS 2002, Madrid, Spain, September 17–20, 2002, Proceedings. Volume 2477 of Lecture Notes in Computer Science, Berlin, Germany, Springer (2002) 326–341
27. Song, D.X.: Athena: a new efficient automatic checker for security protocol analysis. In: CSFW '99: Proceedings of the 1999 IEEE Computer Security Foundations Workshop, Washington, DC, USA, IEEE Computer Society (1999) 192
28. Özkohen, A., Yolum, P.: Predicting exceptions in agent-based supply chains. In this volume. (2006)
29. Yolum, P., Singh, M.: Flexible protocol specification and execution: applying event calculus planning using commitments. In Castelfranchi, C., Lewis Johnson, W., eds.: Proceedings of the First International Joint Conference on Autonomous Agents and Multiagent Systems (AAMAS-2002), Part II, Bologna, Italy, ACM Press (2002) 527–534
30. Yamaguchi, S., Okayama, K., Miyahara, H.: The design and implementation of an authentication system for the wide area distributed environment. IEICE Transactions on Information and Systems **E74** (1991) 3902–3909

Engineering Complex Adaptive Systems Using Situated Multi-agents
Some Selected Works and Contributions

Salima Hassas

LIRIS, Nautibus, 8 Bd Niels Bohr,
Université Claude Bernard-Lyon 1,
Bat Nautibus, 43 Bd du 11 Novembre,
Villeurbanne, 69622, France

Abstract. A complex system is a set of entities interrelated in a retroactive way. The system dynamics is held by the retroactive interactions occuring between its components, making the behaviour, structure or organisation of the global system emergent and non predictable from/non reducible to the individual behaviour or structure of its components. This characteristic of complex systems, makes them more considered from their organisational point of view rather than from the structural/ behavioural aspects of their components. The multi-agent paradigm provides a very suitable tool for modeling/engineering such systems. Many examples exist in the MAS litterature, showing the use of the multi-agent paradigm to develop such systems. However, existing works propose ad hoc approaches/mechanisms. In this paper we discuss some of these works and present a set of intuitive guidelines for engineering self-organising systems, through their positionning at the heart of 3 domains: Complex Adaptive Systems, Non Linear Dynamic Systems and Situated Multi-Agents.

Keywords: Complex Systems, Situated Multi-Agents, Retroactive Interactions, Non Linearity, Self-organisation.

1   Introduction

Recent developments in Information Technology (IT) make us change ou way of thinking computation. Complexity of these systems has grown at a spectacular rate and speed in last decades. We are faced today to:

- the emergence of new environments such as massively large-scale wide area computer networks and mobile ad hoc networks;
- the proliferation of new capacities for storage, access and processing of a huge amount of various kinds of data at lowest costs;
- the emergence of new uses and needs which require the development of sophisticated applications, make use of a huge mass of complex and uncertain data (Genomics, Military/Defence applications, Finance/Economics applications, etc);

O. Dikenelli, M.-P. Gleizes, and A. Ricci (Eds.): ESAW 2005, LNAI 3963, pp. 125–141, 2006.
© Springer-Verlag Berlin Heidelberg 2006

- a rising need for Human-Centered applications, where the user of the IT system is considered as an important component of the system. The system development and evolution are thus guided by the interactions held between the user and its other components (e-learning, e-business, assisting systems, etc);
- the evolution of hardware and software technologies which offers enormous potential for the development of large scale distributed and flexible systems.

The IT system is thus considered as a set of components, interacting together and with their environment.

In this context, thinking the engineering of an IT system requires to have in mind the integration of its complexity as an essential characteristic. The IT system complexity comes from its openness to its environment, which is itself, complex, distributed, dynamic, and uncertain. Considering these aspects, the issue is:

How to Engineer IT Systems, Able to Evolve (Adequately) According to the Evolving of Their Environment?

The systems's environment is here considered at its widest meaning including the level of resources and materials necessary for the system functioning and deployment (physical level) as well as the more abstract higher level of uses and practices which are developped through the system use (conceptual level). The physical level of an environment could be a computer network, or a network of information resources such as the www or a set of documents and ontologies, etc. The conceptual level in this case, could be users profiles, users communities, annotations of shared documents, and the relations between resources (computers, web sites, documents, etc) as traces of actions and interactions. These two defined levels are interrelated:

- at a highest level, the conceptual environment is considered as a place of materialisation of uses and practices;
- at a lowest level, the physical environment, representing a set of physical resources, is considered on one hand as a place of materialization (embodiment) of the computing system, and on the other hand, as a place of marking traces of uses related to actions and interactions. The physical environment could thus be viewed as a complex network of resources.

Effects of actions and interactions held at the conceptual environment, let traces/marks at the lowest physical environment and can influence the topology of the underlying network of resources. For example, the Web/Internet topology expresses some uses like the formation of virtual communities, which are represented by clusters (of pages or nodes) formation.

The IT system is thus considered as a set of interacting entities with retroactive interactions. The challenge of such a system is to find an efficient organisation of its components (self-organisation), into structures that implement a coherent behaviour face to its complex environment dynamics. Natural (living) systems have succeed such a challenge through millions of years. As, defended by Enactivism [29], we think that this capacity of living systems is due to their coupling to their environment. In this paper we develop this idea in section 4 and base on it the proposal, of a conceptual framework for engineering complex adaptive systems using situated multi-agents. Beforehand, we review in section 2 some selected works, taking inspiration from living systems, and point to the common concepts used in these works and analyse them following an enactivist vision. Before concluding the paper in section 6, we present an illustration with a web oriented application in section 5.

2 Review of Some Selected Works Using Living Systems Inspiration for Engineering IT Systems

Face to the growing complexity of IT systems, seeking inspiration from nature has been a fruitful track to follow in different fields of computing systems [5]. Indeed, living systems exhibit many interesting properties, that allow them to adapt to a complex environment. Systems like organisms of cells, colonies of insects or societies of individuals, exhibit global complex behaviours which make them (self-)organise their components into flexible and robust structures. These systems are characterised by high reactiveness, robustness face to individual failures and a high capacity to adapt to a changing environment. In this section, we review some selected works using the living systems inspiration. Inspiration from social insects behaviour is one of the most used in different fields of computing, specially the foraging behaviour metaphor. This metaphor was used to propose the ACO meta-heuristic to solve optimisation problems [9], and to develop ant-like systems using mobile agents with applications in several domains such as computers network routing and load-balancing [30][8][12], computers network security [11][14], information sharing in peer to peer systems [2], and information clustering [16] using social insects collective sorting metaphor [4][19]. Other examples of social insects inspiration have been developed for image processing [5] or manufacturing applications [7]. The main idea in theses works is the use of stigmergy mechanism as a mean to implement a self-organising behaviour as achieved by social insects behaviours. Stigmergy [15] is a mechanism discovered by P.P. Grassé in 1959, which is used in social insects to coordinate individual behaviours, using an environment mediated communication. Coordination is achieved through the influence exerted by persistent effects left in the environment by previous actions, on future actions to be taken by the collective of agents. These effects are physically represented on a spatio-temporal medium (the environment) and are amplified through an auto-catalytic process. In the case of ants foraging behaviour, a pheromone gradient field is used to represent these effects. The idea of gradient field, that allows stigmergic coordination of actions has been used in [27][26] to propose a middleware (called TOTA) for supporting adaptive context-aware activities in dynamic network scenarios. The main idea in this work is the use of a spacial environment for the representation of contextual information and its local spreading through the notion of "computational fields". This allows adaptive interactions between the application components. Other inspirations from biological and living systems are those using immune systems metaphors[13][17], epidemic spreading, rumour propagation [6] and gossiping [20]. Characteristics of these approaches are the use of some mechanisms, that are well-known in biological or natural systems [1], such as: spreading of information, aggregation and replication, balancing diversity and reinforcement, etc. The use of a spatial medium for information diffusion, its aggregation and replication seem to be an important issue in self-organising approaches. Generally, in multi-agent based approaches, with living systems inspiration, agents are used in an ad hoc way, to mimic a natural behaviour. The coupling of agents to their environment is not made explicit, neither are the consequences of this coupling on their behaviours. In this paper, we base a proposal of a conceptual framework for engineering complex systems using MAS, on an enactivist vision [29], through which we explicit this coupling and show how it is related to self-organisation.

3   Enactivism and Autopoesis: On the System Coupling to its Environment

The structural coupling of a system to its surroundings (environment) is an idea developped through the Enactivist philosophy. Enactivism is a philosophical theory of cognition, rooted in a biological vision so as "from the Enactivist perspective epistemology and theories of mind and theories of evolution are very close to being the same thing". [29]. In an Enactivist vision, a system organisation is defined as the set of invariant features allowing an observer to distinguish the system from its surroundings. A system organisation is distinguished from the system structure. the system organisation includes the invariant features without which it would cease to be what it is, whereas its structure includes all its features at a given time. The system tends, during its evolution, to structure its environment, while it is structured by the environment evolution. As mentionned in [29]:

> Systems that continually create themselves are referred to in Enactivism as autopoetic. The components of autopoetic systems "must be dynamically related in a network of ongoing interactions". That is, the components interact in ways which are continually changing, but which at the same time allow for the continuation of interactions so that the system continues to exist. In addition, the interactions of the components of an autopoetic system are responsible for the production of the components themselves. In summary, an autopoetic system is an emergent phenomenon arising from the interactions of components which, by way of these interactions, give rise to new interactions and new components, while preserving the autopoetic character of the system.

Following the perspective of Enactivism and autopoesis, a system as a set of entities evolving in an environment, produces through the ongoing interactions of its components, structures that feed the production of these interactions, in a continuous loop. In the next section, we will see how this ideas could be applied in the context of engineering complex IT systems.

4   Engineering Complex Adaptive Systems Using Situated Multi-agents: Our Vision

4.1   IT System Coupling to its Environment

As presented above, the complexity of IT systems environment, requires to think the engineering of the IT system through its coupling with its environment. IT systems environment presents two levels: a physical lowest level and a conceptual highest level. The two levels are strongly interconnected making the IT system coupling to its environment going through two articulations:

- a physical articulation which corresponds to structural coupling, which determines the IT system structure through its interaction with the environment;
- a conceptual articulation which corresponds to behavioural coupling that determines actions and interactions producing the IT system structure;
- an organisational articulation, expressing retroactive effects of one coupling on the other.

Organisation is the set of invariant features that permits to establish the system identity (autopoesis). It defines rules allowing to couple together, structural and behavioural coupling of the IT system to its environment, following an autopoetic vision.

4.2   Implications on the Multi-agents System Used for Engineering IT Systems

Using Situated Multi-Agents System (MAS) to engineer an IT system which is structurally and behaviourally coupled to its environment, makes the MAS itself subject to the same coupling with its environment. Thus, the implications of the different articulations seen above, have to be considered in the MAS:

- Physical articulation and structural coupling : agents of the MAS represent structurally the components of the IT system. Thus, the structural coupling of the system requires to consider the spatial organisation of the MAS according to the physical environment;
- Conceptual articulation and behavioural coupling: the system behaviour is achieved through the collective behaviour of the MAS, which is itself obtained as an aggregation of agents individual behaviours. Coupling the system behaviour to the environment, needs to consider the social organisation of the MAS with respect to the conceptual environment of the system;
- Organisational articulation and retroaction: to make the whole system have a coherent evolution through its structural and behavioural coupling to the

environment, retroactive effects of one coupling on the other must be correlated. In the MAS which implements the system. It is thus necessary to consider the co-evolution of the MAS social and spatial organisations, during the system evolution.

The design of the situated MAS to engineer a complex adaptive system must thus address both MAS spatial and social organisations, and their co-evolution through the MAS dynamics. This makes self-organisation mandatory.

Example. *In the ants foraging behaviour, ants are collectively able to find shortest paths from their nest to food sources.* **Shortest paths** *appear as* **emergent structures** *on the spatial representation of ants environment. These emergent structures are represented by the* **spatial organisation of ants** *on the environment and are obtained trough a self-catalytic use of paths, which is the* **conceptual materialisation of the social organisation.** *Self-organisation is the way to ensure co-evolution of both organisations, and make the foraging behaviour works. It needs to establish a connection ("glue") between both organisations, to ensure their co-evolution and this is achieved through the stigmergy mechanism.*

4.3   A Generic Framework for Engineering Complex Adaptive IT Systems Using Situated Multi-agents

The IT system is considered as a complex adaptive system represented by a situated MAS evolving in the system environment. Agents are parts of the IT system and are deployed in their living environment. They sense their environment and take behavioural decisions allowing them to face the environment evolution. To engineer such a system, we propose a conceptual framework based on the following main points:

Spatial Representation of the Environment. As a complex adaptive network, highly reconfigurable in presence of intrinsic dynamics and environmental evolution. The dynamics is held by processes running on the network. The network becomes the space of actions and interactions traces and can be used to enhance the network evolution towards a specific organisational structure, with an effect on the network topology. Recent researches work on complex networks emitted 2 statements: 1) [10] "complex man-made networks such as Internet and the world wide web, share the same large-scale topology as many metabolic and protein networks of various organisms..." and 2) [3] "the emergence of these networks is driven by self-organizing processes that are governed by simple but generic laws". The Internet topology has been recently characterized as scale free [28]. A scale free network is a class of a non homogeneous wired network. Such topology is extremely sparse with a few randomly distributed and highly connected nodes (hubs), and many nodes with few connections. A scale-free network also exhibits the so-called small world phenomenon [31], meaning that it has a short average path length allowing each node of the network to reach any other node through a relatively small number of hops.

The scale free topology of the Internet and the world wide web are typical expression instances on a physical level of traces of the use and practices of the conceptual level. the highly connected nodes (hubs) observed in the topology are the effect of a mechanism of preferential attachment: the more a node is connected, the more it gets a chance to be connected in the future. In the world wide web, this expresses the fact that most popular sites, are more and more referenced.

A Collective Behaviour Based Approach Using the Situated Multi-agents Paradigm and Embodied Intelligence. This is characterized by the following points:

- the world is its own model, meaning that there is no symbolic representation of the environment. For instance, in a computer network application, the network is considered as the real environment where agents are launched and have to evolve autonomously. No symbolic representation of the network is provided for agents.
- agents embodiement and situatedness: agents are embodied and situated in their environment following an enactivist vision. Agents' behaviours are spatially and conceptually context aware. The agents structure their environment while their behaviours are themselves structured by the environment evolution.
- agents' activity is held through a sensori-motor (perception-action) loop, meaning that the whole behaviour of the system is coded in terms of non deliberative perceptions-actions of the system agents.

A Stigmergic Mechanism of Communication and Behaviours Coordination. In order to provide stigmergy it is necessary to:

- make use of a spatial control structure, physically represented in the environment. This structure is used to code the system data as well as intermediate results allowing a form of retroactive guiding of the agents behaviours. In that sense, this structure serves to bridge the gap (as a glue) between the agents social and spatial organisation.
- have a set of mechanisms of meta-control allowing the control of the control information like positive or negative feedbacks, control information persistency, control information spreading rate, etc.

The electronic pheromone and all mechanisms based on the construction of gradient field (magnetic fields, pheromone fields, etc.) are an illustration of a spatial structure of control. The main electronic pheromone attributes are:

- *a label to code the nature of the control information;*
- *an intensity corresponding to the amount of pheromone. It measures the importance of the information;*
- *an evaporation rate evaluating the persistency of the control information; The higher the evaporation rate, the lower the persistency of the information;*
- *a spreading rate corresponding to the scope of the control information. The higher the value of the spreading rate, the greater the information scope.*

Balancing Exploration and Exploitation. It is characterized by a strategy for correlating individual behaviours by balancing diversity (exploration) and reinforcement (exploitation) in response to an evolving and unsafe environment. This balancing is crucial and provides a way to correlate the agents distributed behaviours and to obtain a coherent collective behaviour.

5   Illustration on a Web Oriented Application

5.1   The Web as a Complex Adaptive System (CAS): Hollands Properties

As CAS are formed of agents interacting with each other, adapting and co-evolving in their environment, modelling such systems requires a bottom-up approach which consists in identifying the different agents and their rules of behaviours and interactions. Emergent properties will rise from within the system. John Holland identified seven basic elements of a CAS [18]:

- *Aggregation* is the property by which agents group to form categories or meta-agents that in turn can recombine to a higher level (meta-meta-agents) leading to the complex system. The emergence of the meta-agent is due to the interactions between the agents at the lower level. For example on the www, we group content and links (structure) based on some user needs into a web page and web pages into websites, and websites into web communities (meta-agents) that emerge and self organize without centralized control. This self-organisation is a result of a retroactive interaction between usage, content and structure. As web users needs are evolving over time, web page designers are constantly changing the contents and structures of their web pages and web communities are emerging constantly. Aggregate behaviour is also observed in the appearance of hubs and authorities in the web [22].
- *Tagging* is the mechanism that facilitates the formation of aggregates by assigning attributes or tags used for agent identification. A tag could be the main topic of a web community or the word vector bags of words of a specific web page used in text analysis.
- *Nonlinearity* is the property where the emergent behaviour of the system is the result of a non-proportionate response to its stimulus. That means the behaviour resulting from the interactions between aggregate agents is more complex than a simple summation or average of the simple agents. The growth of the web is a nonlinear process.
- *Flows* are physical resources and information circulating through the components of the complex systems without any centralised control.
- *Diversity.* The diversity of skills, experiments, strategies, rules of different agents ensure the dynamic adaptive behaviour of a CAS. The web has a large number of interacting constituents and this diversity in the web is contributing to its robustness. We observe diversity in its usage, structure and content. In [23], users were classified into random users, rational users and recurrent users. Web pages are also diverse in their structure, like hubs

and authorities pages [22], and web pages were divided into five categories: Strongly Connected Components SCC, IN, OUT, tendrils and tubes, and disconnected.

- *Internal models* or schemas are the functions or rules agents use to interact with each other and with their environment. These schemas direct agents behaviours.
- *Building blocks* are the component parts that can be combined and reused for each instance of a model. Identifying these blocks is the first step in modelling a CAS. In [25], the authors showed that sub-graphs motifs form the building blocks for the WWW network and web services are also building blocks for distributed web based applications [21].

5.2   The WACO System

The WACO (Web Ants Content organisation) system, illustrates the use of the conceptual framework described in section 4.3 to engineer a complex adaptive system using situated multi-agents. The web is considered as a complex environment, represented by a complex network of resources (web pages, web sites, servers, etc) inhabited by artificial creatures called WebAnts. These creatures implemented by mobile agents, are embodied in the environment, organized in a colony and mimic some behaviours of natural ants, namely the collective sorting behaviour and the food foraging behaviour. The content of the web is viewed by WebAnts as a potential source of food that needs to be organized and be collected in an efficient way. Four types of WebAnts were created, each assigned a different task (tags associated with each agent):

1. Explorers WebAnts look randomly for web documents to sort;
2. Collectors WebAnts maintain and organize semantically collected documents;
3. Searchers WebAnts reinforce clusters of collected documents by searching the web for similar documents to add to the cluster;
4. Finally, Requests Satisfying WebAnts search for the appropriate cluster based on user requests.

The different groups of WebAnts achieve their tasks and communicate through the stigmergy mechanism. There is no central control dictating their actions and behaviours. Stigmergy is achieved in two ways: 1) using a digital pheromone representing resources contents and 2) using the size of clusters of homogenous contents to enforce specialisation of Searchers WebAnts and regulate the population. WebAnts in WACO are created in a dynamic way and they adapt to their environment and co-evolve. This process requires a mechanism of managing and regulating the population of agents. To do this, a mechanism of energy distribution and consumption is used [24]. WebAnts are sensitive to some notion of order, which is obtained by semantic organisation of the web content. The higher the disorder on the web, the more active are WebAnts. Activity of agents is regulated by a mechanism of energy distribution, provided by the environment and directly associated with the notion of order in the global environment.

Disorder in the environment, generates energy which is captured by agents and increases their activity and number. Based on their fitness function defined by order/disorder, two mechanisms direct their life cycle: duplication (birth) and disappearance (death) (see [16] for more details).

Documents Coding by Synthetic Pheromone Use. Documents contained by the websites are considered as objects to be sorted following their semantic contents, so as to construct semantic clusters, where a cluster is a set of semantically closed documents with respect to a predefined similarity measure. We consider two levels in this application: a higher level corresponding to the extraction of information from documents using any algorithm of text mining and a lower level which use a synthetic pheromone based coding of the extracted information to organise and search the web content. A semantic value is associated to each document. This value is used as a label for a specific pheromone to which WebAnts would be sensitive, when looking for documents with similar semantic values. Each semantic topic is identified by a kind of pheromone. Synthetic pheromone is coded by a structure with these different fields:

- *Label ($W_{||}$)*: characterizes the kind of information coded by the pheromone, which is in our context the semantic value of a document (weighted keyword).

$$W_{||} = L_C.H_C.TF.IDF$$

  TF is the frequency of the keyword in the current document, the H_C is a Header constant ($H_C > 1$ if the word appears in a title, $= 1$ otherwise), which increases the weight of the keyword if it appears in the title of the document, and IDF is the inverse of document frequency. The linkage constant L_C ($L_C > 1$ if the word appears in a link, $= 1$ otherwise).
- Intensity ($\tau_i j$): expresses the pertinence of information; the higher its value, the greater its attractive power. This value is computed on each site i, for each topic j, using the number of documents addressing the same topic, each time ($t + 1$) a new document is added, as:

$$\tau_i j(t + 1) = \rho_j \tau_i j(t) + \Sigma_{k=1}^{|Dij|} \Delta \tau_{ijk}(t)$$

  ρ_j represents the persistence rate (($1 - \rho_j$) the evaporation rate), $\Delta \tau_{ijk}$ the intensity of pheromone emitted by a document k, on the site i for a topic j at time t, and D_{ij} is the set of documents addressing topic j on the site i. -
- Evaporation rate: expresses the persistence rate of information in the environment. The lower its value is, the longer is the influence of the spread information in the environment.

$$\rho_j = \frac{|D_{ij}|}{|D_i|}$$

Dij is the set of documents addressing the topic j on the site i, and D_i is the set of all documents on the site i. The idea here is to make the clustering of documents about a same topic more attractive than isolated documents. If a site contains heterogeneous semantic content, this information is considered as not sufficiently pertinent. So the associated pheromone will evaporate more quickly than emitted pheromone by homogenous content.

- Diffusion rate: expresses the distance to which information is spread in the environment, the higher its value the greater the scope of the information in the environment. We express this distance using the linkage topology information. Indeed, when browsing the web looking for a topic, one explores pages following links addressing the topic of interest. We associate to each site i, a distance d_{ij} for each topic j addressed by i, which is computed as the longest path from the site i to the last site addressing the topic j, following a depth first

$$d_{ij} = Max_k(d_{ij})_k$$

k is the number of links addressing topic j, from a site i.

Coupling of Agents to the Environment and the System Dynamics.
The web represents a complex uncertain environment that WebAnts explore, and structure by interacting with one another. The web structuring, structures the population of agents in return. The web is also the medium of agents interactions, through the deposit and smelling of the synthetic pheromone, the perception of scattered documents and clusters forming. Agents communicate through the stigmergic mechanism, using a multi-structured electronic pheromone. The building blocks are the popuations of WebAnts agents which mimic the collective sorting behaviour and the foraging behaviour. The use of the digital pheromone for information coding corresponds to Hollands tagging mechanism and aggregation is observed through the multi-pheromone structure.

- Explorers WebAnts perceive different kinds of pheromones, corresponding to different semantic values but are more sensitive to the pheromone value of the last document collected;
- Collectors WebAnts compute regularly the synthesis of the site pheromone, and update the values of its associated parameters (label, intensity, persistence rate, diffusion rate);
- Searchers WebAnts are launched, when a cluster reaches a threshold size and Requests Satisfying WebAnts code the user request into a pheromone value, and search in the environment the appropriate cluster, to answer the user request, by following the gradient of the associated pheromone field.

Agents use the collective sorting behaviour through the spreading by sites of their synthetic pheromone characterising their contents. When this pheromone is perceived by Explorer WebAnts, during their random path, they collect the URL of the site and look for an appropriate cluster, by smelling in the environment the appropriate pheromone. If no pheromone is found after a predefined number of jumps, they initiate the clustering operation. Searcher WebAnts accomplish the foraging behaviour through the spreading of a clustering pheromone. When a cluster size reaches a predefined threshold, Searcher WebAnts are created to enforce the clustering operation. These agents leave the cluster, to search in the environment for sites or servers with similar content. During their search behaviour, they propagate the location of the cluster through the deposit of pheromone to guide both Explorer WebAnts and Request satisfying WebAnts in their search for clusters during their collecting or search behaviour. By this operation, the higher the size of a cluster is, the more its location is propagated. A combination of the collective sorting and foraging behaviour enables a permanent structuring of the web into clusters representing a concentration of documents addressing a same semantic topic, and the propagation of this information on the web, making easier the search for pertinent documents during the information retrieval process. This structuring has an effect of the evolution of agents populations. Specialisation of Searcher WebAnts agents occurs through their spatial localisation and the semantic content of their surroundings. The size of agents populations is regulated by the degree of order (efficient clustering) in the environment, which influences itself the specialisation of agents. Simulations were conducted to test this approach in [16]. Some of the obtained results are presented below.

Results

Experiment 1 - Order Increasing and Maintaining in the System: We studied the notion of order on the web. Then, we associate this notion to the emergence of clusters with similar semantic contents. Next, we express the function of order locally, for a given site, by the number of sites in its neighborhood, with a similar content. The similarity is computed with respect to a specified threshold distance between associated weighted keyword vectors. On the figure 1, the x-axis represents the number of iterations (time scale) and the y-axis represents the number of documents. As noticed on this figure, disorder decreases regularly in the system whereas new documents apparition increases. Disorder is measured by the total number of documents minus the number of clustered documents. The clustering of documents consists in registering its address with addresses of pages containing similar content. Thus, a document could be clustered more than once, that is why we could observe negative value for order value.

Experiment 2 - Clusters Formation and Size Evolution: Figure 2 represents the evolution during time (x-axis) of the mean size of clusters (y-axis). We can observe the evolution of clusters formation and the increase of their sizes. This shows the effectiveness of the clustering operation.

Experiment 3 - Energy Distribution and Evolution in the System: In figure 3, we show the mean value of energy of specialized agents (Searcher WebAnts). These agents increase their amount of energy during the formation of clusters. This allows the speeding of the operation of clustering (high activity of specialised agents). When clusters are formed (time 80000), Specialised Searcher WebAnts disappear (energy value $= 0$). We observe at time 100000, a sudden increase of energy of specialised agents that is associated to the apparition of new clusters, as new sites are created or new documents are discovered.

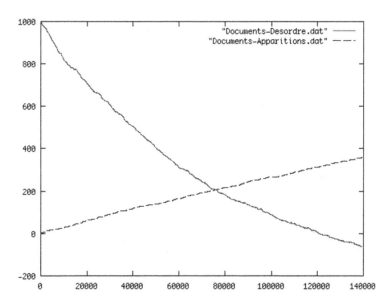

Fig. 1. Disorder decreases while new documents are created, and sorting occurs

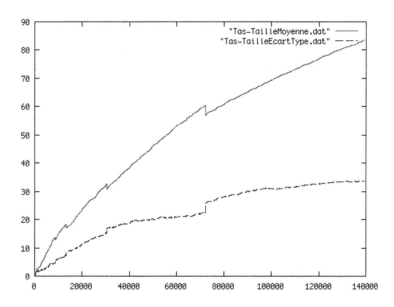

Fig. 2. Clusters mean size and its standard deviation evolution

Experiment 4 - Evolution of Population of Agents and Regulation of Their Activities: Figure 4 (y-axis represents size of population, x-axis represents time) shows the evolution of agents' populations in the system and the proportion of active agents with respect to the whole population.

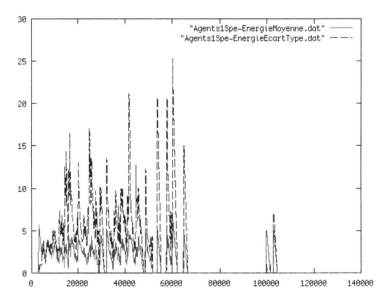

Fig. 3. Mean values and standard deviation values of Searchers WebAnts energy evolution

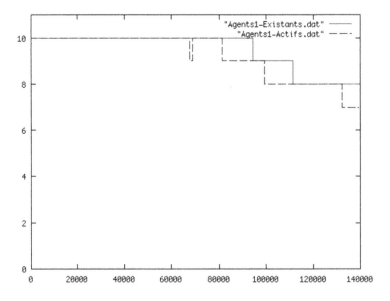

Fig. 4. Population evolution: proportion of active agents/total population of agents

We can observe that until time 80000, which is the time of emergence of a global order, all agents are active, and after this time, the number of active agents decreases. This implies that inactive agents disappear, reducing by this way the number of initial agents. All agents are active again during the formation of new clusters, as new sites are created (time 100000). After this time, we observe the same phenomenon as at time 80000.

6   Conclusion

In this paper, we have presented a vision for engineering complex adaptive systems using situated multi-agents, following an *Enactivist* perspective. IT systems are characterised by an intrinsic increasing complexity, due to their openness on a complex, distributed and uncertain environment. We argued that the engineering of such systems need to be focused on their coupling to the environment, as done in living systems which are generally taken as a source of inspiration for engineering such systems. We have identified three articulations for an IT system coupling to its environment: physical, conceptual and organisational. The physical articulation concerns the structural coupling (co-evolution of the system structure with the environment). The conceptual articulation concerns the behavioural coupling (co-evolution of the system's components behaviours and of the whole system with the environment). The organisational articulation concerns the retroactive effects (autopoesis) of one coupling on the other (co-evolution of system's structure and behaviour through the environment evolution).

When we use a situated multi-agents to engineer an IT system following this vision, the multi-agent system is itself subject to this same coupling to the system environment. As the multi-agent systems are structurally represented by the spatial deployment of agents in the physical environment, the structural coupling is expressed through the spatial organisation in the physical environment. At the conceptual level, the behavioural coupling, which is related to the structural coupling, is represented in the multi-agent system by the social organisation and its coupling to the spatial organisation. The multi-agent system has to maintain its spatial organisation through its social organisation and vice versa (self-organisation).

From the multi-agent perspective, it is necessary to study:

- The relation between spatial organisation and the environment topology (and their retro-active effects). The environment topology (physical level) is generally influenced in its evolution by the conceptual level (cf. scale free networks). This is a kind of reflective coupling between the system structures and their generating processes , like in an autopoetic scheme.
- The relation between spatial organisation and social organisation and their retro-active effects. This expresses the structure-environment coupling, which is mandatory to self-organisation and achieved through self-organisation.
- The reflective effects between the two coupling which expresses the co-evolution of (emergent) organisations and the environment topology.

We believe that understanding these different coupling, and their retroactive relations, is necessary to provide an effective methodology for engineering self-organising systems.

References

1. O. Babaoglu, G. Canright, A. Deutsch, G. Di Caro, F. Ducatelle, L. Gambardella, N. Ganguly, M. Jelasity, R. Montemanni, and A. Montresor. Design patterns from biology for distributed computing. In *Proceedings of the European Conference on Complex Systems*, November 2005. To appear.
2. O. Babaoglu, H. Meling, and A. Montresor. Anthill: A framework for the development of agent-based paeer to peer systems. In *Proceedings of the ICDCS'02*, Vienna, A., July 2002.
3. A. Barabasi and R. Albert. Emergence of scaling in random networks. *Science*, 286:509–512, 1999.
4. E. Bonabeau, G. Théraulaz, V. Fourcassié, and J-L. Deneubourg. The phase-ordering kinetics of cemetery organization in ants. Technical Report 98-01-008, Santa Fe Institute, 1998.
5. C. Bourjot, V. Chevrier, and V. Thomas. A new swarm mechanism based on social spiders colonies: from web weaving to region detection. *Web Intelligence and Agent Systems: An International Journal - WIAS*, 1(1):47–64, 2003.
6. D. Braginsky and D. Estrin. Rumour routing algorithm for sensor networks. In *Proceedings of the Fisrt Workshop on Sensor Networks and Applications (WSNA)*, Atlanta,GA, USA., September 2002.
7. V.A. Cicirello and S. S. Smith. Wasp-like agents for distributed factory coordination. *Journal of Autonomous Agents and Multi-Agent Sytems*, 8(3):237–266, 2004.
8. M. Dorigo and G. Di Caro. Ants colonies for adaptive routing in packet-switched communication networks. *Lecture Notes in Computer Science*, page 673, 1998.
9. M. Dorigo, V. Maniezzo, and A. Colorni. Ant system: Optimization by a colony of cooperating agents. *IEEE Transactions on Systems, Man, and Cybernetics-Part B*, 26(1):29–41, 1996.
10. M. Faloutsos, P. Faloutsos, and C. Faloutsos. On power-law relationships of the internet topology. In *Proceedings of the ACM SIGCOMM'99, Cambridge, MA, USA*, pages 251–262, 1999.
11. S. Fenet and S. Hassas. A distributed intrusion detection and response system based on mobile autonomous agents using social insects communication. *Electronic Notes in Theoretical Computer Science*, 63:21–31, 2002.
12. S. Fenet and S. Hassas. An ant based system for dynamic multiple criteria balancing. In *Proceedings of the Fisrt Workshop on ANT Systems*, Brussels, Belgium, September 1998.
13. S. Forrest, S. Hofmeyr, and A. Somayaji. Computer immunology. *Communications of the ACM*, 1997.
14. N. Foukia, S. Hassas, S. Fenet, and P. Albuquerque. Combining immune systems and social insect metaphors: a paradigm for distributed intrusion detection and response systems. In *Proceedings of the 5th International Workshop on Mobile Agents for Telecommunication Applications, MATA'03*, Marrakech, Morocco, October 2003. Lecture Notes in Computer Science -Springer Verlag.
15. P.P. Grassé. La reconstruction du nid et les interactions inter-individuelles chez les bellicoitermes natalenis et cubitermes, la theorie de la stigmergie - essai d'interpretation des termites constructeurs. *Insectes Sociaux, no. 6*, pages 41–81, 1959.
16. S. Hassas. Using swarm intelligence for dynamic web content organization. In *Proceedings of the IEEE Swarm Intelligence Symposium*, pages 19–25, Los Alamitos, CA, USA, 2003. IEEE Computer Society.

17. S. Hofmeyr and S. Forrest. Architecture for an artificial immune system. *Evolutionary Computation 7(1), Morgan-Kaufmann, San Francisco, CA, pp. 1289–1296*, 2000.
18. J.H. Holland. Adaptation in natural and artificial systems. *MIT Press, Cambridge, MA*, 1992.
19. O. Holland and C. Melhuis. Stigmergy, self-organization and sorting in collective robotics. *Artificial Life*, 5(2):173–202, 1999.
20. M. Jelasity, A. Montresor, and O. Babaoglu. Gossip-based aggregation in large dynamic networks. *ACM Trans. Comput. Syst.*, 23(1):219–252, 2005.
21. M. Kirtland. he programmable web: Web services provides building blocks for the microsoft .net framework. *MSDN Magazine*, 15, 2000.
22. J. M. Kleinberg. Authoritative sources in a hyperlinked environment. *J. ACM*, 46(5):604–632, 1999.
23. J. Liu, S. Zhang, and Y. Ye. Understanding emergent web regularities with information foraging agents. In *Proceedings of the First International Conference on Autonomous Agents and Multi-Agents Systems (AAMAS'02)*, Bologna, Italy, July 2002.
24. F. Menczer and R. K. Belew. Adaptive retrieval agents: Internalizing local context and scaling up to the web. *Machine Learning*, 39(2/3):203–242, 2000.
25. R. Milo, S. Shen-Orr, S. Itzkovitz, N. Kashtan, D. Chklovskii, and U. Alon. Network motifs: simple building blocks of complex networks. *Science*, 298:824–827, 2002.
26. M. Mamei and F. Zambonelli. Programming stigmergic coordination with the tota middleware. In *Proceedings of the Fourth International Conference on Autonomous Agents and Multi-Agents Systems (AAMAS'05)*, pages 415–422, Utrecht, Netherlands, July 2005.
27. M. Mamei, F. Zambonelli, and L. Leonardi. Tuples on the air: a middleware for context-aware computing in dynamic networks. In *Proceedings of the Fisrt International ICDCS Workshop on Mobile Computing Middleware (MCM03)*, Providence, Rhode Island., May 2002.
28. R. Albert and A.-L. Barabasi. Statistical mechanics of complex networks. *Reviews of Modern Physics 74*, 2001.
29. David A. Reid. Enactivism. Available at http://plato.acadiau.ca/courses/educ/reid/enactivism/.
30. R. Schoonderwoerd, O. Holland, and J. Bruten. Ant-like agents for load balancing in telecommunications networks. In *Proceedings of the 1st International Conference on Autonomous Agents*, pages 209–216, February 5–8 1997.
31. D. J. Watts and S. H. Strogatz. Collective dynamics of small-world networks. *Nature*, 393:440–442, 1998.

Techniques for Multi-agent System Reorganization

Gauthier Picard[1], Sehl Mellouli[2], and Marie-Pierre Gleizes[1]

[1] Institut de Recherche en Informatique de Toulouse, Université Paul Sabatier,
118 route de Narbonne, 31062 Toulouse Cedex, France
{gleizes, picard}@irit.fr
[2] Département des Systèmes d'Information Organisationnels,
Université Laval, G1K 7P4, Québec, Canada
sehl.mellouli@sio.ulaval.ca

Abstract. A multi-agent system which operates in an open environment must be able to react to unpredictable events. These events lead, at the system level, to possible system's failures and, inside the system, to agents' failures. Each agent performs several roles which could be unfulfilled in the system in case of agents' failures. To overcome these failure situations, agents could have their interactions and/or roles change during the multi-agent system execution. Doing so, we can prevent from system incoherence and possible deadlocks. Hence, we propose in this paper two techniques such that the first techniques allows to operate changes in agents' interactions and the second technique allows to operate changes in agents' roles in order to build adaptive multi-agent systems. We will illustrate our techniques by applying them to a case study: a timetable design.

1 Introduction

A Multi-Agent System (MAS) which operates in an open environment must be able to react to unpredictable events. Because the environment has its own behavior, all situations a system will be in front of, cannot be exhaustively enumerated. Meanwhile, many troublesome situations could occur in the environment leading to a MAS failure. Nevertheless, the MAS should continue properly operating. Hence, the system must be adaptive to take into account this dynamic. It has to adjust its behavior to its dynamic environment in order to be functionally adequate [2, 3]. The functional adequacy of a system can be defined as the following property: a system which realizes during its life the function which satisfies its environment. For example, the environment can be the user of the system which is functionally adequate if the user is always satisfied by the system behavior. We can say that these systems are useful for stakeholders.

Some of the troublesome situations could make agents unavailable, and could be identified at design level, and hence can be overcome by the designer. Those that could not be identified at design level must be overcome at runtime. So we propose in this paper, two techniques to build adaptive systems: the first technique is based on a dynamic role assignment to agents which is applied at design level by the designer, the second technique is based on cooperative behavior assessment which is applied at runtime. The agents have their roles or interactions which change in order to overcome the troublesome situations.

O. Dikenelli, M.-P. Gleizes, and A. Ricci (Eds.): ESAW 2005, LNAI 3963, pp. 142–152, 2006.
© Springer-Verlag Berlin Heidelberg 2006

The first approach aims at proposing a MAS reorganization to recover from failures that can be identified at design level. Agent's failures occur when roles are unfulfilled. This approach proposes that other agents enroll the unfulfilled roles and so, an agent can see its roles change. Hence, we need a role assignment technique that must be based on parameters describing roles and agents. In this paper, we will provide the needed description to assign roles to agents.

The second approach aims at proposing a MAS adaptive behavior to recover from failures that occur at runtime. A MAS behavior is the result of the behavior of its agents and of their interactions. Changing the interactions between agents induces the modification of the MAS behavior. An agent possesses the ability of self-organization i.e. the capacity to locally rearrange its interactions with others depending on the individual task it has to solve. Self-organization is founded on the capacity an agent possesses to be locally "cooperative", this does not mean that it is always helping the other ones or that it is altruistic but only that it is able to realize cooperative acts if it can and to recognize cooperation failures called "Non Cooperative Situations" (NCS, which could be related to exceptions in classical programs) and to treat them.

This paper is organized as follows: section 2 describes the timetable case study used to illustrate the two techniques. Section 3 presents the technique based on the role change. Section 4 expounds the technique based on cooperative behavior. Section 5 gives a comparison of the two techniques and section 6 concludes.

2   The Timetable Case Study

A case study related to an academic timetable problem has been chosen in order to illustrate the different techniques. In this application, teachers and student groups have to find partners, time slots and rooms to give or to assist at some courses. The groups of students are supposed already done, the realisation of the group is out of the scope of this application and a group stays the same during all the problem solving. A teacher has some constraints about his availabilities, his capabilities and the requirements he possesses about particular pedagogic equipments. A students group must take a particular teaching made up of a certain number of time slots for a certain number of teaching topics. A lecture room is equipped or not with specific equipments and can be occupied or not. Moreover, a teacher or the manager of the rooms or a students group can add or remove constraints at any time during the solving process via an adapted interface.

Such an application clearly needs adaptation and robustness. The system must be able to adapt to environmental disturbances (constraints modifications) and not to compute new solutions at each constraint changing. The correct organization has to emerge from actors interactions.

We propose to solve this application with two kinds of agents. The first ones are representative of teachers or of students and are called representative agent (RA). Moreover, each RA has constraints, ifor each course, which it must take into account. RA aims at satisfying users' constraints. Each RA owns several constraints to fulfill. For example, students must follow many courses during several time slots.

The second ones, called Booking Agents (BA), enable a RA to delegate the task of searching time slots, rooms and partnership. Therefore, a RA owns as much BAs as it has to find a partner for a time slot in a room. In figure 1, all BAs for a teacher are represented by a geometric shape with the label 'Ti' and a colour. For students, one BA for each specific course to receive is represented by a shape (the type of course), a colour and the label 'Si'. For example, the teacher represented by a square has four BAs because it has to give four hours of his course. The group of students represented by the colour yellow and labelled S1 has four BA because it must find four given different lectures (represented by different shape labelled S1).

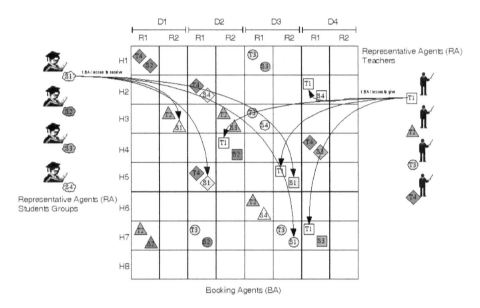

Fig. 1. An example of timetable grid

BAs have to move in a grid to satisfy their users' constraints. This grid can be seen as a set of cells, each of them is constrained (time slots, number of seats, specific equipment...). In figure 1, the grid is realized for two rooms R1 and R2, four days (D1 to D4) and eight time slots (H1 to H8). The grid corresponds to input data to the problem and is fulfilled at the beginning of the problem solving. Some modifications can occur during the solving problem and are reported on the grid, for example a room can become unavailable because the windows are broken. Consequently, we define two kinds of agents which will operate in the future system: RA and BA.

3   Role Assessment

A lot of assignment techniques proposed in the literature do not allow a dynamic role assignment to agents [1, 5, 6, 9, 15]. They do not consider the MAS adaptive behavior. In what follows, we propose a dynamic role assignment to agents that considers the MAS adaptive behavior.

3.1 Dynamic Role Assessment Technique Based on Role Description

Based on role and agent definitions provided in [1, 5, 6, 9, 15], we provide our role description. A role is defined with a set of responsibilities. These responsibilities constitute the objectives of the role. In order to reach its objectives, a role must perform tasks. Moreover, each task needs resources to be well executed; hence the role needs to have access to resources. Nevertheless, a role cannot access to all the available resources due to security and integrity reasons. So, a role has a set of prohibited resources it cannot access to. Finally, in an organization, there are roles more important than others, according to the objectives of the organization. So we need to specify a role priority among roles. The role priority helps to assign unfulfilled roles, in a NCS, to a particular agent. The role with the highest priority is first assigned to a particular agent. Since, our strategy deals only with role assignement and not roles execution, we will not focus on deadlock situations.

Hence, we propose the following role description:

- goals: that are goals the role has to achieve,
- tasks: what the role can do,
- needed resources: the resources needed by the role to be accomplished,
- prohibited resources: the resources the role must not access,
- priority: a role has a priority over roles. This priority can be determined during MAS design.

A role cannot be assigned to an agent ad-hoc. In real organization, each agent is not able to enact all different roles. Nevertheless, each agent will be assigned roles based on some criteria. These criteria are provided by the role and agent descriptions. In the next section, we will present agent description based on existing ones [1, 5, 9, 15].

3.2 Agent Description for the Role Assesment

Agents can see their roles changing during execution. So agents must be able to adopt new roles with their current roles. In fact, there are NCS in which roles cannot be performed. In that case, they must be assigned to existing agents so that the system continues to well operate. To this end, we need to provide an agent description.

Based on the previous descriptions, we introduce our agent description. For security reason, an agent could not be allowed to access resources; it can only access to its needed resources. Hence, an agent is described by the resources that it can access to, and by the resources it cannot access to that are considered as its prohibited resources.

Since we aim at defining a role assignment technique at design level, our agent description does not consider any element related to its execution such that agent beliefs or goals since their content is not known at design level. We limit our agent descriptions to:

- permitted resources: resources it has access to,
- prohibited resources: resources that cannot access to.

In the timetable case study, there are three types of BA: those having the role to satisfy a RA time constraints, those having the role to find a partnership, and those having the role to book a room for lecture.

Now, we have descriptions for roles and agents, we have all the ingredients to define an assignment technique of roles to agents.

3.3 A Technique to Change Role

A role is assigned to an agent when the agent performs the activities that the role is supposed to do. The agent must offer all abilities needed by the role to be executed. In this case, the abilities are the required resources of the roles to be well performed. Nevertheless, several events could occur during MAS execution leading to NCS in which there are failures of agents. In the timetable example, such an event could be one of the NCS to be dealt with is when two agents are in the same cell, and one of the agents becomes not available (due to a particular problem). In the case of a NCS, roles could be missing in the system. Hence, the current system's objectives could not be reached. For identified NCS at design level, the system designer tries to assign the unfulfilled agent's roles to an available agent so that the system continues to correctly operate. This induces MAS reorganization. Thus, for each agent failure, we propose MAS reorganization.

Each agent plays a number of roles r_i ordered according to their priority in the system. For each role r_i that will be assigned to other agents, we first need to know what are its prohibited resources. Doing so, we eliminate all the agents having access to these prohibited resources. Secondly, we eliminate all the agents that do not have access to the resources required by role r_i. Finally, we have to choose one agent from the list of the remaining agents. The technique to choose the agents that will perform the unfulfilled roles is out of the scope of this paper. However, such technique can be based for example on an evaluation cost to perform a particular role. Each agent, able to perform an unfulfilled role, evaluates its cost, such as a communication cost or a bandwidth cost, to enact the unfulfilled role. The agent with the minimum cost will perform the unfilled role.

Somehow, there could be situations in which, the system reorganization is not possible since there is not an available agent to which an unfulfilled role can be assigned. An agent may be unavailable if it is no longer possible to communicate with it. Hence, the designer has to define a way to overcome this situation so that the system continues to properly operate. In that case, we propose to first build a list of agents that are not available but that could enact the role r_i, and then evaluate the cost to provoke events so that the agents' will be reactivated. The cost evaluation formula will be provided by the designer. The role assignment algorithm is presented in Figure 2. In this algorithm, we only considered the priority of the roles as a major constraint to dynamically assign roles to agents. However, other constraints can be added to this algorithm such as two roles may be incompatible, and relations between roles such those defined in [7] and [12]. In this case, an agent cannot perform two roles which are incompatible.

```
Begin
R = {r}, a set of roles;
for each role r {
        Check r's prohibited resources and actions;
        Eliminate all the agents having access to any prohibited resource;
        Eliminate all the agents that do not have access to all the required resources;
        if (no agent is available)
        {
                determine the agents to which the role r can be assigned ;
                for each not available agent, evaluate the cost to provoke an event to
                reactivate it;
                reactivate the agent with the minimum cost;
        }
        else
        {
                Choose the agent that will perform role r;
                Assign the missing role to the chosen agent a;
        }
}
end;
```

Fig. 2. An algorithm for role assignment

In the time table example, there are two types of agents: RA, and BA. There are two types of RA: those having the role to collect a students group's constraints and those having the role to collect a teacher's constraints. It will be associated, for each course, a RA. Also, there are three types of BA: those having the role to satisfy a RA's time constraints, those having the role to find a partnership, and those having the role to book a room for the lecture. The RAs have not access to the grid of constraints. The BAs have access to the grid of constraints.

When designing the MAS, one of the NCS to be dealt with is when two agents are in the same cell, and one of the agents becomes not available (due to a particular problem). For example, let us consider two BAs: a BA associated with mathematic lecture, and a BA associated with English lecture. The two BAs can meet in the same cell. If they meet, each of them detects the other one. Each of them knows what the other agent's role is. One of the NCS that could happen is one of the BA is no longer available. Using our algorithm, we find that each BA can enroll the role of the other BA since they need access to the grid (as a resource). Hence, if we suppose that the mathematics' BA is in failure, then the English's BA will be able to enact the two roles. If an agent has to enroll another agent's role, it must have access to the necessary knowledge to perform this role.

Moreover, this technique is not adequate to be used at system run-time. It only helps the designer to overcome NCS identified at design level before system implementation. In the next section, we will present a technique based on cooperative behavior assessment that will be applied at runtime.

4   Cooperative Behaviour Assessment

4.1   Role Description Used in Cooperation Behavior Assessment

Systems we are interest in are systems where all the interactions a system may have with its environment cannot exhaustively be enumerated; unpredictable interactions can occur during the system functioning and the system must adapt itself to these unpredictable events. The solution provided by the AMAS theory [4,8] is then to rid ourselves of the global searched goal by building artificial systems for which the observed collective activity is not described in any agent composing it. Each internal part of the system (agent) only pursues individual objectives and interacts with agents it knows by respecting cooperative techniques which lead to avoid failures (like conflict, concurrency…), or to act to remove these failures called Non Cooperative Situations (NCS). A cooperative agent has the following behavior: it tries to anticipate NCS and to avoid them or faced with a NCS, it acts to come back to a cooperative state. It permanently adapts itself to unpredictable situations while learning on others. Interactions between agents depend on their local view and on their ability to "cooperate" with each other. Changing these local interactions reorganizes the system and thus changes its global behavior.

More precisely, three kinds of NCS can be detected by an agent:

1. when a signal perceived from its environment is not understood and not read without ambiguity;
2. when the information perceived does not induce the agent to an activity process;
3. when concluding results lead to act in a useless way in the environment.

The first NCS is detected locally by the agent when it receives information (or it perceives information) that it cannot understand. What is cooperative for an agent which is sending information (or which is putting information in the environment) is to inform its acquaintance and, by consequence, to send something understandable by the receiver. The second NCS is also detected locally by the agent. A cooperative agent sends information to other agents if it considers that this information can be useful for the other, otherwise it has no reason to send it. The last one concerns the evaluation by the agent about its actions done in its environment. A cooperative agent has to act at the right time and in a right way, so some situations detected such as conflicts enable it to react in the better way.

In AMAS theory, the role concept is not explicitly present, because the description of the agents and relations between agents are made at a less abstract level. The definition of the roles for each agent is not necessary to develop the system because the agent could change its role during run-time. If the agents in the system can be observed during run-time, the observer can give roles to them.

4.2 Agent Description for the Cooperative Behaviour Assessment

In the timetable application, there are two agent levels: RAs and BAs. In this paper, only the BA architecture is detailed. Cooperative agents considered here are composed of five parts contributing to their behavior:

- *Skills.* An agent's skills represent what it is able to do or *what* abilities it may bring to the collective. A BA has several skills implemented by methods, enable it to move in the grid, to manage its constraints, to manage a room booking, to manage a partnership, to manage the received messages.
- *Representation of itself, of others or of its environment.* These representations are what the agent knows about itself, the others and its environment. A BA has a representation of itself about the status of its booking, its constraints and the state of

its partnership (if it has found or not a teacher for a student group or a student group for a teacher). A BA knows about others the status of the recently met agents. It knows about other BAs of the same RA as it the status of the constraints. Its representation of the physical environment is the information about the cell when it is inside.

- *Social attitude*. It is what enables the agent to change its interactions with others. This social attitude is based on what we call cooperation: if an agent detects a non cooperative situation, it acts to come back to a "cooperative" state. The social is here described as a set of cooperation rules, which are condition-action pairs to solve NCS (like exceptions in classical OOP).
- *Interaction language*. It is what the agent needs to directly communicate or not. In the Internet system, agents could communicate via message passing. Another possible means to communicate is achieved by changing the environment. A BA communicates by message passing when it has a representation of the others. A BA perceives also an other agent and the room properties when it is inside a cell of the grid.
- *Aptitudes*. These attitudes are the capacities an agent possesses to reason on its representations and on its knowledge. A BA is able to book or to cancel a room, to negotiate a booking of a room or a partnership, to establish/cancel a partnership, to send and interpret messages.

4.3 A Technique to Change Interactions

Applying the AMAS theory consists in enumerating, according to the current problem to solve, all the cooperative failures that can appear during the system functioning and then defining the actions the system must apply to come back to a cooperative state [14].

For instance, the NCS for a BA are:

- *Partnership incompetence*: the BA meets another BA that may be an uninteresting partner. The action realized by the agent is to store in its representation, information about the agent met and to move in another cell.
- *Booking incompetence*: the BA is in a cell that is uninteresting to book. The action realized by the agent is to store in its representation, information about the cell and to move in another cell.
- *Message unproductiveness*: the BA receives a message that is not correctly addressed. The message is sent back to the sender.
- *Partnership conflict*: the BA_1 meets another BA_2 that is interesting, but the BA_2 has already a partner. If the BA_1 has more difficulty than BA_2 to fill up its constraints then BA_2 removes its partnership, passes a partnership with BA_1 and informs the other BA of the same RA as it ; else BA_1 moves to find new partners.
- *Booking conflict*: the BA is in a cell that is interesting to book but this cell is already booked; It the cost of booking is lower than the previous booking done then the BA cancels the previous booking, informs its partner if it has and informs the other BA of the same RA as it ; else .. the BA moves to visit new cells.
- *Booking uselessness*: the BA meets its partner: they must separate to efficiently explore more the grid The BA moves to visit new cells.

The action locally performed by a BA at a given time, under specific conditions, changes the organization of the system. Each agent has not a defined representation of the other BAs at the beginning of the execution. This representation is acquired according to the moves of the agent, on the grid, and according to the meeting with others.

For example, let us consider two BAs: one for Mathematics and one for English. The two BAs can meet in the same cell, leading to a schedule conflict. They perceive each other and they know, for instance, that they represent two teachers (one for Mathematics and the other for English). If one of them (Mathematics teacher) has booked the room, the other (English teacher) remembers this fact. The English's BA will move to another cell. If it meets, in another cell, students' BA who searches for a Mathematics teacher, the English teacher BA can inform them that it has met a mathematic teacher's BA in another cell. Hence, the students BA will move to the cell in which the Mathematics teacher's BA was. So the organization will be changed, and a new interaction will be created between students' BA and Mathematics teacher's BA.

The solution of the timetable problem can be viewed as a given organization on the grid. This organization evolves during all the time while the solution is built by the BAs. This evolution, based on a cooperative attitude, guides the locally BAs behaviour to enable to reach a global solution.

5   Discussion

5.1   Centralized/Distributed Decision of the Reorganization

The reorganization in a system can be done at several level of granularity, with a global knowledge or with partial knowledge. In the presented role assessment technique, the reorganization is realized by replacing an agent which cannot play its role. The choice of a new one is done in a global list which stores the roles the agents of the system. In the cooperative behavior assessment, an agent uses a local knowledge to choose to change the way it interacts with others. For example, an agent which had a bad answer to its request by another agent changes its local representation of this agent. Next time for the same request, it will ask another agent.

5.2   Reliability and Robustness

The reliability of a system can be defined as the capability of the system to execute the function it was developed for. The question underlying by the reliability is: "does the system converge towards the function it was developed for?" In our systems, the convergence of the system is linked with the stability of the environment. If the environment is so dynamic, the system always tries to adapt itself and will be not optimal to answer the initial requirements. At present, it is very difficult to prove these properties.

The robustness can be defined by the fact the system continues to run when some problems are encountered. In the two approaches, it is not so easy to prove that all system failures will be repaired. We can assume that agents try to remove NCS. So when a NCS happens, the system continues to correctly operate. So, a system is said to be robust when it continues to operate despite NCS.

5.3 Design Difficulties and Advantages

The most difficult task for the designers in the assessment role is to evaluate the cost to provoke events to reactive agents. In fact, the cost depends on the system under development. Depending on applications under development, the cost can be related to the used bandwidth for the communication between two agents, to the time needed to exchange messages between agents, or to the cost to send an agent to reactivate another one. In the cooperative behavior assessment, the difficulties lie in the fact that designers must find all possible NCS and it is a crucial task. If some NCS are forgotten the system will not run in an optimal way.

The best advantage of the two approaches is the fact that systems can adapt to change in running time without the intervention of designers. Making machines more autonomous is a way to simplify the task of the designer. The system has autonomy to modify itself its behavior at the macro level and this enables to counter the difficulties due to the complexity of the system to be developed. In the role assessment the system has capability to self-repair if failures occur. In the cooperative behavior assessment, the behavior changes at the agent level imply a global function change. The system has the capability to self-repair but also self-adapt to changes in its environment. From a design point of view, the two techniques can be complementary. In fact, the role assessment focuses on NCS that enables to replace one agent by another one when the first one failed, and the cooperative behavior assessment focuses on NCS that leads agents to change their interactions in order to react to a failure.

6 Conclusion

In this paper, two approaches are described to prevent from MAS failure. A MAS failure occurs when it is in a NCS. Each approach can be used at different stages of system development. The first presented approach is used at design level. When the NCS can be identified at design level, the MAS architecture can be proposed to overcome this NCS. However, if the NCS cannot be identified at design level, the system must be able to adapt itself at runtime. The second presented technique allows the MAS to adapt its behavior at runtime when a NCS happens.

As future work, we identify four axes. The first is how to verify that the system will correctly behave after using these techniques. The second is how to ensure that the agents of the system are able to detect a NCS. In fact, in the role assessment technique, in a NCS, an agent can be made unavailable and hence its roles must be enacted by available agents. However, the agent can still be available but for any extra reasons the other agents deduce that it is no longer available. Using the two techniques, the same role can be performed by two different agents at the same moment. Can this introduce inconsistency in the system? In the cooperative behavior assessment, if two agents perform the same role and if this is not desired one of the agents will disappear. The third axe is how to detect the error that induced the NCS, and how to limit the error propagation. The fourth is how to prove the coherent behavior of the system. Finally, we are convinced that the agent-oriented software methodologies must support adaptive MAS, which is not always the case.

References

[1] Becht, M., Gurzki, T., Klarmann, J., Muscholl, M.: ROPE: Role Oriented Programming Environment for Multiagent Systems. In *Fourth IECIS International Conference on Cooperative Information Systems,* 2–4 September, Edinburgh, Scotland, 1999

[2] Bernon, C., Gleizes, M-P., Peyruqueou, S., Picard, G.: ADELFE, a Methodology for Adaptive Multi-Agent Systems Engineering. In *Third International Workshop on Engineering Societies in the Agents World (ESAW-2002),* Madrid, 16–17 September 2002.

[3] Bernon, C., Gleizes, M-P., Picard, G., Glize, P.: The Adelfe Methodology For an Intranet System Design. In *Fourth International Bi-Conference Workshop on Agent-Oriented Information Systems (AOIS-2002),* Toronto (Ontario, Canada) at CAiSE'02, 27–28 May, 2002.

[4] Capera, D., Georgé, J-P., Gleizes, M-P., Glize, P.: The AMAS Theory for Complex Problem Solving Based on Self-organizing Cooperative Agents. In *1st International Workshop on Theory And Practice of Open Computational Systems (TAPOCS 2003) at 12th IEEE International Workshops on Enabling Technologies (WETICE 2003), Infrastructure for Collaborative Enterprises, 9–11 June 2003, Linz, Austria.* IEEE CS, pp. 383–388

[5] Cao, S., Volz, R.A., Loerger, T., Zhang, Y: Role-Based and Agent-Oriented Team Modeling. In *Proceedings of the International Conference on Artificial Intelligence,* IC-AI '02, June 24–27, Las Vegas, Nevada, USA, 2002.

[6] Dastani, M., Dignum, V., Dignum, F.: Role-assignment in open agent societies. In *The Second Joint International Conference on Autonomous Agents and Mulit-Agent Systems (AAMAS'03),* Sydney, Australia, 2003.

[7] Ferber J., Gutknecht O., Michel F.: From Agents to Organizations: an Organizational View of Multi-Agent Systems. In *The Second Joint International Conference on Autonomous Agents and Multi-Agent Systems (AAMAS'03),* Sydney, Australia, 2003.

[8] George J.P., Edmonds B. Glize P.: Making self-organizing adaptive multi-agent systems work. In Bergenti, F., Gleizes, M-P., Zambonelli, F. eds, *Methodologies and Software Engineering for Agent Systems.* Kluwer, 2004

[9] Karageorgos A., Mehandjiev N.: Designing Agent Organizations Using Role Models. In *Knowledge Engineering Review, Special Issue on Coordination and Knowledge Engineering,* 17(4), 2003, 27 pages.

[10] Kendall, E. A.: Role Modeling for Agent System Analysis, Design, and Implementation. In *Concurrency,* Vol 8, No. 2, April–June 2000.

[11] Mellouli, S., Moulin, B., Mineau, W.: Laying the Foundations for an Agent Modelling Methodology for Fault-Tolerant Multi-Agent Systems. In *The Fourth International Workshop Engineering Societies in the Agents World.* October 29–31 2003, London, UK.

[12] Odell, J., Parunak, H. V. D.: The Roles of Roles. In *The Journal of Object Technology,* Vol. 2, No. 1, January–February 2003.

[13] Parunak, H. V. D.: Go to the Ant: Engineering Principles from Natural Agent Systems. In *Annals of Operations Research,* 75 (1997) 69–101.

[14] Picard, G., Bernon, C., Gleizes, M-P.: Emergent Timetabling Organization. In *CEEMAS'05,* Budapest, 2005.

[15] Wooldridge, M., Jennings, N.R., Kinny, D.: Developing Multiagent Systems: The Gaia Methodology. In *ACM Transaction on Software Engineering and Methodology* 12(3): pp. 317–370. 1999.

Implementing a Multi-agent Organization that Changes Its Fault Tolerance Policy at Run-Time

Sebnem Bora and Oguz Dikenelli

Computer Engineering Department,
Ege University, Izmir, Turkey
sebnem.bora,oguz.dikenelli@ege.edu.tr

Abstract. In this paper, we present an approach that supports simultaneously applying different fault tolerance policies in multi-agent organizations. The main strategy of our approach is to implement fault tolerance policies as reusable agent plans using HTN (Hierarchical Task Network) formalism. In this way, different fault tolerance policies such as static and adaptive ones can be implemented as different plans. In a static fault tolerance policy, all parameters related to the fault tolerance are set by a programmer before run-time. However, an adaptive fault tolerance policy requires dynamically adapting resource allocation and replication mechanisms by monitoring the system. Monitoring of a system brings some cost to the system. If all agents in an organization apply the adaptive fault tolerance policy, the monitoring cost will become an important factor for the system performance. Hence by applying our approach, the adaptive policy can be applied only to the critical agents whose criticalities can be observed during the organization's lifetime and the static one can be applied to the remaining agents. This reduces the monitoring cost and increases the overall organization performance. A case study has been implemented to show the effectiveness of our approach.

1 Introduction

Multi-agent systems have recently been widely employed in solving problems faced in distributed and dynamic environments. As distributed systems, multi-agent systems are vulnerable to the failures resulting from the system crash or shortages of system resources, slow downs or break downs of communication links, and errors in programming. Consequently, a fault on an agent may spread throughout a multi-agent system, and cause a degradation of the system performance and even the multi-agent system to fail. Especially, in multi-agent systems, which consist of a number of agents that interact with one-another to achieve a common goal, it may not be possible to achieve the common goal, if a fault occurs on an agent. Therefore, it seems that fault tolerance is a necessary paradigm that must be inserted to the multi-agent develop-ment environment.

In most cases, fault-handling mechanisms and resource management are statically configured in fault tolerant multi-agent systems (MAS). However, effective fault-handling in emerging complex applications in large-scale MAS requires the ability to dynamically adapt resource allocation and fault tolerance policies in response to

O. Dikenelli, M.-P. Gleizes, and A. Ricci (Eds.): ESAW 2005, LNAI 3963, pp. 153–167, 2006.
© Springer-Verlag Berlin Heidelberg 2006

changes in environment, user or application requirements, and available resources. This adaptation process incorporates an observation mechanism that transparently monitors the application's behaviors as well as the resources availability, and adaptively reconfigures the system resources. However, using such an observation mechanism in large-scale MAS naturally causes a computational overhead over the organization and decreases the overall performance of the organization. A better approach is to apply the static policy to less critical agents and agents that shows predictable behaviors, and apply adaptive policies to the critical agents, agents with preknown criticalities, or agents having their criticalities understood during the organization's lifetime.

In this paper, we present an approach to apply adaptive and static fault tolerance policies to different parts of multi-agent organizations at the same time. In order to implement this approach, fault tolerance policies have been implemented as reusable plans using HTN formalism [1]. Hence, other agents or administrators can request an agent to behave as a fault tolerant agent by applying a specific strategy. Moreover, both fault tolerance policies are simultaneously employed in different replica groups of an agent organization.

In our approach, in order to apply a static fault tolerance policy in an organization, the replication degree and strategy is defined before application starts. On the other hand, in adaptive fault tolerance policies the replication degree and strategy are defined at the run time. The details of static and adaptive fault tolerance policies are inserted into reusable agent plans. These plans are designed to implement static and adaptive fault tolerance policies by using the group communication service, the membership service and the replication service that are inserted to FIPA based communication infrastructure of SEAGENT (A Semantic Web Enabled Multi-Agent Framework) agent development framework [2,3,4]. Adaptive fault tolerance policy is applied to the replication group by simply including an observation service. This service was implemented in Agent Communication Channel Module (ACC) defined in FIPA specifications. The responsibility of this service is to gather the system level information such as the number of requests coming to each agent, the message size, and send this information as a FIPA message to the agents applying adaptive fault tolerance policies. An agent applying the adaptive fault tolerance policy decides about its replication degree based on this information by executing the adaptive fault tolerance plan structure.

The remainder of this paper is structured as follows: Section 2 is a review of related work on fault tolerance in multi-agent systems. Section 3 presents SEAGENT overall architecture; Section 4 presents how to support the development of fault tolerant multi-agent system in SEAGENT; Section 5 presents how to embed the observation mechanism into SEAGENT; Section 6 gives the implementation details of fault tolerance policies as reusable plans; Section 7 gives the case study and finally Section 8 gives the conclusion.

2   Related Work

Several approaches to fault-tolerance in MAS are documented in the literature; each focuses on different aspects of fault-tolerance. Kumar et al. present a methodology than can be used to specify robust brokered architectures with capability of recovering from broker failures [5]. Their methodology is based on the theory of teamwork. In their work, brokers are organized hierarchically in teams. Brokers in teams exchange information between them and maintain communications between agents. Their approach can be used for recovering from broker failures but not recovery of agent failures.

Klein proposes an approach based on a shared exception handling service that is plugged into existing agent systems [6]. This service monitors the overall progress of a multi-agent system. When a new agent is created, the "new agent registration" agent takes a description of its normative behavior and creates sentinels to look for the evidence of dysfunctional behavior. When a sentinel detects such faulty symptoms, this information is sent to a "diagnosis" agent that produces a set of candidate diagnoses. These are sent to the resolution agent that defines a resolution plan to take corrective actions.

Hagg uses sentinel agents to guard specific functions or to guard against specific states in the society of agents. The sentinel interacts with other agents using semantic addressing. Thus, it can build models of other agents by monitoring agent communication and by interaction. It can also use timers to detect crashed agents or communication link failures [7].

There are also well-known fault tolerance approaches based on replication techniques for multi agent systems. In order to increase fault tolerance and improve availability and reliability of MAS, Fedoruk and Deters implemented transparent replication via proxies [8]. The proxy as an interface handles all communication between replicas and other agents in the MAS. The proxy also controls execution in a replica group and state management of a replica group. Although this proxy approach handles fault tolerance issues in a multi-agent system, proxy itself is a single point of failure. There is no recovery mechanism introduced in this work when the proxy fails. They chose FIPA-OS agent toolkit as a platform for their implementation. Since FIPA-OS does not provide any replication mechanism, the replication server is implemented as a standard FIPA-OS agent. Moreover, this approach does not support the idea of changing fault tolerance policies at run-time. Therefore, replication is realized by a programmer before the application starts.

Guessoum et al. present an adaptive multi-agent architecture with both agent level and organization level adaptation [9, 10]. The organization's adaptation is based on the monitoring of the system's behavior. The architecture was implemented with the DIMA [11] platform and the DarX middleware [12]. In DarX, software components can be either replicated or un-replicated, and it is possible to change the replication strategy at run time. Although we use the same techniques to implement fault tolerance policies within the organization, the main difference of our approach from this work is that we try to support different fault tolerance policies within the organization at the same time. In addition to this, the fault tolerance policy of an agent can be changed at run-time by sending a request to that agent.

These approaches present useful solutions to the problem of fault tolerance in multi-agent systems. However, the entities used for handling this problem force a specific multi-agent organization and these approaches lack flexibility and reusability. On the other hand, in our case, fault tolerance policies are added to generic behaviors package as reusable plans to make an agent fault tolerant and these plans can be used whenever we need to make an agent fault tolerant. Briefly, our approach provides flexibility and reusability to multi-agent organizations in terms of fault tolerance since it is possible to easily modify existing plans, remove some of plans, or include new plans.

3 SEAGENT Platform Overall Architecture

In this section, SEAGENT's layered software architecture is briefly introduced. Each layer and packages of the layers have been specially designed to provide built-in support for semantic web based multi agent system development. SEAGENT platform architecture is shown in Fig. 1. The bottom layer of the platform architecture is responsible of abstracting platform's communication infrastructure implementation. SEAGENT implements FIPA's Agent Communication and Agent Message Transport specifications [13] to handle agent messaging.

The second layer includes packages, which provide the core functionality of the platform. The first package, called as Agency, handles the internal functionality of an agent. Agency package supports the creation of general purpose and goal directed agents. The second package of the Core Functionality Layer includes service sub-packages, one for each service of the platform. SEAGENT provides all standard MAS services such as Directory Facilitator (DF) Service and Agent Management Service (AMS) following the previous platform implementations and FIPA standards.

Third layer of the overall architecture includes pre-prepared generic agent plans. We have divided these generic plans into two packages. Generic Behavior package collects domain independent reusable behaviors that may be used by any MAS such as well known auction protocols (English, Dutch etc.). On the other hand, Generic Semantic Behaviors package includes only the semantic web related behaviors.

In our case, fault tolerance plans are added to generic behaviors package to make an agent fault tolerant and these plans can be used whenever we need to make an agent fault tolerant.

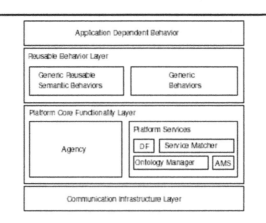

Fig. 1. SEAGENT Overall architecture

4   Implementing Fault Tolerance Services in SEAGENT Platform

Replication is the most efficient way to improve fault tolerance in the presence of failures. It is achieved by incorporating redundant copies of system's hardware or software components. When one of the system components fails, there exists another copy to take over. Replicated agents can provide increased fault tolerance to MAS by adding redundancy. Several replication strategies have been mainly categorized as active replication and passive replication in [14].

In the active replication, there are extra copies of an agent (called replicas or clones) processing client requests and synchronizing internal states with every other replica agents. In order to implement replica coordination in active replication, replicas must communicate via a group communication service which provides multi-point-to-multi-point communication [15].

In passive approach, there are also extra copies (replicas) of an agent. However, primary one responds to client requests. Primary periodically updates replicas' states. If primary fails, one replica can be elected as a primary agent. Each strategy has its own merits. There is a tradeoff between both strategies in terms of recovery speed and overhead [14].

In SEAGENT, we have implemented both passive replication strategy, and semi-active replication strategy which is a subtype of active replication due to the non-deterministic behaviors of agents. In semi-active replication strategy, replicas are organized in a group, and all replicas execute incoming requests. One replica is designated as the primary replica (the leader) and responsible for providing responses.

Active and passive approaches mainly focus on the coordination within the group. In addition to coordination requirements, replication degree which means the number of the replicas within the group is a critical concept for applying fault tolerance policies based on replication. The problem is about how the system will decide the number of replicas at runtime. Replication degree can be identified adaptively or statically. In a static fault tolerance policy, this number is set to the number defined by a programmer at initialization. In adaptive fault tolerance policy, the leader of the group decides the number of replicas based on resources of the system. This process incorporates an observation mechanism that transparently monitors the agents' behaviors as well as the availability of resources, and adaptively reconfigures the system resources by executing the adaptive fault tolerant policy agent plan. The observation mechanism is embedded into Agent Communication Channel (ACC) Module of SEAGENT's communication infrastructure since ACC is responsible from forwarding messages received for one agent to another agent.

There are large numbers of systems and research projects that have proposed a range of services to support replication based fault tolerant systems [16, 17] such as global time service, replication service, group communication service, and membership service. These services form the infrastructure for supporting active or passive replication strategies in multi-agent systems. In order to integrate these services into SEAGENT platform, we have to identify the services which may cause performance bottleneck if they are implemented as reusable plans. These services must be implemented within the internal architecture.

The group membership service maintains a list of agents which are currently in the replica group and uses the failure detector to reach a decision about the group's membership. The membership service incorporates a failure detector which monitors the group members not only case they should crash but also in case they should become unreachable due to a communication failure. The failure detector has a periodic nature based on timeouts that certainly cause performance bottleneck in the case of modeling as a reusable plan. Hence, it is implemented as a part of SEAGENT's internal architecture.

The group communication service provides an ordered multicast to the replication group and the responsibility of this service must be integrated with the multi-agent system communication infrastructure functionality. In our case, SEAGENT agent platform compliant with FIPA standards provides necessary mechanism for multi-casting FIPA messages between agents. Therefore, this mechanism is naturally provided by SEAGENT platform. However, SEAGENT platform does not support the ordering of incoming messages. The ordering of messages is necessary for the coordination between replicas within the group. Since each message changes the internal state of agents, executions of the messages in different orders may cause inconsistencies within the group. Therefore, the ordering scheme is implemented by the dispatcher module which assigns a group specific ascending number to a new request whenever it is received from another agent.

The replication service is responsible for creating new replicas and applying different fault tolerance policies such as static and adaptive fault tolerance policies. This service must provide some subservices such as cloning [18,19], leader election, and uses the other services such as the membership service, the group communication service to achieve its purposes. Internal mechanism of the replication service changes depending on the applied policies such as static and adaptive fault tolerance policies. The replication service is implemented as a reusable plan in SEAGENT agent platform. Therefore, this makes our agents flexible in terms of fault tolerance since it is possible to change a preset plan at run-time via FIPA-ACL (Agent Communication Language) message.

Throughout this paper, we assume that the system is an asynchronous environment and subject to message omissions, agent crashes (fail-silent), and network partitions. We also assume no message corruptions and no malicious faults.

In SEAGENT, each agent can be replicated many times and with different replication strategies. SEAGENT provides the group membership service, the group communication service and replication service to the groups. Each replication group has only one leader which coordinates the replica group and communicates with the other agents. When the leader fails, a replica is selected as a new leader in the replica group. We note that SEAGENT platform itself is not fault tolerant against its components failures. It only supports developing fault tolerant multi-agent organizations.

Due to the space limitation of the paper, the integration of the membership service, group communication and replication strategies to the agency package will not be presented here. Next Section describes how the observation service which implements monitoring is embedded to the SEAGENT's communication infrastructure.

5   Embedding the Observation Mechanism into the SEAGENT's Communication Infrastructure

Monitoring is necessary for acquiring information to determine the criticality of agents in adaptive fault tolerance policies. The information is acquired from either the system-level information such as communication load, processing time etc. or application level information such as the importance of messages, the roles of the agents etc. [12]. In our approach, the number of requests received by an agent and message sizes are the sources of information to determine the agent's criticality.

Monitoring is achieved via an observation mechanism. Next section presents the observation mechanism.

5.1 Observation Mechanism

The observation mechanism is responsible for monitoring the system-level information such as the number of messages and message sizes in our approach. Therefore, we implemented this mechanism in the Agent Communication Channel Module (ACC) of the communication infrastructure. All FIPA messages are received by ACC module and then forwarded to the receiver agents. Since all system-level information can be acquired in this module, we prefer to modify this module.

In ACC, we implemented a data structure which stores data about each individual agent who receives requests for a preset period. This data collection period is set during the initialization of an organization. The data consists of the agent's name and address, the number of requests and the total size of messages received by the agents, its normalized information and criticality from the previous period. The information in the data structure is updated for every new request received by ACC. In addition, when a new request is received by ACC module to forward the message to the receiver agent, it increases the total number of requests and the total size of messages that are sent in the multi-agent system.

During system initialization, a period is set for the organization and a timer module is implemented in ACC. Task of the timer is to monitor this period and calculate the criticality of each agent by using the following formulas:

$$Ratio=[[k*(req\_no)]/(tot\_req)]+[[l*(msize)]/ tot\_msize] \qquad (1)$$

tot_req: The number of total requests that are sent in a multi-agent system;

req_no: The number of requests that are sent to the individual agent;

tot_msize: The total size of messages received by the agents in a multi-agent system;

msize: The total size of messages received by an agent;

k,l: Coefficients for contributions of the number of requests and message sizes to the *Ratio*. The difference between the new value of *Ratio* and the old value of *Ratio* is given below.

$$\Delta Ratio= Ratio_{(new)}- Ratio_{(old)} \qquad (2)$$

Ratio(new): Ratio determined in the recent period;

Ratio(old):Ratio stored in the data structure;

$$W_{new}= W_{old}+ \Delta Ratio \tag{3}$$

W_{new}= New criticality value to be applied in the next period;

W_{old}= Old criticality stored in the data structure and determined in the previous period;

Before the next period begins, *tot_req*, *tot_msize*, and *req_no* and *msize* are set to zero for each agent, then data structure is updated with *req_no*, *msize*, *Ratio(new)*, *Wnew*. In the next step, we determine the normalized criticality as follows:

$$W_{(ratio)}=W_{(new)}/Tot\_W \tag{4}$$

$W_{(ratio)}$: Normalized criticality;

Tot_W: Total criticality of all agents in a multi-agent system.

$W_{(ratio)}$ values are sent to the agents to be used in adaptive fault tolerance plan presented in the next sections.

Fault tolerance mechanisms of an agent are activated when the agent is initialized by the developer. Next section describes how a replication service is implemented as a reusable plan.

6 Implementing Replication Service as a Reusable Plan

As we mentioned previously, the implementation of replication service changes depending on the fault tolerance policies. Fault tolerance policies have been modeled as reusable HTN plans in our approach. In SEAGENT implementation, the leader and its replicas execute different plans for static and adaptive fault tolerance. During system initialization, agent type is set as a leader or replica. Therefore, each agent executes its plan based on its predefined type.

In order to invoke a fault tolerance plan in SEAGENT, the agent must receive a FIPA message which is generated by its failure detector. After a failure detector discards a suspect agent, it generates a specific FIPA message which includes a replication request within its content and sends it to itself. When the agent receives this message, it matches the request to the fault tolerance policy plan. In case of static fault tolerance policy, the replication degree and replication strategy will be set to the values defined during the creation of the agent but it can be changed by sending a FIPA request which includes the "Changing Action Request" within its content such as "The Increase of Replication Degree", "The Decrease of Replication Degree", or "The Change of Replication Strategy". In case of an adaptive fault tolerance policy, in addition to receiving a FIPA message from failure detector, receiving a FIPA message which includes the agent's criticality also invokes the fault tolerance policy plan. In this plan, the replication degree of the group is set to a determined value by considering the criticality of the agent. This plan structure is presented in the next section.

6.1 Applying Adaptive Replication Using the HTN Planning Approach

In the adaptive fault tolerance policy, the leader has the "Adaptive Fault Tolerance" plan in which adaptive replication mechanism is performed. In section 3.1, we mentioned about the observation mechanism embedded into the communication infrastructure. The observation mechanism sends the normalized criticality value to each agent in the content of a FIPA message. When the agent is received this message, it starts to execute the "Adaptive Fault Tolerance" plan and gets its criticality value as a provision. The first task of this plan is to determine the replication degree of the group by using $W(ratio)$ values sent by the ACC module. Since the resources are limited, the replication degree for each adaptive agent is defined as follows:

$$R.D = rounded(W_{ratio}*R_a) \tag{5}$$

Where $R.D$ is the replication degree of a replica group, and R_a is the maximum number of replicas in an organization,

$$R.C = N.R - R.D \tag{6}$$

$N.R$: The number of replicas in the current group;

$R.C$: The number of replicas that must be replicated if $R.C$ is a positive integer or the number of replicas that must be killed if $R.C$ is a negative integer.

If $R.C$ is a positive integer then "Replicate a New Replica" task is executed. The number of replica to be created is sent as a provision to "Replicate a New Replica" task. Hence this task is responsible from generating FIPA messages and sending messages to itself to activate the "Cloning a Replica" plan. This task knows how many replicas will be created through "the number of replicas" provision, and then prepares cloning request messages as much as this number, and sends them itself. After the cloning request messages are received by the leader agent, "Cloning a Replica" plan begins to execute.

"Cloning a Replica" plan structure is shown in Fig. 2. First task of this plan is to ask a suitable host to Agent Management Service (AMS) where new replicas will be placed. (Of course we have changed AMS implementation to make it capable of returning the most suitable host). After the suitable host's address is received, the "clone itself" complex task begins to execute the cloning process. In the first subtask of "Clone itself' complex task, the 'cloning' server at the remote host where the replicated agent will reside is contacted by sending RMI (Remote Method Invocation) message. However, the cloning server and platform must be ready for hosting a new replicated agent at the remote host. Before sending RMI messages to the cloning server, object serialization of the agent state is performed in this subtask. In the "Send Agent State" subtask, several RMI messages are sent to the cloning server at the remote to transfer necessary agent knowledge to perform replication. The RMI messages also contain the paths where the libraries are copied to, and the serialized agent's state which includes all data at the membership vectors, hash tables, and queues related to the operation of the agent to a text file at the host in byte array form. In the last subtask of the "clone itself" complex task, the agent identifier(s) of new replica(s) are inserted to the member and heartbeating vector of the membership service.

When cloning server receives the RMI messages from the original agent, it places the libraries, agent's source code to the paths sent in the messages, and then executes the agent's source code. Whenever the replicated agent starts as a replicated agent, it is registered to only AMS and becomes ready for achieving the goals. It has also any

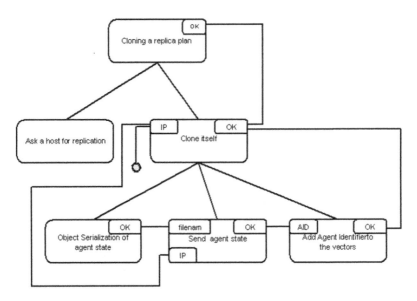

Fig. 2. Cloning a replica plan

information and data state that the original agent has. The only constraint related to the replicated agent is that a replicated agent can not replicate itself and can not give a service to other agents since it is not registered to DF. However, it will have the ability of replicating and responding to the other agents, if it is selected as a new leader when the leader has crashed. Only the leader is registered to the DF, since it gives its services to the other agents.

If R.C is a negative number, a FIPA request for decreasing replication degree is sent to the agent itself. After receiving this FIPA request, the "Decreasing Replication Degree" plan structure is executed. In the first task of this plan, the leader figures out how many removing operations will be performed by checking the request within the content of the FIPA message. Then, the leader prepares FIPA messages as much as the required value and sends each message to itself to activate the "Decreasing replication Degree" complex task. In the first subtask of this complex task, a FIPA message is sent AMS to find out the replica on the host with the worst performance. After AMS returning the agent identifier for the agent to be removed, in the next subtask, the agent is killed and the information related to this agent is removed from the membership service.

In order to give an idea about the fault tolerant multi-agent system developed by using SEAGENT, next we'll give a case study example.

7 Case Study

Our fault tolerance approach presented in this paper has been implemented within SEAGENT's internal architecture. By using our approach, different fault tolerance policies can be simultaneously applied in different replica groups in a multi-agent organization.

For the evaluation of our approach, we designed an agent system which includes some specific agents which are called library assistant agents and some other agents that are specially designed for querying library assistant agents. A library assistant agent holds the library ontology for the books which exist in the library of our department. Instances of this ontology hold the properties of books including name, ISSBN, authors' names and keywords of the books. The library assistant agent is queried by the agents to find out the situation of a specific book. In our case study, the library assistant agent has only one plan that matches the request to the book ontology instance(s) and returns the matched books descriptions within a FIPA message. Two agents have also simple plans that directly query the library assistant agents and present the result returned by the library assistant agent to the user interface. In this case study, the other agents depend on the library assistant agent. Therefore, the library assistant agent is a single of point of failure. Since it is a critical agent for the system operation, it must be initialized as a fault tolerant agent. Although, our agent plan is very simple, in this case study its general characteristic is very realistic in terms of fault tolerance. Therefore it must be implemented as a fault tolerant agent to make the system more robust.

The agent system based on our approach is implemented in two versions. In both versions, the library assistant agents are replicated into groups, and static and adaptive fault tolerance policies are simultaneously applied in different replica groups. In the first version, there are two library assistant agent leaders with their replicas in the number range from 10 to 40 within the organization. One of the library assistant agent leaders applies a static fault tolerance policy, while the other one applies the adaptive fault tolerance policy. In the second version, the number of library assistant agent leaders that apply either static or adaptive fault tolerance policies is changed within the organization in order to show the effectiveness of our approach.

The agent system is implemented in SEAGENT agent platform and Java Version 1.5.0. The tests are performed on nine computers with Intel Celeron CPU running at 1.2 GHz and 256MB of RAM, running Windows 2000. SEAGENT agent platform including ACC module runs on one of the computers. We distribute up to 80 agents, which execute the same plan, to nine computers. Particularly, leader agents and their replicas run on different computers.

The evaluation consists of two tests:

1. In this test, we have evaluated how the increase of the number of replicas effects the response time in two library assistant agent groups managed by different fault tolerance policies. Therefore, we implemented a test bed consisting of two library assistant leaders, their replicas in the number range from 10 to 40, and two agents that query the library assistant agents. In order to see the effects of increasing the number of replicas, querying agents send requests to the leaders. The response time is the time that takes a querying agent to receive the reply from the leader agent after sending its request to the leader. In this test, we try to observe the effect of the increase of the number of replicas to the response time while applying different fault tolerance policies.
2. In this test, we evaluated the effect of the increase of the number of library assistant agents that apply adaptive fault tolerance policies to the overall system

performance. Therefore, we implemented a test bed consisting of a number of library assistant leaders applying either static or adaptive fault tolerance policies, their replicas, and two agents which query each library assistant leader with two hundred requests. In this test, first we observe the multi-agent organization which consists of 30 library assistant agent leaders that apply the static fault tolerance policy and their 30 replicas; and 10 library assistant agent leaders that apply the adaptive fault tolerance policy and their 10 replicas. In order to distinguish this case from others, we call it as "s30d10". Then, we observe the multi-agent organization which consists of 20 library assistant agent leaders that apply the static fault tolerance policy and their 20 replicas; and 20 library assistant agent leaders that apply the adaptive fault tolerance policy and their 20 replicas. We call this case as "s20d20". Finally, we observe the multi-agent organization which consists of 10 library assistant agent leaders that apply the static fault tolerance policy and their 10 replicas; and 30 library assistant agent leaders that apply the adaptive fault tolerance policy and their 30 replicas. We call this case as "s10d30". In this test, we allow the organization clone agents and kill agents in groups managed by the adaptive fault tolerance policy. We again aim to observe the effect of the increase of the number of library assistant agent leaders that apply adaptive fault tolerance to the overall system performance by measuring the time to complete processing two hundred requests for each.

7.1 Discussion

The results of Test1 are illustrated in Fig. 3. The results show a linear increase in the response time as more replicas are added to the system. These results are expected, since the number of messages increases with the number of replicas due to the multicasting of requests and every replica in library assistant group processes each coming request. However, we are interested in the monitoring cost in the organization. We observe that the monitoring cost, which is the difference between the response times of the library assistant agents that apply static and dynamic fault tolerance policies, is almost constant as the number of replicas increases. This result was expected, since there is only one leader library assistant agent that applies adaptive fault tolerance policy and is monitored by the observation mechanism in ACC module.

The results of Test 2 are illustrated in Fig. 4. As seen from the figure, as the number of the leader library assistant agent that applies adaptive fault tolerance policy increases, the overall system performance decreases, i.e. the response time for two hundred requests increases. This result was also expected since as the number of leader library assistant agents that apply the adaptive fault tolerance policy increases, the observation mechanism in ACC module has to continuously monitor more agents, determine the criticality values for them and send these values to the agents. As soon as each agent receives FIPA message including the criticality value within the content of the message, it executes the adaptive fault tolerance policy plan to determine the new replication degree. According to the new value, the agent starts either cloning itself or killing its replicas. Therefore, all these operations increase the response time for certain tasks and decreases overall system performance.

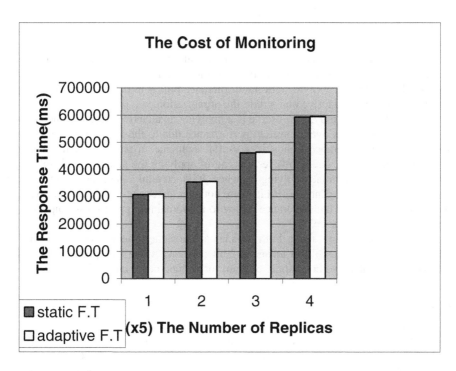

Fig. 3. The Monitoring Cost of the Adaptive Fault Tolerance Policy in a Multi-Agent Organization

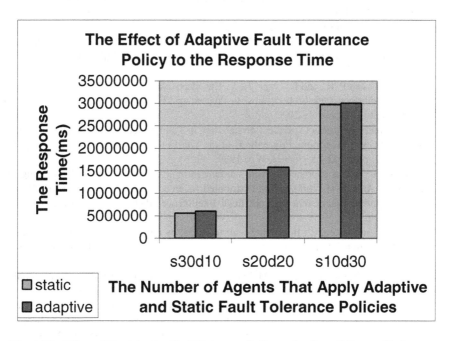

Fig. 4. The Effect of the Adaptive Fault Tolerance Policy to the Overall System Performance

8   Conclusion

In this paper, we presented our approach that allows to simultaneously applying adaptive and static fault tolerance policies in multi-agent organizations. Thus, while some of the agents can apply a static fault tolerance policy in their replica groups, the remaining can apply adaptive one within the organization.

In the applied case study, we observe that applying an adaptive fault tolerance policy to the groups decreases overall system performance due to the monitoring. Of course, the adaptive fault tolerance policy is a useful technique in terms of fault tolerance comparing to the static one. However, instead of applying the adaptive fault tolerance policy in all organization, applying it when it is certainly necessary under some conditions such as the agents' criticalities are not anticipated, or change constantly, etc., and applying the static fault tolerance policy to the remaining groups will improve the overall system performance.

Our approach supports using both policies at the same time within the organization. Moreover, it is flexible in terms of fault tolerance since it is possible to easily modify existing plans, remove some of plans, or include new plans.

References

1. Paolucci M. et al.: A planning component for RETSINA Agents. Intelligent Agents VI, LNAI 1757, N. R. Jennings and Y. Lesperance, eds., Springer-Verlag, 2000.
2. SEAGENT Agent Platform. http://aegeants.ege.edu.tr/current_projects/seagent/
3. Dikenelli O., Erdur R. C., Gumus O., Ekinci E. E., Gurcan O., Kardas G., Seylan I., Tiryaki A. M.: SEAGENT: A Platform for Developing Semantic Web Based Multi Agent Systems. In AAMAS'05, page 1270, 2005.
4. Dikenelli O., Gumus O., Tiryaki A. M., Kardas G.: Engineering a Multi Agent Platform with Dynamic Semantic Service Discovery and Invocation Capability.In MATES 2005, Germany, 2005.
5. Kumar S., Cohen P. R., and Levesque H. J.: The adaptive agent architecture: Achieving fault-tolerance using persistent broker teams. In Proceedings, Fourth International Conference on Multi-Agent Systems, July 2000.
6. Klein M. and Dallarocas C.: Exception handling in agent systems. Etzioni O., Muller J. P. and Bradshaw J. M. editors, Proceedings of the Third International Conference on Agents (Agents'99) pages 62–68, Seattle, WA, 1999.
7. Hägg. S.: A sentinel approach to fault handling in multi-agent systems. In Proceedings of the second Australian Workshop on Distributed AI, in conjunction with the Fourth Pacific Rim International Conference on Artificial Intelligence (PRICAI'96), Cairns, Australia, August 1996.
8. Fedoruk A. and Deters R.: Improving fault-tolerance by replicating agents. In Proceedings of 1st International Joint Conference on Autonomous Agents and Multi-Agent Systems, Bologna, Italy, 2002.
9. Guessoum Z., Ziane M., Faci N.: Monitoring and organizational-level adaptation of multi-agent systems. AAMAS'04, ACM, pp. 514–522, New York City, July 2004.
10. Guessoum Z., Briot J.-P., Charpentier Z., Aknine S., Marin O. and Sens P.: Dynamic and Adaptative Replication for Large-Scale Reliable Multi-Agent Systems, Proc. ICSE'02 First International Workshop on Software Engineering for Large-Scale Multi-Agent Systems (SELMAS'02), ACM, Orlando FL, USA, May, 2002.

11. Guessoum Z. and. Briot J. P.: From active objects to autonomous agents. IEEE Con-currency, 7(3):68–76, 1999.
12. Guessoum Z., Briot J. P., Sens P., and Marin O.: Toward fault-tolerant multi-agent systems. In MAAMAW'2001, Annecy. France, 2001.
13. FIPA. FIPA Specifications. http://www.fipa.org
14. Tanenbaum A. S. and van Steen M.: Distributed Systems: Principles and Paradigms, Prentice-Hall. (2002)
15. G. Chockler V., Keidar I., and Vitenberg R.: Group Communication Specifications: A Comprehensive Study, ACM Computing Surveys 33(4), pages 1–43. (2001)
16. The Transis Project. http://www.cs.huji.ac.il/labs/transis
17. The Horus Project. http://www.cs.cornell.edu/Info/Projects/HORUS/
18. Shehory O., Sycara K., Chalasani P., and Jha S.: Agent Cloning: An Approach to Agent Mobility and Resource Allocation. IEEE Communications, Vol. 36, No. 7, pp. 58–67 (1998).
19. Decker K., Sycara K., and Williamson M.: Cloning for Intelligent Adaptive Information Agents. In ATAL'97, LNAI, pp. 63–75, Springer-Verlag, (1997).

Predicting Exceptions in Agent-Based Supply-Chains*

Albert Özkohen and Pınar Yolum

Department of Computer Engineering,
Boğaziçi University,
TR-34342, Bebek, Istanbul, Turkey
aozkohen@elitsoft.com.tr, pinar.yolum@boun.edu.tr

Abstract. Exceptions take place when one or more events take place unexpectedly. Exceptions occur frequently in supply-chains and mostly result in severe monetary losses. Consequently, detecting exceptions timely is of great practical value. Traditional approaches have aimed at detecting exceptions after they have occurred. Whereas this is important, *predicting* exceptions before they happen is of more importance, since it can ease the handling of exceptions.

Accordingly, this paper develops a commitment-based approach for modeling and predicting exceptions. The participants of the supply-chains are represented as autonomous agents. Their communication with other agents yields creation and manipulation of commitments. Violation of commitments leads to exceptions. We develop two methods for detecting such violations. The first method uses an AND/OR tree to analyze situations in small parts. The second method uses an ontology to generate new information about the environment and checks whether this information may cause any violations. When applied together, these methods can predict exceptions in supply-chain scenarios.

1 Introduction

A supply-chain is composed of producers that are responsible for producing and delivering a service and consumers that receive the produced service [1]. Entities that are involved in supply-chains are autonomous parties and are thus operated independently. To be successful in a supply-chain, entities need to be cooperative but this does not mean that they will not have individual motives or unpredictable operations based on context. Fox *et al.* [2] state that properties such as dynamism, reasoning, readiness to cooperation, interaction and adaptability show us the necessity to use an agent-based structure while modeling supply-chains. Given these properties of supply-chains, the most natural way to model the entities in supply-chains are as autonomous agents that perceive, reason, act and communicate on their own [2, 3]. This is because entities have to be intelligent and to possess enough initiative in order to reason about their situation and about the appropriate action plans.

The elements of a supply-chain can vary from one design to another. Generally, we might say that suppliers, customers, production units, storage units, logistic support units such as shipping companies, technical support units, management departments, all

---

* This research was supported by Bogazici University Research Fund under grant BAP05A104. We thank the anonymous reviewers for their helpful comments.

O. Dikenelli, M.-P. Gleizes, and A. Ricci (Eds.): ESAW 2005, LNAI 3963, pp. 168–183, 2006.
© Springer-Verlag Berlin Heidelberg 2006

can be different agents belonging to a multiagent system. Each agent will have its own set of goals and appropriate action plans to achieve the goal according to the current context.

As in traditional supply-chains, agents follow a protocol to regulate their activities. When protocols rules are violated, exceptions occur. The exceptions have various consequences such as productivity drops, increases in various costs or decrease in customer satisfaction [4, 5]. Because of these consequences, it is crucial to detect and handle exceptions appropriately. The exception handling process is one which requires complex reasoning activities under defined and extendable rule sets. In current practice, exceptions are managed using brain power of working professionals who use the supply-chain management tools. But, this is costly and inefficient because human-based operations are more error prone and more costly compared to automated approaches. For these reasons, there is an ongoing research on automating exception handling in supply-chain management systems [6, 4, 7, 8]. These approaches mostly assume that first exceptions occur and then the approaches recover from these exceptions. What we are proposing here, on the other hand, is to *predict* that the exceptions are going to happen before they actually take place. Depending on how early the exceptions can be predicted, the corrective actions can be taken more appropriately. For example, if a supplier knows that a delivery will not reach its destination several hours before the delivery is due, she might schedule an alternative delivery. However, if she learns that the delivery has not reached its destination at the scheduled delivery time, it may be too late to schedule an alternative delivery.

The exception prediction heavily involves receiving data from outer world (through communication or sensing), which will help the system to infer that an exception is about to happen. To allow exception prediction, we develop an approach based on participants' commitments to each other [9, 10]. Each commitment between participants is broken down into smaller commitments and are placed in an AND/OR graph. Violation of one commitment can lead to violation of other commitments depending on its position in the AND/OR graph. Detecting the first violation is enough to predict that the other commitments will be violated. As a further step, we use an ontology and a rule set to derive facts about the external world. If any one derived facts conflicts with an existing commitment, we conclude that the commitment cannot be fulfilled as promised and predict that an exception is going to take place.

The main contribution of this paper is to develop an approach for predicting exceptions in supply-chains. The approach models supply-chains as multiagent systems in order to enable exception handling. It further defines communications between agents as commitments and detects an exception if a violation of a commitment is perceived. Commitments are placed within an AND/OR tree in order to decide on exceptional cases with a better accuracy. An ontology and domain for the rules existing between agents are defined to reason about the domain and predict if any commitments will be violated. The ontology is useful to predict the occurrence of exceptional cases even before any violation of commitment is detected.

The rest of this paper is organized as follows: Section 2 models exceptional situations using commitments, which exist as nodes within AND/OR trees. Section 3 develops an ontology to represent knowledge about exception scenarios. Section 4 compares our method with other research done in the area. Section 5 summarizes our main contributions and points at directions for further research. Section 6 gives the listing of the ontology for our sample case study.

2   Modeling Exceptions

Different kinds of exceptions can take place in supply-chain systems. Huhns *et al.* [4] group different exception categories such as missed deadlines, errors in product definitions, late payments, and so on. Most exceptions can be viewed as breach of commitments between some of the parties in the supply chain. If a supplier promises to deliver the material on a particular date but misses that deadline, we end up with an exception. Or, if the customer does not pay her debt as he has promised, then again we have an exception. Based on this intuition, we propose to model exceptions as violations of *commitments*.

2.1   Commitments

Commitments are obligations from one party to another to carry out a particular task [11].

Definition 1. A commitment, denoted by $C(debtor, creditor, condition, ADL, FDL)$ shows that the debtor has to satisfy the condition in favor of the creditor before FDL (fulfilling deadline). The commitment has to be activated before the activation deadline (ADL).

After the activation of the commitment, if the condition is discharged before FDL, the commitment C is discharged [11, 9].

Note that while the most of the previous definitions of commitments do not incorporate explicit activation deadlines, because of the domain we are dealing with (supply-chains) such a condition is necessary. That is, in real life many contracts are valid if they are accepted in a certain time-frame.

Example 1. A shipping company APS commits to have the goods delivered to Istanbul before 17:00 only if the contract is finalized before 12:00. Such a commitment can be represented as $C(APS, Ali, goods, 12 : 00, 17 : 00)$.

A commitment is violated when the debtor of a commitment does not carry out the condition of her commitment before the fulfilment deadline. The existence of violated commitments signal exceptions. Commitments exist in all aspects of communications between agents (humans or software) [12]. Commitments are created as a result of agent activities (interaction or communication with outer world).

Commitments can be discharged within time, may be revised, canceled or delegated. In order to work out exceptional situations, it is sufficient to differentiate between fulfilled and violated commitments. When commitments are fulfilled successfully there will not be any exceptions. We exploit this intuition in the paper and develop a method to detect violated commitments in order to decide on exceptions.

Commitments as explained above rarely exist in isolation: they have bonds to other commitments. In many cases, one commitment may be part of a more extensive commitment. For example, if a supplier commits to deliver goods, then the fulfilment of the delivery may be dependent on a carrier company's commitment to deliver the goods. If the carrier discharges his commitment, so does the supplier. Or, rather than being part of a more extensive commitment, two commitments may be alternatives to each other. For example, if both carrier APS or carrier $Aras$ are willing to make a commitment to deliver, then the supplier can choose to activate one of the two commitments.

2.2 Commitment AND/OR Trees

In business life many tasks can be decomposed into smaller tasks. That is, for finishing successfully a task we may have to finish a number of other tasks also successfully. We model this fact by decomposing the commitments into other commitments. For example, if a driver violates his commitment to show up to work on time, most likely the company's commitment of delivering goods at a certain time will be violated, too, unless there is a backup driver.

To capture such dependencies, we propose two commitment variants, conjunctive and disjunctive commitments. A conjunctive commitment is a commitment, which can be fulfilled by fulfilling two separate commitments. These commitments can themselves be conjunctive.

Definition 2. $C(x, y, d, adl, t)$ is a conjunctive commitment if $\exists a, b$ such that $(a \not\equiv b) \wedge (d \equiv a \wedge b)$. A conditional commitment can be decomposed as follows: $C(x, y, d, adl, t) \equiv C(p, q, a, adl_1, t_1) \wedge C(r, s, b, adl_2, t_2)$ such that $(t_1 \leq t) \wedge (t_2 \leq t) \wedge (adl_1 \leq t_1) \wedge (adl_2 \leq t_2) \wedge (adl_1 \leq adl) \wedge (adl_2 \leq adl)$.

The two commitments that make up the conjuncts may not be between the same individuals as the conjunctive commitment. Hence x, p and r may be different agents. Similarly, y, q and s could be different too: Section 2.4 explains this point in more depth.

A disjunctive commitment is a commitment, which can be fulfilled in one of several ways.

Definition 3. $C(x, y, d, adl, t)$ is a disjunctive commitment if $\exists a, b$ such that $(a \not\equiv b) \wedge (d \equiv a \vee b)$. A disjunctive commitment can be decomposed as follows: $C(x, y, d, adl, t) \equiv C(p, q, a, adl_1, t_1) \vee C(r, s, b, adl_2, t_2)$ such that $(t_1 \leq t) \wedge (t_2 \leq t) \wedge (adl_1 \leq t_1) \wedge (adl_2 \leq t_2) \wedge (adl_1 \leq adl) \wedge (adl_2 \leq adl)$.

An AND/OR tree is an n-ary tree where the children of a node are connected with each other with an AND relationship or an OR relationship. If the children of a node are connected with an AND relation, then all the propositions in the children have to be true for the parent proposition to be true. If the children are connected with an OR relations, then at least one proposition in one of the nodes need to be true for the parent to be true [13]. We apply the same idea to model commitments.

Definition 4. A commitment AND/OR tree is a n-ary tree where each non-leaf node is either a conjunctive or a disjunctive commitment and all leaf nodes are commitments that cannot be decomposed further.

The commitments in the leaf nodes are important for hunting down exceptions. The only way that an exception in the non-leaf nodes can be violated is when one of the leaf nodes is violated. Hence, the violations of any of the commitments in the leaf nodes gives us a handle for propagating the error up the tree to detect other exceptions. A commitment in the leaf node is violated when when the fulfilment deadline has passed and the condition that has been committed to is still false. When this is the case, the system easily detects the violation and hence the exceptions. Following this detection, the commitment AND/OR tree is traversed from bottom to up in order to check if the violated commitment will have any other consequences. This is used to predict other exceptions. In other words, if a leaf commitment that has an AND relation with its siblings is violated, then the commitment that lies in the parent node will certainly be violated: There is no need to wait for other sibling commitments to be fulfilled or violated. However, if the leaf commitment has an OR relation with its siblings, then as soon as a leaf commitment is violated, its siblings need to be checked. This kind of an OR relation can be used for modeling alternative plans when violation occurs. Because an alternative plan can be activated when one of the already selected commitments is violated.

The main reason to use AND/OR trees for modeling exceptions is to let us search and find the real non-complying commitment in order to execute the proper corrective action. The system begins with an initial rule configuration. During execution, the system creates a parallel structure for each occurrence of an exception and tries to search within the AND/OR tree for the node(s) where the violation occurs. In system definition phase, commitments have to be entered and labeled accordingly to form the AND/OR tree. This decomposition activity can continue until all debtors and creditors of the commitments are within the boundaries of the multiagent system. If sensing the termination of commitments (successfully or with a violation) cannot be done, then we cannot define commitments for these debtors or creditors. We conclude in this way because we need to know if a leaf commitment is discharged successfully or not, in order to understand that if it is an exception or not and in order to reason appropriately with its curing action plan, or maybe with an alternative OR branch.

2.3 Monitoring Exceptions

To keep track of the commitments that are violated or fulfilled, we envision a monitoring agent (MA) in the multiagent system. The monitoring agent is responsible to record all commitments persistently with their timeout values. When a commitment is discharged by the creditor, the MA is notified and the associated commitment drops form the list of commitments that are waiting to be discharged. Then, MA checks when a commitment is giving timeout. This means the responsible (debtor) agent has not fulfilled its obligation, otherwise MA would have received a fulfilment message. In this case MA sends a message to the creditor that the debtor did not succeed.

2.4 Example

Let us consider the following example depicted in Figure 1, which models the delivery of some goods between a customer and a supplier using alternative methods:

Our simplified MAS contains the following agents:

Supplier: It has a primary goal of arranging that goods reach to the customer on time.
Customer: It waits to receive goods that will be delivered.
Driver-1: Its primary goal is to carry load on time.
Driver-2: Its primary goal is the same as Driver-1.

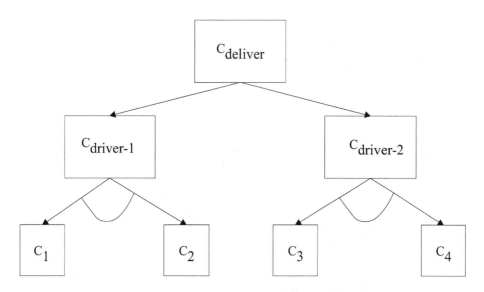

Fig. 1. A commitment AND/OR tree

1. Assume the following commitment

   $C_{deliver} = C(Supplier, Customer, Deliver\text{-}good, ActivationDeadLine, ArrivalTime)$

   is being created with a FDL value as ArrivalTime. If the commitment is not discharged after ArrivalTime, it will mean that it has not fulfilled its preposition
   (Deliver-good) and this will result in an exception. Additionally the commitment
   can not be activated after ActivationDeadLine (ADL).
2. Then MA (see Section 2.3) records $C_{deliver}$ just after the creation.
3. MA tracks any information from Customer notifying if the commitment is fulfilled.
4. If no appropriate reply comes from Customer, and fulfilment-dead-line
   (FDL:ArrivalTime) is reached, then MA understands that Supplier is not complying
   and sends a message to Receiver notifying this problem.
5. For better understanding and examining the non-complying situation one may further decompose the commitment $C_{deliver}$ (or the just happened exception) to linked
   commitments such as $C_{deliver} = C_{driver-1} \vee C_{driver-2}$.
6. The delivering commitment can be further decomposed as follows: $C_{driver-1} = C_1$
   $\wedge C_2$ where

$C_1 = C(Supplier, Driver_1, GiveLoad, adl_1, t_1)$ and
$C_2 = C(Driver_1, Customer, CarryLoad, adl_2, ArrivalTime)$ and
$t_1 < ArrivalTime$ and $adl_1 < ArrivalTime$ and $adl_2 < ArrivalTime$

Alternatively we can state that C_2 is not responsible to the Customer , but to the Supplier. Then we have the following equality

$$C_2 = C(Driver1, Supplier, CarryLoad, adl_2, ArrivalTime)$$

7. We can also divide (from the main OR branching in Figure 1) the driver commitment as follows: $C_{driver-2} = C_3 \wedge C_4$ where

$C_3 = C(Supplier, Driver_2, GiveLoad, adl_3, t_2)$and
$C_4 = C(Driver_2, Customer, CarryLoad, adl_4, ArrivalTime)$
$t_2 < ArrivalTime$ and $adl_3 < ArrivalTime$ and $adl_4 < ArrivalTime$

Alternatively we can state that C_4 is not responsible to the Customer , but to the Supplier. Then we have the following equality

$$C_4 = C(Driver_2, Supplier, CarryLoad, adl_4, ArrivalTime)$$

8. If MA detects that C_1 is non-complying, then the system comes to a result that $C_{driver-1}$ will be false because one of the children resulting false in an AND branch, which makes the parent false too. So an alternative commitment, namely $C_{driver-2}$ can be tried before waiting the result of C_2. That is an alternative path, or may be an alternative action instead of a non-complying branch can be selected in order to fulfill the top-level commitment $C_{deliver}$.
9. Figure 1 shows an example decomposition as an AND/OR graph. The branching paths that are accompanied by an arc are the AND branches and the rest are OR branches.
10. The decomposition yields the AND/OR commitment tree where the leaves can no longer be decomposed. Hence, violation of commitments in the leaves signal exception.

2.5 AND/OR Tree Usage

Our system is composed of agents, which collect and process information. As it is stated above, commitments reside in the nodes of the AND/OR tree and each node is decomposed in other nodes (i.e. other commitments) where these other (child) commitments cause the parent commitment to be fulfilled successfully. As our structure is a tree, it has leaf nodes. Leaf nodes hold these commitments, which are not able to be further decomposed.

Following our previous example, let us suppose that software agents exist in the shipping companies, but they do not exist in the trucks or roads. So our system will not be able to sense about what happened on the roads. It can only know if the driver has arrived to the destination or not. So boundaries of that multiagent system is the shipping companies and the leaf commitment is the arrival of the driver to the destination point.

2.6   AND/OR Tree Manipulation

A supply chain is hardly ever static: New participants enter, some tasks become obsolete, or new operations are added. To keep up with the dynamic structure of the supply-chain, the AND/OR tree has to be updated frequently. This means that new nodes will need to be added or removed as desired.

For adding a node (i.e. a commitment) to the structure we need to specify its prospective parent node in the tree and the operator with the siblings (AND/OR). The rest is a regular tree insertion algorithm. For instance let us assume that the definition of making a delivery is changed and a new commitment C_0 such as paying in advance comes into the picture

$$C_0 = C(Customer, Driver_1, Pays, adl_0, t_0) \text{ where}$$
$$(t_0 < ArrivalTime) \text{ and } (adl_0 < t_0)$$
$$C_{driver-1} = C_0 \wedge C_1 \wedge C_2$$

The new node C_0 has to be inserted as a sibling for C_1 and C_2.

For deleting a node, the specification of its correct place in the tree is enough. The system has to check if there were any siblings for the deleted node. If not, that is if it was the only child of the parent then the parent becomes leaf node. For instance suppose that the agreement with Driver2 is cancelled and no shipment will be done with him anymore. In this case we have to correct the structure of the AND/OR tree, so we have to delete $C_{driver-2}$. This results in deleting that node and all of its children from the tree structure. The system in our example becomes then as follows:

$$C_{deliver} = C_{driver-1} = C_0 \wedge C_1 \wedge C_2$$

A leaf node contains a leaf commitment where further decomposition cannot be done within the given boundaries of the domain. All subsequent actions and plans for handling the exceptions will be initiated from the commitments existing on the leaf nodes.

3   Ontology-Based Exception Prediction

An ontology is a conceptualization of a domain. It is a vocabulary of terms, concepts, rules of inferences and their inter-relationships [3]. To reason about different situations, we developed a supply-chain ontology using OWL, a well-known ontology language [14]. This ontology captures relations between different supply-chain entities, such as drivers, delivery, and so on. It also allows relations to be specified. On top of that, we specify rules, such as business rules, in Semantic Web Rule Language [15]. This enables us to represent a large set of knowledge systematically and effectively. The underlying idea is that if we can get information that can be related to working of any one entity in the supply-chain from the outside world, we can derive knowledge as to whether any one commitment is about to be violated. An illustrative example is that if the system hears that there is a tremendous traffic jam on the highway, it may derive that the truck that will follow that highway is going to be late. This reasoning is done much earlier than the expected arrival time of the truck.

3.1   Reasoning Using the Ontology

Let us give an example reasoning, which is related with Figure 1: We can assume that continuous truck-status information may be given by a truck agent (assuming trucks have agents detecting about the situation or status and broadcast this information while our MA receives it using a predefined format) to our multiagent system. This information can contain a problem about the truck where the driver was carrying our load.

Given the following facts:

- Delivery are done by drivers.
- Drivers drive trucks.
- Trucks can be either in working mode or stopped.

and the following rules:

- If a truck is stopped, its driver cannot drive it.
- A delivery is canceled when drivers cannot drive their trucks.

We can apply the rules on the facts and reason about which drivers cannot drive their trucks. If we can figure out that a driver has a commitment to deliver but cannot drive his truck, we conclude that the driver will not fulfill his commitment. Recall from example given in Section 2.4 that if a driver cannot fulfill its commitment (leaf node), the delivery will not succeed (parent node). Hence, we cascade the effects of our findings to other commitments and predict the violation before it happens.

The inference of the above ontology example can be implemented using various rule-based reasoning systems to the instances of the created ontology. We have tried various reasoner systems available and have decided on KAON2 [16]. We have seen that KAON2 is performing well by combining ontology definition, instance creation, rule definition and querying the ontology with all the instances and rules. A subset of

```
del101 is a delivery
del102 is a delivery
del103 is a delivery
del104 is a delivery
John is a driver
George is a driver
fiat50NC is a truck
bmc is a truck
delivery del101 is done by John
delivery del102 is done by George
delivery del103 is done by John
delivery del104 is done by George
John drives fiat50NC
George drives bmc
fiat50NC's workmode is working
bmc's work mode is working
```

Fig. 2. Assignment of individuals to classes

the OWL and SWRL specification required to run the following example is given in Section 6. The developed system first creates an ontology with the properties and actual instances as shown in Figure 2. The example has four deliveries, namely $del01$, $del02$, $del03$ and $del04$. It has two drivers $John$ and $George$. It has two trucks $fiat50NC$ and bmc. But this information is not enough for defining the instances. It has to specify the drivers, which do the deliveries. For instance it says that $John\ delivers\ del01$. Also it specifies, which trucks are driven by which drivers. Then it mentions the working mode of the trucks, it reads the rules that should be applied on the instances and applies these rules. Finally, the system can be queried for various cases. In the example in Figure 4, when the system is queried for cancelled deliveries, the system responds with the URIs of the canceled deliveries. The ontology creation, reasoning and querying activities are performed through a Java program that we developed using SDK 1.5.0.

3.2   Hybrid System

The ontology works simultaneously with the AND/OR tree as follows. The system receives information from the environment and other agents. Using its inference mechanism, the system tries to infer new facts from the set of information it receives. If the newly derived facts, contradict the proposition of any of the commitments in the system, then the agent can figure out that, the commitment will not be fulfilled. Note that this may happen before the commitment timeout has been reached. It may also be the case that information from the outside world will not help the agents derive facts that violate any of the existing commitments. In this case, the agent will wait for the MA to signal timeouts from commitments to decide that one of its commitments has been violated. Hence, the system can be thought of operating both methods in a hybrid way: Some exceptions are caught by the rules defined in our ontology even before any violation takes place and some exceptions are caught when the timeout takes place. If the exceptions are caught by the ontology rules, then the involved participants have a chance to take corrective actions before the timeout.

We have developed an algorithm which simulates clock ticks and picks time values randomly and checks first if any problem reported using the reasoner which infers based on ruled defined by the ontology. If we have some predictions about any delivery which will be cancelled, then we go to the commitment tree which is created as parallel with the ontology definition and cancel all the commitment which are predict to cause any violation. Alternative paths are selected from-noncancelled commitments in the AND/OR tree, using the smallest accepted activation-dead-line(ADL). In this alternative path selection point different strategies such that minimum delivery time, cost of delivery can be used separately or all together to form a utility function.

If the ontology does not report any problem in that specific time interval, then this time the leave nodes of the tree for all deliveries, four in our example, are searched for a violating commitment. If any violation is reported, i.e. the FDL is equal or less than the current time tick, then again a deactivation / reactivation of alternative paths using some kind of utility function is again performed. Figure 3 shows the initial configuration of a delivery tree. Here, the delivery is shown with Commitment 1. To realize Commitment 1, two alternative commitments exist; hence either Commitment 2 or Commitment 5 needs to be active at any point in time. Initially, Commitment 5 is active and

Initial Tree for delivery del101:

- Commitment 1 =C (Supplier1, Customer1, del01, 10 days as ADL, 40days as FDL) - active
- C1 = C2 OR C5.
  Commitment 2 =C (Supplier1, Customer1, Delivery by John, 20 days as ADL, 30days as FDL) - inactive
- C2 = C3 AND C4.
  Commitment 3 =C (Supplier1, John, Load Good, 20 days as ADL, 17days as FDL) - inactive
- Commitment 4 =C (John, Customer1, Deliver Good, 20 days as ADL, 20days as FDL) - inactive
- Commitment 5 =C (Supplier1, Customer1, Delivery by George, 15 days as ADL, 20days as FDL) - active
- C5 = C6 AND C7.
  Commitment 6 =C (Supplier1, George, Load Good, 15 days as ADL, 18days as FDL) - active
- Commitment 7 =C (George, Customer1, Deliver Good, 15 days as ADL, 20days as FDL) - active

Fig. 3. Initial tree definitions for all four deliveries responding to a query

Query results for the cancelled deliveries ... as time = 20

- Violation detected for delivery 1
  Tree becomes as follows:
- Commitment 1 =C (Supplier1, Customer1, del01, 10 days as ADL, 40days as FDL) - active
- C1 = C2 OR C5.
  Commitment 2 =C (Supplier1, Customer1, Delivery by John, 20 days as ADL, 30days as FDL) - active
- C2 = C3 AND C4.
  Commitment 3 =C (Supplier1, John, Load Good, 20 days as ADL, 17days as FDL) - active
- Commitment 4 =C (John, Customer1, Deliver Good, 20 days as ADL, 20days as FDL) - active
- Commitment 5 =C (Supplier1, Customer1, Delivery by George, 15 days as ADL, 20days as FDL) - cancelled
- C5 = C6 AND C7.
  Commitment 6 =C (Supplier1, George, Load Good, 15 days as ADL, 18days as FDL) - cancelled
- Commitment 7 =C (George, Customer1, Deliver Good, 15 days as ADL, 20days as FDL) - cancelled

Fig. 4. Updates based on exception of not loading the goods

Commitment 2 is inactive. Further, to realize Commitment 5, two separate commitments (Commitments 6 and 7) have to be fulfilled. To enable this, both Commitment 6 and Commitment 7 are marked as active.

After starting the system with the initial configuration, the system can be queried for possible exceptions. The particular exception that we are interested here is the canceling of deliveries. Hence, we formulate our query accordingly. When the system is queried at time 0, the system does not report any exceptions. However, at time 18 the system detects that the goods have not been loaded and hence Commitment 6 cannot be fulfilled. This means that no matter whether Commitment 7 is successful or not, Commitment 5 will fail. For this reason, there is no need to wait for Commitment 7. Hence, the system cancels Commitments 5, 6, and 7. However, notice that even though Commitment 5 fails, this does not mean that Commitment 1 will fail. Since Commitment 1 can be achieved in one of two ways, the system can now activate C2 and its children commitments as shown in Figure 4.

We are also currently working on an enhanced version of our program in order to support various types of queries. Additionally, we are creating a user interface, which lets the user of the system to define number of drivers, deliveries, working modes, and other properties for configuring the system as well as interfaces for generating various types of queries.

4   Discussion

Several approaches have been followed in dealing with supply-chain automation and exception handling supply-chains.

Huhns *et al.* make use of linguistic models for modeling the coordination in supply-chain management [4]. They develop interaction diagrams and they identify the conversations by giving a use case model. From there, they obtain Dooley Graphs. Finally they build the state machines in order to generate agent skeletons. Exception handling is only a step that is taken care in this process. They define the groups of exceptions but no mechanism is proposed for handling or predicting exceptions.

Dellarocas and Klein propose a knowledge base approach instead of the linguistic approach [7]. This work seems targeting in a stronger fashion for dealing and handling exceptions. The taxonomy is an n-ary tree without any relationships between the child nodes of a parent exception. Moreover the relationship between the exceptions is not clearly defined.

Kalakota *et al.* port the supply-chain architecture form static into dynamic architecture [17]. Instead of collecting historical data from customers, retailers, distribution centers, production outlets and so on, and to prepare the knowledge-base according to this gathered information for giving decisions (static infrastructure), they propose to store all information dynamically in local agents and they intend to give quicker decisions in much smaller time intervals, i.e. more frequently (dynamic infrastructure). Their assumption on internal operations is based on each individual agent's definition about the degree of self-determination by using statistical methods. They also propose an example supply-chain ontology but they do not develop methods for the automation of exception handling.

Frey *et al.* successfully show that multiagent infrastructure is suitable for globally flexible and locally autonomous business needs where competition and cooperation have to coexist without disrupting each other. They make use of already existing multiagent projects, which are developed or under development. Each multiagent system is responsible for a different group of tasks, such as negotiation, process planning and scheduling, production planning and controlling. Their work mainly defines the interactions and integration between those sub-systems. Despite all scheduling, tracking, tracing, reliability building efforts, exceptions are not taken into consideration, which empowers the need for special care for exceptions in supply-chain management.

Lesser *et al.* have developed a domain independent coordination framework, namely Generalized Partial Global Planning (GPGP) based on TAEMS [18]. The framework is used to coordinate agents so that the utility of each agent in the multiagent system is maximized. Their proposed coordination framework also make used of AND/OR graphs as we have done; however, they use agents' goals as nodes in the AND/OR tree. This allows their framework to represent decomposition of global goals into local goals that can be achieved by individual agents. Lesser *et al.* do not focus on prediction or handling of exceptions as we have done here.

5   Directions

We have developed an automated tool to predict exceptions in supply-chains. The example illustrated in this paper is simple yet important for showing why it is important to predict exceptions before they occur. We are currently working on more complex examples in order to cover additional aspects for our proposed system. Our model uses a hybrid method, which either uses an ontology to detect proactively if an exception will occur (or conditions show that an exception is about to occur when the relevant timeout comes), or a structured AND/OR tree holding commitments in its nodes detects timeouts.

In this work, we worked with deterministic rules. It will be interesting to enhance this approach by probabilistic rules. For instance if the main road is blocked, the driver may surprise the customer by using a tiny alternative road for reaching its destination although this may have low probability. Hence the sensing from the ontology can further be modeled using a probabilistic approach.

If the system becomes bigger and more complex, it may become difficult and unnecessary to load all commitment data into a single MA. Communication and storage capacity constraints can impose problems. A distributed version of MA can be designed for the performance and privacy reasons. We will investigate these questions in our future work.

References

1. Swaminathan, J.M., Tayur, S.R.: Models for supply chains in e-business. Management Science **49** (2003) 1387–1406
2. Fox, M.S., Barbuceanu, M., Teigen, R.: Agent-oriented supply-chain management. International Journal of Flexible Manufacturing Systems **12** (2000) 165–188
3. Singh, M.P., Huhns, M.N.: Service Oriented Computing—Semantics, Processes, Agents. Wiley (2005)
4. Huhns, M.N., Stephens, L.M., Ivezic, N.: Automating supply-chain management. In: Proceedings of the 1st International Joint Conference on Autonomous Agents and MultiAgent Systems (AAMAS), ACM Press (2002) 1017–1024
5. Becker, T.J.: Putting a price on supply chain problems: Study links supply chain glitches with falling stock price. Georigia Tech Research News (2000) Available at: *http://www.gtresearchnews.gatech.edu/newsrelease/*.

6. Mallya, A.U., Singh, M.P.: Modeling exceptions via commitment protocols. In: Proceedings of the 4th International Joint Conference on Autonomous Agents and MultiAgent Systems (AAMAS), ACM Press (2005) 122–129

7. Dellarocas, C., Klein, M.: A knowledge-based approach for designing robust business processes. In van der Aalst et al., W., ed.: Business Process Management, LNCS 1806. (2000) 60–65

8. Dellarocas, C., Klein, M., Rodriguez-Aguilar, J.A.: An exception handling architecture for open electronic marketplaces of contract net software agents. In: Proceedings of the ACM Conference on Electronic Commerce. (2000) 225–232

9. Yolum, P., Singh, M.P.: Reasoning about commitments in the event calculus: An approach for specifying and executing protocols. Annals of Mathematics and Artificial Intelligence **42** (2004) 227–253

10. Fornara, N., Colombetti, M.: Operational specification of a commitment-based agent communication language. In: Proceedings of the 1st International Joint Conference on Autonomous Agents and MultiAgent Systems (AAMAS), ACM Press (2002) 535–542

11. Singh, M.P.: An ontology for commitments in multiagent systems: Toward a unification of normative concepts. Artificial Intelligence and Law **7** (1999) 97–113

12. Castelfranchi, C.: Modelling social action for AI agents. Artificial Intelligence **103** (1998) 157–182

13. Nilsson, N.J.: Principles of Artificial Intelligence. Springer-Verlag (1980)

14. OWL: Web ontology language specification (2004) Available at: *http://www.w3.org/TR/owl-features/*.

15. SWRL: A semantic web rule language combining OWL and RuleML (2004) Available at: $http://www.w3.org/Submission/2004/SUBM-SWRL-20040521/$.

16. Motik, B.: (Kaon2 infrastructure library for managing owl-dl and swrl ontologies) Available at: *http://kaon2.semanticweb.org/*.

17. Kalakota, R., Stallaert, J., Whinston, A.B.: Implementing real-time supply chain optimization (1996) Available at: *http://cism.mccombs.utexas.edu/jan/sc_imp.html*.

18. Lesser, V., Decker, K., Wagner, T., Carver, N., Garvey, A., Horling, B., Neiman, D., Podorozhny, R., NagendraPrasad, M., Raja, A., Vincent, R., Xuan, P., Zhang, X.: Evolution of the GPGP/TAEMS Domain-Independent Coordination Framework. Autonomous Agents and Multi-Agent Systems **9** (2004) 87–143

6 Appendix

This section outlines the main parts of the ontology used in the system.

```
<?xml version="1.0" encoding="ISO-8859-1"?>
<!DOCTYPE rdf:RDF [
    <!ENTITY owl 'http://www.w3.org/2002/07/owl#'>
]>
<rdf:RDF
    xml:base="http://boun.edu.tr/driver"
    xmlns:a="http://boun.edu.tr/driver#"
    xmlns:owl="http://www.w3.org/2002/07/owl#"
    xmlns:rdf="http://www.w3.org/1999/02/
              22-rdf-syntax-ns#"
    xmlns:rdfs="http://www.w3.org/2000/01/
```

```
                    rdf-schema#"
    xmlns:swrl="http://www.w3.org/2003/11/swrl#">
<owl:Ontology rdf:about=""/>
<owl:ObjectProperty rdf:ID="cancelled">
    <rdfs:domain rdf:resource="#delivery"/>
    <rdfs:range rdf:resource="#truck"/>
</owl:ObjectProperty>
<owl:ObjectProperty rdf:ID="doneBy">
    <rdfs:domain rdf:resource="#delivery"/>
    <rdfs:range rdf:resource="#driver"/>
</owl:ObjectProperty>
<owl:ObjectProperty rdf:ID="drives">
    <rdfs:domain rdf:resource="#driver"/>
    <rdfs:range rdf:resource="#truck"/>
</owl:ObjectProperty>
<owl:ObjectProperty rdf:ID="workMode">
    <rdfs:domain rdf:resource="#truck"/>
</owl:ObjectProperty>
<a:driver rdf:ID="George">
    <a:drives rdf:resource="#bmc"/>
</a:driver>
<a:truck rdf:ID="bmc">
    <a:workMode rdf:resource="#stopped"/>
</a:truck>
<a:delivery rdf:ID="del01">
    <a:doneBy rdf:resource="#George"/>
</a:delivery>
<a:truck rdf:ID="fiat50NC">
    <a:workMode rdf:resource="#stopped"/>
</a:truck>
<swrl:Variable rdf:ID="V"/>
<swrl:Variable rdf:ID="T"/>
<swrl:Variable rdf:ID="D"/>
<swrl:Imp>
    <swrl:head rdf:parseType="Collection">
        <swrl:IndividualPropertyAtom>
            <swrl:propertyPredicate
              rdf:resource="#cancelled"/>
            <swrl:argument1
                rdf:resource="#V"/>
            <swrl:argument2
                rdf:resource="#T"/>
        </swrl:IndividualPropertyAtom>
    </swrl:head>
    <swrl:body rdf:parseType="Collection">
```

```
        <swrl:IndividualPropertyAtom>
            <swrl:propertyPredicate
                rdf:resource="#doneBy"/>
            <swrl:argument1
                rdf:resource="#V"/>
            <swrl:argument2
                rdf:resource="#D"/>
        </swrl:IndividualPropertyAtom>
        <swrl:IndividualPropertyAtom>
            <swrl:propertyPredicate
                rdf:resource="#drives"/>
            <swrl:argument1
                rdf:resource="#D"/>
            <swrl:argument2
                rdf:resource="#T"/>
        </swrl:IndividualPropertyAtom>
        <swrl:IndividualPropertyAtom>
            <swrl:propertyPredicate
                rdf:resource="#workMode"/>
            <swrl:argument1
              rdf:resource="#T"/>
            <swrl:argument2
                rdf:resource="#stopped"/>
        </swrl:IndividualPropertyAtom>
    </swrl:body>
</swrl:Imp>
<owl:Class rdf:ID="delivery"/>
<owl:Class rdf:ID="driver"/>
<owl:Class rdf:ID="truck"/>
</rdf:RDF>
```

Preserving Variability in Sexual Multi-agent Systems with Diploidy and Dominance

Robert Ian Bowers and Emre Sevinç

Boğaziçi University, Bebek, İstanbul
ribowers@gmail.com, emres@bilgi.edu.tr

Abstract. Diploidy and allele dominance are two mechanisms whereby natural organisms preserve genetic variability, in the form of unexpressed genes, from the conservative sway of natural selection. These may profoundly affect evolution, for it is variability upon which natural selection operates. Many multi-agent systems rely on evolutionary processes and sexual reproduction. However, sex in artificial agents often ignores diploidy and dominance. An agent-oriented modelling platform was used to compare the evolution of populations of sexual agents under four models: haploid genetic transmission versus diploid; and with either complete allele dominance versus none. Diploidy fulfils its promise of preserving variability, whereas haploidy quickly commits its possessors to the current niche. Allele dominance too preserves variability, and without sacrificing adaptivity. These results echo consistent findings in classical population genetics. Since both these factors strongly affect evolution, their inclusion in a model may improve both accuracy, and efficacy, according to the modeller's motives.

1 Introduction

Natural selection is a conservative sway. By definition, it consumes variability. It is the favouring of some portion of a distribution of characters over others, such that subsequent generations manifest a range that is, whatever else, shorter than it had been. By this successive shortening of possibilities, if left unchecked, natural selection will eventually dispense of all variability, and the evolving entity—whether species, solution, or programme—will have converged. That is, a population of variants will have been reduced to uniformity.

Though convergence is the aim in most applications of evolutionary computing, it does mean the end of evolution, and so a commitment to a particular variant. The obvious risk is that the chosen variant will be other than optimal. Evolutionary algorithms, particularly those that rely exclusively on local operators, as in natural evolution, carry the risk of converging on a solution that, whether a local optimum or not, is inferior to alternatives elsewhere in the search space. In such cases, convergence is said to be premature. Premature convergence is described as "the preeminent problem" in genetic algorithms [1], and this sentiment resounds in the literature, not only for genetic algorithms, but for evolutionary algorithms in general [2], [3], [4], [5].

O. Dikenelli, M.-P. Gleizes, and A. Ricci (Eds.): ESAW 2005, LNAI 3963, pp. 184–202, 2006.
© Springer-Verlag Berlin Heidelberg 2006

Evolutionary algorithms reliably reach optimal solutions on the condition that sufficient variability is maintained [3]. This point has been demonstrated mathematically for some specific evolutionary algorithms (e.g. [6] for the (μ, λ)-ES, with a class of convex fitness functions; others in [7]), and more recently, for the general case, by analysing convergence in an abstraction of the evolutionary algorithm [5].

The basic approach of dealing with premature convergence by introducing explicit measures to maintain diversity was incited by [2]. Mauldin's [2] solution was to enforce a uniqueness condition on new births: only individuals sufficiently unlike all existing individuals may enter the population. Though this is made less attractive in its requirement for a global operator—both expensive computationally, and cumbersome theoretically—it succeeds in its aim to stave off convergence. Later work corroborates this basic strategy (e.g. [8]).

Nature has its own mechanisms for assuring diversity. Species do not converge, after all, despite the passage of countless generations. An invariant gene pool would not allow a species to evolve, and so leave it vulnerable to potential environmental change [9], or exploitation by parasites [10]. For natural selection to continue to operate, it requires something to provide it with a stream of variability. Mutation does this, but inefficiently. As mutation is nothing other than random copying errors, it is more disruptive than constructive. Hence, increasing mutation rates can be counterproductive, as it blindly unravels what benefit evolution has won [2], [3], [4]. Therefore, mutation is constrained to be slow, and is so in natural organisms [9].

Apart from *creating* diversity, as mutation does, a second effective strategy for avoiding genetic stagnation is to merely slow selection down [1], [11]. The longer the present variability can be held on to, the more thorough will the search have had the potential to be upon convergence. If the processes that deplete variability can be slowed, selection is allowed to proceed without unravelling its spoils, unlike with mutation. Sexual organisms have such mechanisms, by which they retain variability, allowing even a slow stream of it to accumulate.

Here we consider two ways natural sexual organisms preserve variability by maintaining a reservoir of unused genetic material. Natural selection can only kill the variability that it can see. Genes that have no effect on their possessors will not be systematically selected for or against. Unexpressed genes, even those which are harmful when expressed, remain in circulation in the gene pool. Hence, mechanisms that allow genetic material to hide silent in the genome shield variability from the conservative pruning of natural selection, and so promote future evolution.

One such mechanism is diploidy. The haploid genome, as a data structure, is a list of values, one for each trait, that determines the particular qualities of the individual. The diploid genome is a double list, containing two values for each trait, and the possessor's qualities are determined by some function of these two corresponding values. This means that there is a dissociation between the heritable code (genotype) and the way it is expressed (phenotype). This allows some genetic material to remain silent, and so be passed on whatever its effect might have been had it been expressed. Thus, the diploid genome cautiously preserves genetic variation in a way that the haploid genome does not. Regarding the gene pool as a sort of implicit knowledge, the effect of diploidy is to retain a morsel of memory of the search history [12], [13], [14].

Another such mechanism is allele dominance [15]. Each parent provides an allele, a corresponding version of each trait value. In some cases, only one of these alleles is expressed, and the other lies dormant as if in deference: the dominance of one allele over the other is complete. In other cases, the two alleles combine to express an intermediate quality. This is known as codominance. An important difference is that complete dominance shrouds one allele, letting it remain despite the tests of natural selection, in a manner that co-dominance does not. A further important difference lies in the way these functions bias inheritance: complete dominance passes on the most radical interpretation of the parents' genes; codominance, the most conservative.

Here we report upon a comparison of the courses of evolution of four versions of an arbitrary sexual species, the sugar agent, a denizen of the JAWAS agent-oriented simulation toolkit [16]. Agents inherit traits according to one of two models of genetic transmission—the haploid versus the diploid genome—and with either complete allele dominance ("Mendelian dominance") or no dominance at all ("co-dominance").

2   Related Literature

Many multi-agent systems rely on evolutionary processes. In many of these, the model of reproduction is sexual. Apart from most fungi and some algae, almost all sexual organisms are diploid. However, the haploid pattern of inheritance is seen in the artificial agents of most of the multi-agent simulation, packages available for social science research, including JAWAS [16], A-Scape [17], and others. Similarly, sex in artificial agents often ignores the issue of allele dominance. These mechanisms do appear in the artificial life literature, for example, when the explicit object is to model some aspect of sex (e.g. [18]). However, given the ubiquity of these mechanisms in natural organisms, and their significance to a course of evolution, they are bound to be relevant aspects of any model in which reproduction is sexual, and it makes sense to wonder what sort of implicit decisions one is making in leaving them out.

In general, haploidy is the norm in evolutionary computing. Most applications of genetic algorithms [19], [20], genetic programming [21], and evolutionary strategies rely on a haploid model of genetic transmission, and it is this that is given as standard in textbook introductions, e.g. [22], [23]. This model has been set upon very many problems with success, both derived and applied [23]. When the solution sought is not apt to change, and the search space is constrained, as with many situations, haploidy is likely to do well, and the redundancy in diploidy will offer little benefit [19], [24]. Indeed, attempts to apply diploidy to such problems have not always found it to offer an improvement [25], [26].

The motivation[1] for implementing diploidy in genetic algorithms (GAs) came from an attempt to deal with dynamic, time-varying problem environments, on which typical GAs fare poorly [13], [27], [28]. Because diploidy holds on to its variability, it will be more able to adapt to changing demands. If it has begun to settle on a solution, and the goal changes, a haploid GA may have squandered its only potential to adapt, and be stuck in an outdated optimum [2]. Goldberg and Smith [13] demonstrated that diploidy conferred a GA with a sizeable benefit, over a regular haploid GA, on such a problem. Since then, supplementing GAs with diploid representations has been done with similar motives, and the basic findings in [13] have mostly been replicated (e.g. [19]), with various applications (e.g. [29]); with variations on the implementation of dominance (e.g. [14], [30], [31]); as well as with variations on the diploid representation itself (e.g. [32]). For an exception, see [24]. The literature on the use of diploidy in genetic algorithms is concisely surveyed in [12] and in [27]. Kursawe (1991; cited in [33]) is an example of diploidy applied to evolutionary strategies. The overall conclusion to be drawn from this work is that, in problems that change over time, such as when the fitness function is made to oscillate, diploidy follows the moving target, whereas haploidy fails [13], [26], [29]. Survival, to a line of genes, is such a problem.

Evolution for genetic algorithms and evolutionary strategies is unlike that in our multi-agent setup in some relevant respects. To begin, there is no explicit fitness evaluation function, as in GAs. Fitness in an agent world is, as with natural organisms, implicitly determined by many factors in the environment, and can very feasibly change its demands, for instance, at different population densities. So, though not as much as a line of genes, an artificial lineage may find itself having to deal with oscillating fitness demands, the sort of problem in which diploidy most confers an advantage in GAs. Though fitness in the present study is fairly steady, it is somewhat noisier than the fitness function of a typical GA.

Another reason multi-agent methods might get more out of diploidy than do most genetic algorithms lies in the frequency of fitness evaluations. In our artificial world, and others like it, fitness evaluation is continuous. In contrast, fitness evaluation in genetic algorithms is (usually) as rare as once per generation. The especial relevance of this to diploidy and dominance lies, again, in its carriage of unexpressed alleles. As these are unexpressed, they are exempt of evaluation, and this exemption lasts for the entire generation. The more fitness evaluations a quality is allowed to pass dormant, the greater the genome can hold on to its variability, even while exposed qualities are under harsh selection pressures. In this way, frequent fitness evaluation heightens the effect of genes being permitted to hide in diploidy. This point was clarified empirically in [26]. Schafer [26] varied the number of fitness evaluations per generation in a diploid GA. When fitness was evaluated only once each generation, diploidy offered no advantage. When fitness was evaluated twice, a stark advantage was seen. It may not, then, be appropriate to generalise to multi-agent systems, conclusions drawn from work on GAs.

---

[1] Other researchers choose the diploid model uncritically, for the sake of fidelity (e.g. [20]).

As with diploidy, a literature utilising the notion of dominance in genetic algorithms seems to have begun with [13]. Already the conception of dominance had gone beyond that in the present study, with alleles that remember their dominance values. Vekaria and Clack [21] is an attempt to apply a similar approach to dominance with genetic programming. Following [13], various dominance schemes were studied in (diploid) GAs. Some studies developed the representation scheme used (e.g. [30], [34]). The next step was to relax dominance, to begin to allow for incomplete dominance [14]. Then, various schemes by which dominant-recessive relations undergo change were developed [24], [30], [31]. Dominance schemes are reviewed in [27]. As with diploidy, the bulk of this work has been done with GAs, and so attempts to generalise therefrom should be made with caution.

Work on diploidy and dominance are interwoven. Of the studies mentioned in the previous paragraph, all except [21] use a diploid representation. Indeed, there are reasons to think that they would work together, and they largely concur in nature. However, this is all the more reason to pull these two mechanisms apart, and vary them independently of each other, as the current study attempts to do.

Mendelian dominance, as modelled here, is the standard among evolutionary algorithms not explicitly studying dominance. Other studies that approach the issue of allele dominance take the notion beyond the simple dominance scheme modelled here. By our model, a gene that dominates in one case might be recessive in the next. By other models, in contrast, particular alleles are consistently dominant or recessive. Though this is biologically accurate, it skips a computational step, which turns out to have interesting effects of its own. What seems not to have been explicitly modelled and tested before is the entire absence of dominance, as in the case of our codominance condition. The partial dominance in [14] is not codominance. It does not return intermediate phenotypes, for instance. And like other dominance schemes, it is far more complex and derived than the implementations in our model.

We have several requirements of our model of diploidy and dominance, beyond what previous work has provided. We require that it be agent-oriented. Sex is a multi-agent process at essence: it is something that only works in societies of interacting agents. Further, it must be true to nature, and as simple as these processes can be formulated. It must be able to dissociate dominance effects from ploidy effects. And it must be subjected to experiments designed expressly for the sake of studying these effects. We report on such a model here.

3   Haploidy and Diploidy

Almost all of the variability between individuals of sexual species is due to the shuffling of genes in meiosis [15]. Meiosis is the process by which a diploid cell divides into haploid cells. Diploid and haploid refer to the amount of genetic material a cell contains. A haploid cell contains a single complement of genes; a diploid cell contains two. Most species that exclusively reproduce asexually have only haploid cells at all stages. In animals that reproduce sexually, each parent contributes, via meiosis, a haploid sex cell (gamete), and these fuse to form a diploid cell (zygote), which is what thereupon grows into the new individual. Its genome is thus diploid. This is the most familiar form that sexual cycles take, but other sexual organisms, notably fungi [15], do it slightly differently. In such organisms, sexual reproduction follows an analogous passage through diploid and haploid phases, except that it is the haploid cell that develops into the mature, multicellular individual. We abbreviate these two varieties of sexual cycle as the diploid pattern, and the haploid pattern, respectively. In the diploid pattern, the genome of the mature organism is diploid, and the seed or egg is haploid; in the haploid pattern, the genome of the adult is haploid, and the dormant unicellular seed-like phase is diploid.

The difference between these, though subtle, is important: It is the mature organism that must contend with the world—that is to do well or poorly in it—and so upon which natural selection may operate. By the haploid pattern, the expression of one set of genes determines the course of evolution; by the diploid pattern, the expression of two sets of genes does. This has important repercussions, for it allows a gap to appear between what is passed on to the next generation (the genotype), and what is expressed (the phenotype). This allows an allele to remain effectively hidden in the genome, where natural selection cannot act upon it.

The haploid genome keeps just one set of instructions for each trait, whether that is the mothers copy, the fathers, or some function of the two. This directly determines the way the trait is expressed, and so the differentiation between genotype and phenotype is blurred. Selection is operating directly upon the trait that earned the selection advantage. There can be no mistakes. If an individual does well on account of a high score on some trait, it will have nothing other than that same high score to pass on to its offspring. No low scores can get through. It can be said that selection is transparent under these circumstances.

In contrast, by the diploid procedure, there is a clear distinction between the genotype and the corresponding phenotype. The diploid genotype consists of two sets of instructions, one from each parent. The phenotype is again determined by the genotype, but being a function of two values is, of course, less direct than being determined by a single value, as in haploidy. So when a successful agent reproduces, its offspring may well inherit a quality very unlike that expressed in the parent. It is this gap between genotype and phenotype in diploidy that allows it to smuggle unused genes past natural selection.

The algorithms we implemented for haploid-style and diploid-style inheritance are described below. In both haploidy and diploidy, the parents' genotypes are taken as the input to the reproduction function. A genotype and a phenotype are returned as outputs.

3.1 The Haploidy Algorithm

The genome of the haploid agent consists of a list of values, one for each heritable trait. Each value is a real number, between 0 and 1, expressing a probability to behave in a prescribed manner. Recombination, to an agent that is both sexual and haploid, consists of combining such a list from each parent into one, and assigning the resulting array to the offspring as its genotype. Inheritance for such an agent can be described in two steps:

1. For each trait, take the corresponding gene from each parent's genotype.
2. Some function, f, of these two values is assigned to the offspring. In principle, if not in nature, the sort of relation designated by f is not constrained. The resulting value determines, both, how the trait is expressed in the agent (i.e. its phenotype), and also what the agent ultimately passes down to its offspring (i.e. its genotype). For trait X:

$$\text{genotype}[X] \ (= \text{phenotype}[X]) = f(\text{father.genotype}[X], \text{mother.genotype}[X])$$

3.2 The Diploidy Algorithm

The diploid genome consists of a 2-dimensional array. It is a list of pairs of genes. Each heritable trait is represented by a real number for each of two genes, organised in a 2-element array. Inheritance for a diploid agent is a matter of combining the mother's array and the father's array into that of the offspring. This can be described in three steps:

1. For each trait, take one value, randomly selected, from the appropriate array in each parent's genome. This is the analogue of meiosis.
2. The new agent likewise inherits a 2-element array for each trait. This is filled with one gene from each parent. This is the analogue of fertilisation. For trait X:

$$\text{genotype}[X][0] = \text{mother.genotype}[X][0] \text{ OR } \text{mother.genotype}[X][1]$$
$$\text{genotype}[X][1] = \text{father.genotype}[X][0] \text{ OR } \text{father.genotype}[X][1]$$

3. Some function, f, of the two values in the genotype determines how the trait is expressed in the agent (i.e. its phenotype). For trait X:

$$\text{phenotype}[X] = f(\text{genotype}[X][0], \text{genotype}[X][1])$$

4   Dominance

There could be any number of functions for determining how the parents' genes combine to give the offspring's phenotype. One item that differentiates such functions in carbon-based organisms is the issue of trait dominance. In some cases, a disagreement between two genes trying to manifest different values for the same character is resolved by compromising upon an intermediate value. In other cases, one allele dominates over the other. When this happens, only one allele is expressed; the other, recessive allele is carried silently. It is this silent allele by which dominance shields genetic variability from natural selection.

Traits differ in the degree to which alleles dominate over others, from complete dominance, to codominance. Each of these suggest a function for determining trait expression — the f in the above algorithms. By simulating both of these extremes, we attempt to capture this dimension. These functions differ in the way they bias inheritance: complete dominance passes on the most radical interpretation of the parents' genes; codominance, the most conservative.

Note that our model does not include alleles that are consistently dominant or recessive to each other, as in natural organisms. In our model, which value dominates is decided anew with every birth. In pea plants, in contrast, the allele for purple flowers always dominates over the allele for white flowers. This omission makes a difference in the degree that certain genes are shielded. Since consistently recessive alleles are only exposed to selection pressures under specific circumstances, such as when two come together, this insulating effect is heightened as the allele becomes rarer. This means that such alleles are very resistant to extinction. Thus, the results of our model should be regarded as conservative.

4.1 Mendelian Dominance

Some traits are all-or-none. If pea plant A has purple flowers, and pea plant B has white flowers, their offspring would express one of these petal colours, rather than a mixture of the two. This is the famous discovery of Gregor Mendel from 1865 (cited in [15]). In our simulation, under this sort of trait expression, agents express only one of the values that represent each trait: either that inherited from the mother, or that inherited from the father. Hence:

$$f(\text{x, y}) = \text{x OR y}$$

4.2 Codominance

Some traits are the culmination of very many genes. Some of the relevant genes that the mother contributed will dominate; some of the father's will. Overall, the child's phenotype is expected to be the average. If agent C has red petals, and agent D has white petals, and if they are a certain species of snapdragon, all their offspring will have pink petals [15]. This sort of trait expression is simulated here by simply taking the average of the two values that make up the genome for that trait. That is:

$$f(\text{x, y}) = (\text{x} + \text{y})/2$$

5 The Simulation Environment and Agents

Simulations are conducted in VUScape [35], an environment in the JAWAS framework [16]. JAWAS (Java Artificial Worlds and Agent Societies) is an object-oriented, multi-agent systems development framework for implementing artificial societies. The system is implemented in the Java programming language and agents in that system are Java objects. VUScape is based heavily on the SugarScape environment of Epstein & Axtell [36].

VUScape is a virtual world, a 2-dimensional torus-shaped grid, populated by virtual agents all clamouring about in search of a limited, but replenishing resource, essential for their survival. They can sense a unit of the resource at some distance, and consume it when it is near. They spend their acquired stores of nutrients with each time step in order to maintain their existence, as if fuel. In the simulation, time is discrete. Each cycle allows each agent to execute, after which the world's resources are replenished. Each simulation begins with a fixed number of individual agents (1000), scattered randomly over a 50 x 50 cell grid. At the beginning of the simulation, each cell is randomly assigned an amount of resource. Consumed resources are replenished at a fixed rate up to a given maximum.

Those agents that fail to maintain a store of resources expire. Given that the agents also reproduce, the population is continually being added to, and so the resource will be scarce, meaning that the lot of the agents is one of perpetual competition. Competition assures that the agents are being evaluated upon an implicit criterion for differential survival. At the beginning of a simulation, each initial agent is randomly assigned a value for each heritable trait, defining the analogue of a gene pool. Since offspring inherit select traits from parents, differential reproduction is autocatalytic — the more an agent reproduces, the more potential its code will have for further reproduction. Evolution is expected to occur in such a situation upon each trait that is both heritable, and allowed to vary.

The genome of agents in VUScape consists of two traits: Talk and Listen. The simulation is set up to encourage cooperation among the agents. To harvest the resource found in a given cell, there must be enough agents present, working in tandem. Depending on the quantity of the resource present, to harvest a cell might require the combined efforts of up to four agents. To such an agent, "talk" is a plea for help, and "listen" is the act of responding to another agent's plea. Each agent has a Talk value, which indicates the probability that the agent will issue a plea for help whenever it happens upon a cell that is too big for it to harvest alone. Each agent also has a Listen value, which indicates the probability that it will preferentially move to a cell in which another agent has talked. Under such circumstances, natural selection favours individuals that talk and listen more frequently [35], [37]. This is how communication works in VUScape.

For the experiments reported herein, we supplemented the reproductive function of VUScape agents with the methods for genetic transmission described above. The implementation of the haploid-codominant condition (Haploid-CoD) was already present in JAWAS. VUScape's default settings were used, with one exception: we raised the resource growback rate (from 1 to 1.3), so that simulations would support larger populations of agents. Each run was initialised with 1000 agents. Simulations were run for 3000 timesteps each.

6   Design

Two criteria are measured for comparing populations: 1) the average values of each trait, Talk and Listen; and 2) the variance seen in these values. These two numbers represent the way each trait is distributed at each timestep over the course of each simulation. In this way, the behaviour of these two dependent measures for each trait is a good description of how the different models of genetic transmission implemented effect evolution.

Simulations were run with one of two implementations of genetic transmission (haploid versus diploid), and with one of two functions for trait expression (Mendelian versus codominant). These are our two independent variables, for a 2 x 2 experimental design. This yields four sorts of populations: haploid and Mendelian (Haploid-Or); haploid and codominant (Haploid-CoD); diploid and Mendelian (Diploid-Or); and diploid and codominant (Diploid-CoD). Each of these population types were run 15 times (4 of the Haploid-CoD runs were excluded from analyses, on account of early extinction). Each simulation was continued for 3000 timesteps. The mean and variance of each trait (Talk and Listen) were sampled at every 100 iterations.

These data are subjected to two sorts of repeated-measures, 2-factor ANOVA. The factor of primary interest is the sort of population, whether Haploid-Or, Diploid-Or, or Diploid-CoD (3 conditions). The haploid-codominant condition is excluded from analyses on account of the much lower variance in this group — approaching, sometimes reaching, zero. Its inclusion would muddy the statistics used, and unnecessarily, for with no variance, one does not need a statistical test to say that it is different! This condition is highly dissimilar from the other three conditions on all measures.

The other factor is time. When looking at trajectories of evolution over time, or interactions of conditions with time, the entire trend, from initialisation to end, is analysed. Such tests include 31 timesteps (timestep 1, then every 100 iterations). Where the interest is to analyse the end results of evolution, after populations have somewhat settled, only data from the last 6 time samples— from timestep 2500 to 3000—are considered. In previous work with JAWAS (e.g. [37], [38]), simulations were run for 2000 timesteps. Our simulations were run for 3000 timesteps. Bonferroni post hoc tests are used, as a standard test for post hoc effects.

7   Results and Discussion

Both of the heritable traits in our agents' genomes were unambiguously advantageous to their survival. Average trait values were expected to increase over generations. But would they do so at the expense of variability? Figures 1 and 3 show the evolution of Talk, one of the two traits allowed to evolve in the simulations. At the beginning of each simulation, each agent is randomly assigned a number between 0 and 1, which indicates its Talk value. Random assignment of trait values assures two initial conditions: that the average trait value will be roughly 0.5 (Figure 1); and that variance will be artificially high (Figure 3). So the action of evolution over the first several hundred timesteps can be thought of as correcting these impositions. How do these different algorithms make this correction?

First note that the algorithm followed in the Haploid-CoD condition, does not correct it. It rather consolidates the population's initial average trait values.

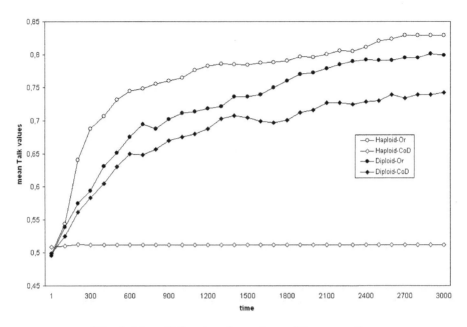

Fig. 1. Mean Talk values for each condition, over time

If these values are good, all is well, but in the present case, agents clearly could have done better. Within the first few hundred timesteps, all agents in the simulation have identical trait values. Traits converged to as low as 0.456 and only as high as 0.577, over 11 simulations (Listen: M = .515, SD = .034, ranging from 0.456 to 0.577; Talk: M = .512, SD = .031, from 0.471 to 0.556). Evolution, for these populations, acts to stifle evolution! This cannot be an apt model for an evolutionary process. However, let us note that despite its poor performance, it does initially strike one as somewhat accurate. Indeed, this is the only method of genetic transmission that we took unaltered from the JAWAS simulation framework. It is in retrospect that we see how it necessarily kills variability. Its comparison with the other three methods is instructive, for it accentuates what is happening differently there.

All of the other three methods allow natural selection to act, and directional evolution is seen to occur. Given that both of the traits that may be so affected are set up to be advantageous to the agents, we expect average values to increase over many generations. This may be regarded as an implicit goal of each of our algorithms: to evolve better harvesters, who use Talk and Listen more often. This clearly occurs in all of these three methods, as can be readily seen in Figures 1 and 2.

Our primary concern, however, is how each method performs on a second implicit goal: retaining variability. This conflicts with the pressure to score highly, for the nearer agents come to some ideal value, the less variable will the population become with respect to that trait. If a population would evolve such that all agents come to have the same top value, it may be said that they are more

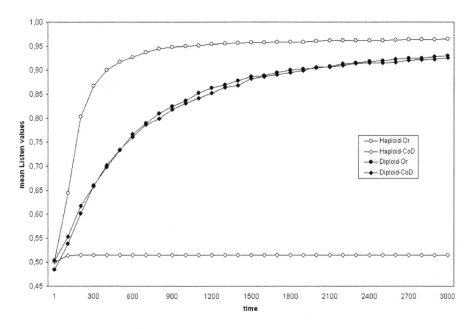

Fig. 2. Mean Listen values for each condition, over time

adapted to their environment, but the species would be vulnerable to potential environmental change [9], or exploitation by parasites [10]. How will each model of genetic transmission resolve these conflicting demands?

7.1   Means

A progressive increase of Listen and Talk values was seen in all Haploid-Or, Diploid-Or, and Diploid-CoD simulations (see Figures 1 and 2). Since the first-generation agents are assigned trait values randomly from 0 to 1, as each simulation begins, the average score is roughly 0.5 (in our 56 simulations, for Listen, $M = 0.498$, $SD = 0.030$). At the end of the simulations, with the passage of 3000 timesteps, mean Listen values had increased to 0.965 for Haploid-Or populations ($N = 15$, $SD = 0.025$, from 0.898 to 0.993); 0.929 for Diploid-Or ($N = 15$, $SD = 0.044$, from 0.847 to 0.996); and 0.926 for Diploid-CoD ($N = 15$, $SD = 0.032$, from 0.879 to 0.996). The corresponding increase in Talk is charted in Figure 1. This rise lagged behind that of Listen, on account of the nature of these capacities, but was no less consistent. At timestep 3000, the average Talk values had risen to 0.829 for Haploid-Or populations ($N = 15$, $SD = 0.071$, from 0.716 to 0.923); 0.799 for Diploid-Or ($N = 15$, $SD = 0.064$, from 0.668 to 0.893); and 0.743 for Diploid-CoD ($N = 15$, $SD = 0.068$, from 0.638 to 0.872).

A repeated-measures, 2-factor ANOVA (31 timesteps × 3 conditions) for each trait, showed main effects and interactions around. Mean values of the two heritable traits increased over generations (Listen: $F(30) = 886.7$; Talk: $F(30) = 170.5$,

p's < .001). The interaction between population type and time proved significant as well (p's < .001), meaning that traits developed according to dissimilar trajectories over time. For both traits, the highest values were obtained in
the haploid-Mendelian condition. Furthermore, these heights are achieved more
quickly than in other conditions. This is starker in the case of Listen (Figure 2),
but apparent in Talk as well, as seen in Figure 1. That groups ultimately reached
dissimilar heights was confirmed with a 2-factor ANOVA (6 timesteps × 3 conditions) for each trait, on the latter portion of the simulations (Listen: $F(2) =$
7.09, p = .002; Talk: $F(2) = 8.16$, p = .001). Post hoc tests show that Haploid-Or

Table 1. Summary of inferential statistics. Results of all eight analyses of variance
reported above are summarised here. Two tests were applied to both mean scores
(Means) and variance of mean scores (Variance) for each dependant variable (Talk and
Listen). One test considers the entire span of the simulations, from the first timestep
to the 3000th (T1-T3000). The other considers only the last 500 timesteps, from the
2500th to the 3000th (T2500-T3000). Each test is a 2-factor ANOVA (3 groups x a
number of timesteps, 31 or 6). F statistics, degrees of freedom (in parentheses), and
probabilities of type 1 errors (p) are listed for each main effect (Groups, Time), and
the interaction of these (Groups x Time), as well as for post hoc tests between groups
(Bonferroni). Three post hoc comparisons are relevant in each case, one between each
pair of groups (e.g. "H-Or & D-Or" is to abbreviate a post hoc comparison between
Haploid-Or and Diploid-Or groups).

	Talk T1-T3000	T2500-3000	Listen T1-T3000	T2500-T3000
Means				
Groups	$F(2) = 12.45$ p < .001	$F(2) = 8.16$ p < .001	$F(2) = 49.73$ p < .001	$F(2) = 7.09$ p < .002
Post hoc comparisons				
H-Or & D-Or	p = .041	p = .513	p < .001	p = .012
H-Or & D-CoD	p < .001	p = .001	p < .001	p = .004
D-Or & D-CoD	p = .061	p = .040	p = 1	p = 1
Time	$F(30) = 170.50$ p < .001	$F(5) = 2.81$ p = .018	$F(30) = 886.70$ p < .001	$F(5) = 15.06$ p < .001
Groups x Time	$F(60) = 2.35$ p < .001	$F(10) = 0.43$ p = .930	$F(60) = 25.50$ p < .001	$F(10) = 2.12$ p < .024
Variance				
Groups	$F(2) = 29.76$ p < .001	$F(2)\ 6.23$ p = .004	$F(2)\ 94.23$ p < .001	$F(2) = 11.64$ p < .001
Post hoc comparisons				
H-Or & D-Or	p < .001	p = .005	p < .001	p < .001
H-Or & D-CoD	p = .122	p = .045	p < .001	p = .025
D-Or & D-CoD	p < .001	p = 1	p < .001	p = .145
Time	$F(30) = 223.63$ p < .001	$F(5) = 1.67$ p = .142	$F(30) = 784.08$ p < .001	$F(5) = 2.06$ p = .072
Groups x Time	$F(60) = 11.69$ p < .001	$F(10) = 0.36$ p = .961	$F(60) = 41.28$ p < .001	$F(10) = 0.64$ p = .783

populations evolved notably higher Listen scores than both diploid conditions (p's < .02), which were similar to each other (p = 1.000). A similar pattern is seen in the evolution of Talk, except that the diploid-Mendelian condition rose to levels nearer to the haploid-Mendelian condition (p > .5), and both of these were significantly higher than the diploid-codominant (p's < .05). Populations that inherited Talk according to the Mendelian function evolved to possess higher trait values than those using the codominance model, though this was not seen in Listen. All inferential statistics are summarised in Table 1.

7.2   Variance

In each condition, as evolution proceeds and trait values go up, variance goes down. Agents become more homogeneous. This is expected, but to what extent will each algorithm relinquish variability for high scores? Two differences can be seen between the trends plotted in Figure 3 and in Figure 4: the rate of their decline; and the extent that they dip to. In both codominance conditions variance drops very rapidly. This is striking in comparison to the much more gradual declines seen in the corresponding Mendelian conditions. Secondly, in both diploid conditions, the decline levels off at a notably higher level than in either of the haploid conditions. (Haploid-Or: M = .007, SD = .006, ranging from 0.000 to 0.022; Diploid-Or: M = .017, SD = .009, from 0.002 to 0.030; Diploid-CoD: M = .016, SD = .010, from 0.000 to 0.040).

Tests conducted on the variance of trait values confirm both of these observations. Groups displayed significantly dissimilar rates of evolution, as indicated

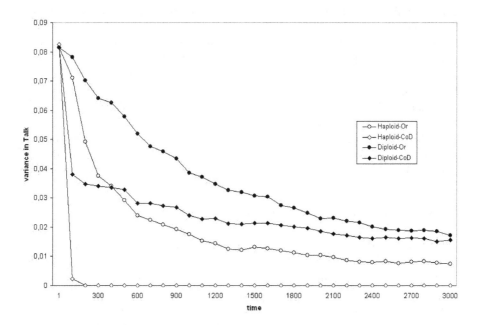

Fig. 3. Mean variance of Talk values for each condition, over time

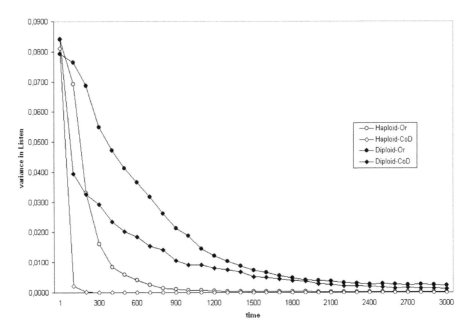

Fig. 4. Mean variance of Listen values for each condition, over time

by strong interaction effects with time (Listen: $F(60) = 41.3$; Talk: $F(60) = 11.7$, p's $< .001$). What level of variability does each method leave one with? Tests just looking at the end of the simulation, from timestep 2500 through 3000, showed significant differences between the three sorts of populations (Listen: $F(2) = 11.64$, $p < .001$; Talk: $F(2) = 6.23$, $p = .004$). Post hoc tests reveal that Haploid-Or populations had less variable trait values than in either sort of diploid population (for Diploid-Or, $p < .006$; for Diploid-CoD, $p < .05$), which did not differ significantly from each other ($p > .1$). See Table 1 for a summary of all the analyses conducted.

Another curious difference that appeared in the Haploid-CoD condition was that it supported fewer agents than any of the other groups (p's $< .001$). On the 3000th time step, the average size of Haploid-CoD populations was 474.9, as opposed to 592.4, 588.5, and 587.2 for Haploid-Or, Diploid-Or, and Diploid-CoD, respectively.

8   Applying Diploidy and Dominance

Since the influences of diploidy and dominance promote evolution, they may benefit certain engineering applications that utilise evolutionary mechanisms. The advantage for finding solutions to problems that these processes are anticipated to confer is in insulating a search from getting stuck at some local optimum. Diploidy does this by preserving a reservoir of variation. The anti-conservative bias in Mendelian dominance will add further reach to the process.

The point that a diploid representation offers benefits in dynamic, time-dependent problem situations with moving optima has been aptly made with the work on diploidy in GAs [27], treated above. The other situation in which diploidy especially helps is when the problem is complex. It is not only moving optima that can trap evolution that moves too quickly, but those that take very much evolution to achieve. "A harder problem requires a larger diversity of structures in the population" [8]. Consider the Listen scores charted in Figure 2. None of the four sorts of populations reached what might be supposed to be the optimum score of 100%, yet at the end of the simulation, haploid populations had entirely converged.

In simpler problems, with fitness definitions that are unambiguous, unimodal, and unmoving, a haploid algorithm may outperform a diploid version [24]. Even the haploid-Mendelian version reported upon here achieved higher scores than the corresponding diploid version, which would most often be the goal (though not, for example, here!). In cases where they perform equally, the haploid is to be preferred as it is somewhat cheaper in terms of, both, time and space.

The redundancy in the diploid genome means that it occupies twice as much memory as the haploid. Though it entails no significant hike in processing costs over the same period, if the intent is to bring it to convergence, the processing demands for the diploid representation will, naturally, be greater. However, it will anyway be of the same order of complexity as the haploid. Dominance, as described here, adds neither space nor time costs over codominance.

The practical benefits afforded by diploidy and dominance invite inventive bastardisations of these ideas. For instance, accepting that the benefit of complete dominance lies in its radical bias, try making the bias even more radical. Instead of "A or B", try "A or B +/−10%". Likewise, in the way diploidy maintains a store, this study invites the engineer to try triploidy or other polyploid strategies. This is not without precedent in nature. In some animals, the sexes even have dissimilar ploidy amounts, demonstrating how fractions are possible, as well, such as the heritability of hymenoptera. Dasgupta and McGregor [32] is such an example of an innovative response to diploidy in genetic algorithms.

9   Conclusions

Some distinct overall conclusions can be drawn from the pattern of results acquired, about how each of the four methods modelled allow evolution to proceed.

Diploidy fulfils its promise of preserving variability. The haploid-Mendelian condition heads for high ground early in the simulation. It compromises variability for high scores. It is easy to imagine situations in which this would be a good strategy, however, it commits its possessors to the current niche. Diploidy, however, seems to make its possessors somewhat shy of the top. Trait values stabilised at a markedly lower level in the diploid conditions. In the face of the conflicting implicit goals of scoring highly, and preserving variability, haploidy chooses the former; diploidy, the latter.

Mendelian dominance, likewise, was seen to preserve variability. The difference is particularly striking nearer to the beginning of the simulations, in the first 1000 time steps (see Figures 3 and 4). Just as the haploid-codominant species loses its ability to improve by throwing away all its variability, the diploid-codominant species, too, squanders much of its initial variability early in the simulation, and ultimately fails to match the average trait value levels achieved in either Mendelian condition (see Figure 1). Much more gradual declines in variability are seen in the corresponding Mendelian conditions. Nor does this insulation of variability come with a compromise to adaptivity. Diploid-Mendelian populations scored at least as highly as the diploid-codominant, and significantly higher in Talk scores. So by both criteria, complete dominance appears to be an improvement over codominance.

The improvement that Mendelian dominance imparts over codominance to the haploid species is more extreme. Indeed, the haploid-codominant species must be faulty, for it forbids directional evolution. The lesson of the haploid-codominant agent seems to be that either of these ways of preserving variability, either dominance or diploidy, rescues it from stagnation. Hence, both the diploid-codominant and haploid-Mendelian conditions performed well.

Mutation was left out of our model. To the extent that diploidy preserves variability, and mutation creates it, the differences observed between the ultimate variability in the haploid genome versus that in the diploid would have been greater had mutation been included. Mutation would have given the diploid genome more diversity to hide; and the haploid, more to squander.

These results echo consistent findings in classical population genetics. Diploidy and dominance strongly affect evolution. If they did not, one would not be obliged to include them in a model. As they do, where accuracy is an issue, a modeller should consider these aspects of sex, particularly where studying evolution in sexual agents. Further, since these influences *promote* evolution, their addition to a model may benefit certain engineering applications.

References

1. Lin, S-C., Punch, W.F., and Goodman, E.D.: Coarse-grain parallel genetic algorithms: Categorization and new approach. In 6th IEEE Symposium on Parallel and Distributed Processing. IEEE Computer Society Press, (1994)
2. Mauldin, M.L.: Maintaining diversity in genetic search. Proceedings of the National Conference on Artificial Intelligence (AAAI-84), pp. 247–250, (1984)
3. Potts, J.C., Giddens, T.D., Yadav S.: The development and evaluation of an improved genetic algorithm based on migration and artificial selection. IEEE Transactions On Systems, Man, And Cybernetics, Vol. 24, No. I (1994)
4. Herrera, F., and Lozano, M.: Adaptation of genetic algorithm parameters based on fuzzy logic controllers. In F. Herrera and J. L. Verdegay, editors, Genetic Algorithms and Soft Computing, pp. 95–125. Physica-Verlag, Heidelberg, (1996)

5. Leung, K-S., Duan, Q-H., Xu, Z-B., & Wong, C. K.: A new model of simulated evolutionary computation-convergence analysis and specifications. IEEE Transactions on Evolutionary Computation, Vol. 5, No. 1 (2001)
6. Rudolph, G.: Convergence of non-elitist strategies. Proc. 1st IEEE Conf. Evolutionary Computation. Piscataway, NJ: IEEE, pp. 63–66 (1994)
7. Fogel, D.B.: Evolutionary Computation: Toward a New Philosophy of Machine Intelligence, 2nd Ed. IEEE Press: New York, USA, (2000)
8. Shimodaira, H.: A diversity-control-oriented genetic algorithm (DCGA): Performance in function optimization. In L.D. Whitley, D.E. Goldberg, E. Cant, L. Spector, I.C. Parmee, & H-G. Beyer (Eds.), Proceedings of the Genetic and Evolutionary Computation Conference (GECCO 2000), Las Vegas, USA, July 8–12, 2000, p. 366, Morgan Kaufmann (2000)
9. Smith, John Maynard: Games, Sex and Evolution. Harvester Wheatsheaf: Hertfordshire, UK (1988)
10. Ridley, M.: The Red Queen: Sex and the Evolution of Human Nature. Maxwell Macmillan: Toronto (1995)
11. Gao, Y.: An Upper Bound on the Convergence Rates of Canonical Genetic Algorithms. Complexity International, vol. 5 (1998)
12. Branke, J.: Memory-enhanced evolutionary algorithms for changing optimization problems. In Congress on Evolutionary Computation (CEC'99), IEEE, Band 3, S. 1875–1882 (1999)
13. Goldberg, D. E., and Smith, R. E.: Nonstationary function optimization using genetic algorithms with diploidy and dominance. In J.J. Grefenstette, editor, Proceedings of the Second International Conference on Genetic Algorithms, 59–68. Lawrence Erlbaum Associates (1987).
14. Ryan, C.: The degree of oneness. In Proceedings of the ECAI workshop on Genetic Algorithms. Springer-Verlag, (1996)
15. Campbell, N.A., Reece, J.B., Mitchell, L.G.: Biology, 5th Edition. Addison Wesley: Amsterdam (1999)
16. JAWAS: Java Artificial Worlds & Agent Societies. Vrije Universiteit, http://www.cs.vu.nl/ci/eci/jawas/ (last seen on 2005-04-14)
17. A-Scape. Brookings Institution, http://www.brook.edu/es/dynamics/models/ascape/ (last seen on 2005-04-14)
18. Jaffe, K.: The dynamics of the evolution of sex: Why the sexes are, in fact, always two? Interciencia 21(6), pp. 259–267 http://www.interciencia.org.ve (1996)
19. Kurup, M.M.: A study of dominance and diploidy as long term memory in genetic algorithms. http://www.kurups.org/papers/GA.ps (last seen on 2006-01-11)
20. dos Santos, J.P.P.R.: Universal service: Issues on modelling and computation. DSc. Thesis, Universite Catholique de Louvain, (1996)
21. Vekaria, K., and Clack, C.: Haploid genetic programming with dominance. Departmental Research Note (RN/97/121) (1997)
22. Langdon, W.B., Poli, R.: Foundations of Genetic Programming, Springer (2002)
23. Russell, S., and Norvig, P.: Artificial Intelligence: A modern approach, 2nd Ed., Prentice-Hall: New Jersey (2003).
24. Yılmaz, A.S. and Wu, A.S.: A comparison of haploidy and diploidy without dominance on integer representations. In the Proceedings of the 17th International Symposium on Computer and Information Sciences, Orlando, FL, October 28–30, 2002, pp. 242–248 (2002)
25. Branke, J.: Evolutionary approaches to dynamic optimization problems: Updated survey. GECCO Workshop on Evolutionary Algorithms for Dynamic Optimization Problems, pp. 27–30 (2001)

26. Schafer, R.: Using a genetic algorithm with diploidy to create and maintain a complex system in dynamic equilibrium. In J.R. Koza (Ed.), Genetic Algorithms and Genetic Programming at Stanford 2003, pp. 179–186 (2003)
27. Singh, A.: Giving genes their voice: A survey of information expression mechanisms in genetic algorithms. http://computing.breinestorm.net/natural+ paradigms+ gas+competent+genetic/ (last seen on 2006-01-11). (2002)
28. Simões, A. & Costa, E.: Using genetic algorithms to deal with dynamic environments: A comparative study of several approaches based on promoting diversity. Proceedings of the Genetic and Evolutionary Computation Conference (GECCO'02), W. B. Langdon et alli (Eds.), Morgan Kaufmann Publishers, New York, 9–13 July, 2002 (2002)
29. Osmera, P.: Evolvable controllers using parallel evolutionary algorithms. Proceedings of MENDEL '2003, Bmo, Czech Republic pp. 126–132 (2003)
30. Ng, K. P. & Wong, K. C.: A new diploid scheme and dominance change mechanism for non-stationary function optimization. In L. J. Eshelman (ed.), Proceedings of the Sixth International Conference on Genetic Algorithms, Morgan Kaufmann: San Francisco, pp. 159–166 (1995)
31. Lewis, J., Hart, E., and Ritchie, G.: A comparison of dominance mechanisms and simple mutation on non-stationary problems. In Parallel Problem Solving from Nature (PPSN V), pp. 139–148 (1998)
32. Dasgupta, D., and McGregor, D. R.: sGA: Structured Genetic Algorithm. University of Strathclyde, Technical Report no. IKBS-8-92 (1992)
33. Ghosh, A., and Dehuri, S.: Evolutionary algorithms for multi-criterion optimization: A survey. International Journal of Computing and Information Sciences, 2 (1), (2004)
34. Schnier, T., and Gero, J.: Dominant and recessive genes in evolutionary systems applied to spatial reasoning. Australian Joint Conference on Artificial Intelligence, 127–136 (1997)
35. Buzing, P.C.: Vuscape: Communication and cooperation in evolving artificial societies. Masters' thesis, Department of Computer Science, Vrije Universiteit, Amsterdam, The Netherlands (2003).
36. Epstein, J. M., Axtell, R.L.: Growing Artificial Societies: Social Science From the Bottom Up. MIT Press (1996)
37. Buzing P.C., Eiben A.E., and Schut M.C., Emerging communication and cooperation in evolving agent societies. Journal of Artificial Societies and Social Simulation, vol. 8(1), (2005)
38. Eiben A.E., Nitschke G., and Schut M.C.: Comparison of reproduction schemes in an artificial society for cooperative gathering. AISB Socially Inspired Computing: Engineering with Social Metaphors Symposium (AISB-SIC 2005), (2005)

Towards a Methodology for Situated Cellular Agent Based Crowd Simulations

Stefania Bandini, Mizar Luca Federici, Sara Manzoni, and Giuseppe Vizzari

Dipartimento di Informatica, Sistemistica e Comunicazione,
Università degli Studi di Milano–Bicocca,
Via Bicocca degli Arcimboldi 8, 20126 Milano, Italy
{bandini, mizar, manzoni, vizzari}@disco.unimib.it

Abstract. This paper introduces a research activity aimed at the definition of a methodology to provide a solid conceptual framework for the development of simulation systems focused on crowd dynamics and based on the Situated Cellular Agent (SCA) model. After a brief introduction of the SCA Model, the general methodological approach is described. The main steps provide the definition of the spatial abstraction of the environment, the definition of its active elements, and the specification of types of mobile agents, the related behaviours with particular attention to their movement by means of the notion of utility. A case study is also briefly described in order to show how the methodology was applied in the modelling of crowd behaviour in an underground station.

1 Introduction

The Situated Cellular Agents (SCA) model [1] is a formal and computational framework for the definition of complex systems characterized by the presence of a set of autonomous entities interacting in an environment whose spatial structure represents a key factor in their choices on their actions and in determining their possible interactions. The model has been successfully applied in different contexts, and in particular its focus on the modelling of the environment as well as its inhabiting agents and their interactions, make it particularly suitable for simulation of actual physical systems. In particular, crowd modelling and simulation requires to model the autonomous behaviour of individuals interacting among themselves (e.g. because they compete over a shared resource, but also because of crowding effects) and the interaction among pedestrian and the environment. In fact in this situation the concept of perception must have a very precise meaning, and it influences the modelling activities as well as the design and implementation of the simulation system.

There are several computational approaches to crowd modelling, ranging from analytical ones, which generally consider humans as particles subject to various forces modelling interactions among pedestrian (see, e.g., [2]), to CA-based models which provide a discrete abstraction of the environment, whose cells encapsulate the possible presence of pedestrian and whose transition rules represent the rules that govern pedestrian movement (see, e.g., [3, 4]). Agent based models are

O. Dikenelli, M.-P. Gleizes, and A. Ricci (Eds.): ESAW 2005, LNAI 3963, pp. 203–220, 2006.
© Springer-Verlag Berlin Heidelberg 2006

more suited than the previous ones to be applied to situations characterized by a certain degree of heterogeneity and dynamism of agents and environment. Moreover, several indirect interaction models provide the possibility of situated agents to leave marks in the environment to influence the behaviour of other mobile entities. This metaphor has been often exploited to model the movement of animals but also humans (see, e.g., [5]). Also situated agents were successfully applied in this context [6], but to our knowledge a methodology for the analysis, modelling and design of crowd simulations through situated agent models does not exist.

Several methodologies for the analysis and design of multi-agent systems have been defined (see, e.g., GAIA [7], INGENIAS [8] and SODA [9]) but they are more focused to the design of general purpose software systems analyzed and structured using the notion of agent, and thus they lack focus to simulate specific issues. Some specific methodological approaches to multi–agent simulation can also be found (see, e.g., [10]) but they are still very abstract and do not provide specific support to crowd modelling. In this paper the first proposal of a methodology for the modelling of SCA based crowd simulations is introduced. In particular, the methodology provides a set of phases for the definition of an abstraction of the structure of the simulated environment, the specification of active elements of the environment able to generate signals facilitating the movement of pedestrian, and types of agents, with the related perceptive capabilities and behavioural specifications. The following Section will briefly introduce the SCA model, while the proposed methodology is defined in Section 3. A specific case study focused on the modelling of pedestrian in an underground station adopting the proposed methodology is described in Section 4. This scenario was chosen in the wider domain of crowd modelling and simulation because it presents very complex behaviours that are not easily found in other typical simulation scenarios such as room evacuation. Conclusions and future developments will end the paper.

2   Situated Cellular Agent Model

The Situated Cellular Agent model is a specific class of Multilayered Multi-Agent Situated System (MMASS) [11] providing a single layered spatial structure for agents environment and some limitations to the field emission mechanism. A thorough description of the model is out of the scope of this paper, and this aim of Section is to briefly introduce it to give some basic notion of the elements that are necessary to describe the methodology.

A *Situated Cellular Agent* is defined by the triple $\langle Space, F, A \rangle$ where *Space* models the environment where the set A of agents is situated, acts autonomously and interacts through the propagation of the set F of fields and through reaction operations. Figure 1 shows a diagram of the two interaction mechanisms provided by the model.

Space is defined as a not oriented graph of sites. Every *site* $p \in P$ (where P is the set of sites of the layer) can contain at most one agent and is defined by the 3-tuple $\langle a_p, F_p, P_p \rangle$ where:

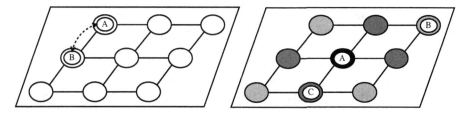

Fig. 1. A diagram showing the two interaction mechanisms provided by the SCA model: two reacting agents on the left, and a field emission on the right

- $a_p \in A \cup \{\perp\}$ is the agent situated in p ($a_p = \perp$ when no agent is situated in p that is, p is empty);
- $F_p \subset F$ is the set of fields active in p ($F_p = \emptyset$ when no field is active in p);
- $P_p \subset P$ is the set of sites adjacent to p.

A SCA agent is defined by the 3-tuple $< s, p, \tau >$ where τ is the *agent type*, $s \in \Sigma_\tau$ denotes the *agent state* and can assume one of the values specified by its type (see below for Σ_τ definition), and $p \in P$ is the site of the *Space* where the agent is situated. As previously stated, agent *type* is a specification of agent state, perceptive capabilities and behaviour. In fact an agent type τ is defined by the 3-tuple $\langle \Sigma_\tau, Perception_\tau, Action_\tau \rangle$. Σ_τ defines the set of states that agents of type τ can assume. $Perception_\tau : \Sigma_\tau \rightarrow [\mathbf{N} \times W_{f_1}] \ldots [\mathbf{N} \times W_{f_{|F|}}]$ is a function associating to each agent state a vector of pairs representing the *receptiveness coefficient* and *sensitivity thresholds* for that kind of field. $Action_\tau$ represents instead the behavioural specification for agents of type τ. Agent behaviour can be specified using a language that defines the following primitives:

- $emit(s, f, p)$: the *emit* primitive allows an agent to *start the diffusion of field* f on p, that is the site it is placed on;
- $react(s, a_{p_1}, a_{p_2}, \ldots, a_{p_n}, s')$: this kind of primitive allows the specification a *coordinated change of state* among adjacent agents. In order to preserve agents' autonomy, a compatible primitive must be included in the behavioural specification of all the involved agents; moreover when this coordination process takes place, every involved agents may dynamically decide to effectively agree to perform this operation;
- $transport(p, q)$: the *transport* primitive allows to *define agent movement* from site p to site q (that must be adjacent and vacant);
- $trigger(s, s')$: this primitive specifies that an agent must *change its state* when it senses a particular condition in its local context (i.e. its own site and the adjacent ones); this operation has the same effect of a reaction, but does not require a coordination with other agents.

For every primitive included in the behavioural specification of an agent type specific preconditions must be specified; moreover specific parameters must also be given (e.g. the specific field to be emitted in an emit primitive, or the conditions to identify the destination site in a transport) to precisely define the effect of the action, which was previously briefly described in general terms.

Each SCA agent is thus provided with a set of sensors that allows its interaction with the environment and other agents. At the same time, agents can constitute the source of given fields acting within a SCA space (e.g. noise emitted by a talking agent). Formally, a field type t is defined by $\langle W_t, Diffusion_t, Compare_t, Compose_t \rangle$ where W_t denotes the set of values that fields of type t can assume; $Diffusion_t : P \times W_f \times P \rightarrow (W_t)^+$ is the diffusion function of the field computing the value of a field on a given space site taking into account in which site (P is the set of sites that constitutes the SCA space) and with which value it has been generated. It must be noted that fields diffuse along the spatial structure of the environment, and more precisely a field diffuses from a source site to the ones that can be reached through arcs as long as its intensity is not voided by the diffusion function. $Compose_t : (W_t)^+ \rightarrow W_t$ expresses how fields of the same type have to be combined (for instance, in order to obtain the unique value of field type t at a site), and $Compare_t : W_t \times W_t \rightarrow \{True, False\}$ is the function that compares values of the same field type. This function is used in order to verify whether an agent can perceive a field value by comparing it with the sensitivity threshold after it has been modulated by the receptiveness coefficient.

3   Methodology for SCA-Based Crowd Modelling

In SCA agents' actions take place in a discrete and finite space. Entities populating the environment are classified in types, which represent templates for the specification of active elements of the environment. The latter are not only mobile entities, but also specific elements of the environment which the modeller wishes to exploit to influence the former (e.g. with attraction or repulsion effects). To model an agent type in SCA means to define the allowed states, perceptive capabilities and behavioural specification. In the proposed methodology, agent's states represent attitudes, in terms of perceptions (in fact, as previously introduced, the state determines the current agent's perceptive capabilities), but also conditions which determine its choices on actions to be selected and carried out. These actions include the definition of influences of the agent on other entities of the environment (e.g. crowding effects) by means of field emissions, the specification of its motory system and movement preferences by means of the notion of movement utility, but also the transitions from one state to another (i.e. a change of attitude towards the perception and action in the environment). While some agents related to active parts of the environment may present a very simple type specifications, mobile entities with different possible movement attitudes might require several states and complex behavioural specifications.

The diagram shown in Figure 2 shows the main phases of the methodology, while in the following subsections the steps that bring to the definition of a complete model for crowding simulations will be introduced. It must be emphasized that the first three steps lead to the development of a computational model which can be adopted in several experiments on an analogous scenario. The last two phases are those that effectively characterize the specific experiment.

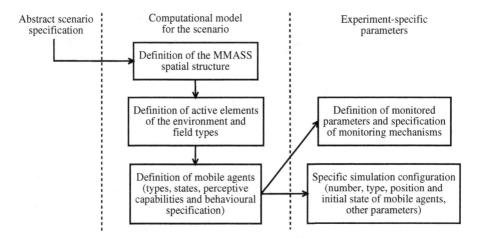

Fig. 2. A diagram showing the main phases of the methodology

Section 4 will then present a concrete case study in which the proposed methodology has been applied.

3.1 Definition of the MMASS Spatial Structure

In order to obtain an appropriate abstraction of space suitable for the SCA model, we need a discrete abstraction of the actual space in which the simulation will take place. This abstraction is constituted of nodes connected with non-oriented arcs (i.e. a non oriented graph). Nodes represent the positions that can be occupied by single pedestrian once per time. Some of the nodes can be occupied by some agents that constitute part of the environment (doors, exits, shops etc), and that cannot be occupied by other individuals. Arcs connect nodes, representing the adjacency of one node to another. Individuals can move by single steps only from one node to other nodes that are in its immediate adjacency, so arcs and adjacency constraint agents' movement. However, as previously mentioned, the spatial structure of the environment also constraints field diffusion.

SCA space represents thus an abstraction of a walking pavement, but it has to be sufficiently detailed to be considered a good approximation of the real environment surface, and it allows a realistic representation of the movements and paths that individuals would follow. As for other crowd modelling and simulation systems we assume that a single node is associated to the space occupied by a still person [3], but the choice on the dimension of what must be considered the atomic element of the environment (a single cell) depends on the specific simulation scenario and on the related goals.

In general, in the definition of SCA space, different solutions can be adopted to represent agents' environment. For example, physical constrains such as obstacles could be represented by adjacent nodes occupied by unmoveable, inactive agents, but one could also choose simply not to represent them. In other words they can

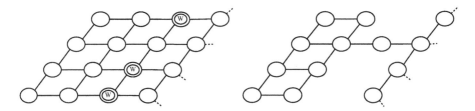

Fig. 3. Two possible ways to model a wall. The one on the left does not block field diffusion.

be represented by gaps of the discrete structure and by the absence of arcs among nodes, as shown in Figure 3. The difference between the two approaches is that in the first case the occupied node does not stop field diffusion. Thus this choice is less suited to represent hard obstacles, such as walls, which should not only prevent movement of agents but also the diffusion of signals.

3.2   Definition of Active Elements of the Environment and Field Types

As previously introduced, in this framework we assume that specific elements of the environment can be perceived as reference points influencing (or even determining) the movement of pedestrians. The SCA model provides a simple mean of generating at-a-distance effects that can be exploited to generate attraction or repulsion effects: the field diffusion-perception-action mechanism. However, only an agent can be the source of a field, and thus the proposed methodology requires the reification of objects or abstractions exploited to generate attraction/repulsion effects as immobile agents that are able to emit fields.

In this phase active objects in the environment have to be selected, and field types have to be assigned. Attention must be paid not only to physical objects of the environment which constraint agent movement (and that can thus be considered as reference points), but also to objects that somehow transmit conceptual information (e.g. exit signs or indications). This phase comprises two main operations:

– *selection of active elements*: the objects of the environment that are considered relevant for our simulation have to be identified. An element is considered relevant if, by a process of abstraction from reality, it can be considered as representing a target, or if it is possible to assume that it does exert an influence on the individuals that act in the environment;
– *assignment and design of field types*: the type of the fields emitted by the objects must be specified, in terms of emission intensity, diffusion and composition function, in relation to the desired extent of influence.

It must be noted that a field represents a signal and *per se* it does not imply an effect on agents' behaviours, in fact the possible reaction to the perception of a signal is provided by the agent type specification; moreover the actual behaviour of an agent is influenced by its current state. In this way, it is possible to model an environment as a source of different indications that are exploited in different ways by different agents to determine their paths. For instance, the window of a shop could be modelled as the source of a field diffusing outside the shop; such a field could cause a movement towards the shop for agents which consider interesting the represented goods, but could also be completely ignored by other agents. Moreover, different fields can be spread over the environment, and thus agents may perceive them and combine their effects according to a private criteria for action selection. In this way agents are not provided with a sort of script specifying their movement paths, a predefined map, or in general a strict behavioural specification, but they are provided a simple mean for evaluating the available actions against their current attitude in a more autonomous way.

In order to effectively exploit this approach to generate agent movement, the number, position and diffusion range of these fields generated by active objects must be carefully designed. This activity is strictly related to the definition of the spatial abstraction: first of all it defines the positions that can be occupied by active objects, and moreover it deeply influences the definition of field types (which in turn provide the specification of diffusion functions) and the choice on field emission intensity. In fact, the diffusion of fields is guided by the spatial structure of the environment, and the set of sites involved in a diffusion operation is determined by the emission intensity, the diffusion function for the related field type, and by the morphology of the space. This activity is strongly dependant on domain and simulation specific factors, so a general strategy for the choice of field types and active objects, their placement in spatial abstraction of the environment, and the definition of their parameters cannot be given. However, specific modules of the SCA platform, supporting a visual definition of active elements of the simulation environment, is currently being designed.

3.3   Definition of Mobile Agents

Once the spatial abstraction has been defined, and the active elements of the environment and the related fields have been specified, the third phase of the methodology is to define the behaviour of the pedestrian. The model allows to define heterogenous agents thanks to the notion of agent type, which comprises the definition of related state, perceptive capabilities and behavioural specification. However, the modelled behaviour can be quite complex, as an individual may be endowed with several distinct attitudes towards movement and action selection that are activated in different contexts.

The behaviour of an agent type can thus be segmented in relevant states. The more complex is the behaviour that we want to capture, the higher will be the number of states that an agent can assume. This definition can be summarized in the two phases below:

- *definition of agent type's states*: in this phase of the modelling it must be established the number of states that each agent can assume. Each state represents diverse priorities, and a different attitude of the agent. For each state must be determined the field emissions of the agent type (i.e. the influence of agents of this type towards other entities in the system), and the sensitivity to fields emitted by other agents. In addition to these elements, that are required for every SCA agent type, this methodology also provides the definition of the utility value for every field type, as a measure of the relevance of the perception of this field on agent's choices on its own movement;

– *definition of conditions for states transition*: the change of the state of an agent is related to the perception of a specific condition in its current context that determines a transition from a movement attitude towards a different one. These conditions must thus be carefully defined and modelled by means of a *react* or a *trigger* operation.

To exemplify these phases, the case of a student moving in a University will be considered. Different behaviours will be activated according to the current state and goals of the related agent: a student situated in a lecture hall during a lesson is not sensitive to fields emitted by doors. By changing state, at the end of the lesson, the student may become sensitive (and more precisely) attracted by, exit doors. To deal with such a composite kind of behaviour, the methodology exploits specific agents states to partition their behavioural specifications. According to the model, the state of an agent determines its current perceptive capabilities, but it also influences its behaviour. In fact it can be included in the preconditions of actions that compose the behavioural specification $Action_\tau$ for agent type τ. In the model, $Action_\tau$ is made up of a flat set of actions and an action selection strategy. In this framework, we propose to reify the possible attitudes of that type of agent as specific states and to specify the actions that can be selected only for agents in that state. For instance, an agent related to the previously introduced student would require three states: GoingToLesson, AttendingLesson, GoingHome.

In these states its perceptive capabilities can be differentiated, but also its preferences on possible available moves. This can be modelled by means of a *utility function* which computes a sort of "desirability" value for every site in which the agent might move, in relation to its current state. Utility functions represent a flexible mean of combining different aspects influencing the selection of actions [12] and in this specific case these aspects are represented by different fields. In fact, fields are related to entities, either mobile (i.e. other pedestrian) or immobile (e.g. doors), that influence mobile agents' motion in a different way according to their context. It is thus necessary to specify, for each agent state, what is the impact of the perception of each field type on the desirability of the related place. The overall utility of a place is the aggregation of all these influences, that can have a positive, negative or null impact on the total value. The basic agent strategy for the choice on single movement action is thus to select the adjacent free place with highest utility value. According to the specific scenario, the possibility to remain still could be considered acceptable, penalized or even not allowed.

Before the conclusion of this paragraph we must specify that the specification of utility values and the action modelling are not properly phases, but are activities that permeate the whole process of the construction of a simulation. The focus of these activities is the constant revision of the simulation (a process that in some cases is referred to as simulation calibration) in relation to realism considerations and to the comparison of the simulation results with data collected by means of empirical observations.

3.4   Specific Simulation Configuration

The configuration for an experiment in a specific simulation scenario, not only in the case of crowd simulation, is a crucial phase that has to be performed carefully. In particular the effort of conceptualization carried out in the previous passages is wasted unless a realistic configuration for the experiment is defined. In fact, the data that are obtained through the execution of simulations are obviously strongly dependant on the starting conditions, as well as on the modelling of the simulated reality.

To configure a crowd simulation means to set the following parameters:

- *agents number and starting positions*: the number of the mobile agents that will populate the simulation must be decided in relation to the crowd scenery that is being represented; their positions must also be specified;
- *agents' initial states*: the initial state of every agent has to be specified. The decision to assign to an agent an initial state or another is taken in relation to the goals of the specific simulation: in fact, this parameter determines the initial movement attitude of the agent in the environment;
- *field emission intensity*: field emission intensity is a parameter that allows to modulate stronger or weaker influence effects; the choice on this parameter (together with the diffusion functions to be adopted for various field types) also determines the extent of the effects. The possibility to tune these parameters is a key factor in the definition of specific effects, both at individual level (e.g. amplifying or attenuating the field emission intensity of a specific agent) as well as on the collective scale (for instance modifying the intensity of fields related to elements of the environment).

3.5   Definition of Monitored Parameters and Specification of Monitoring Mechanisms

This phase represents a formal statement of what is the goal of the simulation, a precise specification of what has to be observed and how. When simulating crowd dynamics in an evacuation scenario, the average number of turns required for agents to exit from a room is a crucial parameter to be monitored, while it can be of no interest when the goal of simulation is to observe the behaviour of pedestrian in a shopping centre. Other possible observable parameters could be average crowd density, average (or maximum) number of people waiting in a queue, occurrence of specific events, and many others dependant on the specific simulation context.

The variety of possibly monitored parameters, and thus also the number and heterogeneity of distinct monitoring mechanisms, does not allow to define specific guidelines for this phase.

4   A Case Study: The Underground Station

An underground station is an environment where various crowd behaviours take place. In such an environment passengers' behaviours are difficult to predict, because the crowd dynamics emerges from single interactions between passengers, and between single passengers and parts of the environment, such as signals (e.g. current stop indicator), doors, seats and handles. The behaviour of passengers changes noticeably in relation to the different priorities that characterize each phase of their trips. That means for instance that passengers close to each other may display very different behaviours because of their distinct aims in that moment. In a crowd dynamic behaviours of the singles can also constitute a hindrance for the purpose of someone else. Passengers on board may have to get off and thus try to reach for the door, while other are instead looking for a seat or standing beside a handle. Moreover when trains stop and doors open very complex crowd dynamics happen, as people that have to get on the train have to allow the exit of passengers that are getting off. Passengers have to match their own priority with the obstacles of the environment, with the intentions of other passengers, and with implicit behavioural rules that govern the social interaction in those kind of transit stations, in a complex mixture of competition over a shared resource and collaboration to avoid stall situations. Given the complexity of the overall scenario, we decided to focus on a specific portion of this environment in which some of the most complex patterns of interaction take place: the part of platform in presence of a standing wagon from which some passengers are attempting to get off while other waiting travellers are trying to get on.

However the value of the realized simulation is not the main goal of this work, as our main aim is to show how the proposed methodology was applied in this case study. The goal of a complete simulation system in this context would be the possibility to support expert users in the detection of critical problems of the structure of the station, as bottlenecks, wrong disposition of the exits and so on, by offering the modelling instruments able to capture interaction between passengers and the environment, simultaneously on board and on the waiting platform. Such a tool would be of great aid for the prediction of security measure in situations of overcrowding or in presence of an unexpected hazard.

To build up our simulation we made some behavioural assumptions, now we will make some brief examples of the kind of behaviours we wanted to capture. Passengers that do not have to get off at a train stop tend to remain still, if they do not constitute obstacle to the passengers that are descending. Passengers will move only to give way to descending passenger, to reach some seat that has became available, or to reach a better position like places at the side of the doors or close to the handles. On the other hand in very crowded situations it often happens that people that do not have to get off can constitute an obstacle to the descent of other passengers, and they "are forced to" get off and wait for the moment to get on the wagon again. Passenger that have to get off have a tendency to go around still agents to find their route towards the exit, if it is possible. Passengers on the platform enter the station from the ingress points (station entrances) and tend to distribute along the threshold line while waiting

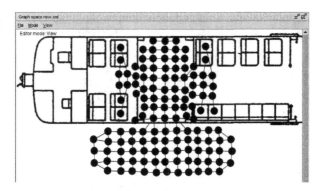

Fig. 4. Discretization of a portion of the environment for the underground station scenario

for a train. Once the train is almost stopped they identify the entrance that is closer to them and move towards it. If they perceive some passenger bound to get off, they first let them get off and then get on the wagon.

4.1   Environment Abstraction: An Underground Station

To build an environment suitable for SCA platform, first of all we need to define a discrete structure representing the actual space in which the simulation is set. In our case study we started from an available diagram of an underground wagon. A discrete abstraction of this map was defined, devoting to each node the space generally occupied by one standing person; as shown in Figure 4 this activity is supported by software. Arcs connecting nodes are not necessarily uniform across the space: in fact we decided to allow some specific movement opportunities to agents in critical positions of the environment. However a thorough analysis of the effects of this kind of heterogeneity in the spatial structure on field diffusion is needed, and will be the object of future works.

4.2   Active Elements of the Environment: Train and Station

In our simulation fields are generated by elements of the environment but also by agents that represent passengers. We identified the following objects as active elements of the environment: *Exits*, *Doors*, *Seats* and *Handles* (see Figure 5 for their disposition).

Now we give a brief description of the kind of fields that those static agents emit. Station exits emit fixed fields, constant in intensity and in emission, that will be exploited by agents headed towards the exit of the station. Exits could also constitute entry points for agents that arrive on the platform. Agent-doors emit another field which can guide passengers that have to get off towards the platform, and the same field can guide passengers that are on the platform and are bound to get in the wagon. Seats may have two states: occupied and free. In the second state they emit a field that indicates their presence. An analogous

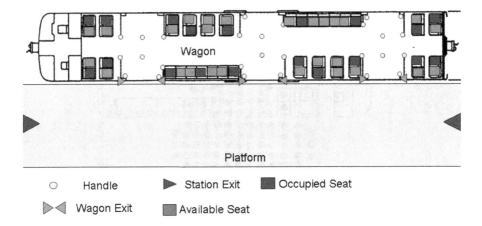

| ○ | Handle | ▶ | Station Exit | ■ | Occupied Seat |
| ▶◀ | Wagon Exit | ■ | Available Seat | | |

Fig. 5. Immobile active elements of the environment defined for the underground station scenario

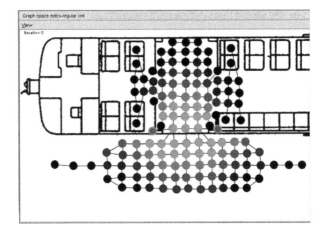

Fig. 6. Extension of fields diffused by door agents in the underground station scenario

field is emitted by handles, which however are sources of fields characterized by a minor intensity. As shown in Figure 6, the positioning of field sources and the definition of parameters for field emission is partly supported by a software module.

4.3 Mobile Entities: Passengers

We have identified the following states for agent of type passengers: *waiting* (w), *passenger* (p), *get-off* (g), *seated* (s), *exiting* (e). In relation to its state, an agent will be sensitive to some fields, and not to others, and attribute different relevance to the perceived signals. In this way, the changing of state will determine a change of priorities. A state diagram for passenger agents is shown in Figure 7. State w is

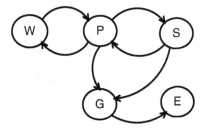

Fig. 7. A diagram showing various states of agent type passenger

associated to an agent that is waiting to enter in the wagon. In this state agents perceive the fields generated by the doors as attractive, but they also perceive as repulsive the fields generated by passengers that are getting off, in other words those in state g. In state w the agent "ignores" (is not sensitive to) the fields generated by other active elements of the environment, such as exits' attractive fields, chairs attractive field and so on. Once inside the wagon, the agent in state w changes its state in p (passenger), through a trigger function activated by the perception of the maximum intensity of field generated by agent-door type. Agent in state passenger is attracted by fields generated by seats and handles, and repulsed by fields related to passengers that are getting off. It does not have any sensitivity for the attraction field of the doors. In state g the agent will instead emit a field warning other agents of its presence, while it is attracted by fields generated by the doors. Once passed through the wagon door, or in immediate proximity (detected by means of specific thresholds on related field intensity), the agent in state g changes its state to e (exiting) and its priority will become to find the exits of the station. The agent in state e is thus attracted by fields related to exits.

Table 1 summarizes the sensitivity of the passenger to various fields and it also sketches a first attribution of the utility of the presence of these field types on empty nodes considered as destination of a transport action. In particular, cells provide the indication of the fact that the related field is perceived as attractive or repulsive and the priority level (i.e. relevance) associated to that field type.

Table 1. The table shows, for every agent state, the relevance of perceived signals

State	Exits	Doors	Seats	Handles	Presence	Exit press.
W (getting on)	not perc.	attr. (2)	not perc.	not perc.	rep. (3)	rep. (1)
P (on board)	not perc.	not perc.	attr. (1)	attr. (2)	rep. (3)	rep. (2)
G (getting off)	not perc.	attr. (1)	not perc.	not perc.	rep. (2)	not perc.
S (seated)	not perc.	attr. (1)*	not perc.	not perc.	not perc.	not perc.
E (exiting)	attr. (1)	not perc.	not perc.	not perc.	rep. (2)	not perc.

*The door signal also conveys the current stop indication.

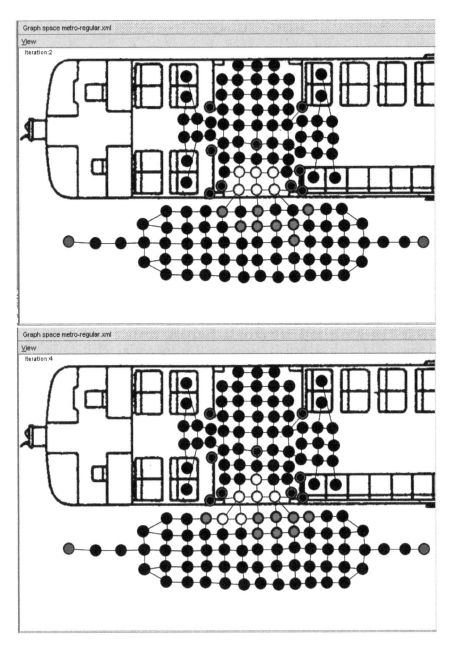

Fig. 8. Two screenshots of the underground simulation. On the first one light gray agents are inside the train and going to get off, while dark agents are standing outside and are going to get on. On the second, the latter have made some rooms for the former to get off.

All passengers except those in state g emit a presence field that generally has a repulsive effect, but a lesser one with respect to the "exit pressure" generated by agents in get-off state.

4.4   Preliminary Results and Lessons Learned

A sample simulation based on this case study was designed and implemented exploiting the MMASS framework [13] (please note that SCA is a particular class of MMASS model): only a subset of the overall introduced model was implemented, and more precisely active objects of the environment and passenger agents in state w, g, e, p. Figure 8 shows a screen-shot of this simulation system, in which waiting agents move to generate room for passenger agents which are going to get off the train.

The system is synchronous, meaning that every agent performs one single action per turn; the turn duration is about one third of second of simulated time.

The goal of this small experimentation was to qualitatively evaluate the modelling of the scenario and the developed simulator. The execution and analysis of several simulations showed that the behaviour of the agents in the environment is consistent with a realistic scenario, and fits with our expectations. In particular, we executed over 50 simulations in the same starting configuration, which provides 6 passengers located on a underground train in state g (i.e. willing to get off), and 8 agents that are outside the train in state w (i.e. waiting to get on). This small simulation campaign is motivated by the fact that an agent having two or more possible destination sites characterized by the same utility value makes a non deterministic choice. In all simulations the agents achieved their goals (i.e. get on the train or get out of the station) in a number of turns between 40 and 80, with an average of around 55 turns.

Nonetheless we noticed some undesired transient effects and more precisely:

- oscillations and "forth and back" movements;
- static forms providing "groups" facing themselves for a few turns, until the groups dispersed because of the movement of a peripheral element.

These phenomena, which represent minor glitches under the described initial conditions, could lead to problems in case of high pedestrian density in the simulated environment. This points out the need of additional mechanisms correcting the movement utility. In particular, some possible improvements to the basic movement utility mechanisms are:

- introduce a notion of agent *facing*: the SCA model does not provide an explicit facing for agents because is not always relevant or even applicable (consider for instance the modelling of immune system cells [14]); however in this specific simulation scenario this is a relevant factor for agents' choices on their movement. Instead of modifying the general model, a possible way of introducing this notion is to allow agents to keep track of their previous positions, in order to understand if a certain movement is a step back. The utility of this kind of movement should be penalized, in order to discourage this choice;

- *penalize immobility*: in order to avoid stall situations, or simplify the solution of this kind of situation, an agent should generally move, unless it has attained the goal for a movement attitude (i.e. agent state). To obtain this effect, the memory of the past position, introduced in the previous point, could be exploited to penalize the utility of the site currently occupied by the agent whenever it was also its previous position.

While these correctives can be easily modelled and implemented, to apply this approach to problems in larger scale scenarios, such as those related to malls or multi-floor buildings, it could be necessary to introduce some additional elements for the specification of agents' behaviours. In particular, in order to endow agents with the possibility to select in a more autonomous way those signals that are relevant to direct their movement, it could be necessary to introduce some form of abstract map of the environment. However the introduced methodology is focused on supporting the modelling of situations in which there is a strong focus on specific spots of a spatial structure, such as a hall or a part of a building floor, in specific situations (e.g. evacuation).

5   Conclusions and Future Developments

This work has presented the first proposal of a methodology for the modelling of crowds through the SCA model. The main phases of this methodology were introduced, and in particular the first two provide the definition of an "active environment", able to support simple reactive agents in the navigation of its spatial structure according to their behavioural specification. A case study related to a complex modelling scenario was introduced in order to show how the proposed methodology can be applied in a concrete case study.

Future developments are aimed at refining both the methodology and the MMASS platform, in order to better support the modeller/user, in the construction of complex simulation scenarios. In particular the platform provides basic user interfaces and modules aimed at supporting the definition of an active environment, and parameters for specific simulations, but improvements are under development. Moreover specific libraries for active objects and paradigmatic pedestrian behaviours could be defined after a thorough analysis of psycho/sociological studies of crowd behaviors.

Another part of the project in which this work has been developed provides the generation of effective forms of visualization of simulation dynamics to simplify its analysis by non experts in the simulated phenomenon. In particular, the developed simulator can be integrated with a 3D modelling and rendering engine (more details on this integration can be found in [15]), and a sample screenshot of the animation of the simulation dynamics is shown in Figure 9. A more through analysis of modifications to the basic utility approach that must be introduced to correct minor glitches in agents' movement (i.e. oscillations) is particularly relevant in this case. The analysis of the most suited mechanisms to correct these issues are thus object of current and future work.

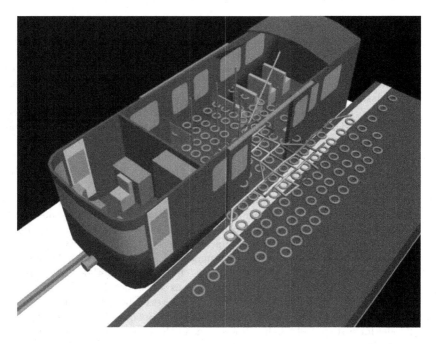

Fig. 9. A screenshot of the 3D modelling of the simulation dynamics

Acknowledgements

This work is preliminary result of the Social Mobile Entities in Silico (SMES) project, and was partly funded by the New and Old Mobility Analysis and Design for the Information Society (NOMADIS) laboratory, in the context of the Quality of Life in the Information Society (QUA_SI) multi-disciplinary research programme in Information Society.

References

1. Bandini, S., Mauri, G., Vizzari, G.: Supporting Action-at-a-distance in Situated Cellular Agents. Fundamenta Informatic Fundamenta Informaticae **69** (2006) 251–271
2. Helbing, D.: A Mathematical Model for the Behavior of Pedestrians. Behavioral Science (1991) 298–310
3. Schadschneider, A., Kirchner, A., Nishinari, K.: CA Approach to Collective Phenomena in Pedestrian Dynamics. In Bandini, S., Chopard, B., Tomassini, M., eds.: Cellular Automata, 5th International Conference on Cellular Automata for Research and Industry, ACRI 2002. Volume 2493 of Lecture Notes in Computer Science, Springer (2002) 239–248
4. Dijkstra, J., Jessurun, J., Timmermans, H.J.P.: A Multi-Agent Cellular Automata Model of Pedestrian Movement. In: Pedestrian and Evacuation Dynamics. Springer-Verlag (2001) 173–181

5. Helbing, D., Schweitzer, F., Keltsch, J., Molnár, P.: Active Walker Model for the Formation of Human and Animal Trail systems. Physical Review E **56** (1997) 2527–2539

6. Bandini, S., Manzoni, S., Vizzari, G.: Situated Cellular Agents: a Model to Simulate Crowding Dynamics. IEICE Transactions on Information and Systems: Special Issues on Cellular Automata **E87-D** (2004) 669–676

7. Zambonelli, F., Wooldridge, M.J., Jennings, N.R.: Developing Multiagent Systems: The GAIA Methodology. ACM Transactions on Software Engineering and Methodology **12** (2003) 317–370

8. Pavón, J., Gómez-Sanz, J.J.: Agent Oriented Software Engineering with INGENIAS. In Marík, V., Müller, J., Pechoucek, M., eds.: CEEMAS. Volume 2691 of Lecture Notes in Computer Science, Springer-Verlag (2003) 394–403

9. Omicini, A.: SODA: Societies and Infrastructures in the Analysis and Design of Agent-based Systems. In Ciancarini, P., Wooldridge, M., eds.: Agent-Oriented Software Engineering: First International Workshop, AOSE 2000. Volume 1957 of Lecture Notes in Computer Science, Springer-Verlag (2001) 185–193

10. Campos, A.M.C., Canuto, A.M.P., Fernandes, J.H.C.: Towards a Methodology for Developing Agent-based Simulations: The MASim Methodology. In: 3rd international Joint Conference on Autonomous Agents and Multiagent Systems (AAMAS 2004), Washington, DC, USA, ACM Press (2004) 1494–1495

11. Bandini, S., Manzoni, S., Simone, C.: Dealing with Space in Multi–Agent Systems: a Model for Situated MAS. In: Proceedings of the first international joint conference on Autonomous agents and multiagent systems, ACM Press (2002) 1183–1190

12. Russell, S.J., Norvig, P.: Artificial Intelligence: A Modern Approach (2nd ed.). Prentice Hall (2002)

13. Bandini, S., Manzoni, S., Vizzari, G.: Towards a Specification and Execution Environment for Simulations Based on MMASS: Managing At–a–distance Interaction. In Trappl, R., ed.: Proceedings of the 17th European Meeting on Cybernetics and Systems Research, Austrian Society for Cybernetic Studies (2004) 636–641

14. Bandini, S., Celada, F., Manzoni, S., Puzone, R., Vizzari, G.: Modelling the Immune System with Situated Agents. In: International Workshop on Natural and Artificial Immune Systems. Lecture Notes in Computer Science, Springer–Verlag (2006) (in press)

15. Bandini, S., Manzoni, S., Vizzari, G.: Crowd Modelling and Simulation: Towards 3D Visualization. In: Recent Advances in Design and Decision Support Systems in Architecture and Urban Planning, Kluwer Academic Publisher (2004) 161–175

QoS Management in MANETs Using Norm-Governed Agent Societies

Jeremy Pitt[1], Pallapa Venkataram[2], and Abe Mamdani[1]

[1] Intelligent Systems & Networks Group,
Dept. of Electrical & Electronic Engineering,
Imperial College London, London, SW7 2BT, UK
[2] Protocol Engineering & Technology Unit,
Dept. of Electrical Communication Eng.,
Indian Institute of Science, Bangalore 560012, India

Abstract. Mobile ad-hoc networks (MANETs) are self-created and self-organized by a collection of mobile nodes, interconnected by multi-hop wireless paths in a strictly peer-to-peer fashion. Such networks offer unique benefits and versatility with respect to bandwidth spatial re-use, intrinsic fault tolerance, and low-cost rapid deployment. However, Quality of Service (QoS) provisioning to applications running in such networks is intrinsically difficult. In this paper, we consider a QoS framework for MANETs which monitors network resources and application requirements, and feeds information to agents, who coordinate efficient resource allocation on a social basis (in this case, decision-making according to normative policies and protocols). Thus we propose a framework for QoS management in MANETs which converges network-centric events, metrics and parameters with organizational intelligence offered by norm-governed multi-agent systems, as a step towards realising a vision of *ubiquitous networking*.

1 Introduction

Mobile ad-hoc networks (MANETs) are self-created and self-organized by a collection of mobile nodes, interconnected by multi-hop wireless paths in a strictly peer-to-peer fashion. Such networks offer unique benefits and versatility with respect to bandwidth spatial re-use, intrinsic fault tolerance, and low-cost rapid deployment. However, Quality of Service (QoS) provisioning to multimedia applications running in such networks is intrinsically difficult, since the dynamic network topology renders centralised solutions based on complete and perfect information out of scope.

In this paper we propose a framework for efficient Quality of Service (QoS) management in Mobile Ad Hoc Networks (MANETs). The framework consists of two main components: underneath, the Multimedia Network Support Platform (MNSP), which is an advanced multimedia transport service for transmission and reception in mobile multimedia application, and, running over MNSP, a norm-governed multi-agent system (MAS) which effectively constitutes a deliberative assembly. The MNSP communicates information about network events and

O. Dikenelli, M.-P. Gleizes, and A. Ricci (Eds.): ESAW 2005, LNAI 3963, pp. 221–240, 2006.
© Springer-Verlag Berlin Heidelberg 2006

behaviour to the MAS, the MAS makes decisions according to norm-governed policies and protocols, and these decisions are communicated to the MNSP for implementation.

The paper is structured as follows. In Section 2 we describe in more detail the particular features and challenges of MANETs for QoS provisioning of multimedia services and applications. In Section 3 we discuss why norm-governed multi-agent systems (open agent societies) are an appropriate technology for addressing these features and challenges. In Section 4 we present the architecture of our proposed QoS management framework, including discussion of the MNSP layer and the agents layer, and in Section 5 we give an example of a session-sharing mechanism which can be addressed in this framework. These sections collectively motivate the application domain (ad hoc networks), the specific problem (QoS provisioning), and the proposed solution (a two layer QoS framework). For this paper, Section 6 then gives a correspondingly detailed consideration of the norm-governed protocols for enacting this solution in the agents layer of the framework. Finally, we conclude with a discussion of some areas of further research, and comment that this proposed framework, which converges network-centric events, metrics and parameters with organizational intelligence offered by norm-governed multi-agent systems, has significant potential for QoS management in MANETs. In particular it can serve as a contribution towards realising a vision of *ubiquitous networking*.

2   MANETs and Multimedia

Wireless networking technologies, as well as the widespread use of mobile devices such as PDAs, cell phones, and laptops, are making pervasive (or ubiquitous) networking a reality. Many applications such as email and micro-browsers can now successfully run in mobile wireless networks. However, while issues such as ad hoc routing [1] and security [5] have been well researched, the issue of QoS for mobile multimedia over MANETs needs further consideration. There are three main sources of problems: *mobility, wireless-ness, and multimedia* [24]. It is well-known that multimedia contents, especially audio and video, require a much higher network bandwidth. The topology of mobile ad-hoc networks is likely to be highly dynamic, due to unpredicted mobility of network nodes and consequent dynamic topology of the network itself. The limited bandwidth of wireless channels between nodes further exacerbates the situation, as message exchange over-heads of any QoS-provisioning algorithms must be kept to a minimum. In addition, other wireless and mobility features cause further problems, such as varying bandwidth, variable bit error rate, possibly asymmetric connectivity, and unexpected quality degrade during handoff.

For smooth running of mobile multimedia application four QoS parameters: *bandwidth, cost, delay bounds, and security*, need to be appropriately set (or allocated) so that throughout the application the end-user gets the data as per his/her requirement. These factors are the important parameters for making adaptation decisions in MANETs. Among these four parameters, bandwidth is the most important measure and is usually monitored in any type of application. Cost and security factors are rarely mentioned in literature about mobile applications, and it is difficult to measure them too. Delay bound is another important measure, especially for mobile multimedia applications, since streaming media is very sensitive to latency. Besides bandwidth and latency, error rate is also a very important measure for mobile multimedia applications because multimedia compression is very sensitive to errors.

In order to achieve QoS guarantee for mobile multimedia applications in MANETs, at least three network measurements, namely bandwidth, latency and error rates, need to be monitored. To precisely represent these network quality measures in applications, a standard measure of application-level data quality for mobile multimedia applications is also required, as well as a mapping scheme between this application measure and the network measures. For example, the degree to which a data item used by a mobile client matches a reference copy, is used as a measure of data quality. It is mapped to the available bandwidth of a MANET.

Since network conditions may change very quickly in MANETs, to measure these parameters we need network monitoring methods for mobile multimedia applications to be able to detect changes as fast as possible. Active monitoring, in addition to competing with applications for scarce bandwidth, causes large delay to get results, therefore it is inappropriate for agile network monitoring.

Besides network monitoring, we need also some special requirements for mobile multimedia applications. For example, streaming media applications require timely delivery of data and use protocols like RTP and RTSP [19]. Therefore, many TCP-based network monitoring techniques cannot be applied to streaming media applications. The RTP Control Protocol (RTCP) can be used to get feedback including packet loss and jitter information from the receivers of an RTP media stream. However, packet loss or jitter can be found in the feedback from a MANET, caused by either congestion or error in the radio links. If the sender cannot distinguish congestion from error, it may apply inappropriate QoS adaptation methods and the problem will remain.

Some of the key requirements of QoS adaptation for mobile multimedia applications are: automated data format adaptation without user intervention, graceful quality degradation, seamless handoffs across networks during roaming, and high QoS with low jitter, delay, and guaranteed bandwidth. To fulfil these requirements, a number of different approaches can be applied to achieve QoS adaptation for mobile multimedia. Given the nature of the problem, some attempts have been made to deploy mobile agents for solving these dynamically adaptable problems [14, 15]. This is the basis of the multimedia network support platform (MNSP) [25].

However, as with routing, QoS provisioning critically depends on cooperation between nodes. However, it is possible that some nodes can behave 'selfishly' and drop other applications' traffic in order to preserve its own multimedia service and application requirements and/or resources (cf. [27]). Since nodes in a MANET communicate on a peer-to-peer basis and operate without a centralised authority (which could monitor, detect and prevent/punish 'selfish' behaviour), we need a distributed approach to achieving a 'fair' allocation of resources. Naturally agents are a compelling paradigm for this style of distributed problem solving, but in this case the notions of 'selfishness', 'fairness', 'judgement' and 'punishment' are all socio-legal concepts determined relative to a 'code of conduct' (which presumably a node agrees to when it joins a MANET). Therefore we also require a conceptual understanding of agents at a higher level abstraction: in this case, we use the abstraction offered by norm-governed multi-agent systems.

3   Norm-Governed Multi-agent Systems

A software agent is generally considered to be a software process embedded in an electronic environment, which encapsulates a state, reacts to changes in the environment depending on that state, and asynchronously communicates with other embedded agents. A multi-agent system is a useful design abstraction which focuses on the *logical* distribution of responsibility and control (as opposed to the *physical* distribution of resources and methods), interoperability between heterogeneously designed components and composition of independent services, interaction at the knowledge level (rather than mere data transfer), and autonomic policies (i.e. policies which deal with recovery from errors or other unexpected events).

A norm-governed multi-agent system refers to any set of interacting agents whose behaviour is regulated by norms, where a norm is a rule which prescribes organizational concepts like permission, obligation, sanction, and so on [11]. The advantages of norm-governed systems are the abilities to provide formal (logical) definitions of responsibility and control, to represent interoperability in terms of external, executable specifications, and to reason about non-ideal states of the system (i.e. the system state as it is, not as it should be), and so facilitate self-repair.

Any set of networked nodes with a dynamic topology that features distributed functionality, asynchronous communication decentralised command and control, partial knowledge, local decision-making, delegated responsibility and autonomous action can be regarded as an instance of a multi-agent system. These are all general features of mobile ad hoc networks. Therefore it is reasonable to consider an agent-based approach to MANETs.

There are however three further characteristics of MANETs. Firstly, each component is opaque (there is no direct access to its internal state), so there is no notion of global utility (components may act in their own self-interest), and behaviours and interactions are unpredictable in advance. For these reasons, it may be that a component in a MANET fails to comply with the system specifications, either by design, by accident or from necessity. Secondly, because of the dynamic, open and even volatile nature of the system, the design-time specifications may need to be modified at run-time; and thirdly, because of the complex and unpredictable nature of the system, the system specifications may only be partially given at design-time, and the components themselves complete the specifications at run-time. Dealing with non-compliant behaviour, self-modifying code and incomplete specifications can be addressed by the norm-governed approach, where appropriate behaviour can be stipulated using concepts stemming from the study of legal and social systems: e.g. permissions, obligations and other normative relations such as power, right and entitlement. Therefore it is reasonable to consider a *norm-governed* multi-agent system for MANETs.

What we propose here is to converge 'heavyweight' agents, which operate in the domain of norms and 'codes of conduct' *about* QoS provision, with the multimedia network support platform (MNSP) whose processes operate in the domain of network-centric events and parameters in *providing* QoS itself. This is the basis of our QoS Management Framework presented in the next section.

4   QoS Management Framework

4.1   Design Challenges

To build agents for QoS management in MANETs that should combine their cognitive and reactive abilities for QoS management tasks. Furthermore, designed agents should be self-adaptive (i.e., capable of playing several roles). Such an agent-based system will provide automated provisioning of QoS that relies on an intelligent analysis of network QoS events and a corresponding automatic reconfiguration of agents in order to ensure guaranteed QoS (cf. [20, 26]). Effectively we are trying to solve a type of dynamic consensus problem in MANETs (cf. [7]).

In order to meet system's functional requirements, modelling of multi-agent system for QoS management is faced with several design challenges. The provisioning and support of adequate QoS for a large and diverse user population (running many different applications with different wireless devices) is not a simple process. Agents should track the QoS distribution of observed flows, compare the QoS-related parameters of real-time flows against the negotiated QoS, detect and locate possible QoS degradation, and then tune and reconfigure network resources accordingly to sustain the delivered QoS. In order to accomplish that goal a multi-agent system has to use QoS distribution monitoring that provides information about QoS characteristics experienced by the real-time flow in different network segments. In contrast to conventional end-to-end QoS monitoring, QoS distribution monitoring is able not only to detect possible QoS degradation, but also to provide more information for locating and predicting that degradation.

The designed agents for QoS management should satisfy different kinds of service level agreements/policies that define qualitative and/or quantitative characteristics of QoS between service providers and application users as well as among service providers themselves. One of the main issues regarding the implementation of service level agreements is the diversity of used architectures, technologies and protocols in MANETs as well as their continuous change. It is evident that such a trend in development of communication networks makes it difficult to guarantee agreed QoS to a user application.

4.2 MANET Structure

The proposed multi-agent system based QoS framework assumes that the structure (topology) of the MANET is that it has been clustered and each cluster has a *Cluster-Head (CH)* to administer the activities of the cluster. Some of the assumptions are:

- The CH is selected based on its rich network resources availability and its communication range covers all the hosts in the cluster.
- The CH in the set of clusters effectively provide the MANET backbone, other nodes in range of more than one CH are gateways between clusters.
- If the CH moves out of the cluster or is running short of resources, another host will be selected as CH [9].
- The CH is aware of all the applications running on all the hosts of the applications.
- The multi-agent system based QoS framework is implemented on the CH.

Figure 1 shows a cluster of MANET with a cluster-head (CH) and four hosts. The CH supports different sets of multimedia applications running on all its hosts but their data pass through the cluster-head of the cluster, CH.

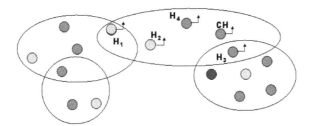

Fig. 1. MANET with Clusters; Cluster with Hosts

Note that one of these assumptions, the appointment of the Cluster Head, is a classical problem for norm-governed systems. In particular, the appointment of a node to Cluster Head is a role assignment, which if correctly performed assigns certain powers, permissions and obligations to the node (by virtue of it occupying this role, cf. [2]).

4.3 Architecture of the QoS Framework

The multi-agent based QoS framework consists of two layers: the top layer is a a norm-governed multi-agent system (MAS), which runs over the bottom layer which is the multimedia network support platform (MNSP) [25] (itself running over a modified TCP (M-TCP) protocol, which we do not consider further here).

In the top layer, one process for each host, there are the socially-organized 'intelligent' agent who coordinate their activities according to the norms of the society and the needs of the applications running on their respective host. In operation, the Cluster Head creates an agent which is called the chair-process (CHCP), for reasons which will be discussed below, and initialises a number of processes for running the communications between the MAS-layer and the MNSP-layer (see below).

The bottom layer, the MNSP, is an intelligent multimedia transport service for transmission and reception in mobile multimedia applications like VoIP and video conferencing, Education-on-Demand (EoD), etc., but can also be used as a general service for a multimedia market place. Services offered include specialised Video-on-Demand (VoD), hypervideo, video-rating, conventional publishing services (infography, animation, design assembling, etc.,) and electronic commerce on virtual gallery and education.

The MNSP consists of five components which runs at the cluster-head (CH). Each of these components is designed with Intelligent Network based concepts and real time communication features. These components are: *Synchronization API, Quality of Service (QoS) API, Call Admission Control (CAC) API, Buffer Management (BM) API and Playout system.* These components allow the MNSP to support in implementation the decisions taken by the agents in the MAS-layer.

Communication between the MAS-layer and the MNSP-layer is through a number of lightweight processes, some of which are 'static' and some of which are mobile (and can either be implemented as intelligent packets or mobile 'agents'). These processes include:

- Resource-monitoring process (*RM-proc*), is a static process which monitors regularly the host's multimedia applications' requirements and reports to the Cluster Head RM-Proc;
- Session-Registry process (*SR-proc*) is a static process which registers all the sessions established on all the hosts of the cluster;
- Network Status collection process (*NStat-proc*), which is a mobile process[1] [14, 15] which visits all the hosts and collects network status information, including congestion, data loss, delays, etc. for a specified duration;
- Request-collection process (*Req-proc*), which are mobile processes that deliver the resource requests from the hosts. These include the requirements for immediate needs and predicted requirement.
- Vote processes (*V-proc*), which are mobile processes that collects votes (on requests) from each host in the cluster and communications the outcomes of each vote.

Note that static processes RM-proc and SR-proc run at each Host, the mobile processes are initiated at the Cluster Head and execute at each of the hosts.

In the next section, we illustrate the functioning of the QoS framework through a shared-session mechanism, and then show how the need for sharing sessions can be identified in the MNSP-layer, communicated to the MAS-layer by the lightweight processes, and resolved in the MAS-layer by the intelligent, 'normative' agents.

---

[1] We use the term process to distinguish these from the normative agents in the MAS-layer, but in [14, 15] these processes are referred to as (mobile) agents.

5   Session-Sharing Mechanism

Mobile multimedia applications generally carry huge data from the source to the destination, while either the source or destination or both are on the move. Generally, these applications are divided into set of sessions for the better management of the data in the MANETs. Sometimes, a single host may be receiving the data from a single server for its set of end-users by creating separate parallel sessions which costs heavily for service providers.

To discuss session sharing, let us assume a user starts watching a football match (live) on a PC. This transaction may be broadly divided into the following events: *the capturing video and audio at the ground, A/D conversion, Receiving and on-line editing at studio, data-recording, sending on the Internet, audio/video stream is read, demultiplexed, decoded, and played-out.* In other words, this system has ten events in its event-flowgraph (see Fig. 2).

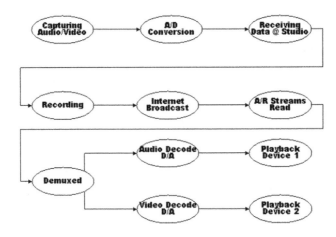

Fig. 2. Event Flowgraph

Figure 2 depicts an event-flowgraph of watching of a football match, a mobile multimedia application. However, there is a possibility of several end-users scenarios: two of them are:

- the user that initiated the playback simultaneously wants to watch the football match using a second device as audio/video output – for instance a mobile system. Or another user wants to join watching the match on a different system, maybe at a different location.
- two users want to watch the match on the same screen while listening to different audio tracks (e.g. different languages) with a mobile device.

In both cases, there are events in the flowgraphs for the delivery of multimedia content to the second device which are *shared* with the flowgraph depicted in Fig. 2. Sharing of sessions is necessary in cases where only a single device exists to perform a certain operation, but sharing can also be used to leverage efficiency by sharing computational resources among tasks. Therefore, we create an event-flowgraph for every registered session. Events of this flowgraph and implicitly edges connecting events can be marked as sharable to be reused by other applications within their event-flowgraphs as shared sessions (cf. [6]).

We have therefore designed a session sharing mechanism (SSM) in the QoS framework. The SSM can initiated by the CHCP whenever it gets the signal for session sharing from the session registry processes (SR-proc). The general mechanism is as follows:

- New session request S_i arrives at host H_m
- SR-proc at H_m derives the the event flowgraph of S_i
- if the derived event-sequence matches with an existing session S_j, then SR-proc at H_m requests to SR-proc at CHCP for a shared session; otherwise it registers S_i as an individual session with SR-proc at CHCP;
- SR-proc at CHCP passes the request to the multi-agent deliberative assembly (see the next section).

Session sharing is the mechanism which allows new requests of a host to join in the middle of a session to cater the requests of its end-users. For example, consider that a session S_1 as illustrated in Fig. 2 which is in progress, and S_2 is another session which needs to be started but has the last four events in common. The Registry agent analyses the event-flowgraph of S_2 and determines that parts are shareable with S_1. It then signals to signals SR-proc for SSM initiation. The SR-proc defers the decision to the MAS-layer using a Req-proc process, and if a favourable outcome is achieved (as discussed in the next section) the SSM waits for an appropriate session event on both event-flowgraphs and starts the session S_2 from that event onwards.

6   Multi-agent Deliberative Assemblies

This section gives a (partial) formal specification of the norm-governed MAS layer. We begin with an overview of the treatment of the MAS layer as a multi-agent deliberative assembly, consider the interaction between the MNSP and the MAS layer, and then define the actions required to make decisions in the MAS layer. This definition will use axioms specified in the Event Calculus [12]: while the exposition here is (or tries to be) self-contained the work in [18, 17] does provide useful background. We conclude this section with a broad discussion of a number of open issues.

6.1   Overview

All the requests for session sharing or individual sessions are passed up to the MAS-layer for deliberation and decision. Essentially we are doing resource allocation and coordination, but by passing requests from the MNSP-layer to the MAS-layer, we are decentralising the decision-making process and allowing local network conditions to determine the outcome. In this way, the MAS-layer acts as a kind of deliberative assembly as studied in [18, 17], but the decisions about whether to accept shared sessions (or not) are taken collectively, based on *local* decision-making and/or other policies. There are a number of policy decisions that can be made here, in particular we need to determine:

- Under what conditions do we want to manage resource allocation in existing sessions based on some kind of appointed chair, floor control protocol and system of entitlements (cf. [2])?
- Under what conditions do we want to manage resource allocation in existing sessions based on voting protocols (cf. [17])?

With each of these options, there are further questions: for example, with the floor control approach, do we want the floor assignment to be chaired or non-chaired. With the voting protocol approach, do we want specially-designated (e.g. heavily-loaded) hosts get a veto rather than a vote? Fine-tuning the precise operation of the resource allocation decision-making mechanics is a subject for further investigation. Finessing these finer details for the moment, the rest of this section is concerned with establishing the broad details of the operation of the MAS-layer, which can be used as a base from which these finer details can be 'tweaked'.

6.2   MNSP-Layer to MAS-Layer

All the hosts collect information on their new applications to be scheduled and their resource requirement, existing running applications and their usage, remaining net resources, etc. This information is periodically sent by each host by its RM-proc to the RM-proc at CHCP. The SR-agent assists the CHCP in registering all the sessions created by all the hosts of the cluster. The chair-process collects the host requests and network status, and periodically calls a meeting. The meeting schedule is broadcast by a V-proc to all the hosts with an agenda. At the time of meeting, the chair initiates discussion and optionally gives an opportunity for every host to present their case to all the other hosts. Later the CHCP sends a V-proc to collect the vote on the decision (i.e. their opinion on resource allocation). The CHCP concludes the meeting by giving the rulings based on the consensus and this is communicated by a V-proc to all hosts. The decisions are passed to MNSP to implement in the next time interval.

The primary decisions which need to taken are over session sharing. Abstractly, the problem is this. Suppose agent a_1 has established a session with a flowgraph of x events thus:

$$e_1^1 — e_2^1 — e_3^1 — \ldots — e_x^1$$

Now suppose agent a_2 requests a new session and the derived flowgraph for the sessions has y events, thus:

$$e_1^2 — e_2^2 — e_3^2 — \ldots — e_y^2$$

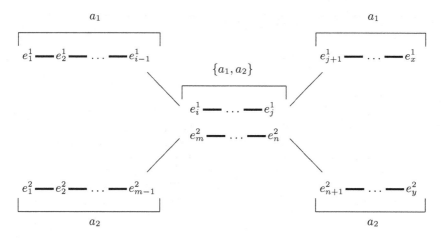

Fig. 3. Shared Flowgraphs

and suppose further that the flowgraph shares events $e^2_m \ldots e^2_n$ in common with $e^1_i \ldots e^1_j$. We now want to set up a collective flowgraph as shown in Figure 3, in which the event chains $e^1_i \ldots e^1_{i-1}$ and $e^1_{j+1} \ldots e^1_x$ are 'owned' by a_1, the event chains $e^2_1 \ldots e^2_{m-1}$ and $e^2_{n+1} \ldots e^2_y$ are 'owned' by a_2, and the shared events are owned jointly by a_1 and a_2. Then, when new sessions are started, it is only those agents who 'own' specific events who get to vote on whether or not they should be shared.

The CHCP operation is specified in Algorithm 1. A voting protocol required for steps 8-10 has been analysed and specified in [18, 17], while a resource allocation protocol required step 11 has been similarly analysed and specified in [2]. In the next section, we consider a formal specification which effectively merges these these two protocols and allows the agents to organise the sharing of sessions between themselves.

6.3   Formal Specification

For the sake of simplicity, we will not consider the complete voting protocol as defined in [18, 17]. For our purposes here, we can define (informally) the required steps as:

- a session is opened;
- a number of motions are tabled;
- each motion in turn is proposed;
- the chair calls for a vote on each motion (opens a ballot);
- the agents empowered to vote (in a sense made explicit below) cast their votes;
- the chair closes the ballot;
- the motion is declared carried, or not, as determined by the votes cast and the standing rules (e.g simple majority);
- after all motions are processed, the chair closes the session.

Algorithm 1. Functioning of CHCP

1: Begin
2: Chair-process of CH (CHCP) is activated
3: **while** true **do**
4:    **if** a Req-proc arrives or NStat-proc reports on MANET changes **then**
5:       Begin
6:       Initiate the meeting.
7:       Inform the hosts: H1, H2,....Hn, about the meeting time.
8:       During the meeting consider the following: Urgent requests(URs) and/or Shared Sessions(SSs) and/or Individual Requests(IRs).
9:       Chair-process requests for vote and is collected by V-agent.
10:      Chair-process gives a ruling on allowing: URs and/or SSs and/or IRs.
11:      The decision is implemented by the MNSP as per the ruling.
12:      End
13:   **else**
14:      Wait for next set of requests.
15:   **end if**
16: **end while**
17: End

In particular, note we do not anticipate motions being seconded or open for discussion, e.g. for agents to present their cases.

Given this informal specification, all that remains is to modify the formal specification given in [18, 17] to accommodate these changes. The modifications required are as follows:

- to request a shared session: this requires proposing a motion to share each event in the flowgraph;
- to grant sharing an event: the event in the flowgraph is shared and the requesting agent is now a joint 'owner' of the event (this is equivalent to gaining shared access to a controlled resource, as in the resource allocation protocol studied in [2]);
- to enforce sharing an event: this can be 'dictated' by the chair in response to Urgent Requests or in the case where there is an entitlement to share an event which pre-empts a vote;
- to release ownership of an event: on session termination an agent voluntarily gives up ownership of a shared event;
- to revoke ownership of an event: the chair may also revoke ownership of an event, e.g. as a sanction on an agent for inappropriate behaviour.

We next give axiomatic specifications in the Event Calculus for each of these actions.

Shared Session Request. The session is started with the status of each motion tabled to be *pending*, e.g. for the sharing of events in the two sessions above, we would have:

$$\text{initially } status(share(a_2, e_i^1)) = pending$$
$$\text{initially } status(share(a_2, e_{i+1}^1)) = pending$$

$$\vdots$$

$$\text{initially } status(share(a_2, e_j^1)) = pending$$

From the derived flowgraph for a_2's session, it is known that event e_i^1 is to be shared with e_m^2, and if this motion is carried, it is that sharing of the two event that is communicated to the MNSP layer.

Then, for each motion, the propose action sets in train the sequence of steps in the protocol outlined above, for example, a specific instance of this axiom would be:

$$propose(a_2, share(a_2, e_i^1)) \text{ initiates } status(share(a_2, e_i^1)) = proposed \text{ at } T \leftarrow$$
$$\mathbf{pow}(a_2, propose(a_2, share(a_2, e_i^1))) \text{ holdsAt } T$$

In other words, if a_2 has been empowered (by some role assignment protocol, not discussed here) to make proposals in this MANET, the action above will change the status of a tabled motion so that the chair can call for a vote on it. Note that a_2 is empowered if it occupies the role of proposer, and the motion has the appropriate status, i.e.:

$$\mathbf{pow}(a_2, propose(a_2, share(a_2, e_i^1))) \text{ holdsAt } T \leftarrow$$
$$status(share(a_2, e_i^1)) = pending \text{ holdsAt } T \ \wedge$$
$$role\_of(a_2, proposer) = true \text{ holdsAt } T$$

Granting Shared Event. Once a motion has been voted on, and if it has enough votes (according to the standing rules of the MANET) to carry, then the chair is empowered to declare that it has carried (indeed, in the formalisation given in [18, 17], the chair is not just empowered but also *obliged* to exercise that power). As a result, we also want the declaration to grant (joint) ownership of the event, as follows. (Note unlike the axiom given above, this is a generic instance, where A and C take the value of an agent, E the value of an event, and so on.)

$$declare(C, share(A, E), carried) \text{ initiates } granted(A, E) = true \text{ at } T \leftarrow$$
$$\mathbf{pow}(C, declare(C, share(A, E), carried)) \text{ holdsAt } T$$

Whether or not an agent has been granted ownership of an event determines if the agent has (or has not) the power to vote on a motion when the chair opens the ballot on that motion. Recall that agents only vote on shared events that they 'own' (have been granted), so the required axiom is:

$$\mathbf{pow}(V, vote(V, share(A, E))) \text{ holdsAt } T \leftarrow$$
$$status(share(A, E)) = voting \text{ holdsAt } T \ \wedge$$
$$role\_of(V, voter) = true \text{ holdsAt } T \ \wedge$$
$$granted(V, E) = true \text{ holdsAt } T$$

Enforcing Shared Event. There may be occasions when the agents are required to circumvent the 'niceties' of the voting protocol and the chair can simply override the rules. Two occasions are firstly, when there is an urgent request, and secondly, when there is an entitlement (to a resource or event) which may have been established by some pre-existing contract like a Service Level Agreement (SLA). On such occasions, we want to allow that the chair agent may simply *assert* that the requesting agent be granted ownership of the event, as follows:

$$assert(C, share(A, E)) \text{ initiates } granted(A, E) = true \text{ at } T \leftarrow$$
$$status(share(A, E)) = pending \text{ at } T$$
$$\mathbf{pow}(C, assert(C, share(A, E))) \text{ holdsAt } T$$

C is empowered in situations specified by the following axioms:

$$\mathbf{pow}(C, assert(C, share(A, E))) \text{ holdsAt } T \leftarrow$$
$$role\_of(C, chair) = true \text{ holdsAt } T \land$$
$$status(share(A, E)) = pending \text{ holdsAt } T \land$$
$$urgent(share(A, E)) = true \text{ holdsAt } T$$
$$\mathbf{pow}(C, assert(C, share(A, E))) \text{ holdsAt } T \leftarrow$$
$$role\_of(C, chair) = true \text{ holdsAt } T \land$$
$$status(share(A, E)) = pending \text{ holdsAt } T$$
$$entitled(A, E) = true \text{ holdsAt } T$$

Note that the assert action also immediately updates the status of a motion to be resolved, without going through all the intermediary steps of the voting protocol:

$$assert(C, share(A, E)) \text{ initiates } status(share(A, E)) = resolved \text{ at } T \leftarrow$$
$$status(share(A, E)) = pending \text{ at } T$$
$$\mathbf{pow}(C, assert(C, M, carried)) \text{ holdsAt } T$$

Release Shared Event. Once an agent's session has terminated it no longer has need of the event/resources allocated to that session. It can 'gracefully' withdraw by *releasing* its ownership, so that it no longer gets a vote on sharing this event:

$$release(A, E) \text{ initiates } granted(A, E) = false \text{ at } T \leftarrow$$
$$\mathbf{pow}(A, release(A, E)) \text{ holdsAt } T$$
$$\mathbf{pow}(A, release(A, E)) \text{ holdsAt } T \leftarrow$$
$$granted(A, E) = true \text{ holdsAt } T$$

Revoke Shared Event. Finally, we want to allow for the chair agent to revoke 'ownership' of an event, e.g. to reclaim resources or as a sanction applied as a consequence of 'inappropriate' behaviour on the part of the granted agent.

Therefore we also require the axiom:

$$revoke(C, A, E) \text{ initiates } granted(A, E) = false \text{ at } T \leftarrow$$
$$\textbf{pow}(C, revoke(C, A, E)) \text{ holdsAt } T$$

and the chair is empowered to revoke under the conditions outlined above.

6.4 Further Issues

A key advantage of MANETs is that the nodes communicate directly in peer-to-peer fashion; it then follows that the agents do too. Arguably, this then becomes a disadvantage, because there is an absence of any stable infrastructure components, in particular the cluster head (the chair agent). This complicates the issue of handoff: if the cluster head becomes unavailable it has to be replaced. One way to do this of course is to organise a candidate election, however, the existing voting protocol can be used directly. In such an election, it is possible for candidates to have a manifesto: one issue is to examine whether cluster head-handoff should include continuity of the existing management policies or could encompass a vote on alternatives. This might allow other 'QoS attributes' to be evaluated: e.g. responsiveness, fairness, and so on.

The specification can be animated to reason dynamically about the agents' normative positions (i.e. a characterisation of their powers, permissions, obligations and so on). One aspect of further research is to link the agents' knowledge of their normative positions with respect to the 'code of conduct' for the MANET (which may also get a formal, contractual representation) to their actual QoS resource commitments (current and predicted) to inform the decision-making algorithm which outputs the actual vote ('yes' or 'no'). There are also strategic considerations which could be accommodated in this decision. Some of these aspects are addressed by related works considered in the next section.

7 Related Work

The issue of QoS in general and in MANETs in particular has received considerable attention since the technology has been deployed and ever greater demands, especially for multimedia, has been placed on it. Several research groups have adopted a multi-agent approach to developing a solution. In this section, we consider a representative cross-section of this work and relate it the current proposal.

7.1 Strategy-Centric Adaptive QoS

Suganuma et al. [21] develop a multi-agent system architecture with a strategy-centric adaptive QoS control mechanism. The application considered is video-conferencing, and the problem addressed is to ensure smooth operation in the light of changing user requirements, system and network environments. In particular, it was inappropriate to demand that users manage this operation for themselves. Therefore the 'intelligence' to respond to changes was to be found in agents, and the developed system worked by tailoring the QoS control strategy to the characteristics of detected changes.

The system architecture model conceptually comprised two layers:

- the *domain cooperation layer*: specific knowledge and protocols (to interact between agents) are applied to satisfying QoS, as determined by the currently selected strategy; and
- the *strategy selection layer*: given a class of problems and library of strategies, agents select the most appropriate strategy for a 'given' problem (current operating conditions). The strategy is selected by negotiation.

The strategy-centric QoS control operates by transitions between the two modes of operation, according to event which change the parameters and/or class of 'problem'.

This two layer architecture broadly corresponds to the two-layer framework proposed here. The MNSP corresponds to the domain cooperation layer, i.e. it is concerned with multimedia transport; and the MAS layer corresponds to the strategy selection layer, i.e. it is concerned with the meta-level decision-making with respect to the cooperative behaviour that is essential for multimedia QoS provisioning in MANETs.

Note, however, that the norm-governed specification described above needs to be informed by an appropriate decision-making module which effectively determines the way in which to vote. These strategies and associated algorithms to implement them have not been addressed in the current work. However, we could expect that the strategies could be derived from this work, suitably moderated to take into account the normative aspects of cooperative behaviour, and indeed other socio-cognitive and/or socio-economic factors (e.g. trust, reputation and recommendation [16].

7.2   3-Level QoS Control

Iraqi et al. [10] present a 3-level multi-agent architecture. Their application is wireless ATM and the specific problem is network congestion control. While ATM and congestion control are only loosely related to our concerns here, the agent architecture for a self-regulating control mechanism does relate closely to our proposal.

The 3 layers of this proposed architecture are hierarchically organised as:

- a 'lower' system level layer, composed of switch agents, which monitor network component behaviour (i.e. the local ATM switch and its associated buffers) and control that behaviour according to directives stemming from the 'upper' layer;
- an 'upper' domain level layer, composed of domain agents, which are responsible for intelligent processing and decision-making based on more global knowledge about network conditions;
- a 'super agent', which is responsible for an entire management domain and the implementation of management policies within that domain.

The advantages of this architecture are that, firstly, the delegation 'down' the hierarchy of performance management to the appropriate level (i.e. the switches) and so minimising control information exchange; and secondly the aggregation 'up' the hierarchy of information which provides end-to-end knowledge which informs management decisions which become delegated actions. It is precisely these advantages that we seek to leverage by having lightweight mobile agents in our 'lower' layer (the MNSP) and heavier normative agents in the 'upper' layer.

Thus this 3 layer architecture also broadly corresponds to the framework proposed here. Clearly the switch agents correspond to the mobile agents in the MNSP, and the domain agents correspond to the normative agents in the MAS layer. The super agent corresponds to the chair agent running on the cluster head (CHCP).

However, the most substantive difference is in the perception of the chair agent versus that of super agent. The 3-layer model views the super agent as having a management policy it can delegate to other agents to enact. Our model views the chair agent as a *primus inter pares* (first amongst equals) and so neutral with respect to decisions made by the cluster. It can only coordinate decisions, it cannot dictate them (except, as we have seen, in the case of entitlements).

As an aside, Iraqi et al. note that for the task (we would say 'role') of a super agent "The DAs [domain agents] can also elect one special agent for this task. This process is out of the scope of this study." The mechanisms for robust voting/election are precisely those outlined here and in [18, 17].

7.3 QoS Routing in MANETs

Mantilla and Marco [13] address the problem of QoS routing in MANETs, i.e. finding a source-destination path with the necessary resource available, meeting constraints on bandwidth, delay, packet loss, etc., subject to the dynamically changing link conditions of the network.

In this work, two classes of agent are identified, Solicitor Agents and Supplier Agents. The solicitor agent consults routing tables and sends out messages (calls for proposals, or cfp) to adjacent nodes (and so on until the destination), while Supplier Agents consult available resources at the node to determine how to respond.

In our terms, agents consulting routing tables and checking available resources are pro-active functions of the MNSP. Furthermore, we would not distinguish between classes of agent, these are both agents who happen to occupy different roles in the contract-net protocol (of which the cfp is the initiating message). Note that a full and comprehensive analysis of the contract-net protocol, using norm-governed agents, is given in [3].

7.4 MAS for QoS Management

Trzec and Huljenic [22] apply an agent-oriented software engineering methodology to QoS management, using MESSAGE (an agent-oriented extension of UML). This work gives a functional definition of the system from the organizational, goal, role, interaction and domain perspectives. From this analysis, they draw a 4-layer architecture, with communication, QoS, collaboration and service layers. In our framework, we would expect that the functionality of the communication and QoS layers to be supported by the MNSP, while the functionality of the collaboration and service layers should be provided by the MAS layer. The use of Service Level Agreements, like management policies, is a very interesting idea.

However, leaving aside the fact that we find it very difficult to take an organizational perspective without considering any form of norm, the main problem here is what happens to the system when agreements are not fulfilled. One of the major motivations for the norm-governed approach is the requirement to deal with behaviour that deviates from the ideal. In other words, malfunctioning, either by intent or circumstance, is to be expected. The application of software engineering methodologies is generally concerned with the development of 'correct' systems which function correctly, and don't consider that a system can still function, even if that functioning is sub-ideal or non-normative. How to detect and recover from such situations is essential; detection is of course an an integral part of the norm-governed approach; but for recovery we use the idea sanctions; while there is also a link here to related work on forgiveness [23].

8   Summary, Further Work and Conclusions

We have proposed a framework to provide QoS management to multimedia applications in MANETs (cf. [4]). In particular this framework was based on a two-layer architecture; a MAS-layer which made decision according to norm-governed policies and protocols, and a network-layer (the MNSP) which provided network-centric information up to the the MAS-layer and enacted decisions made at the MAS-layer. The glue between the two layers were a number of static and mobile processes. We believe that the mobile multimedia applications and wireless Internet services can significantly benefit from the framework. The framework exhibits several enabling properties: QoS awareness, to manage service components according to agreed-on QoS levels; location awareness, to enable runtime decisions based on network topology; and the current status of involved resources.

At this stage of our research we emphasise that in effect this paper is a *specification* of a proposed system. Quite clearly, what is required in the next stage of research is experimental evaluation, simulation and mathematical modelling and analysis. We are in the process of implementing this proposed QoS framework with the intention of pursuing two further lines of inquiry: firstly, simulation experiments; and secondly, physical implementation. Simulation can be performed with respect to existing protocols, e.g. RSVP, for comparative evaluation; while actually building and running the system should provide unexpected insights and highlight issues that are in need of further investigation (it has been reported before that real world operation of MANETs can be substantially different from simulated networks, e.g. [8]). This will also permit consideration of the many issues involved in handover, e.g. of roles, sessions, and powers (by delegation).

Furthermore, the present telecom/datacom services will have to meet a number of QoS requirements resulting from rapidly changing markets and technologies. Within this open market of services, the aspects of their customisation and instant provision are of fundamental importance. The intrinsic features of norm-governed multi-agent systems make it possible to address a number of problems related to the diversity of telecom/datacom infrastructure and services. In particular, in this paper has initiated an investigation into the extent to which norm-governed multi-agent systems can be used for self-determination of QoS management in MANETs. As such this is a contribution to the realisation of the vision of *ubiquitous networking*, the idea that (unlike ubiquitous computing, where essentially the devices are invisible) we acknowledge the presence (and limitations) of the device, and seek to render the network itself invisible and yet ensure the device is transparently, and permanently connected.

Acknowledgements

This Indo-UK collaboration has been supported with the assistance of UK EP-SRC Overseas Travel Grant (OTG) GR/T20328. The comments of the anonymous reviewers have been especially useful and this is gratefully acknowledged.

References

1. M. Abolhasan, T. Wysocki, and E. Dutkiewicz. A review of routing protocols for mobile ad hoc networks. *Ad Hoc Networks*, 2:1–22, 2004.
2. A. Artikis, L. Kamara, J. Pitt, and M. Sergot. A protocol for resource sharing in norm-governed ad hoc networks. In J. Leite, A. Omicini, P. Torroni and Pinar Yolum, editors, *Proceedings of the Declarative Agent Languages and Technologies (DALT) Workshop*. LNCS 3476, pp. 221–238, Springer-Verlag, 2005.
3. A. Artikis, J. Pitt, and M. Sergot. Animated specifications of computational societies. In C. Castelfranchi and L. Johnson, editors, *Proceedings AAMAS'02*, pages 1053–1062. ACM Press, 2002.
4. J. Bolliger and T. Gross. A framework-based approach to the development of network-aware applications. *IEEE Trans. on Software Eng.*, 24:376–390, 1998.
5. S. Capkun, J.-P. Hubaux, and L. Buttyan. Mobility helps security in ad hoc networks. In *MobiHoc'03: Proceedings of the 4th ACM international symposium on Mobile ad hoc networking & computing*, pages 46–56, 2003.
6. D. Carlson and A. Schrader. Seamless media adaptation with simultaneous processing chains. In *ACM International Conference on Multimedia.*, pp. 781–788. 2002.
7. D. Cavin, Y. Sasson, and A. Schiper. Consensus with unknown participants or fundamental self-organization. In I. Nikolaidis, M. Barbeau, and E. Kranakis, editors, *Proceedings Third International Conference on Ad-Hoc, Mobile, and Wireless Networks, ADHOC-NOW*, pages 135–148, 2004.
8. K.-W. Chin, J. Judge, A. Williams, and R. Kermode. Implementation experience with manet routing protocols. *SigComm Comput. Commun. Rev.*, 32(5):49–59, 2002.
9. X. Du. Qos routing based on multi-class nodes for mobile ad hoc networks. *Ad Hoc Networks*, 2(3):241–254, 2004.

10. Y. Iraqi, R. Boutaba, and A. Leon-Garcia. QoS control in wireless ATM. *Mobile Networks and Applications*, 5:137–145, 1999.
11. A. Jones and M. Sergot. On the characterization of law and computer systems: The normative systems perspective. In J.-J. Meyer and R. Wieringa, editors, *Deontic Logic in Computer Science*. John Wiley and Sons, 1993.
12. R. Kowalski and M. Sergot. A logic-based calculus of events. *New Generation Computing*, 4(1):67–96, 1986.
13. C. Mantilla and J. Marzo. A QoS framework for heterogeneous wireless networks using a multiagent system. In *5th European Wireless Conference*, pp. 61–67. 2004.
14. S. Manvi and P. Venkataram. Qos management by mobile agents in multimedia communication. In *DEXA Workshop*, pages 407–411, 2000.
15. S. Manvi and P. Venkataram. Mobile agent based online bandwidth allocation scheme for multimedia communication. In *GLOBECOM 2001 IEEE Global Telecommunications Conference*, pages 2622–2626. IEEE, 2001.
16. B. Neville and J. Pitt. A computational framework for social agents in agent mediated e-commerce. In A. Omicini, P. Petta, and J. Pitt, editors, *ESAW*, volume 3071 of *Lecture Notes in Computer Science*, pages 376–391. Springer, 2004.
17. J. Pitt, L. Kamara, M. Sergot, and A. Artikis. Formalization of a voting protocol for virtual organizations. In F. Dignum, V. Dignum, S. Koenig, S. Kraus, M. Singh, and M. Wooldridge, ed., *Proc. 4th AAMAS'05*, pp. 373–380. ACM, 2005.
18. J. Pitt, L. Kamara, M. Sergot, and A. Artikis. Voting in online deliberative assemblies. In A. Gardner and G. Sartor, editors, *Proceedings 10th ICAIL*, pages 195–204. ACM, 2005.
19. H. S. A. Rao and R. Lanphier. RFC 2326 Real Time Streaming Protocol (RTSP). IETF RFC2326.txt (http://www.ietf.org).
20. S. Choi and K. Shin. Predictive and adaptive bandwidth reservation for handoffs in qos-sensitive cellular networks. In *Proceedings ACM SIGCOMM'98*, pages 155–166. AAAI Press, 1998.
21. T. Suganuma, S. Lee, T. Kinoshita, and N. Shiratori. An agent architecture for strategy-centric adaptive QoS control in flexible videoconference system. *New Generation Computing*, 19(2):173–192, 2001.
22. K. Trzec and D. Huljenic. Intelligent agents for QoS management. In C. Castelfranchi and L. Johnson, editors, *AAMAS'02*, pages 1405–1412. ACM Press, 2002.
23. A. Vasalou and J. Pitt. Reinventing forgiveness: A formal investigation of moral facilitation. In *iTrust*, pages 146–160, 2005.
24. P. Venkataram, editor. *Wireless Communications for the next Millennium*. McGraw-Hill, 1998.
25. P. Venkataram, R. Rajavelsamy, S. Chaudhari, T.Ramamohan, and H. Ramakrishna. A wireless rural education and learning system based on disk-oriented MPEG streaming. *International Journal of Distance Education Technologies*, 1(4):20–38, 2003.
26. P. Venkataram and P. Sureshbabu. A QoS adaptation algorithm for multimedia wireless networks. *Journal of Indian Institute of Science*, 80(3):195–215, 2000.
27. Y. Wang, V. Giruka, and M. Singhal. A fair distribution solution for selfish nodes problem in wireless ad hoc networks. In I. Nikolaidis, M. Barbeau, and E. Kranakis, editors, *Proceedings Third International Conference on Ad-Hoc, Mobile, and Wireless Networks, ADHOC-NOW*, pages 211–224, 2004.

Collaborative Agent Tuning: Performance Enhancement on Mobile Devices

Conor Muldoon[1], Gregory M.P. O'Hare[2], and Michel J. O'Grady[2]

[1] Practice & Research in Intelligent Systems & Media (PRISM) Laboratory,
School of Computer Science & Informatics, University College Dublin (UCD),
Belfield, Dublin 4, Ireland
{conor.muldoon}@ucd.ie
[2] Adaptive Information Cluster (AIC), School of Computer Science & Informatics,
University College Dublin (UCD), Belfield, Dublin 4, Ireland
{gregory.ohare, michael.j.ogrady}@ucd.ie

Abstract. Ambient intelligence envisages a world saturated with sensors and other embedded computing technologies, operating transparently, and accessible to all in a seamless and intuitive manner. Intelligent agents of varying capabilities may well form the essential constituent entities around which this vision is realized. However, the practical realization of this vision will severely exacerbate the complexity of existing software solutions, a problem that autonomic computing was originally conceived to address. Thus we can conjecture that the incorporation of autonomic principles into the design of Multi-Agent Systems is indeed a desirable objective. As an illustration of how this may be achieved, a strategy termed Collaborative Agent Tuning is described, which seeks to optimise agent performance on computationally limited devices. A classic mobile computing application is used to illustrate the principles involved.

1 Introduction

Complexity: in a word, the primary reason for the recent upsurge of interest, both academic and commercial, in the area of autonomic and self-managing systems. Autonomic implies a number of fundamental features including: self-configuring, self-healing, self-optimising and self-protecting [1]. Augmenting software with such properties is seen as essential to addressing this critical issue of complexity. It is anticipated that the arrival of the ubiquitous computing era will give rise to a radical reappraisal of how software should be developed, managed and optimised in an era of unparallel pervasive access to computational technologies.

A spectatular rise in the use of mobile computing technologies has been witnessed in recent years. Various interpretations of the mobile computing paradigmn, for example ubiquitous and pervasive computing and more recently, Ambient Intelligence (AmI) [2], have all been the subject of much research. Revenue projections suggest the provision of applications and services to mobile users will become an increasingly important revenue generator for many enterprises in the coming years. Thus the task of differentiating products and services is one that will increasingly challenge and

O. Dikenelli, M.-P. Gleizes, and A. Ricci (Eds.): ESAW 2005, LNAI 3963, pp. 241–258, 2006.
© Springer-Verlag Berlin Heidelberg 2006

preoccupy service providers. One approach to this may well involve the utilisation of intelligent techniques. While a number of candidate technologies exist, intelligent agents are being increasingly seen as offering a viable approach towards realizing intelligent solutions within the technological confines that characterize mobile computing.

A mobile computing landscape populated with multiple agent communities is characterized by complexity and heterogeneity. Conceptually, this landscape could be viewed as consisting of agents operating in small ecosystems, which themselves may be perceived as nodes in a much larger networked agent society. Such nodes would be invariably mobile as they would predominantly operate on people's mobile phones and PDAs. Overtime, however, an increasingly static component would emerge, as small dedicated Multi-agent Systems (MASs) would be increasingly embedded within objects in the environment, as per the AmI vision. Both mobile and static communities would increasingly have to interact and cooperate so as to realize a world of pervasive and transparent service provision, as well as facilitate seamless and intuitive end-user interaction.

Both AmI and standard mobile computing operating environments are characterized by limited computational resources, at least when compared to a classic desktop scenario. To address the problem of executing agents within such environments a strategy termed Collaborative Agent Tuning is introduced. The Tuning approach aims at providing a methodology by which agents can collaborate to optimize the limited computational resources available to them.

The remainder of the paper is structured as follows: In Section 2, some sources of complexity in mobile computing are explored in further detail. The intelligent agent paradigm is considered in Section 3, including related research in resource optimization using agents. The Collaborative Agent Tuning approach is illustrated in Section 4. Experimental results are presented in Section 5. A discussion of the pertinent issues is presented in Section 4 after which the paper is concluded.

2   Some Sources of Complexity in Mobile Computing

Engineering applications and services for mobile users both exacerbates acknowledged difficulties with the software development process and introduces a new set of problems for resolution. As an example, consider the dynamic nature of the end-users' situation. It is well known that the possibility of ascertaining a user's status at any given time provides significant opportunities for enhancing and personalizing applications or services resulting in a more satisfactory end-user experience. In academic circles, the entwined concepts of context and context-aware computing have been proposed as a framework through which the identification and incorporation of various aspects of a user's current situation can be incorporated into applications and services. Though capturing all aspects of a user's context is impractical, it is feasible to capture salient aspects and to use these in a prudent and intelligent manner to adapt the behavior of an application or service appropriately. In the case of the mobile user, the following aspects of a user's context might be considered:

- Device: A plethora of multiple devices exist – all differing in fundamental ways including operating system, CPU, memory, interaction modality and screen size.

The onus is on the application developer or service provider to ensure that their products can *adapt* to the various device contexts. How best to achieve this, of course, remains an open question.

- Network: A wireless network is essential for mobile computing. However, the Quality of Service (QoS) supported by individual networks can vary considerably. Again, this is an aspect of a potential end-user's context that needs careful consideration. Unfortunately, end-users, conditioned by the reliability and performance of fixed network applications, may find wireless networking an unsatisfactory experience. A key challenge facing the designer is to adopt strategies that seek to give the illusion of low latency and infinite bandwidth. One approach to this, termed *intelligent precaching*, may be found in [3].

- User: No two users are alike. This indisputable fact is the basis of ongoing research in areas like personalization and user-adapted interaction. In each case, various aspects of a user's context are considered, for example, their language, previous experience and current objectives. Using these characteristics, models can be constructed for individual users, which in turn provide a basis for further system adaptation.

Incorporating the necessary logic that captures the context in these three cases alone is a significant undertaking and fraught with difficulty. Yet it is obvious that successfully capturing and *intelligently* interpreting the rich and diverse aspects of a user's context, will result in a more rewarding end-user experience, and potentially, a satisfied customer. However, modeling an effective solution is a non-trivial task and this problem becomes more acute when the limited computational resources of the average mobile device are considered. Such resources are at a premium in mobile computing and their effective management is of paramount importance. Thus the use of autonomic precepts offers significant scope for effective resource management. Though traditionally associated with large scale computing clusters, such precepts can be applied in alternative domains. In this paper, discussion will focus on the intelligent agent paradigm in a mobile computing scenario.

3 Intelligent Agents

Intelligent agents encapsulate a number of characteristics that make them an attractive and viable option for realizing AmI applications. At a basic level, their autonomous nature, ability to react to external events, as well as an inherent capability to be proactive in fulfilling their objectives, make them particularly suitable for operating in complex and dynamic environments. Should an agent be endowed with a mobility capability, its ability to adapt and respond to unexpected events is further enhanced.

More advanced agents may possess a sophisticated reasoning facility. An example of such agents includes those that conform to the Belief-Desire-Intention (BDI) architecture [4]. BDI agents follow a sense-deliberate-act cycle that, in conjunction with their other attributes, makes them particular adept and flexible in many situations or, to coin a phrase: agile.

Agents rarely exist in isolation but usually form a coalition of agents in what is usually termed a Multi-Agent System (MAS). Though endowed with particular responsibilities, each individual agent *collaborates* with other agents to fulfill the objectives of the MAS. Fundamental to this collaboration is the existence of an Agent Communications Language (ACL), which is shared and understood by all agents. The necessity to support inter-agent communication has led to the development of an international ACL standard, which has been ratified by the Foundation for Intelligent Physical Agents (FIPA). More recently, FIPA has been subsumed into the IEEE computer society and forms an autonomous standards committee with the objective of facilitating interoperability between agents and other non-agent technologies. As shall be demonstrated in Section 4.2, it is this innate communications ability that provides the basis for realizing autonomic behavior in intelligent agents.

3.1 Collaborating Agents: A Basis for Autonomic Behavior

Agents, through their collaborative nature, inherent intelligence and awareness of their environment (and themselves), are particularly suitable for modeling the complex situations that frequently arise in mobile computing. As an illustration of this, a number of prototypes have been developed here in our laboratories including Gulliver's Genie [5], EasiShop [6] and the ACCESS architecture [7]. However, it became apparent that maximum use was not being derived from the limited processing power of the average mobile device, and as such, a more holistic and altruistic approach was demanded. It was therefore necessary to identify a strategy that would allow agents cooperate in such a manner that they could operate satisfactorily within the prevailing operating conditions on the mobile devices without compromising their individual goals and objectives. One strategy that has been developed for achieving this has been termed *Collaborative Agent Tuning*.

3.2 Related Research

A number of approaches seeking to optimize the use of computational resources are reported in the literature. In [8] the authors describe a system in which agents negotiate and collaborate to gain access to computational resources. The agents use Case Based Reasoning (CBR) to learn, select and apply negotiation strategies. The negotiation protocol described is argumentation-based whereby the initiating agent attempts to persuade the responding agent to give up a resource by iteratively supplying supporting arguments.

The NOMADS mobile agent framework [9] provides support for controlling the rate and quantity of resources consumed by agents. The system has been build on top of a modified Java Virtual Machine (JVM) and an agent execution environment known as Oasis. Control over the CPU in NOMADS is handled by a scheduler thread that converts the amount of CPU percentage assigned to an agent to the number of bytecodes that may be executed per millisecond. If the scheduler thread observes that the CPU utilization of an agent has increased, the number of bytecodes per millisecond limit is lowered and vice-versa. A Guard agent is provided that performs high-level monitoring of agent consumption. If an agent is excessively using the CPU the Guard agent reduces the amount of computational resources assigned to it.

AutoTune [10] is a generic agent developed for performance tuning that has been built on top of the ABLE [11] agent development environment. AutoTune uses a control loop to manage various tuning parameters within the system. Users interact with the target system by issuing work requests and receiving services. The controlled target system is exposed to the AutoTune agent by providing interfaces to its tuning controls and metrics. The AutoTune agent inputs these metrics and based on policies specified by system administrators determines new values of the tuning control settings as the application executes.

The DIOS++ architecture [12] consists of sensors and actuators, which monitor and adjust system state. An autonomic agent permits self-management and dynamic adjustment of rules and policies at runtime to allow the system to alter and optimize its performance. A decentralized market based protocol in which agents compete for scarce computational resources is described in [13]. An automated auction procedure is used to determine prices of tasks and resources traded between agents. Empirical evidence is presented that exhibits how the system converges to a solution when the consumers' bids are sufficiently high.

Though sharing the same broad objectives of these systems, Collaborative Agent Tuning differs in that it is based on the BDI paradigm and employs the formal notions of joint intentions and mutual beliefs. Joint Intention Theory [14][15] prescribes a way by which a team of agents may execute an action jointly. It requires the establishment of mutual belief within the team that the joint action is starting and subsequently another mutual belief about the completion, irreverence, or impossibility of the action. Joint Intentions are expressed here in terms of joint commitments. Joint commitments differ from the concept of a social commitment [16]. Within a social commitment a debtor agent has a one-way commitment toward a creditor agent to perform an action but the creditor does not have the same commitment toward the debtor. When two agents are jointly committed to one of them performing an action the commitment is binding on both agents. If either of the agents comes to privately believe that the action is completed, irreverent or impossible, a similar response for both agents is prescribed. Thus if one of the agents believes that an action is no longer possible, it is in its interest to inform the other agent of this fact because it is jointly committed to the action. It is for this reason that joint commitments reduce resource wastage and are resilient to failure.

Thus the Collaborative Agent Tuning approach to the development of a resource optimization mechanism differs from the other systems mentioned above in that it coerces agents to communicate with each other and to act as a team. In this manner joint commitments increase the utility of the system by enforcing a collaborative approach rather than a non-cooperative competitive one. For the purposes of this discussion, we focus on the case of a MAS operating on a mobile device. The particular case of load balancing and the general case of applying the tuning approach to a MAS that incorporates a fixed network component is beyond the scope of this paper.

Deploying agents on mobile devices has been receiving increasing attention over the last few years. A number of platforms have been documented in the literature that claim to enable the deployment of solutions based on intelligent agents on PDAs and such devices. Some have been designed as extensions of well-known agent development environments thus enabling interoperability with legacy systems while others have been designed specifically for a mobile device context. MicroFIPA-OS [17] is a classic example of a platform that evolved from a system that was originally designed for a traditional workstation setting, namely the well-known open source platform FIPA-OS [18]. Tacoma [19], LEAP-JADE [20] and 3APL-M [21] are other examples. From a BDI perspective, JACK [22] and AgentSpeak [23] are additional examples. For the purposes of this research, Agent Factory [24][25] was augmented with explicit support for Collaborative Agent Tuning. In next section, a brief overview of Agent Factory is presented.

3.3 Agent Factory

The Collaborative Agent Tuning approach has been developed using a pre-existing deliberative agent framework, namely Agent Factory. Agent Factory supports the development of a type of software agent that is: autonomous, situated, socially able, intentional, rational, and mobile. In practice, this has been achieved through the design and implementation of an agent programming language - Agent Factory Agent Programming Language (AF-APL), and an associated interpreter. Together, the language and interpreter facilitate the expression of the current behaviour of each agent through the mentalistic notions of belief and commitment. These are augmented with a set of commitment rules that describe the dynamics of the agents' behaviour through the definition of the conditions under which the agent should adopt commitments. This approach is consistent with the well-documented Belief-Desire-Intention (BDI) agent model. The framework itself is comprised of four-layers that deliver:

1. an agent programming language;
2. a distributed run-time environment;
3. an integrated development environment;
4. a development methodology.

Additionally, the system contains an Agent Management System (AMS) agent and a Directory Facilitator (DF) agent in compliance with the FIPA specifications. Agent-oriented applications implemented using Agent Factory use these prefabricated agents to gain access to the infrastructure services provided by the run-time environment, for example, a yellow and white pages service and a migration service.

Agent Factory supports the development of abstract agent roles that developers may use to capture generic agent functionality. Agent implementations may extend these abstract roles with application specific functionality. The roles contain a list of commitment rules that govern the behavior of agents that use the role. Additionally, they specify perceptors and actuators that enable the agents to perceive and act upon their environment respectively. When extending abstract roles, developers add additional commitment rules, actuators, and perceptors as necessitated by the application. In this manner Agent Factory provides a mechanism to enable the reuse of abstract application functionality.

4   Collaborative Agent Tuning

Collaborative Agent Tuning is an autonomic procedure by which agents collectively alter their response times to adapt to the dynamic performance requirements of their environment. Computational overhead is used as a metric to indicate an agent's workload and as a trigger in altering its response time. Once an agent's computational load changes, rather than taking unilateral action, the agent adopts a commitment to make its desire to alter its response time mutually believable. The framework is based on Joint

Intention Theory, which coerces agents into forming coalitions and to act as a team. This prevents the creation of prisoner dilemma type scenarios whereby agents making locally optimal decisions espouse socially unacceptable behaviour patterns as an inevitable consequence of rational choice. With Joint Intention Theory, agents are forced to communicate with each other to prevent such situations occurring, and in doing so, create a system that is resilient to failure and that reduces resource wastage [26][27].

To elucidate further: consider an agent with a high computational load. To maintain an adequate QoS, it must of necessity have a fast response time. In other words, the time interval between its deliberation cycles must be small. Once this agent's load drops, it may not need to deliberate as often to maintain a satisfactory Quality-of-Service (QoS). Thus, it may seek to decrease its response time (increase the time between deliberation cycles!) and, in this way, free resources for other uses. Acting in an altruistic manner, it begins a collaborative process with other agents on the platform to have its response time decreased, that is, the time it takes the agent to process requests will be increased. Other agents may not necessarily want the agent to respond in a slower manner and may autonomously reject the request, despite the fact that additional computational resources would be made available to them. This is because if they needed to collaborate with the agent in the future, they would have to wait a longer time to receive a response! Thus if the requesting agent's response time was decreased, it would have the subsequent effect of reducing their own responsiveness, since collective decisions can only be made as fast as the slowest decision maker! Therefore, it would not be in the interest of the MAS if the agent were to decrease its response time even though this may seem counter-intuitive to the requesting agent. Had the agent taken unilateral action, even if it were attempting to act in the best interest of the team, the overall utility of the system would be lower as the agent would be unaware of its teammates' own internal beliefs and commitments.

```
TuningProcedure{
        // Establish Mutual Belief
        for(i=1;i<NumberOfAgents;i++){   //local
                Boolean response
                response=request(adopt,Agent[i],<<Self>>,<<tuningParameter>>)
                inform(belief,Agent[i],<<Self>>,tuningEvent)
                If(response==FALSE)return
        }

        // Adopt Joint Commitment
        Self.adoptJointCommitment(<<tuningParameter>>)

        Self.tune(<<tuningParameter>>) // Change sleep speed value

        if(BELIEF commitment: impossible or irreverent or completed){

                Self.dropJointCommitment(<<tuningParameter>>)
                Self.reset // Reset sleep speed value

                // Drop Joint Commitment
                for(int i=1;i<NumberOfAgents;i++){
                        inform(drop,Agent[i],<<Self>>,<<tuningParameter>>)
                        inform(belief,Agent[i],<<Self>>,dropped)
                }

        }

}
```

Fig. 1. Collaborative Tuning Process

Fig. 1 outlines the pseudo code for the collaborative tuning process. Initially an agent communicates with the other agents on the platform to create a joint commitment to have its response time altered. If all agents agree, the commitment is adopted and the agent will adjust the time between deliberation cycles appropriately. The agent will then continue to execute at this new deliberation-cycle frequency until the particular task that it is performing is completed, impossible, or irreverent. Conversely, if any of the agents on the platform do not agree to adopt a joint commitment, the requesting agent has two options. It either iteratively attempts to repeat the process altering the values of the tuning parameters until agreement is reached, or drops the commitment to have its response time altered. The choice made is application specific and is determined by how the particular agent has actually been implemented. During execution, if any of the agents comes to believe that the requesting agent should no longer be operating at the new deliberation-cycle frequency, the joint commitment will be dropped. The agent that causes the commitment to be dropped subsequently maintains a persistent goal to achieve mutual belief on this issue.

4.1   Example: Video Rendering on a Mobile Device

To illustrate collaborative agent tuning, we shall describe a multi-agent system that is delivering a context-sensitive service on a mobile device, and that requires dynamic

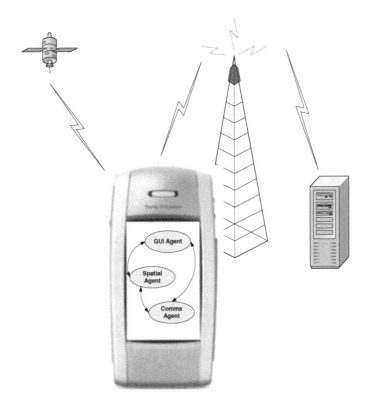

Fig. 2. Architecture of the MAS

allocation of computational resources. The service delivered by the MAS is simple, namely the rendering of video at various physical locations. It can be easily envisaged how such a service could form a constituent part of numerous applications, a mobile tourist guide and mobile learning system being two obvious candidates.

The application comprises three agents, namely the GUI Agent, the Spatial Agent, and the Communications Agent (Fig. 2). As the user explores some city or other physical environment, the Spatial Agent perceives the user's position through the use of a GPS device. This information is channeled to the Communication Agent, which uses it in pre-caching content (available on a fixed networked server) based on the user's current context. The GUI Agent signals to the user when content becomes available. As this content is in the form of a video clip, and should the user decide to view it, the device will typically not have the requisite processing capabilities. This is true even if the agents are operating with a reasonably slow response time. Thus all three agents on the device must collaboratively degrade their processor utilization in order to make additional computational resources available for the video rendering process. In addition to reducing their deliberation cycles, the agents must also alter other aspects of their behavior so as to adapt to the new environmental conditions created due to the temporary lack of resources. For example the Communications Agent will refrain from downloading emails while the video is playing.

In summary: throughout execution, the beliefs and intentions of the agents change, thus at various stages an agent may no longer wish to adhere to previously negotiated agreements. When this occurs, the agent adopts a commitment to make its intention to alter the tuning parameters known to the other agents. In BDI-type agents, the deliberation component often consumes most resources. Therefore, the timeout, or sleep parameter, between deliberation cycles must be increased if resources are to be increased. Other parameters may be adjusted according the particular implementation of the agent in question. Ultimately, if consensus is achieved, the agents will adjust their response times accordingly.

4.2 Tuning Agent Role

The requisite behavior patterns that enables agents to collaborate with each other and to alter their response times is encoded within a generic tuning role that application-specific agents must extend so as to make use of the framework. The initial version of this tuning role has been designed for use with agents operating on the Sony Ericsson P800 mobile phone (Fig. 3), hosting the Connected Limited Device Configuration (CLDC) Java platform augmented with the Mobile Information Device Profile (MIDP).

To illustrate the various issues related to collaborative agent tuning, three scenarios are now considered. In each case, it is assumed that the application incorporates a video component. Issues facing a prospective software engineer are also considered.

4.2.1 Scenario I: Each Agent Adopts a Unilateral Approach
In this case, each agent acts in a unilateral approach in the fulfillment of its tasks. Granted, the agents are interdependent in that information is shared. However, when undertaking a task, a selfish approach is adopted and the agent proceeds to fulfill its immediate objective, irrespective of the effect of its actions on the performance of its fellow agents. Thus the responsive-ness of the application as a whole will be degraded in an unpredictable manner.

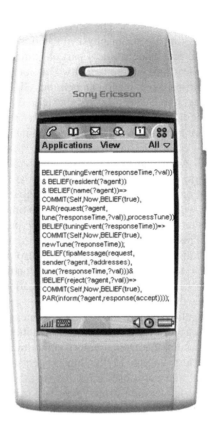

Fig. 3. An illustration of the commitment rules for implementing a Tuning Agent Role on using the Agent Factory runtime environment on a Sony Ericsson P800 emulator

From the software engineer's prospective, this scenario is straightforward to design and implement. In circumstances where computation resources are not foreseen as being at a premium, this approach may well be adequate. However, in a normal mobile computing space, this is most certainly not the case. Resources are scarce and must be used efficiently. If not, the usability of the resultant application will be adversely affected, with the negative usability, and ultimately financial consequences. By carefully identifying the essential tasks during the design, a software engineer may well alleviate some of the performance difficulties. Ultimately, however, they cannot guarantee that the software will operate even in a sub-optimum manner.

4.2.2 Scenario II: A Singular Tuning Approach is Adopted

An agent may adopt a policy of modifying its deliberation cycle in accordance with ongoing activities. In this case, once a video has started to play, the agent decreases its own deliberation cycle for the duration of the video. Some performance benefits may accrue from this approach. Should the agent pause its deliberation cycle for the entire duration, there is a risk of a bottleneck arising elsewhere in the system. Ultimately, the performance will deteriorate but not as much as in the previous scenario. As to whether the improvement will be discernable will depend on a number of factors. However, it is unlikely to be predictable or prolonged, as the other agents remain ignorant of what is happening and have no policy in place to alter their behavior while a resource-intensive task is being performed.

Such an approach can be adopted during implementation without any significant effort on the software engineer's behalf. However, the key problem of coordinating the optimum use of system resources remains.

4.2.3 Scenario III: A Collaborative Agent Tuning Approach is Adopted

Collaboration is an essential activity in a Multi-Agent System (MAS) if the MAS is to fulfill its objectives as a whole. In the video rendering example, the goal of the MAS is to ensure that the video is rendered appropriately and it is the responsibility of each agent in the MAS to contribute this by adopting suitable polices and strategies. Ultimately, it is the responsibility of the software designer to ensure that each agent is imbued with a strategy to facilitate this. In this case, it is envisaged that each agent in the MAS implements what has been termed the *agent tuning role*. In enabling the agent to fulfill its role, the designer must carefully consider the tasks each agent will perform in the MAS, as well as the temporal relationship between the tasks. After doing this, the designer can derive the necessary rules for each agent such that the goals of the MAS are not compromised and the limited resources are used efficiently.

To demonstrate the collaborative agent tuning process, the key steps are now described and illustrated through the documentation of the appropriate rules that must be adopted at various stages in the process. A summary may be seen in Fig. 4(a).

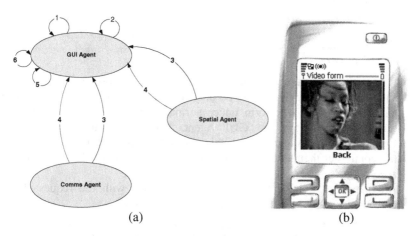

(a)   (b)

Fig. 4. (a) The GUI agent initializes and completes the tuning process in collaboration with the Communications Agent and the Spatial Agent. (b) Video playing in the Nokia emulator.

1. During the course of the agents' execution, some event may trigger the commencement of the agent tuning process. A commitment rule is then triggered by the appropriate agent:

```
BELIEF(tuningEvent(?responseTime,?val)) &
BELIEF(resident(?agent)) & !BELIEF(name(?agent)) =>
```

```
COMMIT(Self,Now,BELIEF(true), PAR(request(?agent,
tune(?responseTime,?val)), processTune)).
```

On adopting this rule, two processes commence in parallel: the first causes the agent to request the other collaborating agent(s) to adjust their *tuning parameters* accordingly. Tuning parameters represent dynamically self-configurable agent characteristics. In this case, it is the time between deliberation cycles that is the principal tuning parameter. Note that there could be others, depending on the domain in question. The second process causes the agent to prepare for forthcoming responses from the other agent(s) collaborating in the process. In the video-rendering example, prior to the user making a request to view a video, this rule is fired. This causes the GUI Agent to issue a tuning request to both the Communications Agent and the Spatial Agent. In parallel the GUI agent will prepare to process the responses from both these agents.

2. The requesting agent uses a second rule to store the requested response time in a persistent internal object. The agent changes its response time to this value when the requested tuning parameters have been accepted[1] by all collaborators:

```
BELIEF(tuningEvent(?responseTime,?val))=>
COMMIT(Self,Now,BELIEF(true),newTune(?reponseT
ime,?val));
```

In the case of the GUI Agent, the time between deliberation cycles will be increased thus freeing additional computation resources for rendering.

3. In the case of an agent agreeing to the tuning request, it proceeds to inform the requesting agent of its assent:

```
BELIEF(fipaMessage(request,sender(?agent,?addresses),
tune(?responseTime,?val))) & !BELIEF(reject(?agent,?val))=>

COMMIT(Self,Now,BELIEF(true),PAR(inform(?agent,response(acce
pt(?val)))));
```

It may of course engage on an appropriate course of action that reflects the new situation. For example, it may be only feasible to undertake a subset of those tasks that it would perform under normal circumstances. On receiving the tuning request from the GUI Agent, both the Spatial Agent and the Communications Agent will fire this rule if the requested tuning parameters do not contradict their own objectives and adjust their individual response times accordingly.

4. Alternatively, if an agent anticipates difficulties with the requested tuning parameter, it will reject the request:

```
BELIEF(fipaMessage(request,sender(?agent,?addresses),
tune(?responseTime,?val)))& BELIEF(reject(?agent,?val)) =>
COMMIT(Self,Now,BELIEF(true),
PAR(inform(?agent,response(reject))));
```

Should the Communications Agent or Spatial Agent be unhappy with the request, they will inform the GUI agent of their rebuff.

---

[1] Acceptance in this case is a predicate rather than proposition and thus the system supports variable levels of acceptance rather than a fixed Boolean truth-value.

5. When the agent receives a tuning response, the following rule is triggered causing the agent to process the informed values. After verifying that all responses have been received, the agent can determine whether to proceed with the tuning process or otherwise.

```
BELIEF(fipaMessage(inform,?sender,response(?val)))=>
COMMIT(Self,Now,BELIEF(true),tuneResponse(?val));
```

When the GUI Agent has received a response from both the Communications Agent and the Spatial Agent, it determines whether the process has been successful or not.

6. Assuming that the agents all respond positively to the initial tuning request, the requesting agent is now in a position to proceed and adjust its response time:

```
BELIEF(accepted(?val,?responseTime)) & BELIEF(?val)=>
COMMIT(Self,Now,BELIEF(true),tune(?responseTime));
```

When both the Spatial Agent and the Communication Agent indicate their acceptance of the tuning request (by reducing their response times), the GUI Agent can now proceed to decrease its own response time. The video rendering process can now commence.

7. Should one of the agents respond negatively and another positively, the tuning event cannot take place. This fact must be broadcast so that those agents who gave prior approval to the original tuning request can reset their parameters to their original states.

8. After the process that caused the tuning procedure is complete, it beholds the agent that initiated the process to monitor it and to inform the other agents of its completion, thus allowing them to reset their tuning parameters to their original values. In the video rendering scenario, the GUI Agent thus informs the Spatial Agent and the Communications Agents when the video process has terminated, in order that they may restore their previous tuning parameters. On completion, the Spatial Agent resumes interpreting the user's spatial context and the Communications Agent start processing normal communications requests again.

5 Experimental Results

To test the validity of the collaborative agent tuning approach, some initial experiments were undertaken using one popular smartphone currently on the market, namely the Nokia 6630. Periodic measurements of the responsiveness of the system were taken at regular intervals. To do this, a control point was placed in the code and associated with point at which the deliberative process began. The time at which each subsequent cycle commenced was then recorded. This was repeated 20 times for each agent, after which the results were calibrated and averaged.

When tuning is disabled (Fig. 5), the responsiveness of the system remains reasonably consistent throughout. This is as expected. However, it should be recalled that a number of trade-offs may have been necessary to achieve this. The designer may have been obliged to experiment with a number of different settings for the deliberation-cycle parameter before finding a combination that gave a satisfactory response. Because of this, the overall responsiveness of the system is quite low though the video will render at an appropriate rate. The responsiveness decreases further albeit momentarily, when the video buffering process commences.

Two different strategies were implemented to demonstrate the collaborative agent tuning approach. In the first case, a pre-emptive approach was followed. The agents mutually negotiated a collaborative agent-tuning strategy when the program was launched and this was adhered to for its entire duration. In the second case, a Just-in-Time (JIT) approach was adopted and the agents negotiated immediately prior to the video being rendered. The results obtained in each case may be seen in Fig. 6. Some critical points have been enumerated on the graph and these are now described.

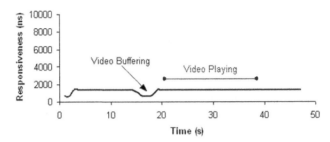

Fig. 5. Measured responsiveness without Collaborative Agent Tuning enabled

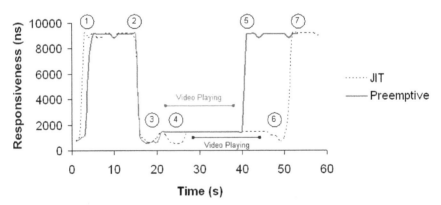

Fig. 6. Measured responsiveness with Collaborative Agent Tuning enabled

1. When the application is launched, it can be seen from the graph that there is a noticeable latency between the two strategies. The JIT approach launches faster while the pre-emptive approach is slower as the agents must negotiate their

tuning strategy during the startup phase. Once this completed, there will be no need for further negotiation, at least concerning collaborative tuning.

2. At some point during the execution, it will be necessary to play a video. In the pre-emptive case, the tuning approach is agreed between the agents so they can now proceed to immediately implement their tuning strategy. In contrast, the agents that have adopted a JIT approach must complete some negotiations before the tuning policy can be implemented.

3. In each case, the responsiveness drops. In the pre-emptive case, pre-loading and rendering of the video can commence immediately. This is not the case with the JIT approach. The responsiveness drops somewhat slower but, more importantly, there is an additional delay as a result of the late negotiation before preloading of the video can occur and the rendering process commence.

4. As a vivid illustration of the differences between the two approaches, the video is being already played in the pre-emptive approach while in the case of JIT collaborative tuning, the video is still being buffered.

5. In the pre-emptive case, the video is now completed and the status quo is restored quickly. The video is still playing in the JIT scenario.

6. Only now is the video complete in the JIT case. However, the agents must then collaboratively reset their tuning parameters. In a pre-emptive scenario, the response times are already restored to their original values.

7. Now, the agents in both cases are operating with their original parameters intact and with identical response times.

In both pre-emptive and JIT collaborative agent tuning scenarios, agents can now operate with a far quicker overall response time as they can now respond to particular events and adjust their responsiveness accordingly. Thus, the agents' performance can be significantly increased over the lifetime of the application, rather than being artificially restricted to operating with a lower response time in anticipation of certain events that would consume processor cycles. Once the agents have completed the collaborative tuning process, the responsiveness of the system is approximately the same as the situation when no tuning occurred. However, once the video has been displayed, the tuning parameters are reset and the responsiveness of the system returns to its original value.

6 Discussion and Future Work

Collaborative agent tuning has been conceived as a strategy for maximizing agent performance over the lifetime of an application. In particular, it is perceived as being useful in environments of limited computational capacity, mobile phones being one particular instance. The two strategies examined – pre-emptive and JIT, offer the software designer some options for consideration; their ultimate choice is dependent on the application in question as well as its target deployment environment. In the video rendering example, it could be that an end-user may not always choose to play the video. In this case, the JIT approach would be appropriate as computational resources would not be wasted on the negotiation process in cases where the user does not play the video. Alternatively, the video component may be an indispensable feature of the application in which case a pre-emptive approach would be preferred as it would reduce the latency of video execution. Agents could also proactively monitor user behavior and decide between pre-emptive and JIT tuning based on a model of user behavior developed over time.

While satisfied that collaborate agent tuning is, in principle, an approach that would yield performance benefits, there is one key difficulty that limits its potential. A metric describing computational load needs to be identified. At a minimum, such a metric would be a tuple of processor state and system memory. The Java Runtime object provides a mechanism to determine the amount of free memory available to the JVM however no such metric exists for computational load. The likely reason for this is because the JVM hides processor specific implementation details from the programmer to facilitate platform independent development. J2ME does not support the Java Native Interface and therefore does not provide a mechanism to enable the developer to write platform specific native code to access such data. To get around this problem future work will associate additional meta-data with tasks being performed by agents. This meta-data will provide and an indication of a tasks computational overhead and will be obtained by the software engineer through system profiling. Using the meta-data and a model of their processing capabilities agents will be empowered with true autonomic behavior. In future work it is also planned to conduct further experiments that compare the collaborative agent tuning approach with other approaches, for example that adopted by DIOS++.

In the broader context of agent communities and societies, there are a number of aspects of collaborative agent tuning that warrant further investigation First of all, it is a unilateral process by the MAS as a whole. Further investigation is needed as to the implications of using a subset of the MAS for the process. For example, are there any measurable gains from allowing a subset of the MAS collaborate in the tuning process, what are the tradeoffs? The implications for scalability need to be considered. In the small ecosystems that comprise ambient intelligent services, this is not necessarily a significant problem. However, it is not clear at this time what the implications would be if the population of the MAS increased.

7 Conclusion

Within this paper we have explored how ambient intelligent systems may be imbued with autonomic properties. The paper draws upon work undertaken by the authors in the use of BDI agents in the delivery of personalized content to mobile users. Accommodating such strong agents on computationally challenged devices places ever increasing demands on the computational real estate that is typically available.

Specifically, collaborative agent tuning is a process whereby cohabiting agents may collaboratively negotiate access to the processor. This process delivers system adaptivity by which agents may voluntarily permit the degradation of their deliberative deductive cycle in order to facilitate the activities of fellow agents. Such benevolence is typified when mutual benefit is derived from such negotiations. Collaborative agent tuning offers a glimpse into those autonomic properties that may be delivered via an agent collective and, furthermore, illustrates how relatively simple autonomic properties may yield important performance enhancements in environments that are computat-ionally limited such as the broad mobile and ubiquitous application sector.

Acknowledgements

Gregory O'Hare and Michael O'Grady gratefully acknowledges the support of Science Foundation Ireland under Grant No. 03/IN.3/1361.

References

1. Kephart, J.O., Chess, D.M. The Vision of Autonomic Computing, IEEE Computer, 36 (1), January 2003, pp. 41–50.
2. Aarts, E., Marzano, S. (editors), The New Everyday: Views on Ambient Intelligence, 010 Publishers, Rotterdam, The Netherlands, 2003.
3. O'Grady, M.J., O'Hare, G.M.P.: Just-in-Time Multimedia Distribution in a Mobile Computing Environment, IEEE Multimedia, vol. 11, no. 4, pp. 62–74, 2004.
4. Rao, A.S., Georgeff, M.P.: Modelling Rational Agents within a BDI Architecture. In: Principles of Knowledge Representation. & Reasoning, San Mateo, CA. 1991.
5. O'Hare, G.M.P., O'Grady, M.J.: Gulliver's Genie: A Multi-Agent System for Ubiquitous and Intelligent Content Delivery, Computer Communications, 26 (11), 2003, 1177–1187.
6. Keegan, S., & O'Hare, G.M.P., EasiShop – Agent-Based Cross Merchant Product Comparison Shopping for the Mobile User. Proceedings of 1st International Conference on Information & Communication Technologies: From Theory to Applications (ICTTA '04), Damascus, Syria, 2004.
7. ACCESS: An Agent based Architecture for the Rapid Prototyping of Location Aware Services, Strahan, R., O'Hare, G.M.P., Phelan, D., Muldoon, C., Collier, R. Proceedings of the 5th International Conference on Computational Science (ICCS 2005), Emory University Atlanta, USA. 2005.
8. Soh, L.-K., Tsatsoulis, C.: Agent-Based Argumentative Negotiations with Case-Based Reasoning, AAAI Fall Symposium Series on Negotiation Methods for Autonomous Cooperative Systems, North Falmouth, Mass, 16–25, 2001.
9. Groth, P. T., Suri, N., CPU Resource Control and Accounting in the NOMADS Mobile Agent System, Technical Report, Institute for Human & Machine Cognition, University of West Florida, 2002.
10. Bigus, J.P., Hellerstein, J.L., Squillante, M.S. Auto Tune: A Generic Agent for Automated Performance Tuning, Proceedings of the International Conference on Practical Application of Intelligent Agents and Multi-Agents (PAAM), 2000.
11. Bigus, J.P., Schlosnagle, D.A., Pilgrim, J.R., Mills III, W.N., Diao, Y., ABLE: A Toolkit for Building Multiagent Autonomic Systems, IBM Systems Journal, 41 (3), 350–371, 2002.
12. Liu, H., Parashar, M., DIOS++: A Framework for Rule-Based Autonomic Management of Distributed Scientific Applications, Proceedings of the 9th International EuroPar Conference (Euro-Par 2003), LNCS. 2790, 66–73, 2003.
13. Walsh, W.E., Wellman, M.P. A market protocol for decentralized task allocation: Extended version. Proceedings of the Third International Conference on Multi-Agent Systems (ICMAS-98), 1998.
14. Cohen, P.R. and Levesque, H.J. Intention Is Choice with Commitment. Artificial Intelligence, 42, 213–261, 1990.
15. Levesque, H.J., Cohen, P.R., and Nunes, J.H.T. On Acting Together, Proceedings of AAAI-90, 94–99, 1990.
16. Singh, M. P. 2000. ASocial Semantics for Agent Communication Languages. In Issues in Agent Communication, Vol. 1916. Edited by F. Dignum and M. Greaves. Springer-Verlag, Berlin, pp. 31–45.

17. Tarkoma, S., Laukkanen, M. Supporting Software Agents on Small Devices, Proceedings of the First International Joint Conference on Autonomous Agents and Multi-Agent Systems (AAMAS-2002), Bologna, Italy, July 2002.
18. Foundation for Intelligent Physical Agents (FIPA), http://www.fipa.org.
19. Johansen, D., Lauvset, K., Van Renesse, R., Schneider, F., Sudmann, N., Jacobsen. K., A Tacoma Retrospective, Software Practice and Experience, 32 (6), 2002, pp. 605–619.
20. F. Bergenti, F., Poggi, A., LEAP: A FIPA Platform for Handheld and Mobile Devices, Proceedings of the 8th International Workshop on Agent Theories, Architectures and Languages (ATAL-2001), Seattle, WA, USA, August 2001.
21. The Agent Oriented Software Group, http://www.agent-software.com.
22. Koch, F., Meyer, J-J., Dignum, F., Rahwan, I., Programming Deliberative Agents for Mobile Services: the 3APL-M Platform, AAMAS'05 Workshop on Programming Multi-Agent Systems (ProMAS05), Utrecht, Netherlands, July 2005.
23. Rahwan, T., Rahwan, T., Rahwan, I., Ashri, R., Agent-based Support for Mobile Users using AgentSpeak(L), Agent Oriented Information Systems (AOIS2003), LNAI 3030, 45–60, 2004, Springer-Verlag.
24. O'Hare G.M.P., Agent Factory: An Environment for the Fabrication of Multi-Agent Systems, in Foundations of Distributed Artificial Intelligence (G.M.P. O'Hare and N. Jennings eds) pp. 449–484, John Wiley and Sons, Inc., 1996.
25. Collier, R.W., O'Hare, G.M.P., Lowen, T., Rooney, C.F.B., (2003), Beyond Prototyping in the Valley of the Agents, in Multi-Agent Systems and Applications III: Proceedings of the 3rd Central and Eastern European Conference on Multi-Agent Systems (CEEMAS'03), Prague, Czech Republic, Lecture Notes in Computer Science (LNCS 2691), Springer-Verlag.
26. Jennings, N.R. Controlling Cooperative Problem Solving in Industrial Multi-Agent Systems using Joint Intentions. Artificial Intelligence, 75(2):195–240, 1995.
27. Kumar, S., P. R. Cohen, and H. J. Levesque. 2000a. The Adaptive Agent Architecture: Achieving Fault-Tolerance Using Persistent Broker Teams. In Proceedings of Fourth International Conference on Multi-Agent Systems (ICMAS 2000), Boston, MA. IEEE Press, pp. 159–166.

Cultural Agents: A Community of Minds

Michael D. Fischer

University of Kent

Abstract. Intelligent agents embedded in cultural processes demonstrate remarkable powers of creation, transformation, stability and regulation. As G.P. Murdock said in his 1971 Huxley Lecture, culture and social structure are not divine law within which individuals simply satisfy their assigned objectives and then die. Culture gives agents the power to hyper-adapt: not only can they achieve local minima and maxima, they modify or create the conditions for adaptation. Culture transcends material and behavioural contexts. Cultural solutions are instantiated in material and behavioural terms, but are based in large part on 'invented' symbolic constructions of the interaction space and its elements. Although the level of 'intelligence' required to enact culture is relatively high, agents that enact culture create conditions to which other, less intelligent, agents will also adapt. A little culture goes a long way. We will consider culture design criteria and how these can be represented in agent-based models and how culture-based solutions might contribute to our global management of knowledge.

1 Introduction

Human culture is a creative and transformative natural force. Although culture is associated mainly with humans, and in a sense had to be 'created' by humans in the course of their evolution, it is nevertheless a natural force that has tremendous potential to affect every physical system that humans contact.

From the standpoint of the sciences, culture has emerged from being an exotic curiosity in the 1930s associated with South Seas islands, tropical Africa or Highland New Guinea to underlying practical workaday methods, first in economic development projects, then industrial settings and more recently in software systems design relating to human-computer interfaces and human factors design.

As evidenced by this meeting, in the development of agent-based software design a natural approach to organising agents is implementing concepts such as society within which to embed agents. However, culture, the system of activities and resources that support human social organisation, is scantly considered in the computational agent literature outside anthropological, sociological and occasionally economic or business models. Where culture does arise in the literature, it is most likely to relate to agents that relate directly or on behalf of people as cultural agents. So while there is some relevant literature that demonstrates considerable potential for the inclusion of culture-related concepts in mathematical and computational modelling, this is the product of a very small group of researchers. Even among anthropologists formal work exploring how culture 'works' is undertaken by few and explicitly eschewed by a sizable minority.

O. Dikenelli, M.-P. Gleizes, and A. Ricci (Eds.): ESAW 2005, LNAI 3963, pp. 259–274, 2006.
© Springer-Verlag Berlin Heidelberg 2006

As an anthropologist I have to consider these issues. Is culture, despite its tenure in anthropology, just too 'fuzzy'? Or is it perhaps suitable for describing actual human groups, but not really as a means for constructing artificial, purposeful, systems? At the same time, there is no doubt that human behaviour driven by culture is responsible for the collective achievements of humans - transcending the technologies of stick, stone and bone a million years ago towards the technologies of genetic engineering, nanoengineering and quantum level computing which will permit us to further radically modify our lives, the world, and some day perhaps the universe.

I will argue that culture is indeed represented, implicitly, within many agent-based systems. It appears in the form of solutions that are inspired by the cultural knowledge of the system designers, in the conception of how agent societies should operate, and by including some of the mechanisms of communication, peer reaction and defining values that we can associate with cultural systems. Making explicit representations of cultural systems will bring these 'hidden' design elements into view as a formal part of the agent framework, making possible more powerful agent-based solutions.

2 The Culture Concept

2.1 A (Very) Brief History of the Culture Concept

Anthropologists generally conceptualise societies as groups composed of individuals who coordinate in a holistic distributed manner through elaborated social behaviour and shared patterns of values. Culture is the term used to describe the resources requred to support this interaction. Anthropologists have proposed a range of definitions for culture over the past century. The development of the 'culture concept' is illustrated in Figure 1. In The shift from exclusively behavioural criteria to the inclusion of ideational components represents both development in anthropological theory as well as the impact of cybernetics and systems theory. In particular, culture must:

> maintain and distribute knowledge in a population of agents
> produce the conditions by which cultural knowledge is useful
> set the terms of reference within which behaviours or actions take place

Prior to WWII cultural properties often traded under the descriptor "superorganic". Murdock [1] argued that culture was "superindividual ... beyond the sphere of psychology ... It is a matter of indifference to psychology that two persons, instead of one, possess a given habit. It is precisely this fact that becomes the starting point of the science of culture" [1](207). When the concept of a system became available in the 1940s [2], anthropologists were able to progress their framework considerably as they now had a language for describing the relationship between complex unseen systems of thought and the expression of these as behaviour. Behaviour could be conceptualised as an inscription of individuals interacting driven by complex systems of thought.

2.2 Culture-Based Systems

Culture as a systemic concept has rapidly become pervasive outside anthropology in many cognate social sciences and humanities subjects. Despite this anthropologists are generally unable to define precisely what is meant by culture, nor do those who do precisely define culture agree. One explanation for difficulty in definition is that culture is not defined by a single process or system, but is the conjunction of many aspects of human cognition and organization [3]. These would include processes or systems relating to communication, learning, adaptation, representation and trans- formation. In short, what anthropologists, and increasingly others, now refer to as culture is an emergent phenomena (or perhaps even an apparent category of phenomena) - the result of interaction of different systems which are, at least in part, orthogonal to each other [4].

This was not unanticipated. Fischer, Lyon and Read [5] note that:

> G. P. Murdock, in ... "Anthropology's Mythology", argued that neither culture nor social structure can be reified to serve as an explanation. Rather these are our characterization of patterns of interactions between individuals, not the source of these interactions. ... Murdock was introducing a program ... focusing ... theory on diversity of individual experience and choice, not commonality and conformance. Fischer and Lyon [6] on Murdock [7].

Marvin Minsky, in The Society of Mind, commented, "What magical trick makes us intelligent? The trick is that there is no trick. The power of intelligence stems from our vast diversity, not from any single, perfect principle" [8](308). Of course Minsky is referring to a single mind. To represent the diverse principles underlying cultural systems we might conceptualize culture as "the community of minds".

As Murdock and Minsky argue, culture cannot be represented in terms of uniform static structures; culture is dynamically enacted and constituted differently by different culture-enacting agents, but with results that are comprehensible, if not acceptable, to other agents. It is critical that we understand how cultural systems become distributed within a population in such a way that most agents can agree on what is a part of a culture and what is idiosyncratic. To connect a diverse community of minds culture must be relational; different agents will behave differently based on their relationship to other agents. Culture is enacted differently by different cultural agents, each of which has an understanding of how the other agents operate under different projections with respect to different relationships.

Fischer [9] relates some of the context for how implicit and explicit theories of culture have changed in recent decades, in particular the tensions between those who see structure and pattern and those who deny these in favour of performance, improvisation and smorgasbord emergent culture. Fischer observes this tension is resolved if we recognize that not least of the outcomes of cultural processes is to recreate the conditions for cultural technologies of thought and objects to operate, symbolically and materially. From this Fischer develops the principle of 'powerful knowledge', knowledge that is deontic, enabling the management and exploitation of processes which emerge from interacting cultural agents and their knowledge.

Fischer and Read [10] outline an approach to focusing on culture in a way that the duality between ideation and behaviour could be represented in concrete models. The basic concept is simple; that we can represent culture as a collection of discrete symbolic systems, possibly not logically consistent with each other. These systems of symbols are shared between agents to varying degrees of detail and consistency. It is when agents instantiate these within a common interaction space into a set of behaviours that commonalities and inconsistencies are reconciled. Indeed, the patterns of behaviour that emerge that are recognised as culture may emerge from underlying symbolic systems that are apparently at odds with each other, both within the same agent and between agents.

2.3 Hyperadaptation

One of the properties of a cultural system is that it supports hyperadaptation. Hyperadaption basically refers to a process of behaviourally modifying the local material context so that a range of new adapations become possible. Hyperadaption occurs in species other than humans, such as 'social' insects, birds or higher primates, but is the principle form of human adaptation.

Adaption involves optimising around some set of resources. Hyperadaptation effectively 'changes the rules', reordering or reorganising the relationship between agent and 'environment' to support a new adaptation. This can be done by reconceptualisation or classification (e.g. learning to exploit features of the environment), but more usually hyperadaptation will involve some modification that must be repeated to support the new adaptation.

The repeated effect can be considered as a technology. Tools are associated with many technologies, themselves probably the product of further adaptation to the original hyperadaptation. Tools are difficult to develop and replicate - only humans have done so with minor exceptions. Technologies often lead to distribution of the replication process.

Human hyperadaptivity appears to be unique both in its character and pervasiveness. There is hardly a aspect of human life that does not rest on a hyperadaptation.

2.4 Approaches to Computational Culture

The 2004 European Meetings for Cybernetics and System Research included sessions relating to cultural systems with contributions exploring the use of culture in mathematical and computational models. These were not new approaches in the sense that the researchers concerned have been working with and promoting these ideas for some time. They are finally beginning to have traction.

Reynolds and Peng [11] demonstrate how a simple model of culture can be instantiated in an agent population to adaptively solve 'real world' optimization problems. They outline a method based on the evolutionary Cultural Algorithms approach originated by Reynolds [12] that models an agent population using diverse symbolic knowledge to adaptively converge towards solutions to optimization problems. In this case they demonstrate that CA can be applied to solving problems in engineering design as a result of emergent features based on adaptive cultural systems with the ability to learn and adapt at a more abstract level than conventional genetic algorithms.

Reynolds and Peng situate culture within the evolutionary process by expanding an agent's phenotype to include acquired characteristics associated with knowledge-based solutions; an individual's fitness is now associated with both their hereditary fitness and their cultural fitness. The latter includes their individual ability to use cultural resources and the fitness bestowed on them by others within the cultural 'swarm' by others' modifying and expanding the knowledge and belief resources in the system adaptively over time. Thus individual fitness is not only about individual's transmitting their individual phenotypes across generations, but about transmitting their knowledge adaptations as well. Furthermore, individual fitness is directly linked to modifications that the individual agent and other agents introduce.

Using the three principles of cognitive relativity, rationality and clarity, Ezhkova [13] addresses culture by an examination of shared experience and how asymmetric but inter-adapted 'clarity' emerges from these shared experiences. Taking culture as a self-organizing complex phenomenon, she notes that as a result of cognitive relativity a culture can be examined from a number of different observer perspectives, where a culture is observed as a unitary 'actor', the community of individual actors who enact a culture, or indeed in a comparative sense as one of a set of cultural systems. Furthermore, these different perspectives can be nested by a single observer such that all are available simultaneously, producing a continuum of composite perspectives and potential actions to be taken.

Ezhkova argues that rationality is thus a relative condition: "Rationality rests on the particular nest of action in which one must exercise decision." Clarity is how Ezhkova denotes the ability to differentiate and classify the variety of inputs agents are exposed to; effectively underlying the ability to create categories. She outlines several approaches to measuring and implementing clarity. Ezhkova proposes the process of seeking clarity as a key cognitive navigational tool, the driver for adaptation in order to maximize success. Culture is a tool for recognition of key stable patterns, using clarity to situate culture in an evolutionary context: "the evolutionary meaning of clarity: what is clear survives". This is a very important point, particularly in a cultural context. Culture emerges, in large part, because of the distribution of a shared sense of clarity rather than specific shared bits of knowledge which tends to be distributed.

Ballonoff [14] presents a three level framework of measurements relating to a culture driven system, i) corresponding to material processes, ii) the impacts of cultural operators on i), and iii) measurements relating to the evolution of ii). That is, in an "ethnographic view", population and genetic statistics are the base phenomena (I), culture modifies these measures over time as events (II), and the pattern of change is governed by measurements of II (as per work of Ezhkova). With respect to a "real" system G related to some set of cultural systems C instantiation is "prediction or computation from the cultural system to create a particular instance of the real system". G evolves forward under evolutionary operators, and C under cultural evolutionary operators, and the effects of both these must occur on the same real systems in concert, clearly constraining each other. He concludes that these constraints can filter the huge lattice of possible relationships between G and C, making it possible to predict possible future cultural structures realizable in the real system.

Hunters and gatherers in Arctic societies undergo strong selection in an adaptationist paradigm. Read [15] uses one such society, the Netsilik, in his formal analysis of the role of resilience and robustness in increasing the adaptive capacity of human societies. Read uses Netsilik Inuit data as an extreme example of the cultural adaptations which allows individuals to modify environmental constraints; their adaptation to an Arctic environment exemplifies the way in which behaviour has both a material and an ideational/cultural dimension. Human societies, Read argues, have developed both resilient and robust responses to shocks in order to satisfy environmental imperatives and cope with culturally generated tensions. Using the basic subsistence challenges of living in inhospitable Arctic conditions along Hudson Bay, Canada, Read shows how relatively simple cultural solutions to real problems sometimes have longer term consequences which require some kind of resolution. The resolution to one problem, in turn, may lead to further dilemmas which then need some form of resolution.

Read stresses the importance of self-monitoring of a system as part of the system's resilience, particularly cultural systems with group level benefits due to difficulty maintaining a stable configurations of behaviour with respect to social and cultural relationships between individuals. Behaviours such as seasonal fishing and hunting are relatively stable while ideational behaviours are far less so, requiring repeated and frequent monitoring by individuals of their relationships with other individuals. "People do what is required to make a cultural model work in the real world" even if it means violating ordinary norms of behaviour. Individual instantiation of cultural models results in group-level behaviour that benefits those individuals.

Read presents a dynamic mathematical approach for studying "real world" systems with interacting material and ideational processes and an insightful explanation for specific cultural behaviours which, when taken in isolation, may seem difficult to fathom; when understood as part of a complex cultural system that provided the Netsilik Inuit with sufficiently robust responses to shocks to retain some continuity of collective notions of who and what the Netsilik were, with resilient responses that provided the flexibility to survive unstable situations.

Employing the deontic logic of permissions and obligations rather than the imperative logic of possibility and necessity, Fischer [9] argues that domain knowledge need not be true, it need only be enabling or effective - what he calls "powerful knowledge". Transforming information or experience into knowledge is a role associated with culture but people embedded in a culture have many ways of carrying out these transformations. An understanding of culture cannot be derived from treating an instantiation as if it were an underlying principle. Indeed, he suggests that when looking at the level of instantiation it is both plausible and sometimes likely that underlying principles will not be expressed in favour of contingent events.

Reynold's and Peng, Ezhkova, Ballonoff and Read advance our understanding of cultural systems of agents, demonstrating that models based on diverse symbolic knowledge in concert with a population that uses this knowledge can apply that knowledge in a dynamic manner to solve new material problems. They identify additional requirements for this knowledge: diverse knowledge domains that are distributed across the population. There are adaptive advantages to having a distributed and diverse knowledge environment both for the population as a whole and the individuals within it, even those that are themselves less adapted. These models demonstrate that even in a highly constrained environment with somewhat unforgiving evolutionary forces at work, cultural systems require more than one type and distribution of knowledge to learn and adapt.

3   Cultural Instantiation

Fischer and Read [10] initiates a programme to develop instantiation of an ideational system as a basis for formally describing relationships between ideational and material processes and increasing the efficacy of using more integrated models and agent-oriented simulations for understanding cultural processes in particular.

In the crudest terms an instantiation of an ideational system is the production of an instance of behaviour conditioned by an ideational system within a given material context, which may include other agents each instantiating the same or a different ideational systems of their own - the reduction of the possible to a presence. Instantiation is an interface between ideas and action, conception and creation, thinking and doing. Models embedding both material and ideational themes are important if we are to advance our understanding of human lives embedded in the world. Many of the problems anthropologists investigate relate to an ideational structure or process embedded within a material context (or vice versa).

Ideational models are critical in human groups to support hyperadaption. Basically hyperadaptive agents need a 'story' to go with the actions that replicate the conditions for hyperadaptation. The critical feature the story must have is that it is logically consistent, otherwise it is difficult to transmit with fidelity within a group. If the story can be reproduced with fidelity this helps to stabilise the associated knowledge of technique and translation (instantiation) necessary to produce behaviours from the story.

It is the behaviours that actually produce the effects that agents have adapted to. Instantiation is the process of translating these 'stories' to actions - what I call 'powerful knowledge'. Powerful knowledge is not true or false (nor are the stories) but is valued with respect to its effects. Powerful knowledge changes more easily than the stories.

Other, non-cultural, agents also adapt to the changes that hyperadaptive agents introduce. This includes both other humans (in other groups), as well as members of a group, and other 'species' of agent altogether. This is, in part a consequence of the need to distribute 'expertise' that is necessary to maintain the hyperadaptive invention.

Ideational systems considered in isolation are difficult to evaluate. Behavioural processes are difficult to interpret. By embedding material and ideational components within an integrated model, the properties of ideational systems, and observable indices of these, may be identified. In this way we can create models that both take account of how the physical context limits the application of ideational resources and how ideational resources influence the structure and recreation of important aspects of the physical context. This is important because considering ideational resources in the context of their application solves many of the philosophical problems that arise when considering the ideational or material issues alone (such as infinite regress, reflection, non-determinism, non-essentialism). Although there are a large number of ways for an ideational resource to be instantiated in a given material context, these will generally be far fewer than the number of ways in which it can be imagined to instantiate. Additionally, the same basic ideational resource can/will be instantiated differently in different contexts.

In modelling instantiation, we represent a group of people as a collection of individual agents, not an abstract aggregate. This makes it possible to study why and how patterns emerge, which cannot be done if we only consider the aggregate that exhibits the pattern. Instantiation is a process that mediates the mapping from ideational structures to physical effects. Behaviour is not a direct result of ideational systems, but of the 'rules' of instantiation of an ideational system. Cultural schema need not be directly linked to behaviour, nor need they be functionally dependent on 'what works', at least until a system of instantiation can no longer reliably connect cultural schema to material requirements - a condition that we posit is relatively infrequent. Thus cultural schema can be relatively stable and conservative while being adaptive to context and supporting relatively rapid adaptation by modifying the pattern of instantiation rather than the pattern of fundamental ideas and thought. Also, instantiation occurs whenever idea contacts the world. The result may stem more from the external context than from what was 'intended' or 'desired'. That is, cultural instantiation is a process of ideational principles of multi-agents interacting together, often within a material context. The result, whatever it is, is the instantiation. Agents rarely fulfil their goals in full, and sometimes not at all.

For example, Read [18] relates our use of instantiation in research on a universal cultural category, kinship terminologies. In the course of developing a computer program, Kinship Algebra Expert System (KAES) [19], to assist in the production of algebraic models of kinship terminology we made a number of important discoveries. Following Leaf [20], a kinship terminology can be represented entirely in terms of native thinker judgements of the relationships between terms without reference to external genealogical concepts [18].

KAES identifies an underlying algebraic structure for this representation of the terminology (if there is one... so far all complex terminologies we have tried are amenable). Based on graphical input relating to a given kinship terminology and knowledge about the relationships between terminologies (in terms of the terminology only) KAES produces results that can be instantiated in a given real or model population, based exclusively on internal properties of the kinship terms and indigenous judgements of lexical properties of the terms and very basic relationships between terms based on entirely internal criteria. Unlike most attempts at formal modelling our approach make no recourse to hypothetical external reference frameworks such as a genealogical grid.

This is not the first model to be based on lexical properties of kinship terms. The componential systems developed in the 1960s (cf. [21]) were based on lexical properties associated with kin terms, and were formal in a trivial sense. They did not result in structures which were general because the formal model used had no analytic capacity beyond establishing that the relationships in a given terminology were consistent. Fischer [22] implemented a general formal representation suitable for instantiation, but while formally based, the fundamental properties it depended on were assumed to be given. Other algebraic approaches to terminological analysis have be extant for 50 years, but have either fitted terminologies to prescribed structures, or been difficult to instantiate on actual populations... there was no easy way to relate the algebraic account and the instantiation of kin terms in groups of people. Additionally these systems tended to depend on considerable algebraic creativity and understanding on the part of the analyst.

Our model is algebraic and algorithmic. That is, the models are algebras, and producing these algebras is done following a algorithm. We have developed a computer program loosely based on Read and Behren's earlier KAES [23], but rather than an expert system which assists in making decisions towards creating an appropriate algebraic account, our program generates the algebras directly from the source data (lists of terms and indigenous judgements on relationships between terms), with only a single decision in the process whether to represent sex as a feature of individual terms, or whether to treat sex as a bifurcation whose associated productions are structurally equivalent. We have retained the KAES label for historical continuity.

Although doubtless a bit abstract for some, KAES is significant. Most important is the result that is emerging from using KAES: the strong suggestion that most, if not all, elementary and complex kinship terminologies can be described in terms of an algebraic structure. This is significant, because there are many more terminologies possible that do not possess such a structure. That the human mind should settle on the more limited set implies some deep commonalities in the forms of logic that humans employ. It is also significant because:

   it is a formal model of an ideational system derived entirely from judgements on
      terminological relationships, not on an instantiation in a population,
   the ideational model contains possibilities that specific populations (e.g. American,
      Shipebo and Trobrian groups) do not exhibit,
   this model can be instantiated over a specific population, and
   will produce results that are predictive of the set of instantiated relationships in
      specific populations.

It is also significant because it is a good example of how the results of the analysis of an ideational system can be directly introduced into subsequent models without transformation or 'tailoring' for the purpose. That is, it provides a means of representing the potentialities of a cultural system and relating these to specific contexts without performing the reductions a particular context would normally require - reductions are properties of the process of instantiation.

One thing that almost all kinship terminological systems have in common is that they must be instantiable to be useful and to reproduce themselves. Being instantiable implies certain properties that an instantiable system must have to 'become present'. Among these is some extent of stability. Most systems can change relatively easily and remain a system. Although it is possible to modify an algebra and have a result that is an algebra, this is much 'harder' to do. Therefore systems that must be stable will benefit if they must also be logically equivalent to an algebra (this would not be unique to algebras but a property to any system of symbols with internally defined rules of production). Beyond this we found that the approach that Read used to identify the algebraic structures underlying terminologies itself could be improved and better understood by taking instantiation into account. That is, by taking into account the need to be instantiable and stable, the algorithm became simpler and more understandable, and this could be used as an evaluation metric for choosing one approach over another. The resulting algorithm from this approach was much more unified than Read's earlier attempts, suggested ways of dealing with terminological systems that had previously been resistant to explanation (classificatory terminologies) and the role of gender was significantly improved.

The most remarkable outcome, from our perspective at least, is that by combining a small subset of knowledge about the ideational properties of the terminology, the generating terms of the algebra, and a small subset of the knowledge about instantiation, how the generating terms are instantiated, that the structure of the complete terminology can be generated [19] precisely. To our knowledge this is the first example of a predictive model of a symbolic system that can be based entirely on data consisting of relational judgements of the relationships between tokens. This result is not possible by looking at the behavioural data alone, nor by construction of an ideational model alone, only by combining aspects of both in a single model.

In some ways this returns to the distinction between competence and performance proposed by Chomksy [24]. Perhaps this is where we often go wrong. He notes that we cannot simply analyse the structures that occur, because there are 'errors' and little variants that will 'spoil' any formal description. But this is not the real reason. We cannot analyse narrow behaviour because it is only a tiny fragment of what is going on, and a single behaviour can potentially impact many different ideational schemas, but is what results because of instantiation. That is, contrary to Chomsky's conjecture that separated the analysis of competence from that of performance, the point of instantiation between these is critical in analysis from either ideational or material perspective. Ideational analyses that ignore altogether issues of instantiation cannot account for either the variation or stability in culture, nor can materialist analyses that ignore the principles of instantiation of practice or behaviour.

4 Describing Cultural Processes Using Deontic Logic

Most cultural systems cannot as easily be represented by 'pure' algebrae as kinship terminologies. However, our conjecture regarding cultural domains [9] only requires that a significant component of a cultural domain be logically equivalent to a model governed by an internally consistent set of principles.

The logics generally underlying models based on statistically derived aggregated variables and their interactions operates on the assumption of direct or indirect causality where probability is an integral property of variables. Either a variable causes effects on another variable (e.g. number of calories ingested and energetic capacity), or the variable's value is proportional to another (perhaps unknown) variable that causes (is responsible for) some of the variation in the second (e.g. age and grey hair). The result is a causal logic operating on probabilistic relationships. While this approach is tractable with small models, it does not scale up well to larger models, and often leads to confusion in interpreting the contingent results of the model - whether these are to be attributed to the model or to factors outside the model. The resulting models are not well suited to supporting multi-agent models.

We can enhance this logic by adding deontic principles in addition to causal principles. Deontic argumentation originally grew out of moral philosophy, with the first modern formulation as a logic by Mally ([25]. See Lokhorst and Gobel [26] for a discussion of Mally's logic), who developed a logic based on propositions that assert that certain actions or states of affairs are morally obligatory, morally permissible, morally right or morally wrong - a logic of what ought to be given moral principles. There were serious problems with Mally's logic, but other deontic approaches have been developed (e.g. Endorsing [27], Maibaum [28]) with respect to obligations and permissions. Deontic logic can be applied both to ideational domains with respect to knowledge-based rules (Fischer and Finkelstein [29], Fischer [22]), as well as to material systems [28]. Deontic logic as I am using it follows Maibaum [28], which implements it by adding modal operators to a conventional predicate logic.

Deontic operations (obliged and permitted) are based on enablement and constraint as the basic principles for describing relationships, and can account for some apparent indeterminacy in a phenomena in terms of enabling and constraining the application of logical formulae (some *f* leading to actions or states). Weak determinism is denoted using the operator obliged ('do *f* when permitted'), stronger determinism by OBL ('do everything possible to do *f*') and constraints on statements by ~not permitted (~permitted) to prohibit a future instantiation of an action or result. The permitted operation is likewise indeterminant.- permitted does not require an action, it only allows (or enables) it at some future point. For example, if we have the following model of a process:

```
~permitted B -- constrain B
Loop:generate A -- a generator of condition A
if A then obliged B -- if condition A the proposition B iif B not constrained.
if B then halt -- exit this segment
generate C -- a generator of condition A
if C then permitted B - enable B
if B then halt -- exit this segment
goto loop
```

Fig. 2. A simple deontic model

Using deontic principles to interpret the statements, the model will execute Loop once, but halt at the second halt statement, since at the first conditional B is constrained, and cannot be expressed until the constraint is lifted. However, once B is permitted, B is expressed (if the first conditional is still valid) because it then obliged. In a variant formulations it is possible to use a weaker definition of oblige that applies only at the time of the conditional. In this case the model would execute Loop twice, and exit at the first halt statement on the second iteration. The first approach is representative of a parallel/declarative architecture. The second (weaker) is typically procedural.

The practical consequences of the deontic approach for modelling is that it provides tools for incrementally building models of processes, is adaptable to incorporation of agent-based description as well as aggregates, and more cleanly separates contingency accounted for within the model from contingency external to the model.

Fischer and Finkelstein [29] employed a deontic logic developed by Maibaum [28] called Modal Action Logic (MAL). Rules are expressed '(IN CONTEXT c) WHEN agent is performing action a THEN result'.

For example, ignoring some details of quantification, one observation derived from our case study of arranged marriages in Pakistan was:

in_public(girl) : [sing(girl,suggestive(lyrics))] -> character(girl, bad).
(gloss: if the girl is singing suggestive lyrics in public then the girl
has bad character).

In essence there is a governing proposition that is action related, defining a context frame for further conditions, which in turn contextualise the action. The use of this formulation solved a number of problems in representing processes because conditions and outcomes could be better organized in terms of the actions in the process. More important, it facilitates a formal representation of ethnographic data in a manner that is closer to the data as it is collected. Ethnographic data are not usually collected in the form of rules - rules are the result of analysis. Ethnographic data are more often in the form of sequences of declarative propositions. It is only after considerable observation and inquiry that the preconditions and results of these actions in specific contexts can be assessed. Thus we can further explore the action: sing(girl, suggestive(lyrics)) in:

> at_mindhi_of(girl,bro):[sing_to(girl,family(bride))]->
> permit(sing(girl,suggestive(lyrics)))
> (gloss: when a girl is attending the mindhi (pre-marriage eve) cere-
> mony of her brother and the girl is singing about the brides' family
> then the girl is permitted to sing songs with suggestive lyrics).

This approach facilitates the incremental development of rules from propositions. Processes with many concurrent actions can be represented. There is independence between the logic and the possibly stochastic events the logic applies to. These features make this formulation ideal for multi-agent modelling.

We can quantitatively evaluate these models without resort to aggregation by using evaluating changes in entropy between the expanded ideational structure and the instantiated structures (see Fischer [31] following Gatlin [30]). Of course, applying information theory [32] to our analysis depends on our capacity at some point to at least enumerate states possible for a given variable (to determine maximum uncertainty), and ideally to identify probabilities (or statistical proxies) for each state to calculate the minimum uncertainty. Deontic logic has no direct capacity to process this information. So why is it relevant to using information theory as a means to assess the interrelationships between the variables used to monitor or describe a particular context?

Within a flow of independent (or external) stochastic events, a logical model employing the deontic operators obliged, ~obliged, permitted and ~permitted to actions/states can modulate the flow of logic in response to these events using much simpler models that than would be required if we were to insist on a local causal model incorporating both variable values and variable degrees of applicability.

Deontic logic thus provides tools for representing not only direct causality, but also to describe in greater detail the context or conditions under which a causal relationship operates. For example, in Figure 2. if we designate stochastic parameters for the generate statements for A and C, their correlation with B is co-dependent. Given a data set consistent with Figure 2. the outcome of this co-dependence as expression of B might be described using only conventional statistical methods (such as multiple or partial correlation). However, Figure 2. proposes that the intrinsic correlation between A and B should approach 1 in isolation, (and the correlation between A and C could be zero) but within the wider model this expression is mediated by C. C thus controls the expression of the relationship between A and B, and the relation between B and C can only be expressed (in Figure 2.) given A. The deontic framework for modelling allows us to express in greater detail how the different variables interact with each other than simpler structural logics such as typically underlay causal path analysis or other conventional quantitative analysis in use. But, importantly, deontic logic is consistent with these; it merely permits more mechanical detail in processes which have structural constraints.

A deontic model formulation requires finding/constructing absolute enabling conditions, which can have a complex underlying aetiology. In other words, we have to either have enough detail on the process under investigation to posit and test constraints, or we have to attempt to predict constraints from the 'holes' in the conventional structure. However, constructing deontic models can be done incrementally in its concurrent/ declarative formulation which makes it convenient to implement as independent statements that 'communicate' based on changes by the statements to the global data set. Such models are typically easier to produce and interpret than models based on first order linear causal interactions. Indeed the use of a distributed deontic framework for situating data collection and analysis may prove to be a useful starting point for progressing more detailed quantitative approaches.

5   Conclusion: Applications to Multi-agent Modelling

Most of this paper has related a view of how human agents utilise cultural resources to produce technical effects on the environment. This reflects much of my experience with multi-agent modelling, which has been principally oriented to modelling human agents in different social and environmental contexts.

Does this approach have anything to offer to multi-agent modelling in general, particularly for the production of engineering applications and the production of useful software systems? Drawing on my prior experience as a software developer and engineer, I will argue that it does for most non-trivial classes of applications.

The weaker argument is that most applications are oriented to results that are embedded in cultural processes, be these traffic control, language understanding, regulating nuclear reactors or operating a factory. If the cultural processes are complex, then the application must take that complexity into account in some way. One potentially powerful way is to identify the principle cultural systems and their organisation, and to incorporate this into the applications. I argue that this is implicitly what is done in any case.

Applications are created using some combination of techniques that work together for a desired result. The gross combination and sequence is often known for an application type, but detailed implementation usually requires some considerable adjustment in configuring the technology to the specific conditions of the implementation, especially in the early stages of a technology. For example, in microelectronics it takes one to two decades for a new technical development to make the transition from first implementation to wide application [22]. Part of this delay simply reflects the development and diffusion of knowledge relating to a new technology, but perhaps more important, it is over this time that the technology itself is refined to make it more adapted to a wider range of contexts of application by practitioners who possess less and less knowledge by incorporating accumulated knowledge of these contexts of use into the technology itself. This is similar to the pattern of development of scientific innovations, where initial demonstration of an effect often appears in a very restricted and difficult to produce context, but as the context becomes better understood, so is the effect easier to demonstrate. This process in engineering is a result of gradually describing the many contingencies that make applications difficult, and adapting the technology so that the materials, tools and techniques incorporate knowledge relating to these contingencies and thus tend to work better across the contingent range.

Technology is often a blend of knowledge about how to interact with material systems, knowledge about the interaction and knowledge about what can and can't be done in different circumstances and how to adapt to different circumstances (deontic or instantiating knowledge, usually referred to as 'contextual' knowledge, although the latter usage is descriptive rather that analytic). Circumstantial adaptations are more often in need of revision as the kinds of circumstances that can arise change often in contrast to underlying principles, which may not change at all during the period of adaptation. Instantiating knowledge is necessary to produce results from the former two, and thus must be kept dynamically in 'tune' with contemporary circumstances. But perhaps more significantly, without incorporation of instantiating knowledge, we are in fact not importing useful knowledge at all because the powerful things that the knowledge enacts in its origin context are not present.

The stronger argument takes this point further. I suggest that multi-agent modelling as a method operates under similar constraints to human groups. If we are developing an application that performs some simple task for which an accepted mathematical model exists, then we are perhaps free of this constraint, but then we do not require multi-agent modelling this these cases. Multi-agent models are used in situations where we perceive complexity and a need for non-linear, non-sequential response in order to produce the application desired. This is precisely the area where our usual ways of expressing relationships and processes fails. Conventional propositional calculus and mathematics can only approximate results in these cases, often in a highly fragile form. Multi-agent models are not directed by a single logical system, but by many interacting with each other. In some cases these different systems are logically independent in the sense that each system interacts with the overall application process in ways that do not directly impact each other. However, in most real-world cases these different systems are not independent, and the interaction between systems usually requires considerable tuning and even 'hacking' to produce the desired behaviour in the application, and this often limits the case use of the application.

The cultural-based architecture I have described is a working example of how human groups deal with the problem of adaptively 'tuning and hacking' in maintaining a group over time. By separating the logic of ideation from the logic of instantiation we make explicit the adjustments necessary to produce a consistent solution. The logic of instantiation represents the part of the application that corresponds to the 'real-world' task at hand, producing satisfactory results in different contexts. The logics of the different ideational systems corresponds to the data structures combined with the relationships between the data items and the constraints on their use. Formally separating the two produces a system that is far easier to debug, develop and maintain.

Designing along these lines for each type of agent we should have two different systems, one that formally defines the ideational component and another that formally defines the instantiation of the former. Deontic logic is ideal for describing the ideational logics and procedural logic more suited for describing instantiation, though there are cases where the deontic extensions may be suitable. Deontic logic is well suited for explicitly mixing ideational frameworks with instantiation frameworks, keeping the two apart but permitting one to act on the other. It is also a way to formally represent what is already a major part of what practitioners do in engineering and software design. Although the story is 'science', the instantiation often is not. In this way we can separate the story from the instantiation.

To conclude, in reverse order - you are already doing 'cultural' programming. Cultural agents refers to design which permits a wide range of stories with ways of mapping these to actions. Hyperadaption is essential for intelligent adaptive systems.

References

Murdock, George Peter (1932). The Science of Culture. *American Anthropologist* 34(2):200–215.

D'Andrade, Roy G. (1995). *The Development of Cognitive Anthropology.* Cambridge University Press: Cambridge.

Leaf, Murray (2005). The Message Is The Medium: Language, Culture, And Informatics. *Cybernetics and Systems* 36:8.

Chit Hlaing, F. K. L. (2005) On the "Globality Hypothesis" About Social-Cultural Structure: An Algebraic Solution. *Cybernetics and Systems* 36:8.

Fischer, Michael D., Stephen Lyon and Dwight Read (2005). Introduction to Special Issue on Cultural Systems. *Cybernetics and Systems* 36:8.

Fischer, M. D. and Lyon, S. M. (2004). George Peter Murdock. In V. Amit (ed) *Biographical Dictionary of Social and Cultural Anthropology.* London: Routledge. pp. 367–369.

Murdock, G. P. (1971). Anthropology's Mythology. *Proceedings of the Royal Anthropological Institute of Great Britain and Ireland*:17–24.

Minsky, M. (1988). The Society of the Mind.

Fischer, Michael(2005). Culture and Indigenous Knowledge Systems: Emergent Order and the Internal Regulation of Shared Symbolic Systems. *Cybernetics and Systems* 36:8.

Fischer, M.D. & D. Read (2001). Final report to the ESRC on Ideational and Material Models. Canterbury: CSAC.

Robert G. Reynolds and Bin Peng (2005). Cultural Algorithms: Computational Modeling of How Cultures Learn to Solve Problems: an Engineering Example. *Cybernetics and Systems* 36:8.

Reynolds, G. R. 1994. An Introduction to Cultural Algorithms. In *Proceedings of the 3rd Annual Conference on Evolutionary Programming*, 131–139: World Scientific Publishing.

Ezhkova, Irina (2005). Nesting Perspectives: Self-Organizing Representations. *Cybernetics and Systems* 36:8.

Ballonoff, Paul (2005). Correspondence Among Mathematical Treatments Of Culture Theory. *Cybernetics and Systems* 36:8.

Read, Dwight (2005). Some Observations on Resilience and Robustness in Human Systems. *Cybernetics and Systems* 36:8.

Klover, Jorgen and Christina Stoica (2005). On The Nature Of Culture And Communication: A Complex Systems Perspective. *Cybernetics and Systems* 36:8.

Lyon, Stephen (2005). Culture And Information: An Anthropological Examination Of Communication In Cultural Domains In Pakistan. *Cybernetics and Systems* 36:8.

Read, Dwight (2006). Kinship Algebra Expert System (KAES): A Software Implementation of a Cultural Theory. *Social Science Computer Review* 24:1.

Read, Dwight and Michael Fischer (2004). *Kinship Algebra Expert System*. Centre for Social Anthropology and Computing, Canterbury. http://kaes.anthrosciences.net (accessed 10/10/2005)

Leaf, Murray (1971) The Punjabi Kinship Terminology as a Semantic System. *American Anthropologist* 73:545–554.

Lounsbury, Floyd (1964). The Structural Analysis of Kinship Semantics. In *Proceedings of the Ninth International Congress of Linguists*. H. Hunt, ed. Pp. 1073–1093. The Hague: Mouton.

Fischer, M. D. (1994). *Applications in computing for social anthropologists*. London: Routledge.

Read, Dwight W., and Clifford Behrens (1990). KAES: An Expert System for the Algebraic Analysis of Kinship Terminologies. *Journal of Quantitative Anthropology* 2:353–393.

Chomsky, Noam (1957). *Syntactic Structures*. Mouton, The Hague.

Mally, Ernst (1926). Grundgesetze des Sollens: Elemente der Logik des Willens. Graz: Leuschner und Lubensky, UniversitRts-Buchhandlung, viii+85 pp. Reprinted in Ernst Mally, Logische Schriften: Groles Logikfragment, Grundgesetze des Sollens, edited by Karl Wolf and Paul Weingartner, pp. 227–324, Dordrecht: D. Reidel, 1971.

Lokhorst, Gert-Jan C., and Lou Goble (2004) Mally's deontic logic, *Grazer philosophische Studien*, vol. 67, pp. 37–57.

Anderson, Alan Ross (1967) Some nasty problems in the formal logic of ethics, *No×s*, vol. 1, pp. 345–360.

Maibaum, T. S. E. (1986) *A Logic for the Formal Requirements specification of Real-Time/Embedded Systems*. Alvey FOREST Deliverable Report 3. Chelmsford:GEC Research Laboratories.

Fischer, M. D. & A. Finkelstein (1991). Social knowledge representation: A case study. In *Using Computers in Qualitative Research*. N. G. Fielding & R. M. Lee. London, Sage. 119–135.

Gatlin, L. (1972). *Information theory and the living system*. Columbia University Press: New York and London.

Fischer, M.D. (2004). Integrating anthropological approaches to the study of culture : The 'Hard' and the 'Soft'. in '*Cybernetics and Systems*'. 35:2/3 pp. 147–162

Shannon, C. E. & Weaver, W. (1963) *The Mathematical Theory of Communication*. First published 1949. Urbana: University of Illinois Press.

Language Games for Meaning Negotiation Between Human and Computer Agents

Arnaud Stuber, Salima Hassas, and Alain Mille

CExAS Team - LIRIS,
Université Claude Bernard Lyon 1,
Bâtiment Nautibus - 8 bd Niels Bohr,
69622 Villeurbanne
{astuber, hassas, amille}@liris.cnrs.fr
Tel./Fax number: (+33/0) 4 72 43 26 51/4 72 44 83 64

Abstract. We present a hybrid system that allows an actor to reuse her individual experience during a cooperative activity. The actor is member of a community which share a computer environment to assist their work. Firstly, an operational issue exists to capture, to represent and to manipulate the experience: we propose an formal grammar-based model. A semantic issue then exists to express the meaning of the experience: we detail our approach based on the mechanisms of the emergence of language. A prototype is presented to illustrate our proposal, some experiments are to come.

Keywords: Emergence of Language, Multi-Agent System, Trace Based-Reasoning.

1 Introduction

In this paper, we consider a human actor who performs a task using a computer environment. We intend to help the actor to achieve her task by providing a contextual access to her individual experience; more precisely, the problem treated here is to build a personal assistant which helps the actor to reuse her past experience in the context of the current task. The individual experience is represented by use traces, which are the observations of the actor activity, expressed as the system's state changes, produced by occurring events. Before to retrieve past experiences, the assistant has to identify the elements of the current trace which are significant for the current task. To do so, some meanings need to be shared by the actor and her assistant to allow their mutual understanding during this interpretation of the current trace.

In consequence, the fundamental issues are 1) to model the experience captured by observing the interactions between the actor and the computer environment, and mostly 2) to have a way to share the interpretations of the traces in the context of the current activity. The first approach to adapt information retrieval is to personalize the assistance. The personalization relies on some dimensions of adaptability defined beforehand; however, in our case, we do not

O. Dikenelli, M.-P. Gleizes, and A. Ricci (Eds.): ESAW 2005, LNAI 3963, pp. 275–287, 2006.
© Springer-Verlag Berlin Heidelberg 2006

know initially what will be significant for the actor. On the other hand, the amount of interactions required before the assistant starts retrieval constitutes a condition of its usefulness. Our proposal is to transpose the principles of the emergence of language to achieve the meaning negotiation between the actor and her assistant, reusing by this way the past negotiations, and without any predefined interpretation.

Here, the emergence of language is chosen to obtain a shared communication system between an actor and her personal assistant. This problematic is a particular case of a more general one: the assistance to a group of human actors, who are concerned about a common task, to share, to exchange and to co-construct a common experience. Our system is the first step of this line of research. Its principles could be extended to the communication between personal assistants in order to assist cooperation.

In the rest of the paper, we first detail the principles of our approach, we situate it in comparison to related works. Next we explain how the experience is represented by use traces, and the structure of the language *symbols* relies on this representation. The mechanism for meaning identification by the assistant is then introduced, defining the representation of *meaning* in the language. The mechanisms of negotiation are finally detailed, and the language games are presented to explicit how common symbols and meanings are obtained.

2   Experience Tracing in a Hybrid Context with Human and Computer Agents

2.1   Principles

To manage the individual experience base, we use the trace-based reasoning (TBR) paradigm, an extension of the case-based reasoning (CBR) paradigm to unstructured cases, i.e., the traces. The individual experience is captured by observing interactions between the user and the system, and it is represented in the system by use traces. To retrieve past experience, a reasoning by analogy between the current trace and the past ones is performed considering a given interpretation.

On the other hand, the multi-agent paradigm is adopted to directly represent the actor interacting with her personal computer assistant (further called *alter ego agent*): the system we consider is a hybrid system. More specifically, in order to obtain an interpretation shared by the actor and her alter ego agent, we apply the mechanisms of the emergence of language considering the interactions between them as a negotiation process about trace meaning. This approach requires a symbolic representation of the trace, the construction of symbols from trace sequences to have a medium of communication, the identification of assistance meanings and the agreement between the actor and her alter ego agent on some symbol-meaning relations to be able to talk about meanings using symbols. The resulting language contains all the interpretations used for trace retrieval.

2.2   Related Works

Our trace model relies on the MUSETTE model defined in [1]. We enrich it with some control elements to ease the trace handling. The syntactical level for trace description, presented in section 3.2, has similar principles of those presented in [2] for intrusion detection systems (IDS). With a CBR approach, [3] presents an ascendant mechanism to elaborate cases, which has similarities with the mechanism of signature identification presented in section 3.3.

The assistance personalization, we are aiming by introducing the alter ego agents, leads to the problematic of *interface agent* presented in [4, 5]. However, in our case, the user modeling is not defined beforehand since we do not know what will characterized the actor in the context of the collective task. We propose to get the required adaptivity by generating a communication system. The mechanisms of emergence of language are presented in [6]. They constitute a frame for the interactive behaviour of the alter ego agent with its actor. In this line of research, applied to ontology alignment between agents, [7] presents different strategies of reinforcement used to build a shared communication vocabulary; these strategies can be applied to the mechanism of reinforcement learning detailed in section 3.4 and used for the signature identification presented in section 3.3.

Concerning the reasoning by analogy in a collaborative context, several studies [8, 9] and also [10] are some important starting points for structured cases; indeed, several efficient case sharing policies are studied. However, in our context, a collaborative experience is made up of a set of individual experiences (stored in traces), and there is any dimension known beforehand to isolate cases, and to exploit them in a Case-Based Reasoning (CBR) framework. Thus, the alter ego agents need some tools to manipulate the traces, and have to consider actors' interactions as the preferential way to construct contextual case structures.

In the field of recommendation systems, our approach differs from the systems for implicit culture support (SICS) [11] by the fact that it is based on the principles of the emergence of language. Thus, the underlying rule-based domain theory used in SICS to suggest actions have no direct counterpart in our approach.

3   Experience Representation

3.1   Environment Representation

The environment is composed of a software used by each actor during the considered activity, in order to manipulate some documents. The documents are supports for the different tasks of the activity; they gather the potentially useful informations for the actors, according to their roles.

Document and Activities: The documents are activity dependant. They are standardized and made up of different fields, which contain activity-specific *keywords*. A keyword represents a *concept*, and all the concepts are organised hierarchically

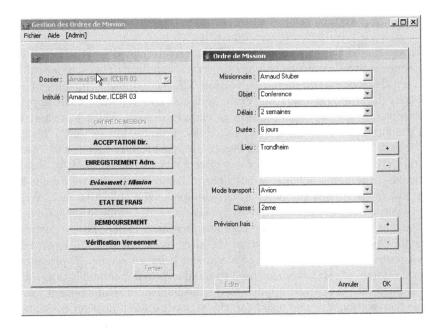

Fig. 1. The computer environment: a prototype of portal for document management. The activity considered is a collective administrative procedure in our laboratory. On the left, the different steps of the collective process; on the right, a document representing a step. The documents are described by a set of fields, which contain keywords defined in a thesaurus.

in a thesaurus. This is introduced to have a measure of semantic similarity between keywords and concepts.

Target Application: The *actions* that an actor can perform in the environment introduced above are: *edition, consultation* and *research.* We do not make any restrictive assumption on how works the target application; thus several actions can be jointly performed. An illustration of environment is given on the figure 1, we consider this environment in the rest of the paper to illustrate our proposal.

3.2   Use Trace Modeling

The trace model presented here is based on the MUSETTE model [1], proposed by our team, for assistance systems. A *use trace* is defined by an alternate sequence of states and transitions. The *objects of interest* observable for the considered task are described in a use model, they are either entities or events. A *use trace* describes the changes that occur in the system, and that are observable by the actor. A state is made up of the observable objects considered as stable. The transitions correspond to the action of an actor, and they are defined by events and eventually some additional entities. To manipulate the traces, the assistant must recognize some situations; an *explained task signature*

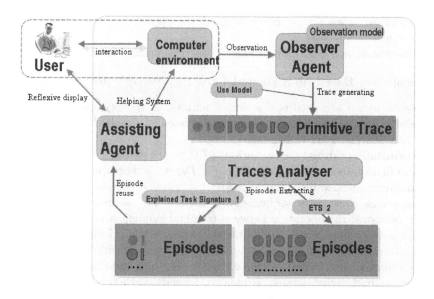

Fig. 2. The MUSETTE model

(or signature) is a recurrent pattern in the traces, made up of at least one significant event for a given situation. When a part of a use trace verifies a signature,
it constitutes an *episode* which can be reused in similar situations. The principles of the MUSETTE model for assistance systems are represented on the
figure 2.

However, consider an actor performing an action on a given document. To
do his action, he has a personal method to use the functionalities of the computer environment. Thus a use trace has a high variability if we consider two
actors performing the same action by different ways. This variability is an issue
for use traces manipulation and constitutes a limit for the comparison of traces.
However, the functionalities constitute a common basis for the users' operations.
In [12], we present a formal grammar-based trace structure where the call of a
functionality is represented by a *tag* added in the trace. Operators are introduced to define the sequences of observations, which are employed to construct
the symbols presented in section 3.3. The trace structure presented below expresses explicitly the call of a functionality to perform an action; the operators
and their properties express the similar forms of use traces for a given action. A
filtering of the trace can also be done in order to extract the actions we want to
consider.

For the actions we take into account, it is possible to decompose an action in: an *initial sequence*, a set of sequences representing the use of functionalities of this action, and a *final sequence*. Among the intermediate
sequences, some are permutable between themselves, they are called *alternative
sequences*; others express events which can not be permutated, they are called
static sequences. This description is added to the use model of the MUSETTE

framework; so, when a trace is constructed, the appropriate *tag* is associated to each sequence.

Below the formal definition of these properties using a formal language.

A Formalism Based on a Formal Language to Interpret Use Traces

- **Sentence:** a sentence is a series of actions. If the actions are performed jointly in several windows, the same approach is applied to each window. These sentences are called *traces*.
- **Terminal symbols:** the transitions (T) and the states (S) are considered as terminal symbols. Among them T_I, T_A, T_S, et T_F represent some transitions containing respectively the tags for the *initial* sequence, some *alternative* sequences, some *static* sequences and the the *final* sequence of an action.
- **Operators:** the operators between terminal symbols are $\cdot$ and $+$, with the properties that $\cdot$ is not commutative, et that $\cdot$ has priority on $+$. A series of states and transitions only separated by $\cdot$ is then indivisible, the notion of *sequence* is so formally defined. Conversely, $+$ is used between sequences; the commutativity between sequences depends on their respective status as it is defined is the introduction of this grammar.
- **Non-terminal symbols:** a *trace* is a series of actions; it is made up of an initial sequence ($Sequence_I$), some intermediate sequences and a final sequence ($Sequence_F$). The intermediate sequences are either alternative ($Sequence_A$) or static ($Sequence_S$); the alternatives can be permuted only if they constitute an uninterrupted series.
- **Production rules:**

$$Trace ::= Action^*$$
$$Action ::= Sequence_I + IntermSeq^* + Sequence_F$$
$$IntermSeq ::= PermSeq \mid Sequence_S$$
$$PermSeq ::= Sequence_A \mid PermSeq + Sequence_A \mid Action$$
$$Sequence_x ::= T_x \cdot S \; [\; \cdot T \cdot S]^* \quad with \;\; x \in \{I, A, S, C\}$$

The figure 3 illustrates the use trace structure. In a sequence, here of minimal size (i.e., one transition and one state), where at least one transition contains the *tag of functionality* and where all elements contain a description of the changes in the environment caused by the functionality; these changes are represented by the difference between the next state and the previous state. Thus the states describe the context between significant events. The trace is bounded by two transitions representing the login and the logout in the environment by the actor.

However, with this trace structure, we do not know the elements that we have to take into account to express an experience.

3.3   Symbolic Trace Representation

An *explained task signature* represents a situation known by the alter ego agent and having a meaning for the actor. To express the signatures, we introduce an

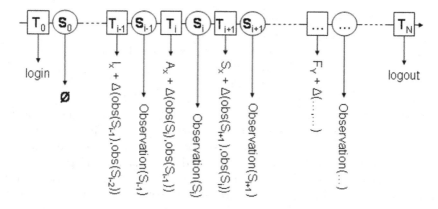

Fig. 3. An instance of trace respecting the formal grammar

intermediate layer made up of local patterns, called *symbols*; a symbol comes
from a sequence, where the actor has specified the elements to consider using an
appropriated GUI. A signature is defined by a group of symbols. The symbols
and the signatures evolve during the interactions, according to the negotiation
mechanisms detailed in section 3.4. A symbol replicates the structure of the
sequence it comes from: a series of state and transitions, with a tag, and where
the observations are partial with the generic dimension defined below.

Through the assistant GUI, the actor has the possibility to specify to his
alter ego agent which element of sequence is important for his current task. An
element is important either by itself (any other is interesting) or for its type

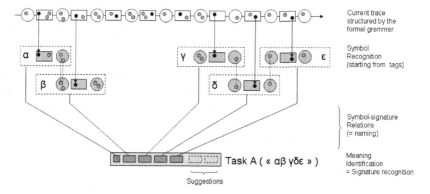

Fig. 4. Principles of ascendant signature recognition: the *tags* guide symbol identification which is finally obtained by matching the different partial observations of a
candidate symbol on the considered sequence. When some symbols are identified, a
signature including enough symbols is candidate for episode retrieval. The result is
proposed to the actor. A label is associated to each symbol (here, α, β...) and each
signature (here, *task A*) to express their respective meaning.

(elements of the same type are interesting). To match a partial observation of a symbol with an observation of a sequence, we require a way to express this abstraction. We introduce *generic nodes* to express it in the observations of a symbol: to match, a generic node must have the same type of the target node; the type definition is domain dependant.

The signature recognition is ascendant and starts by observing the tags present in the current use trace. For a given tag in a sequence, the associated symbols are tested by matching their partial observations to the observations of the sequence. After the identification of symbols in the the trace, the signatures including enough identified symbols are candidates for episode retrieval. The figure 4 gives an illustration of this recognition process. A label is associated to each symbol and each signature to express their respective meaning in natural language. The current trace is reformulated with the recognized symbols and presented to the actor with their labels. The labels of the signatures are use to explain the task identification and to situate the retrieved episodes. For a signature, the retrieved episodes are order by semantic similarity with the current trace and proposed to the actor (see Fig. 6 for an illustration).

3.4   Emergence of Meaning

The principles for the episode extraction presented above do not ensure the meaning adequacy between a recognized signature and actor's intentions. The signature have to ensure this adequacy in order to provide a suitable assistance. However, the alter ego agent can use the interactions with the user to reduce the ambiguities. To do so, we propose to consider the interactions between the actor and her assistant as negotiation process about meanings of the manipulated objects. We then transpose the mechanisms of the emergence of language presented in [6].

In this section, we describe the principles of the emergence of meaning with a use scenario. We consider an actor who performs a series of operations on a document until he needs an assistance to continue his activity. Then he calls his alter ego, which has interpreted his operations according to the ascendant process detailed above. The interpretation is done using current symbols and signatures. Firstly, the interpretations of the current trace are proposed to the actor, so that he can compare them, and finally select one. The figure 5 gives the GUI associated to this step, we consider a list of signatures and the detail of an interpretation on the current trace.

By selecting on a signature, the actor can access to the retrieved episodes in a second interface. In this window, the selected interpretation of the current trace is displayed on the top; below, a list of the retrieved episodes is proposed to the actor. When an episode is chosen, the detail of its interpretation with the considered signature is displayed. The symbols which are not yet found in the current trace are present in the episodes; this constitutes the contextual assistante proposed to the actor, who can then benefit from indications to continue his activity. In the lower part, two panes gives the descriptions of symbols selected either in the current trace or in an episode; the definition of a symbol

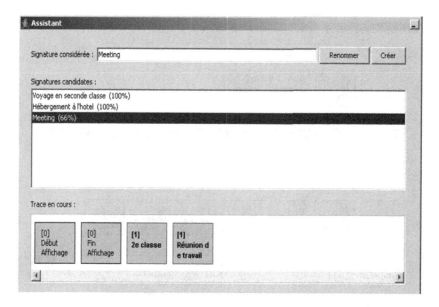

Fig. 5. The interpretation GUI: a list of signature (three signtaures are proposed here) and the detail of the interpretation of the current trace for the selected signature (here, two symbols with their labels in boldface)

or of a not identified section is displayed in a hierarchical form. The user can interact with this description, and thus modify the definition of the associated symbol. After some interactions, the actor calls his alter ego to refresh its proposal. Then, a negotiation starts between them in order to disambiguate the modified or new symbols and the new signature definition, this is done in comparison to last alter ego's language state. Indeed, the interactions can lead to symbols that are similar or equal to already existing ones, the same situation can occur with the signature. This negotiation is done to indicate to the alter ego how to consider the new language elements. After this negotiation, the elements are included in the language and a new interpretation can start. See the figure 6 for an illustration of the signature negotiation GUI.

The Language Games. The emergence of language is based on the agreement between agents (here, the actor and his alter ego agent) on:

- a *repertoire of symbols*, used as a "communication medium" between the agents;
- a *repertoire of meanings* (i.e., signatures), representing some abstractions of the reality;
- a *repertoire of symbol-meaning pairs*, to be able to "talk" about meanings using symbols.

The agreement is obtained automatically by executing iterations of language games, which are respectively the *imitation game*, the *discrimination game* and

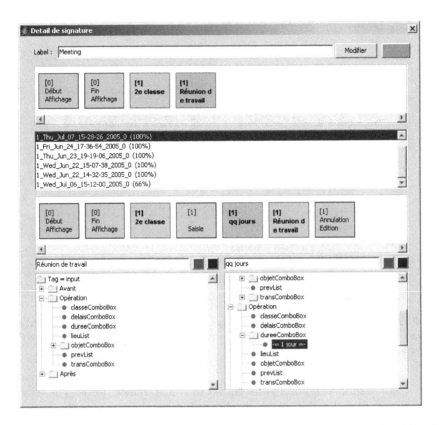

Fig. 6. The negotiation GUI. From top: the label of the signature considered by the assistant, the current trace with a symbolic representation, the list of episodes retrieved by the assistant, the symbolic representation of a selected episode, and in the lower part two trees describing the instantiation of the selected symbol: on the current trace (left) and on the selected episode (right). When the user asks his alter ego agent to update its proposals, he has to disambiguate the modified symbols and to verify the definition of the signature.

the *naming game*. [6] surveys recent work on modeling the origins of communication systems.

We introduced above two symbolic levels: the signatures and the symbols in the symbolic trace. Since a meaning is expressed using several symbols, we can not exactly talk about symbol-meaning pairs but rather about a relation of $1..n$ cardinality.

During signature recognition, an iteration of imitation game is initiated for each recognized symbol, and an iteration of naming game for each symbol-signature relation. At the time of assistance refresh, the iterations are completed according user's reactions. The symbols successfully recognized (i.e., accepted by the user in the new definition of the considered signature) are reinforced, the rejected symbols are inhibited, otherwise the iterations are not completed since we do not know how to consider the symbols that are recognized but not used.

Some symbols can be created, their scores are set to an initial value. During the interactions with the symbols definitions, the user can define an already existing symbol; in this case, the identical symbols are merged after the user has defined a common label. Symbols with low score are eliminated.

With the symbols accepted by the user to define the signature, the iterations of naming are completed. The relations between the considered signature and the accepted symbols are reinforced, the relations with rejected symbols are inhibited, otherwise the iterations are not completed. For new symbols or for the existing symbols added for the first time to the signature, new relations are created with an initial score. By this way, a signature is defined by numerous relations with respective scores; in the mechanism for signature identification (see section 3.3), we only consider the relations with a score above a given threshold as the relations defining a signature. During the signature definition, the user can define an already existing signature (i.e., a signature made up of the same symbols with scores above the threshold); in this case, the signature are merged and the relations of the previous signatures are merged to define the resulting signature with a user defined label. New signatures can be created.

In [6], the discrimination game is done to obtain a conceptualization of the world, and is performed individually by each agent. In our case, the signatures (the meanings expressed by strings in natural language) are defined by the user, but are shared with the alter ego agent. We consider that only the user can perform the discrimination, for this reason any discrimination game is introduced.

On the basis of the analysis detailed in [6], we discuss the introduced mechanisms. Four principles are considered to allow the emergence of a communication system, namely *reinforcement learning*, *self-organisation*, *selectionism* and *structural coupling*. The principle of reinforcement learning does not allow only in itself the emergence of symbols and symbol-meaning relations.

For the imitation game, the principle of self-organisation is obtained with the positive feedback between the correctness of symbol recognition and its utility for the actor. The selectionism is expressed by the score of the symbols, which have a tendency to survive in the repertoire when they have high scores; the variation comes from unknown user actions, where objects of interest are consider as significant for a symbol.

The naming game for symbol-meaning relations also requires these principles: reinforcement learning is based on success or failure in the assistance as a whole, which corresponds to a communication attempt about an assistance meaning using symbols. The self-organisation is due to the positive feedback loop between use and success: when a symbol-meaning relation is successful, its score goes up. The score of a relation between a recognized symbol and a signature influences the signature relevance, and so, they are likely to be reuse; this leads to their greater success. The selectionism is expressed by the limits of the alter ego agent: if a situation cannot be reliably recognized, the signatures and symbols introduced to capture its description have less chance of survival. In addition, the structural coupling due to the iterations of language games, which generate symbols and meanings reinforced or not according to their success, leads to a co-evolution between the repertoire of symbol and the repertoire of meaning; this is the adaptivity we are looking for to capture efficiently experience meaning.

The emergence of a language is not yet experimentally demonstrated. Nevertheless, the conditions of this emergence as they are defined in [6] are fulfilled. The experimentation has to rely on an appropriate use scenario since the emergent language, we intend to obtain, would have the property to evolve and to adapt to the use.

4 Conclusion and Future Work

We present a personal and contextual assistant which provides to an actor a personalized access to her individual experience. The actor is member of a community, its activity is situated in a complex collective task. A computer environment is shared by the community to report its activity. A formalism to represent actor's experience as individual use traces is presented. The use traces are obtained by observing actor's interactions with the common computer environment.

We then detail our proposal for emergence of meaning in the trace, which constitutes the critical issue to allow access to experience. To obtain this emergence, we propose to consider the interactions between an actor and her assistant as meaning negotiations, and to apply the principles of the emergence of language in order to benefit from their adaptation properties. The mechanisms (reinforcement learning, selectionism, auto-organisation, structural coupling), which are necessary for this adaptation, are implemented in a prototype. Some experiments are to come.

In this line of research, the sharing of individual experience between actors will be studied with the principles of language games between alter ego agents. For the collective experience, we will have to consider it as a combination of individual traces, and some internal agents may be introduced to build collective traces. The results of the research on implicit culture may also be useful to build a collective experience. Finally, the research on the emergence of grammar has also to be considered in order to improve the expressivity of the signatures.

References

1. Champin, P.A., Prié, Y.: Musette: uses-based annotation for the Semantic Web. In: Annotation for the Semantic Web. OIS Press (2003)
2. Gorodetski, V., Kotenko, I.: Attacks against computer network: Formal grammar-based framework and simulation tool. In: Proceedings of the 5th International Conference "Recent Advances in Intrusion Detection", Zrich, Switzerland, Springer Verlag (2002) 219–238
3. Martín, F.J., Plaza, E.: Ceaseless case-based reasoning. In Funk, P., González-Calero, P.A., eds.: ECCBR. Volume 3155 of LNCS. (2004) 287–301
4. Maes, P.: Agents that reduce work and information overload. Communications of the ACM **37** (1994) 30–40, 146
5. Lieberman, H.: Autonomous interface agents. ACM Conference on Human-Computer Interface [CHI-97], Atlanta, March 1997 (1997)

6. Steels, L.: Language as a complex adaptive system. Lecture Notes in Computer Science. Parallel Problem Solving from Nature - PPSN **4** (2000)
7. van Diggelen, J., Beun, R.J., Dignum, F., van Eijk, R.M., Meyer, J.J.: A decentralized approach for establishing a shared communication vocabulary. In: International workshop on agent mediated knowledge management 2005, held with AAMAS2005. (2005)
8. Martin, F.J., Plaza, E., Arcos, J.L.: Knowledge and experience reuse through communication among competent (peer) agents. International Journal of Software Engineering and Knowledge Engineering (1998)
9. Ontan, S., Plaza, E.: Learning when to collaborate among learning agents. In: Machine Learning: EMCL 2001. Lecture Notes in Artificial Intelligence 2167. (2001) 394–405
10. Kanawati, R., Malek, M.: A multi-agent system for collaborative bookmarking. In: Proceedings of the first international joint conference on Autonomous agents and multiagent systems, ACM Press (2002) 1137–1138
11. Blanzieri, E., Giorgini, P., Massa, P., Recla, S.: Implicit culture for multi-agent interaction support. In: Cooperative Information Systems, 9th International Conference – CoopIS 2001. Volume 2172 of LNCS, Springer-Verlag (2001)
12. Stuber, A., Hassas, S., Mille, A.: Combining multiagents systems and experience reuse for assisting collective task achievement. In McGinty, L., ed.: ICCBR-2003 Workshop : From structured cases to unstructured problem solving episodes for experience-based assistance. (2003)

Using Socially Deliberating Agents in Organized Settings[*]

Ioannis Partsakoulakis and George Vouros

Department of Information and Communication Systems Engineering,
83200 Karlovassi, Samos, Greece
{jpar, georgev}@aegean.gr

Abstract. Recently there is an increased interest in social agency and in designing and building agent organizations. In this paper we view an organization as a set of interrelated groups. Each group has an explicit structure in terms of positions and their interrelations. Agents in groups deliberate socially, distinguishing between their individual and group attitudes: Each agent is able to agree on and *accept* certain attitudes as attitudes of the groups it belongs. Acting as group member, an agent must be able to act on the basis of these group mental attitudes rather than on the basis of its individual beliefs and goals. This issue, although ultimately important, it has not given much attention in agent community. The objective of this paper is (a) to propose a generic design pattern for building agent organizations in which the constituting groups build and maintain their own group goals and beliefs according to their needs and the environmental conditions, (b) to present the functionality of social deliberating agents that act as group members in organized settings, and (c) to report on the development of a prototype system that comprises agents that implement such a kind of social deliberation.

1 Introduction

Recently there is an increased interest in social agency, as well as in designing and building agent organizations. Unfortunately, there is no wide consensus on the definition of an organization [5]. In this paper we view an organization as a set of interrelated groups that pose specific constraints on the behaviour of their members. We are focusing on groups that have an explicit structure in terms of positions and interrelations between them. Each agent occupies one or more positions and each position corresponds to a specific role. More precisely, a group can be defined as in [18]: *A group or multiagent system is a system of agents that are somehow constrained in their mutual interactions. Typically, these constraints arise because the agents play different roles in the group, and their roles impose requirements on how they are to behave and interact with others.*

In this paper we distinguish between individual and group attitudes. On the one hand, each individual has a set of beliefs and a set of goals. On the other hand, each group has a set of group beliefs and a set of group goals. In organized settings, group goals are not

---

[*] This research is supported by the Pythagoras grant no. 1349 under the Operational Program for Education and Initial Training.

O. Dikenelli, M.-P. Gleizes, and A. Ricci (Eds.): ESAW 2005, LNAI 3963, pp. 288–302, 2006.
© Springer-Verlag Berlin Heidelberg 2006

always in correspondence to the individual goals of group members, since they may have been formed by a (typically small) subset of "authorized" members that determine the goals and the beliefs of the group as a whole. However, it is usually required that in organized settings groups to act as single entities. Successful group action presupposes the *acceptance* of group goals and the acceptance of group beliefs from each agent. Furthermore, agents must be able to act as group members rather than as individuals. Acting as a group member [22] each agent must be able to distinguish between the goals and beliefs that it *holds* individually, from the goals and beliefs that it *accepts* as a group member. This issue, although ultimately important, has not been given much attention within agent community.

The concept of acceptance has been discussed lately in the philosophical literature [2, 26, 6, 21] and two kinds of acceptances have been identified [21]: One that aims at truth and one that aims at utility. According to Tuomela [21], when we are talking about group belief of structured groups, the utility-based concept of acceptance is more applicable (called *proper* group belief). Acceptance of this kind differs from individual belief in important ways. What if of most importance here is the fact that (a) acceptance is voluntary (or intentional) in contrast to belief that is a kind of disposition and (b) the set of acceptances (in contrast to the set of beliefs) is not subject to an ideal of integration or agglomeration. Therefore, an agent can hold conflicting acceptances, when it participates in different groups. We do not claim here that consistency is not important. An agent should seek to participate in groups that are close to its personal beliefs and goals. However, we assume that once an agent is a member of a group then it does not "select" the group attitudes that fit best to its personality, but it is a group member in the core sense.

The objective of this paper is threefold:

(a) to propose a generic design pattern for building agent organizations in which the constituting groups build and maintain their own group goals and beliefs according to their needs and the environmental conditions,
(b) to present the functionality of social deliberating agents, acting as group members in organized settings, and
(c) to report on the development of a prototype system that comprises agents that implement such a kind of social deliberation.

Agents live in a social context that comprises a set of groups that affect their behaviour or that agents have an interest in. The social position of agents is specified by the roles they play in one or more groups inside their social context. Agents must be able to exploit the specific organizational structures and policies in order to *pro-actively* participate on the formation of group beliefs and goals, and to act on the basis of these group attitudes.

The aim of our research is to build a design methodology for human-centred systems towards empowering humans to deliberatively form and manage their social context and position via socially deliberating agents. It must be emphasized that designing and implementing human-centred systems is a hard task: Our approach does not aim to tackle all the related issues: In [4] it has been argued that the development of human-centred systems must take the triple *people-machine-context* as the unit of analysis. It involves studying people capacities, capabilities and goals, computational mechanisms, interface capabilities and context. Our approach does not focus on human-computer interaction, but rather on empowering humans to act in organized contexts, according to their capabilities, goals and context. Particularly, we investigate the social deliberation abilities of software agents that represent humans and form their "digital analogue" within organizations. Agents exploit two types of contexts:

(a) The *social context*, which comprises the organizations that exist in agent's environment, the roles that an agent plays in one or more organizations, the relations between roles, responsibilities and certain organizational policies, and

(b) The *context of action* or *intentional context*, which comprises the *intentional activities* that agents follow in order to play their roles.

The rest of this paper is organized as follows. Section 2 presents a real-life scenario that motivates our research towards empowering humans to act consistently as group members. Section 3 presents a normative model for the specification of the structural and behavioural elements of an organization, describes the overall architecture of a prototypical implemented system, and presents the architecture and the overall functionality of a socially deliberating agent. Section 4 presents related works and finally, section 5 concludes the paper.

2 Motivating Scenario and Requirements

This section presents a real-life scenario that motivates our work and is representative of most of our considerations for incorporating socially deliberating agents in human-centred systems.

Mike is a newcomer engineer in a large company and he is employed in the engineering department. A short time ago, the personal agent of Mike found a new position in this company. This position was found to be consistent with other roles that Mike plays (e.g. the role of student and the role of patient in the local Medical Treatment institution). The agent presented this new position to Mike, who gave the authority to his personal agent to inform the organization and settle the details of undertaking this role. Mike communicated with the company for the last details and now he is one of the newest members in the company.

The job of Mike consists of getting customer orders, designing custom products by gathering the best available parts according to regulations and standards, and, together with more experienced colleagues, providing instructions to the manufacturing unit for getting the final product. The company, as well as the department in which Mike belongs, has certain responsibilities. Some of these responsibilities are addressed to individuals while others are responsibilities of departments or of the company as a whole. The latter are called collaborative responsibilities and, in contrast to the individual responsibilities, they require every group member to contribute and collaborate towards their fulfilment.

Being a newcomer, Mike is not aware of his colleagues' regular activities, has not hands-on experience on the tasks he must perform and he does not posses proper knowledge on how problems are handled when they arise. Mike's capabilities (e.g. designing and engineering products), permissions (e.g. access to information sources), organizational context (e.g. individual responsibilities and collaborative responsibilities that he shares with colleagues, roles he plays and groups he participates in) and intentional context (individual and group activities, constraints and permissions related to these activities) drive the way Mike fulfils his responsibilities.

The digital representative of Mike is an agent that holds knowledge concerning the capabilities of Mike, as well as his social and intentional context. This agent represents Mike in the digital counterpart of the company, which is a multi-agent system comprising the digital representatives of company members. When Mike enters or leaves the company, then his digital representative enters or leaves this multi-agent system as well. It is this agent that presents to Mike all the necessary information about the organization (e.g. the organizational structure, roles and responsibilities of associated roles, methods for achieving these responsibilities etc.) and helps him achieve his goals individually or in collaboration with his colleagues.

Due to security restrictions or to constraints imposed by the organization, information is distributed to company members. This affects organization member's decision-making: They must combine different pieces of information in order to reach agreements about the need to achieve certain goals. For instance, let us assume that according to organizational policies, Mike, as well as all the members of the engineering department, need different and complimentary pieces of information to reach a decision about the design of a product. When group members in the engineering department receive these pieces of information, then they must form a commonly accepted view about the design of this product. As already pointed, this is an important prerequisite for the group to act as a single entity, especially when group members posses conflicting pieces of information. Having an agreed view of the world, representative agents can help humans to pursue their responsibilities, exploiting the organizational structure and the organizational practices.

Concluding the above, we distinguish between three modes of helpful behaviour that a personal agent can offer to its user towards the fulfilment of a specific responsibility. In the first mode, the user decides to fulfil the responsibility alone. In this case, the personal agent helps its user by keeping an agenda of his responsibilities and it does not act on behalf of the user. To exhibit helpful behaviour, the personal agent must be knowledgeable about the organizational and intentional context of its user. In the second mode, the user delegates the responsibility to the agent. In this case, the personal agent must not only be knowledgeable about the organizational context of the user, but it must also have the appropriate capabilities and knowledge to fulfil the delegated responsibility. In case the delegated responsibility is a collaborative one, then the agent must have collaboration abilities and must be able to cope with the distribution of knowledge. Finally, in the third mode, the user collaborates with the agent for the fulfilment of the responsibility. This collaboration is independent on whether the responsibility is collaborative, as it concerns the relation between the user and his representative. In this case the user and the agent commit to proceed to the fulfilment of the responsibility together. The agent must be able to track the activity of the user and must form decisions with him about the fulfilment of responsibilities. In this paper we concentrate on the fulfilment of responsibilities and the collaboration between agents that is a major step towards the realization of the above modes of helpful behaviour.

3 The Overall Architecture

Although there are many methodologies for designing distributed systems as well as human-centred systems (e.g. [28]), complimentarily to these we propose a generic design pattern that incorporates personal agents acting as representatives of human agents: A personal agent that represents a human is "surrounded" by organizations to which it participates via role-playing. These organizations constitute the social context of the agent. A personal agent helps its user to undertake and play these roles in the corresponding human organizations.

The structure of each organization can be the subject of deliberation of "authorized" organizational members. Therefore, it can be dynamic. In this paper, we are working on a specific snapshot of an organization and therefore we do not deal with the dynamics of the organizational structure but rather with the dynamics of the agents towards achieving group goals and forming beliefs while they operate in a given organizational structure.

3.1 Specification of an Organization

The structure of an organization is defined in terms of organizational positions and is based on a formal organizational model that is specified in terms of interrelated roles. Positions are defined as formally recognized role assignments and are important for the design of effective agent organizations [11]. Fig. 1 shows an example of the specification of an organization. The organizational model defines a generic organizational structure. For example, the organizational model in Fig. 1 specifies that a group of type "company" can contain three types of departments, and each department type can contain specific types of individuals. This organizational model specifies that a customer department contains sellers and customers, but the exact number of positions that correspond to each role is determined in the organizational structure. A more detailed description of the model can be found in [13].

Paying special attention to the specification of collaborative behaviour, our model incorporates roles that can be played not only by individuals but also by groups. Roles comprise social laws and applicability conditions, which are necessary for checking consistency between roles [15], as well as responsibilities and recipes for fulfilling responsibilities. A responsibility comprises a condition s and a goal state g[1] and can be represented by a rule of the form $s => g$. When s is considered to hold by an agent or by a group with the corresponding responsibility, then the agent or the group must attempt to achieve g.

As already pointed, due to the inherent distribution of information and to access restrictions to information sources, an organization needs to have policies in order agents to act coherently as a group. Recognition recipes (r-recipes) represent organizational policies for groups to form acceptances concerning world states (e.g. voting, or accepting the opinion of the more experienced group member). These policies help agents to reconcile individual views and form a common view that comprises a set of acceptances [23, 26] shared by the group members. Achievement recipes (a-recipes) represent policies (organizational practices) for the group to achieve

---

[1] States are atomic first-order logic formulae.

goal states collaboratively. As it will be explained in subsequent paragraphs, both types of recipes are necessary for groups to pursue collaborative responsibilities.

A recipe is assigned to a specific role (called the *relevant role*) and comprises a *recipe state* and the *recipe body*. Additionally, a-recipes have *applicability conditions*. The body of a recipe consists of elements of the form $\rho_{ind}:Q$, where ρ is a recipe internal role, *ind* is an indicator, and Q is a set of states for r-recipes and a set of responsibilities assigned to the role ρ for a-recipes. Each internal-role in a recipe is either contained (via the relation "*contains*") to the relevant role or is the relevant role of the recipe indicated by "*self*". The indicator is a quantifier for the players of ρ and it can take the value *all, one* or *most,* indicating *all* the players of ρ, at least *one* of them, or *most* of them respectively. Examples of recipes are provided in the paragraphs that follow.

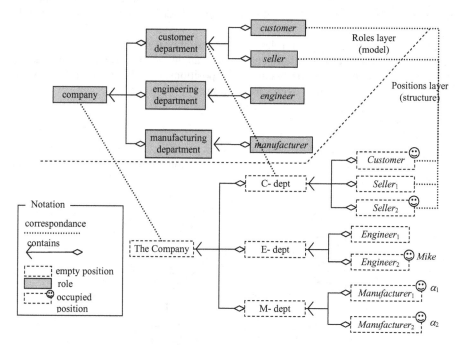

Fig. 1. The structure of an organization is defined in terms of positions and follow a formal organizational model specified in term of roles

Dealing with responsibilities of groups, we must distinguish the case where a group is considered as a *list of individuals* and the case where it is considered as a single *meta-agent* entity [17]. Based on this distinction, we distinguish between three types of responsibilities associated to organizational roles corresponding to groups: individual, collaborative and hybrid.

If $s => g$ is an *individual responsibility* of a role and *Gr* is a group that plays this role, then every agent that is a member of *Gr* must check whether it recognized that state s holds, i.e. whether it believes s. In such a case, it must attempt to establish g.

No communication or coordination is required between group members during the elaboration of their individual responsibilities.

If *s => g* is a *collaborative responsibility*, then the group members, using an r-recipe, must attempt to form a group belief and accept *s*. If this happens, then the group members must attempt to achieve *g* collaboratively.

Finally, if *s => g* is a *hybrid responsibility*, then group members attempt to form an a group belief and accept *s*. When they accept *s*, group members attempt to establish *g* individually.

For example, let us assume that "pending-order(*p,c*)" denotes the fact that a specific product *p* has been ordered by a specific customer *c* and it has not been processed yet. The state "m&s(*p,c*)" denotes the fact that the product *p* has been manufactured and it has been shipped to the customer *c*. Then the responsibility "pending-order(P,C) => m&s(P,C)", where P and C are variables, represents the responsibility of a company to manufacture and ship every product that has been ordered by some customer, when the order is pending.

It must be noticed that certain roles in an organizational model comprise managerial responsibilities. Such responsibilities enable the changing of the organizational structure under certain circumstances, by opening new positions, closing opened positions and deciding on the assignment of agents to positions.

3.2 Overall Architecture

The overall architecture of the system is shown in Fig. 2 and comprises personal agents and facilitator agents. We describe the functionality of each agent type in the following section.

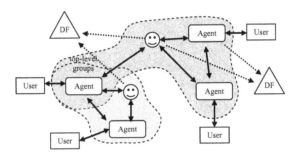

Fig. 2. The overall architecture comprises personal agents (ovals), and facilitator agents with newspaper services (smiley faces) and yellow-page services (triangles). Solid arrows represent communication links. Dotted arrows represent registrations to yellow-page services.

3.2.1 Personal Agents
Personal agents serve/represent specific humans, occupy organizational positions, and populate groups that act in organizational positions. When an agent takes a position in the digital organization, then the corresponding human is assigned to that position in the corresponding human organization, and vice versa. Personal agents help their owners to play their roles (i.e. pursue the role responsibilities), maintain their social context and manage their position in their social contexts, providing a quite intuitive

analogue of human organizations. Personal agents, acting as representatives, may search for new roles within organizations and further check the consistency of the roles played. The minimum conditions for a set of roles to be consistent are specified in [15].

The main functionality of a personal agent acting as a role player is to pursue the responsibilities of the role it plays. However, an agent that plays a role ρ is considered to be a member of each group that plays the roles in which ρ is contained. So, when the personal agent of Mike plays the role "engineer", it must also contribute to the responsibilities of the role "engineering-department" and of the role "company".

The general functionality of a personal agent related to the pursuit of responsibilities is shown in Fig 3: An agent possesses mechanisms for the individual and collaborative recognition of responsibility conditions, and mechanisms for achieving goal states individually or collaboratively (depending on whether the responsibility is an individual or a collaborative one). The following sections present in more detail the process of collaborative recognition that a state holds and the process of the collaborative achievement of a goal state.

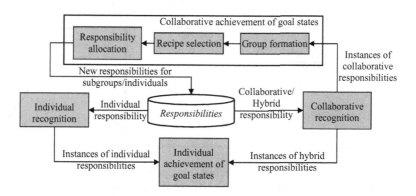

Fig. 3. The elaboration of the different types of responsibilities

Collaborative Recognition of Whether a State Holds. The collaborative recognition of whether a state holds, i.e. the formation of a group belief for a state and its acceptance as a belief of the group by all group members, is based on policies specified by r-recipes and on the contributions of agents towards the state in question. A state may contain free variables. In this case it is a template and there may be many instances that hold simultaneously. In this case group members shall recognize all instances of the state that hold. For example, having the responsibility "pending-order(P,C) => m&s(P,C)", where P and C denote variables for products and customers respectively, group members shall try to contribute towards forming group beliefs for instances of the state "pending-order(P,C)" that refer to specific products and customers. At the end of this process the group will share a common view of the pending orders, i.e. a set of ground instances that are shared by all group members concerning the specific products that have been ordered by specific customers.

For agents to form a group belief about a ground state of the form "pending-order(*p,c*)" they must know specific r-recipes for the state "pending-order(P,C)".

Fig. 4(a) shows two r-recipes that serve as the building blocks for constructing the policy shown in Fig. 4 (b). In [13] we present specific algorithms for the formation of group beliefs that are based on the concept of personal and group contribution.

A *personal contribution* of an agent to a state *s* is a path in a policy for *s*, from *s to* a leaf state unified with a belief of the agent. The leaf node must correspond to a role played by the agent. Personal contributions are communicated between agents that play the same role (e.g. sellers). Personal contributions that are identified by a sufficient number of agents (according to r-recipes' elements indicators) are called *group contributions* because they can affect the beliefs of a group. Group contributions are communicated between the agents that share the same policy. This makes possible for agents to check whether the requirements of the policy are satisfied. This is done by checking whether the distinguished paths of a policy can be unified with the set of group contributions (as Fig. 4 (c) shows). This method aims to be applied in distributed settings and does not assume any agent playing a coordination role during the formation of acceptances. Although this is more robust for functioning in open settings, it is difficult to be applied for large teams of agents due to the quadratic magnitude of messages required [14].

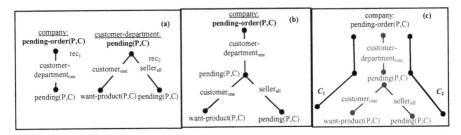

Fig. 4. (a) Examples of state recognition recipes (r-recipes): Relevant roles are underlined and recipe states are in bold typeface. A recipe element is represented by an arc. (b) A policy constructed by these recipes and (c) Group contributions C_1 , C_2 that are unified with the distinguished paths of the policy.

Collaborative Achievement of a Goal State. When an instance of the condition of a collaborative responsibility is accepted by a group of agents, then this group will attempt to establish the corresponding instance of the goal state of the responsibility collaboratively. In this section we assume that when a group recognizes that an instance of a condition holds, then the resulting goal state is a group state, i.e. a state that contains no free variables. In the following, when we refer to a goal state we mean a ground state.

Towards the collaborative achievement of goal states, we assume a multi-step protocol incorporating *group formation*, where agents recognize that the goal state does not hold, *recipe selection*, where agents select an a-recipe for achieving the goal state, and *responsibility allocation*, where agents adopt additional responsibilities specified in the a-recipe in order to achieve the goal state.

When agents enter in the group formation state they attempt to form a group belief on the negation of the goal state of the responsibility. Accepting, as a group, that the goal state does not hold is a pre-requisite for the group to try to achieve that goal state. When such an acceptance is made, group members proceed to the next step of the protocol, which is the selection of an appropriate recipe for the establishment of the goal state.

Fig. 5 shows an example of an a-recipe for the goal state "m&s(P,C)". This recipe contains variables and can be used for the establishment of every instance of state "m&s(P,C)". For an a-recipe to be selected by a group, its applicability condition must be accepted by this group. To achieve this we assume that each agent that enters the recipe selection step it tries to contribute to the acceptance of the applicability condition of each recipe that can be used for the establishment of the state "m&s(P,C)" i.e. for each relevant recipe. During this state, agents may recognize one or more applicable recipes for achieving the goal state. There are many different ways to select one of the recipes that are accepted as applicable. For simplicity, we assume that each group has a recipe manager that can be determined dynamically by some convention. That agent selects one of the applicable recipes and announces its selection to all group members. When a recipe has been selected, group member proceed to the next step of the protocol, which is the allocation of responsibilities of the selected recipe.

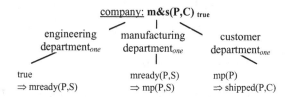

Fig. 5. An example of an a-recipe: Relevant roles are underlined and recipe states are in bold typeface. A recipe element is represented by an arc.

Subsidiary responsibilities according to a-recipe specifications are assigned to individuals and/or subgroups and can by individual, collaborative or hybrid. For example, for the achievement of the state "m&s(P,C)", the group "The Company" may select the recipe specified in Fig. 5. According to this recipe, the responsibility of seeing to it that the manufacturing instructions are ready for the product ("mready(P,C)") is assigned to one of the engineering departments, the responsibility of seeing to it that the product has been manufactured according to the specifications of the engineering department ("mp(P,S)") are assigned to a manufacturing department, and finally the responsibility of seeing to it that the product has been shipped to the appropriate customer ("shipped(P,C)") is assigned to a customer department. In case "The Company" has many applicable recipes and/or many departments, then it must select one recipe for achieving the goal state and one department according to recipe specifications.

Currently, the selection of an appropriate sub-group is done by a group member that is selected by convention, similarly to the selection of an applicable recipe. This agent collects the preferences of group members and it announces the selected subgroup or agent. We call the selection of sub-groups for pursuing responsibilities as *responsibility allocation* stage.

If a subsidiary responsibility of an a-recipe is a collaborative one, then a new collaboration cycle begins for the subgroup that undertakes this collaborative responsibility. This subgroup will recognize instances of the condition of the responsibility and must select an a-recipe for the achievement of the corresponding goal states. In that way, every group member constructs a tree composed by responsibilities and goals, as shown in Fig. 6. This is an *intentional context* towards the top-level responsibility and it is built incrementally.

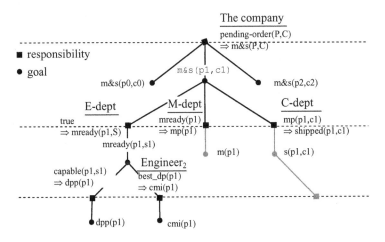

Fig. 6. An intentional context towards fulfilling a responsibility. The agent "Mike" records only the nodes and arcs in black.

The collaborative achievement of a goal state is not a linear process [10, 25]. When a group is in the recipe selection or the responsibility allocation step, group members continue to monitor whether the negation of the goal state continuous to hold, and if that is not the case, then the group stops its attempt to achieve the goal state. Similarly, when the group is in the responsibility allocation step, it continues to monitor the applicable recipes, and since the set of applicable recipes may change, the selected recipe may change as well.

3.2.2 Facilitator Agents

Facilitator agents offer two important services: A *yellow-page* service and a *newspaper* service. Subsections that follow describe these services.

The Yellow-Page Service. Directory facilitators provide yellow-page services for agents to locate each other based on the services they provide. A directory-facilitator agent, as shown in Fig. 2, is not in the scope of any organization. Directory facilitators keep records for the registration of agents in different organizations, and their lifecycle is independent from any of the organizations. A yellow-page service is essential in open settings in order new agents to be able to search and locate other agents. The functionality of a yellow-page service is according to the FIPA specifications.

The Newspaper Service. Typically, the positions in a human organization, the agents in each position and their responsibilities are kept in regulatory documents and contracts. Such documents enable agents to know the organization, keep their knowledge about the organizational structure and population consistent, circumscribe their responsibilities and regulate their behaviour within the organization. A newspaper service, shown in Fig. 2, provides information to the agents that are interested about the state of an organization: The organizational structure, the sub-groups within each group and the assignments of personal agents to positions. For an organizational change to be valid within the organization, it must be announced by the newspaper service.

Using the yellow-page services, an agent can locate agents that provide newspaper services. Agents can ask up-to-date information from a newspaper service, or register to it, in order to be kept informed about an organization. A typical request of this type concerns new positions of a certain role in the organization. It must be pointed out that a newspaper service is not a bottleneck for an organization, because each agent maintains organizational knowledge in a local repository. Therefore, if for some reason the newspaper service malfunctions, the organization can keep functioning although no organizational changes can be announced.

4 Related Work

The development of tools and systems that support humans to work together effectively has found much attention in the last few years: Workflow management systems (WfMS) as well as agent-based systems for supporting humans to accomplish common tasks are emerging paradigms. The research reported in this paper complements efforts for the development of WfMS, as in a greater extend than these systems it aims to cover collaborative activity in settings where flexibility to the fulfilment of responsibilities is important and where information is inherently distributed among members of a group. Agents, in our approach, acting in organized settings must recognize the potential for fulfilling collaborative responsibilities in a distributed way, agree on the appropriate recipe to be used, and allocate responsibilities for the achievement of commonly accepted goal states dynamically. Doing so, they incrementally build a shared intentional context that is distributed among individuals.

As already mentioned, several multi-agent systems aim to support humans to perform collaboratively or at least in coordination. Unlike WfMS that aim to support humans in tasks with well-defined structure in terms of predefined information flow and communication paths, multi-agent systems typically support ill-structured tasks, in which steps to be followed, coordination and information flow cannot be totally specified in advance.

E-ELVES [1] is a sophisticated multi-agent system that integrates a range of technologies that can support a variety of tasks within a human organization: scheduling meetings, arranging lunch, and locating other people. In E-ELVES each human owns a personal agent that interacts with its user and communicate with the others agents. Agents in E-ELVES coordinate using TEAMCORE [16], a domain-independent, decentralized, teamwork-based integration architecture. Although in E-ELVES agents are organized using a role aggregation hierarchy like the one defined in our model, this organization structure is hidden from the participants. Furthermore, although E-ELVES agents collaborate to each other, the aim of the system is not to support human collaborative problem solving activity.

There are several efforts and approaches for building systems of collaborating agents (or teams of agents). Closer to our approach are systems like GRATE* [9], STEAM [20], RETSINA-MAS [19], and CAST [27], in which collaboration is based on a general model of collaborative activity. Although STEAM, RETSINA-MAS, and CAST use the role concept in modelling teamwork, none of them (including GRATE*) offers an adequate model for representing human organizations. Roles in these systems are not interconnected to form a concrete role model and are not used to build more complex organization units. This paper specifies complex organization structures using composite roles and provides separate models for building an organizational model. Also, none of the above systems makes a distinction between beliefs and acceptances. This enables our systems to incorporate several real life situations met in human organizations.

Grosz points on the importance of having specific decision-making mechanisms for establishing group decisions [8]. According to Grosz, the definition of a group decision-making mechanism specifies the legal inputs that a participant can make, the conditions under which an agent can make each kind of input, and rules for how certain combinations of agent inputs serve to establish a group decision. Such a mechanism is analogous to that of a finite state machine with the transitions of the machine corresponding to communicative acts and the final states corresponding to established group decisions. These mechanisms can be considered similar to the policies for accepting a group state proposed in [14]. However, in [8] those mechanisms are not formally specified and are not integrated to any formally defined organizational model. Therefore, this approach seems more suitable for small and unstructured groups rather than organizations.

5 Concluding Remarks

Collaborative activity between agents is a complex group activity that requires sharing of knowledge and communication. Although there are generic models that concern several aspects of collaborative activity [3, 7, 12, 25], building systems with generic mechanisms for collaborative problem-solving and action is quite complicated. In this paper we focus mainly on collaborative activity in well-organized, distributed and dynamic settings. In such settings, agents must not only coordinate their activities for the achievement of their shared goals, but must be able (a) to establish common views of the world based on organization policies, (b) distribute responsibilities dynamically among members of the organization based on specific needs that arise during the course of action and (c) share a context of action that binds the members of groups together towards the achievement of their goals.

The objective of this paper is (a) to propose a generic design pattern for building agent organizations in which the constituting groups build and maintain their own group goals and beliefs according to the needs and the environmental conditions, (b) to show the required social deliberation that is needed for agents to act as group members in such settings, and (c) to report on the development of a prototype system that comprises agents that implement such a kind of social deliberation. Our research aim is to build systems that empower humans to manage their social context, reason about their responsibilities, create common awareness about important states of the world, form agreed goals, and achieve goal states.

This paper emphasizes, more widely than the existing approaches, on the deployment of organizational structures in group activity. It describes how an explicitly stated and shared organization structure can enhance collaborative activity in a distributed and dynamic setting via the specification of role responsibilities and policies (recipes) for the recognition of the need for collaboration and achievement of goal states.

The organizational elements presented are by no means complete. There are many aspects of a real-world organization that can not be modelled using the constructs proposed. For instance, different types of relations between roles, resources available to groups and agents, benefits and utilities of agents are not taken into account. The emphasis in this paper is on the role construct, roles' responsibilities and policies of groups for pursuing their agreed goals. The enrichment of the organization model towards building systems that support more complex human organizations is an ongoing research.

A prototype system has been implemented in Prolog that comprises the mechanisms for elaborating responsibilities and for checking the consistency of a set of roles. The elaboration of responsibilities comprises mechanisms for groups of agents to form acceptances and intentional contexts.

References

[1] H. Chalupsky, Y. Gil, C. A. Knoblock, K. Lerman, J. Oh, D. V. Pynadath, T. A. Russ, and M. Tambe. Electric Elves: Agent Technology for Supporting Human Organizations. *AI Magazine*, 23(2), 11–24, 2002.

[2] J. Cohen. *An Essay on Belief and Acceptance*, Oxford University Press, Oxford, 1992.

[3] P. R. Cohen and H. J. Levesque. Teamwork, *Nous*, 25, 487–512, 1991.

[4] R. Hoffman, P. Hayes and K. M. Ford. The triples rule. *IEEE Intelligent Systems*, May/June 2002, pp. 62–65.

[5] K. M. Carley and L. Gasser. Computational Organization Theory. In Gerhard Weiss (ed.) *Mutliagent Systems: A Modern Approach to Distributed Artificial Intelligence*, MIT Press, 1999.

[6] P. Engel. Believing, Holding True, and Accepting. *Philosophical Explorations*, I, 2, pp. 140–151, 1998.

[7] B. J. Grosz and S. Kraus. Collaborative plans for complex group action. *Artificial Intelligence*, 86, 269–357, 1996.

[8] B. J. Grosz and L. Hunsberger. The Dynamics of Intention in Collaborative Activity. 2004.

[9] N. R. Jennings. Controlling cooperative problem solving in industrial multi-agent systems using joint intentions. *Artificial Intelligence*, 75, 1995.

[10] B. Dunin-Keplicz and R. Verbrugge. Evolution of Collective Commitment during Teamwork. *Fundamenta Informaticae* 56, pp. 329–771, 2003.

[11] J. J. Odell, H. Van Dyke Parunak, and Mitchell Fleischer. The Role of Roles in Designing Effective Agent Organizations. In *Software Engineering for Large-Scale Multi-Agent Systems*, A. Garcia, C. Lucena, F. Zambonelli, A. Omicini, J. Castro (eds.), LNCS 2603, 2003.

[12] P. Panzarasa, N. R. Jennings, and T. J. Norman. Formalizing Collaborative Decision-making and Practical Reasoning in Multi-Agent Systems. *Journal of Logic and Computation*, 11(6), pp. 1–63, 2001.

[13] I. Partsakoulakis and G. Vouros. Building common awareness in agent organizations. In *Proceeding of the AMKM workshop (AAMAS)*, 2005.

[14] I. Partsakoulakis and G. Vouros. Policies for common awareness in organized settings. In *Proceeding of the CEEMAS conference*, 2005.

[15] I. Partsakoulakis and G. Vouros. Personal agents for Reliable Participation in Social Context. In *Proc. of the Coordination in Emergent Agent Societies workshop* (ECAI), Spain, 2004.

[16] D. Pynadath, M. Tambe, N. Chauvat, and L. Cavedon. Towards team-oriented programming. In *Intelligent Agents VI: Agents Theories Architectures and Languages*, Springer, pp. 233–247, 1999.

[17] N. Rescher. *The logic of commands*. Routledge, 1966.

[18] M. P. Singh, A. S. Rao, and M. P. Georgeff. Formal Methods in DAI: Logic-Based Representation and Reasoning. In Gerhard Weiss (ed.) *Mutliagent Systems: A Modern Approach to Distributed Artificial Intelligence*, MIT Press, 1999.

[19] K. Sycara, K. Decker, A. Pannu, M. Williamson, and D. Zeng. Distributed intelligent agents. *IEEE Expert, Intelligent Systems and Applications*, 11(6), pp. 36–45, 1996.

[20] M. Tambe. Towards flexible teamwork. *Journal of Artificial Intelligence Research*, 7, 1997.

[21] R. Tuomela. Belief Versus Acceptance. *Philosophical Explorations*, 2, pp. 122–137, 2000.

[22] R. Tuomela and M. Tuomela. Acting as a Group Member and Collective Commitment. In *Protosociology*, 18–19, pp. 7–65, 2003.

[23] R. Tuomela. Group Knowledge Analyzed. *Episteme* 1(2), 2004.

[24] G. Vouros, I. Partsakoulakis and V. Kourakos-Mavromichalis. Realizing Human-Centred Systems via Socially Deliberating Agents. In *Proc. of the HCI International*, vol. 4, pp. 1223–1227, 2003.

[25] M. Wooldridge and N. R. Jennings. Cooperative problem solving. *Journal of Logic and Computation*, 9, 563–592, 1999.

[26] K. Brad Wray. Collective Belief and Acceptance. *Synthese* 129, pp. 319–333, 2001.

[27] J. Yen, J. Yin, T. R. Ioerger, M. S. Miller, D. Xu, and A. Volz. CAST: Collaborative Agents for Simulating Teamwork. In *Seventeenth Proceedings of the Joint International Conference on Artificial Intelligence (IJCAI)*, pp. 1135–1142, 2001.

[28] J. Zhang, V. L. Patel, K. A. Johnson, J. W. Smith and J. Malin. Designing Human-Centered Distributed Information Systems. *IEEE Intelligent Systems*, pp. 42–47, September/October 2002.

Author Index

Lecture Notes in Artificial Intelligence (LNAI)

Vol. 3763: H. Hong, D. Wang (Eds.), Automated Deduction in Geometry. X, 213 pages. 2006.

Vol. 3755: G.J. Williams, S.J. Simoff (Eds.), Data Mining. XI, 331 pages. 2006.

Vol. 3735: A. Hoffmann, H. Motoda, T. Scheffer (Eds.), Discovery Science. XVI, 400 pages. 2005.

Vol. 3734: S. Jain, H.U. Simon, E. Tomita (Eds.), Algorithmic Learning Theory. XII, 490 pages. 2005.

Vol. 3721: A.M. Jorge, L. Torgo, P.B. Brazdil, R. Camacho, J. Gama (Eds.), Knowledge Discovery in Databases: PKDD 2005. XXIII, 719 pages. 2005.

Vol. 3720: J. Gama, R. Camacho, P.B. Brazdil, A.M. Jorge, L. Torgo (Eds.), Machine Learning: ECML 2005. XXIII, 769 pages. 2005.

Vol. 3717: B. Gramlich (Ed.), Frontiers of Combining Systems. X, 321 pages. 2005.

Vol. 3702: B. Beckert (Ed.), Automated Reasoning with Analytic Tableaux and Related Methods. XIII, 343 pages. 2005.

Vol. 3698: U. Furbach (Ed.), KI 2005: Advances in Artificial Intelligence. XIII, 409 pages. 2005.

Vol. 3690: M. Pěchouček, P. Petta, L.Z. Varga (Eds.), Multi-Agent Systems and Applications IV. XVII, 667 pages. 2005.

Vol. 3684: R. Khosla, R.J. Howlett, L.C. Jain (Eds.), Knowledge-Based Intelligent Information and Engineering Systems, Part IV. LXXIX, 933 pages. 2005.

Vol. 3683: R. Khosla, R.J. Howlett, L.C. Jain (Eds.), Knowledge-Based Intelligent Information and Engineering Systems, Part III. LXXX, 1397 pages. 2005.

Vol. 3682: R. Khosla, R.J. Howlett, L.C. Jain (Eds.), Knowledge-Based Intelligent Information and Engineering Systems, Part II. LXXIX, 1371 pages. 2005.

Vol. 3681: R. Khosla, R.J. Howlett, L.C. Jain (Eds.), Knowledge-Based Intelligent Information and Engineering Systems, Part I. LXXX, 1319 pages. 2005.

Vol. 3673: S. Bandini, S. Manzoni (Eds.), AI*IA 2005: Advances in Artificial Intelligence. XIV, 614 pages. 2005.

Vol. 3662: C. Baral, G. Greco, N. Leone, G. Terracina (Eds.), Logic Programming and Nonmonotonic Reasoning. XIII, 454 pages. 2005.

Vol. 3661: T. Panayiotopoulos, J. Gratch, R. Aylett, D. Ballin, P. Olivier, T. Rist (Eds.), Intelligent Virtual Agents. XIII, 506 pages. 2005.

Vol. 3658: V. Matoušek, P. Mautner, T. Pavelka (Eds.), Text, Speech and Dialogue. XV, 460 pages. 2005.

Vol. 3651: R. Dale, K.-F. Wong, J. Su, O.Y. Kwong (Eds.), Natural Language Processing – IJCNLP 2005. XXI, 1031 pages. 2005.

Vol. 3642: D. Ślęzak, J. Yao, J.F. Peters, W. Ziarko, X. Hu (Eds.), Rough Sets, Fuzzy Sets, Data Mining, and Granular Computing, Part II. XXIII, 738 pages. 2005.

Vol. 3641: D. Ślęzak, G. Wang, M. Szczuka, I. Düntsch, Y. Yao (Eds.), Rough Sets, Fuzzy Sets, Data Mining, and Granular Computing, Part I. XXIV, 742 pages. 2005.

Vol. 3635: J.R. Winkler, M. Niranjan, N.D. Lawrence (Eds.), Deterministic and Statistical Methods in Machine Learning. VIII, 341 pages. 2005.

Vol. 3632: R. Nieuwenhuis (Ed.), Automated Deduction – CADE-20. XIII, 459 pages. 2005.

Vol. 3630: M.S. Capcarrère, A.A. Freitas, P.J. Bentley, C.G. Johnson, J. Timmis (Eds.), Advances in Artificial Life. XIX, 949 pages. 2005.

Vol. 3626: B. Ganter, G. Stumme, R. Wille (Eds.), Formal Concept Analysis. X, 349 pages. 2005.

Vol. 3625: S. Kramer, B. Pfahringer (Eds.), Inductive Logic Programming. XIII, 427 pages. 2005.

Vol. 3620: H. Muñoz-Ávila, F. Ricci (Eds.), Case-Based Reasoning Research and Development. XV, 654 pages. 2005.

Vol. 3614: L. Wang, Y. Jin (Eds.), Fuzzy Systems and Knowledge Discovery, Part II. XLI, 1314 pages. 2005.

Vol. 3613: L. Wang, Y. Jin (Eds.), Fuzzy Systems and Knowledge Discovery, Part I. XLI, 1334 pages. 2005.

Vol. 3607: J.-D. Zucker, L. Saitta (Eds.), Abstraction, Reformulation and Approximation. XII, 376 pages. 2005.

Vol. 3601: G. Moro, S. Bergamaschi, K. Aberer (Eds.), Agents and Peer-to-Peer Computing. XII, 245 pages. 2005.

Vol. 3600: F. Wiedijk (Ed.), The Seventeen Provers of the World. XVI, 159 pages. 2006.

Vol. 3596: F. Dau, M.-L. Mugnier, G. Stumme (Eds.), Conceptual Structures: Common Semantics for Sharing Knowledge. XI, 467 pages. 2005.

Vol. 3593: V. Mařík, R. W. Brennan, M. Pěchouček (Eds.), Holonic and Multi-Agent Systems for Manufacturing. XI, 269 pages. 2005.

Vol. 3587: P. Perner, A. Imiya (Eds.), Machine Learning and Data Mining in Pattern Recognition. XVII, 695 pages. 2005.

Vol. 3584: X. Li, S. Wang, Z.Y. Dong (Eds.), Advanced Data Mining and Applications. XIX, 835 pages. 2005.

Vol. 3581: S. Miksch, J. Hunter, E.T. Keravnou (Eds.), Artificial Intelligence in Medicine. XVII, 547 pages. 2005.

Vol. 3577: R. Falcone, S. Barber, J. Sabater-Mir, M.P. Singh (Eds.), Trusting Agents for Trusting Electronic Societies. VIII, 235 pages. 2005.

Vol. 3575: S. Wermter, G. Palm, M. Elshaw (Eds.), Biomimetic Neural Learning for Intelligent Robots. IX, 383 pages. 2005.

Vol. 3571: L. Godo (Ed.), Symbolic and Quantitative Approaches to Reasoning with Uncertainty. XVI, 1028 pages. 2005.

Vol. 3559: P. Auer, R. Meir (Eds.), Learning Theory. XI, 692 pages. 2005.

Vol. 3558: V. Torra, Y. Narukawa, S. Miyamoto (Eds.), Modeling Decisions for Artificial Intelligence. XII, 470 pages. 2005.

Vol. 3554: A.K. Dey, B. Kokinov, D.B. Leake, R. Turner (Eds.), Modeling and Using Context. XIV, 572 pages. 2005.

Vol. 3550: T. Eymann, F. Klügl, W. Lamersdorf, M. Klusch, M.N. Huhns (Eds.), Multiagent System Technologies. XI, 246 pages. 2005.

Vol. 3539: K. Morik, J.-F. Boulicaut, A. Siebes (Eds.), Local Pattern Detection. XI, 233 pages. 2005.